REMEMBERING 1759

The Conquest of Canada in Historical Memory

This companion volume to *Revisiting 1759* examines how the Conquest of Canada has been remembered, commemorated, interpreted, and reinterpreted by groups in Canada, France, Great Britain, the United States, and, most of all, Quebec. It focuses particularly on how the public memory of the Conquest has been used for a variety of cultural, political, and intellectual purposes.

The essays contained in this volume investigate topics such as the legacy of 1759 in twentieth-century Quebec; the memorialization of General James Wolfe in a variety of national contexts; and the re-imagination of the Plains of Abraham as a tourist destination. Combined with *Revisiting 1759*, this collection provides readers with the most comprehensive, wide-ranging assessment to date of the lasting effects of the Conquest of Canada.

PHILLIP BUCKNER is a professor emeritus in the Department of History at the University of New Brunswick and a senior fellow at the Institute of Commonwealth Studies and the Institute for the Study of the Americas at the University of London.

JOHN G. REID is a professor in the Department of History and a senior fellow at the Gorsebrook Research Institute at Saint Mary's University.

Remembering 1759

The Conquest of Canada in Historical Memory

EDITED BY
PHILLIP BUCKNER AND JOHN G. REID

UNIVERSITY OF TORONTO PRESS
Toronto Buffalo London

© University of Toronto Press 2012
Toronto Buffalo London
www.utppublishing.com
Printed in Canada

ISBN 978-1-4426-4411-3 (cloth)
ISBN 978-1-4426-1251-8 (paper)

Printed on acid-free, 100% post-consumer recycled paper with
vegetable-based inks.

Library and Archives Canada Cataloguing in Publication

Remembering 1759 : the conquest of Canada in historical memory /
edited by Phillip Buckner and John G. Reid.

Includes bibliographical references and index.
ISBN 978-1-4426-4411-3 (bound). – ISBN 978-1-4426-1251-8 (pbk.)

1. Québec Campaign, 1759 – Anniversaries, etc.   2. Plains of Abraham,
Battle of the, Québec, 1759 – Anniversaries, etc.   3. Collective memory –
Québec (Province).   4. Collective memory – Canada.   I. Buckner, Phillip A.
(Phillip Alfred), 1942–   II. Reid, John G. (John Graham), 1948–

FC386.R45 2012   971.01'88   C2012-901838-4

This book has been published with the help of a grant from the Canadian
Federation for the Humanities and Social Sciences, through the Aid to
Scholarly Publications Program, using funds provided by the Social Sciences
and Humanities Research Council of Canada.

University of Toronto Press acknowledges the financial assistance to its
publishing program of the Canada Council for the Arts and the Ontario
Arts Council.

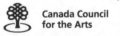 Canada Council   Conseil des Arts
for the Arts   du Canada

 ONTARIO ARTS COUNCIL
CONSEIL DES ARTS DE L'ONTARIO

University of Toronto Press acknowledges the financial support of the
Government of Canada through the Canada Book Fund for its publishing
activities.

Contents

Preface

On 14 September 1759 British and French troops fought a battle on the Plains of Abraham, just outside what was then the capital of the colony of Canada, Quebec City. There was nothing inevitable about the victory of the British forces under General James Wolfe and it was not irreversible. Indeed, the British forces met defeat at the Battle of Ste-Foy in April 1760 and only the arrival of a British rather than a French fleet later that spring ensured that Quebec remained in British hands. Conversely, even if Wolfe had been defeated on the Plains of Abraham, Quebec might still have fallen to the much larger British force slowly making its way north from the thirteen colonies in 1759–60 under the command of General Jeffery Amherst. And, of course, Canada might have been returned to France during the peace negotiations had the war gone slightly differently in Europe and the West Indies. Even after the Treaty of Paris of 1763 secured for the British what they had won on the battlefield, it was not inconceivable that France might have returned or assisted the thirteen colonies during the American Revolutionary War in taking from Britain what Britain had taken from France. But, as it turned out, the French cession of 1763 was never overturned. The Battle of the Plains of Abraham therefore had been decisive in enabling Britain to take possession of Canada. Renamed the province of Quebec in 1763 and subsequently divided into Upper and Lower Canada in 1791, what had been the colony of Canada eventually became part of the Dominion of Canada in 1867.

Because of the significance of the Battle of the Plains of Abraham in 1759, it seemed appropriate to hold an academic conference to mark the two hundred and fiftieth anniversary of the event in September 2009. The conference on '1759 Revisited: The Conquest of Canada in

Historical Perspective' was held at the University of London and co-sponsored by the Institute of Commonwealth Studies and the Institute for the Study of the Americas, both part of the School of Advanced Studies at the University of London, and by the Gorsebrook Research Institute at Saint Mary's University in Halifax, Nova Scotia. We would also to like to acknowledge the assistance provided by Richard Dennis, chairman of the London Conference of Canadian Studies, and by Olga Jimenez, the events manager at the Institute for the Study of the Americas, and to thank the Canadian High Commission in London for allowing us the use of Canada House as a site for the conference and also the Canadian Department of Foreign Affairs and International Trade for financial support. After three intensive days of the conference, we faced the difficult task of identifying a necessarily small number of the many high-quality papers that had been presented. Thematic unity was an important criterion, and after a great deal of agonizing we chose twenty-one papers to be revised for publication. This would still have made for a large and somewhat unwieldy volume. Fortunately, the papers given at the conference divided naturally into one of two categories: those that focused on the Conquest and its immediate aftermath and those that focused on the historical memory of the Conquest. We therefore decided to produce two volumes of essays: *Revisiting 1759: The Conquest of Canada in Historical Perspective* and *Remembering 1759: The Conquest of Canada in Historical Memory*. Each volume can be read on its own, though the two, of course, are interrelated. In their different ways, both volumes offer new and revealing insights into the impact, implications, and long-term significance of Wolfe's victory on the Plains of Abraham in 1759.

As the volumes took shape and moved through the publication process, we were reminded again of our good fortune in publishing with the University of Toronto Press. We thank Len Husband, history editor, who guided the books assuredly through the early parts of the process; and Wayne Herrington, associate managing editor, who then steered them through to publication. Barry Norris's excellent copy editing of both volumes brought about many improvements.

Some of the chapters included lengthy French-language quotations. In order to make the collections as useful a teaching tool as possible, we decided that all the quotations would be translated into English, but that where the quotation was a lengthy one, we would also include the original French version in the accompanying endnote.

Phillip Buckner and John G. Reid

REMEMBERING 1759

The Conquest of Canada in Historical Memory

1

Introduction

PHILLIP BUCKNER AND JOHN G. REID

On 14 September 2009, the day following the two hundred and fiftieth anniversary of the Battle of the Plains of Abraham, the *BBC History
Magazine* carried a blog entry by Dan Snow, a British popular historian
and broadcaster who was in Quebec City for the anniversary. It was,
he declared, a 'strange day.' A large re-enactment had been cancelled
because of protests from 'French Canadian-Quebecois-Separatists,'
and instead all the commemorations were 'low key.' A small monument was unveiled to 'all the combatants,' accompanied by a public
recital of poetry on the battlefield. A few re-enactors wandered around
dressed in white Bourbon coats and even 'one brave Fraser Highland-
er.' A 'gaggle of Quebec separatists' staged a march. Snow interviewed
'several' of them and reported that only a small minority had any idea
of 'the significance' of the anniversary: 'They reminded me of the anti-
Catholic rioters of the 18th century who roared "No Popery" with little
idea of who or what it was.' It was a 'far cry' from the nine hundred and
sixtieth anniversary of Hastings that Snow had attended or the sixty-
fifth anniversary of the Battle of Britain or even the two hundredth anniversary of Trafalgar. 'At commemorations of D-Day or the battle of
Britain,' he noted, 'the tone is one of thanksgiving, of delivery from a
deadly threat to our way of life.' But in Quebec the occasion had been
turned by the separatists into a symbol of 'subjugation.' How different it all was, Snow mused, from the anniversary of the Battle of the
Plains of Abraham in 1909, when 'the great and the good of the British
imperial project arrived to bathe in self-confident celebration' and the
'steel giants of the Royal Navy' anchored off Quebec City: 'There was
no ambiguity; onlookers believed that the battle had been a defining
moment in an empire that was self evidently a great civilising force in
the world.' But in 2009, although there was a 'flutter of protest,' people

mainly 'walked their dogs, and ate picnics in the Battlefield Park.' A few 'jostled to lay claim to the battle's legacy, most people had simply forgotten it.'[1]

It is not immediately clear why Snow expected that a city in which the English-speaking minority composes about 1.5 per cent of the population and which advertises itself as the most French city in the world outside France would have been likely to celebrate the Conquest of 1759 or in what sense the francophone population could have interpreted the Battle of the Plains of Abraham as delivering them from a deadly threat to 'our' way of life. For Snow, the Plains of Abraham may have symbolized a notable victory; for many French Canadians, even the description of 'the southern part of the promontory' as 'the Plains of Abraham' was 'the work of the conqueror, the holder of power. He magnanimously proposed reconciliation, in memory of both generals who died as heroes. Through creation of the park, however, and in the stones of the fortifications and monuments, he indelibly inscribed the memory of his 1759 victory.'[2]

Snow's reference to the 1909 celebrations is also somewhat misguided. In fact, the ceremonies to which he refers took place in 1908. The governor general of Canada, Earl Grey, was well aware that he could not 'unite a nation by loudly commemorating a French defeat,' and so the celebration of the one hundred and fiftieth anniversary of the Battle of the Plains of Abraham in 1759 was paired not only with a celebration of the 1760 Battle of Ste-Foy, at which the *Canadiens* defeated the British, but also with the three hundredth anniversary of the founding of Quebec City in 1608.[3] The ceremonies surrounding this joint anniversary were far from unambiguous and certainly not uncontested. It is impossible to know how many people Snow interviewed in 2009, although one can perhaps understand why they might not have responded enthusiastically to someone from the BBC asking if they understood the 'significance' of 1759. Perhaps they simply told him what he appeared to want to hear or sought politely to shrug off the question. Whatever the reason, it seems unlikely that most of the *Québécois* he encountered had 'simply forgotten' what had happened on the Plains of Abraham two hundred and fifty years earlier.

The past has accurately been described as 'a foreign country.'[4] As when visiting a foreign country, our perceptions of the past are shaped partly by the perspective from which we view it and partly by the intellectual baggage we carry with us, and our understanding of it is always incomplete and subjective. Yet memories of the past help us to define ourselves and our place in society and the wider world. Indeed, a sense of a shared past helps to define what it means to be part of a family, a community, an ethnic group, or a nation. Popular memory – a term coined by Michel Foucault in 1974 – is, of course, not the same as history; it is primarily concerned with the implications of the past for the present and is highly selective in what it chooses to remember and also to forget. But although academic historians seek to achieve greater detachment and to base their study of the past on a firm evidentiary foundation, they are also affected by the climate of opinion in which they function, and are usually very aware of the implications for the present of what they write about the past. Sometimes popular memory and academic history work in harness; at other times they may draw apart. But both involve an ongoing, dynamic process of reinterpreting the past to make it relevant to the present. This is not a neutral process. Collective memories, like personal memories, are not simply reproduced; they are constructed. There is a good deal at stake in conflicts over who has the right to 'claim the cultural authority to define the public memory' and to decide what history will be promoted in public institutions and taught in schools.[5] As Michael E. Geisler notes, the meanings attached to past events are 'constantly recycled, actualized, challenged, renegotiated, and reconfirmed or rewritten depending on changes in public consensus or the ability or inability of a particular hegemonic group to maintain its hold on the public imaginary.'[6] The eleven chapters that follow in this collection focus on one historical event, the Conquest of Canada in 1759, and the various ways this event has been commemorated, interpreted, reinterpreted, and remembered among various groups in Canada, France, Britain, the United States, and, most of all, in Quebec itself.[7]

It was, of course, inevitable that the historical memory of the Conquest would vary greatly among the descendants of those who participated in the events of 1759. For the British, for the Americans, and for those who later formed part of the English-Canadian majority in the Dominion of Canada, 1759 could hardly be viewed other than as a great victory. To some extent, for the British, the Conquest of Canada was overshadowed by the loss of the thirteen colonies in 1783. Indeed, Britain's hold over the remnants of its North American empire remained precarious, and during the War of 1812 Upper Canada nearly fell into American hands. But the Treaty of Ghent restored the *status quo ante bellum*, and after the final defeat of Napoleon in 1815 the British emerged as the dominant European imperial power with a vast empire extend-

ing around the globe – one that grew steadily vaster over the ensuing
century. In their contribution to this collection, Joan Coutu and John
McAleer point out that, as soon as news of Wolfe's death reached Britain, Pitt the Elder began to 'manufacture' a memory of Wolfe that would
entrench his victory on the Plains of Abraham 'in the fabled popular
history of British imperial might.' Benjamin West's iconic painting of
The Death of Wolfe contributed greatly to this effort, and during the nineteenth century Wolfe was always included in the pantheon of imperial
heroes who were seen as the founders of what came to be known as the
Second British Empire – although Wolfe was somewhat overshadowed
by Lord Nelson, with whom he shared the distinction of dying at the
moment of his greatest victory.

For most of the nineteenth century, few new monuments were erected in Wolfe's honour in Britain, but late in that century and early in
the twentieth century, as Canada and the other dominions came to be
seen as increasingly important to the British imperial system and as the
links between Canada and Britain grew stronger, there was, as Coutu
and McAleer show, another outburst of memorialization. In 1909, during the one hundred and fiftieth anniversary of Wolfe's death, tablets
were erected in St Alfege Church in Greenwich, where Wolfe is buried, and at the house in Blackheath where Wolfe's parents had lived.
In 1911, a statue of Wolfe was raised in Westerham, Kent, where he
was born, and funds were gathered for a statue in Greenwich Park that
was finally completed in 1930. There would be no new monuments
after this time, but in British schools students continued to learn about
Wolfe and his glorious victory on the Plains of Abraham. Generations
of British (and English-Canadian) children read books such as G.A.
Henty's *With Wolfe to Canada; or, The Winning of a Continent* (originally
published in 1880). When they grew up, those who attended an imperial event such as the British Empire Exhibition at Wembley in 1924
were bound to find Wolfe 'in the cavalcade of stalwarts lauded for
painting the globe red.'[8]

Yet, as the British Empire receded into history and Canada came to
be seen not as an integral part of a wider British world but as a foreign country, the British public's memory of Wolfe gradually weakened. Quebec House, his Westerham birthplace, though a National
Trust property, is overshadowed by nearby Chartwell, once the home
of Winston Churchill. In a 2002 BBC poll to identify the greatest Britons of all time, Nelson ranked ninth, while Wolfe did not even make it
into the top one hundred.[9] Even the two hundred and fiftieth anniver-

sary of Wolfe's victory saw few public ceremonies. The most significant was the Westerham Wolfe Weekend, where, on 12–13 September 2009, one could see a special exhibit at Quebec House that included an original of the Benjamin West painting (borrowed from another National Trust property), attend a ballet entitled 'Soldiers Three' about Wolfe and his family, visit a fair that included forty stalls, a hog roast, and an art exhibition by a local primary school on the theme of James Wolfe and aboriginal culture, and participate in a banquet with wine brought from the Montcalm vineyards in the south of France. The highlights of the weekend included a re-enactment on the Saturday of the Battle of Montmorency Falls (at which the French defeated the British) and on the Sunday a re-enactment of the Battle of the Plains of Abraham. On the Monday, the Westerham Wolfe Society held its annual dinner to 'honour the pious and immortal memory of Wolfe'; set in the Grand Hall of Chelsea Hospital, the dinner was addressed by the duke of York. Yet, despite the weekend's success in attracting some three thousand five hundred people,[10] it was essentially a Westerham event, praising the town's most famous son. Wolfe's victory and 'immortal memory' attracted little interest in the national press.

Wolfe and the Battle of the Plains of Abraham have not, of course, been entirely forgotten. The battle honour *Quebec 1759* is still borne by seven British regiments and the National Army Museum recently raised £300,000 to prevent J.S.C. Schaak's portrait of Wolfe – which is claimed to be the most authentic portrait of the general at the time and place of his death – from being sold to a private collector abroad.[11] The events of 1759 continue to attract the attention of British military historians, and two major scholarly studies of Wolfe and the battle – both more favourable to Wolfe's reputation than are most recent Canadian studies – as well as a handful of derivative popular histories appeared in time for the two hundred and fiftieth anniversary.[12] Yet the number of British scholars with any interest in Canada or Canadian history has dwindled over the years, and in this sense Coutu and McAleer are right to refer to the 'malleable nature of Wolfe's victory' and of his fame in the land of his birth.

In the United States, Wolfe's fame has also withered. Wolfe's invasion force included several companies of American rangers, and volunteers from the thirteen colonies formed a substantial part of the army led by General Jeffery Amherst that took Montreal in 1760. Throughout the thirteen colonies, the Battle of the Plains of Abraham was welcomed enthusiastically for putting an end to the French menace on their borders.

Wolfe was praised in speeches, in literary works, and in a number of
Anglo-American folk songs, and in New Hampshire the town of Wolfe-
boro was named in his honour. During the American Revolution, the
Americans naturally sought to generate and commemorate their own
'national' heroes. Ironically, one of the first to receive this treatment
was General Richard Montgomery, killed on 13 December 1775 in the
revolutionaries' attempt to seize Quebec City from the British. But even
during this period, Wolfe remained a popular figure, partly because
he had died tragically on the battlefield.[13] A famous folk song written
in his honour, 'Brave Wolfe,' appeared in many New England broad-
sides and songbooks in the late eighteenth and nineteenth centuries.[14]
Moreover, as tensions with Britain diminished in the nineteenth century, Americans increasingly began to stress their Anglo-Celtic roots and
to see themselves as the heirs of the British in North America. Many
prominent Americans came north to visit the site of Wolfe's victory on
the Plains of Abraham, and on 13 September 1859, the centenary of the
battle, the New England Historic Genealogical Society invited Lorenzo
Sabine to deliver a tribute to Wolfe in the Hall of the House of Representatives of Massachusetts. Describing Wolfe as 'this British Achil-
les,' Sabine put his achievement succinctly: with Wolfe's victory, 'the
Gaul resigned the New World to the Briton.'[15] This triumphalist tone
is also apparent in Francis Parkman's classic seven-volume history of
the struggle between France and Britain for North America, which concludes with Wolfe's victory and the comment that 'England imposed
by the sword on reluctant Canada the boon of rational and ordered liberty.'[16] When William Waldorf Astor built the Exchange Court in New
York City in 1898, he commissioned for the facade on the third floor
four ten-foot-tall statues: three were of famous New York residents, the
fourth was of James Wolfe. An article in the *New York Times* in 2007
called this a 'peculiar choice.'[17] But it is peculiar only in retrospect.

Yet as Americans acquired their own empire and a growing belief in
their exceptionalism as a people and as a nation, they ceased to think
of themselves as heirs of the British or of their colonial past as part
of the expansion of Britain overseas. Interest in Wolfe and his victory
inevitably declined. In 1950, when the Exchange Court in New York
was remodelled, Wolfe's statue was offered to a church in London, England. When the offer was declined, the statue apparently languished
in a junkyard until purchased by Eric Harvie, a Calgary collector, who
donated it to the city of Calgary, which placed it in front of the Calgary
Centennial Planetarium as part of the Canadian centennial celebrations

in July 1967.[18] Among professional historians in the United States, those who made up the much-misunderstood 'imperial school' had little interest in anglophilia, much less in triumphalism, and concentrated their efforts on placing American history in a framework of imperial institutions and governance. The exception was Lawrence Henry Gipson, but Gipson's fifteen-volume history of the British Empire before the American Revolution was more remarkable for its monumental size than for exerting any real historiographical influence.[19]

More recently, there has been a revival of American interest in the Seven Years' War, but with a very different interpretation of the importance of Wolfe and the Battle of the Plains of Abraham. In his recent and much-praised study, *Crucible of War*, Fred Anderson devotes only twenty-eight pages out of seven hundred and fifty to the Battle of the Plains of Abraham, and declares that the 'action' of 13 September 1759 'was no more a decisive battle than a brilliant one.' He has little respect for either Montcalm or Wolfe; indeed, the latter comes across as a kind of chancer with a death wish. Anderson's concern is to explain the evolution of the American Empire, not the British: 'To see the Seven Years' War and the Revolution together as epochal events that yoked imperialism with republicanism in American political culture may therefore enable us to take another step toward understanding a national history in which war and freedom have been intertwined.' Given this perspective, it is hardly surprising that the Conquest of Canada and its integration into the British Empire is seen a minor footnote to the story; what matters is that, after the Seven Years' War, the French and their indigenous allies could no longer prevent the American colonies from expanding west.[20] As Warren Hofstra notes in *Cultures in Conflict*, the Seven Years' War has become transformed from the war for empire into 'the war that made America.'[21] Anderson also turns Parkman's analysis of the nature of the British and French empires on its head. It is the French Empire that was the more liberal because of its attitude towards the aboriginal peoples: 'the most Christian King's empire in North America had been less a French dominion than a multicultural confederation knit together by diplomacy, trade, and the necessity of defending against English aggression.' Britain's empire, on the other hand, 'had not developed into the kind of expansive multicultural community that France's had; instead, English settlers explicitly predominated in the British colonies, exercising political, economic, and social hegemony with the backing of an otherwise detached king in Parliament.'[22] 'Brave Wolfe' thus has become an agent of oppression rather than the great liberator.

Even in English Canada, where one might have expected Wolfe's fame to endure, his importance in historical memory has gradually waned. In 1792 the first lieutenant-governor of Upper Canada, John Graves Simcoe, named Wolfe Island at the eastern end of Lake Ontario in Wolfe's honour, and there are coves and counties and rivers named after him in several provinces, as well as streets and schools in numerous Canadian cities. The ballad of 'Brave Wolfe' survived in oral tradition in Newfoundland and Nova Scotia well into the twentieth century and was recorded a number of times in the 1950s and 1960s.[23] Indeed, a song that remained popular in Canada until comparatively recently was 'The Maple Leaf Forever,' which praises 'Wolfe, the dauntless hero' for planting 'firm Britannia's flag on Canada's fair domain.'[24] Yet, as a founding moment, the Battle of the Plains of Abraham was flawed even for English Canadians, and had to compete with other major turning points, including the adding of Nova Scotia to the British Empire in 1713, the founding of Halifax in 1749, the arrival of the Loyalists in the Maritime colonies and Upper Canada during the 1780s, and even the War of 1812. Indeed, the War of 1812 gave Upper Canadians their own imperial hero, General Sir Isaac Brock, whose death in 1812 – like Wolfe's, in battle – was memorialized in a huge statue, much larger than anything ever erected to Wolfe, raised in 1859 on Queenston Heights, though this was probably the last memorial erected to a military figure whose ties with Canada were so tenuous. Even before Confederation, the British North American colonies sought to honour those native-born heroes who had fought and died in the Crimean War and the Fenian raids and, after Confederation, those Canadians who fought and died in the North-West rebellion and the South African War. Few of these monuments resonate today, having been long overshadowed by those erected to commemorate the far larger number of Canadians who died in the two world wars.

There has also been a desire, certainly on the part of successive Canadian governments, to avoid reopening old wounds. When the first monument to Wolfe in Quebec City was unveiled in 1827, the Reverend Dr. Mills, in his blessing, focused on the heroism of both Wolfe and Montcalm.[25] This attempt to reconcile French Canadians to their defeat had limited effect, however, for under the surface the tensions remained. In his *Centenary Lecture on the Life of General Wolfe and the Conquest of Canada*, delivered in Montreal on 13 September 1859, Andrew Bell, editor of the *Montreal Pilot*, lamented that his efforts to organize a major event to celebrate the centennial of the 'battle which caused Canada to pass from the domination of France to the rule of Great Britain' had been 'denounced, mocked or carped at' in the French-Canadian press. Rejecting the idea that the battle of Ste-Foy – 'that bootless battle which French Canadians call the "second" battle (and victory over the British!) of the Plains of Abraham' – should be given equal attention with Wolfe's glorious victory, Bell advised French Canadians to remember the 'benefits' brought by the British victory, and quoted an old British proverb that declared, 'When two men ride the same horse, one of them needs content himself with a place behind the other.'[26]

This barely submerged triumphalism made it difficult to turn the Plains of Abraham into a national shrine for Wolfe. Two of the chapters in this collection focus on this issue. Alan Gordon notes that, following Wolfe's victory, Quebec City became a major destination for tourists from across the English-speaking world. They were attracted partly by the hinterland around the city and natural wonders such as Montmorency Falls and the cataract on the Chaudière River. But the main appeal of the town was that it was near the site of Wolfe's great victory, which had come to be described as the 'Plains of Abraham,' although the definition of what constituted the 'Plains of Abraham' remained unclear. The actual battle had ranged over a wider territory than is included in today's National Battlefields Park, and the suburban growth of Quebec gradually encroached on the battlefield site and turned it into a place for horse races, circuses, and even public executions. Gordon points out that the first 'monument' on the Plains was the rock against which it was believed Wolfe had 'lain dying.' But pilgrims picked away at the rock, which continued to diminish in size until Governor General Lord Aylmer had a small column inscribed with the words, 'Here Died Wolfe Victorious,' erected near the spot in 1832; this, in turn, was replaced by a more elaborate fenced monument in 1849. The steady stream of English-speaking visitors to the site of the battle did not, however, much admire the town itself, which remained small, with an undeveloped tourist infrastructure. Gordon describes how interest in the 'historic' character of the town began to rise in the 1830s as the travel literature began to 'recast the battle as one of many events in a more robust reading of local history.' Much of the pressure for this change came from the city's English-speaking residents, who peaked at about 40 per cent of the population during this period: 'Using the language of liberalism, even if only briefly, English-speaking residents brokered a new understanding of Quebec City's urban space, one that at once promoted their vision of a progressive city and paradoxically shifted attention away from the Plains of Abraham and memories of 1759.'

In his chapter, J.I. Little uses many of the same sources and makes some of the same points as Gordon but for very different purposes. Whereas Gordon is concerned to show how the vision of Old Quebec increasingly was linked to liberal notions of progress, Little focuses on Quebec as a place of memory, using British, American, and Canadian travellers' accounts to show how the Plains of Abraham were transformed in the public memory over time. For most of the nineteenth century, the battlefield remained a largely untended space whose main attraction was the spot where Wolfe was said to have died. Indeed, most of the early travellers were disappointed by the lack of a substantial monument to Wolfe and particularly dismissive of the small wooden statue in the town carved by a local entrepreneur in the 1770s. The 1849 monument was overshadowed in 1867 by the building of a large prison nearby. Despite tourists' complaints that the site of the battle had been profaned, the Plains of Abraham 'continued to receive relatively little attention as a physical space.' This was, of course, well nigh inevitable so long as the site was seen essentially as place where the British established their supremacy over the French. To downplay this interpretation, successive governors began to emphasize the bravery and sacrifice of Montcalm. After Confederation, the need to create a sense of national identity that both French Canadians and English Canadians could share led to an even greater emphasis on reconciliation, a major theme of the 1908 celebrations that linked the founding of Quebec City in 1608 with the anniversary of the Battle of the Plains of Abraham. Even Henri Bourassa admired Governor General Grey's skill 'at turning a festival of the birth of French Canada into a great memorial to the Conquest.'[27] Every effort was made to portray the Plains of Abraham as a place where, Emily Weaver declared in 1907, 'two rival races, under two rival leaders, unconsciously joined hands.'[28] But this effort never had much chance of success, since French and English Canadians were bound to have different interpretations of the meaning of 1759, which would resurface in times of tension.

Although the First World War brought such tensions to the surface, most English-Canadian historians writing in the twentieth century tried to promote reconciliation between anglophones and francophones. But though they were more sympathetic than was Parkman to French-Canadian society before the Conquest, they continued to stress that the Conquest, however devastating and tragic it had been for the inhabitants of

New France, gave to French Canadians the blessings of parliamentary institutions and British liberal traditions. This basic assumption was shared by all of the most prominent English-Canadian historians even after the Second World War, whether they were conservatives like Donald Creighton and W.L. Morton or liberals such as A.R.M. Lower and J.M.S. Careless. It was embodied in all of the English-Canadian history surveys of the period and in the history that was taught in the schools and universities in English Canada – including English-language schools in Quebec – where students absorbed what Brian Young, in his chapter in this volume, calls 'an easy sense of the superiority of British institutions.' This was a more benign version of the Conquest than that embodied in Bell's centenary lecture or Parkman's volumes. As Daniel Francis has pointed out, '[t]here was nothing triumphalist about it. As an English Canadian of Irish extraction, I was not taught to take pride in the fact that "we" whipped the French on the Plains of Abraham. The Québecois [*sic*] were never presented as a vanquished enemy.' Such an interpretation obviously would have hindered the evolution of a 'myth of unity: that French and English were partners, co-operating in building the same Canada.' Francis admits, however, that, although they could not 'lord it' over the *Québécois*, English Canadians had evolved a series of stereotypes about French Canadians that infantilized them.[29] Catherine Desbarats and Allan Greer describe such attitudes as part of a long tradition of Orientalism in English-Canadian scholarship on French-Canadian history.[30] More than simply memories of 1759 have shaped and divided English- and French-Canadian perceptions of each other.

Indeed, by the second half of the twentieth century, Wolfe's victory on the Plains of Abraham had become an increasingly remote event in the historical memory of most English Canadians. 'O Canada' gradually replaced 'The Maple Leaf Forever' as Canada's informal national anthem and was adopted formally as the national anthem in 1980, and anniversaries of the 1759 battle passed by without much comment. Even the two hundredth anniversary in 1959 attracted limited attention outside Quebec, and not all that much in Quebec. One of the few references in the English-Canadian press was a short article in the *Globe and Mail* by Berkeley Rhodes, a history teacher at the University of Toronto High School, who pointed out that, in the monument on the Plains of Abraham, '[t]he delicate subject of the British conquest is handled with disarming tact: both Wolfe and Montcalm emerge as heroes.'[31] Ironically, that same year C.P. Stacey published his masterful study, *Quebec*,

1759: The Siege and the Battle, a critical account of the tactics of both Wolfe and Montcalm during the battle. In the introduction to a new edition in 2000, Donald E. Graves proclaims that 'Stacey wrote from the point of view of a Canadian – a citizen of a nation with a shared British and French heritage – not solely from a British point of view.'[32] But this implies that the book was more radical than was the case. Stacey was critical of Wolfe but not of the British army, which he saw as the real heroes of the battle. In the introduction to the 1959 edition, Stacey praised Parkman's *Montcalm and Wolfe* as 'a magnificent book, which can still be read with the greatest profit,' and declared that 'the events of 1759 mark the greatest turning point in the history of Canada.'[33]

Lack of interest in the battle by English-Canadians in the past few decades partly reflects the weakening of older British loyalties and growing Canadian nationalism. In 1965 even Britannia's flag, which Wolfe had planted so firmly on Canadian soil, was replaced by a new flag that lacks any imperial symbolism.[34] Like their counterparts in the other dominions, Canadians of British origin preferred to play down memories of their imperial past in favour of the evolution of a distinctive national identity shorn of its imperial roots,[35] an approach pursued by successive Canadian governments in the past half-century. When the federal government decided to restore the National War Memorial, which originally was intended as a tribute to Canadians who had served in the First World War, it chose to add a series of statues honouring famous military figures from Canadian history. The decision not to include Wolfe and Montcalm initially was justified by the fact that 'they weren't Canadians. They were fighting for Britain and France.'[36] Ironically this Canadians-only policy was not rigorously applied. When the Valiants Memorial was unveiled in 2006, the comte de Frontenac and General Brock were among the fourteen individuals chosen to show 'how certain key turning points in our military history contributed to the building of our country.'[37] But neither Wolfe nor Montcalm made the grade.

During the 1960s, English-Canadian historians also lost interest in their country's imperial past and began to focus on social history and the more limited ethnic, regional, class, and gender identities of Canadians. Few were interested in the history of New France and fewer still chose to focus on the Conquest of Quebec and its consequences. The most distinguished historian of New France writing in English at that time undoubtedly was W.J. Eccles, but although he wrote an important revisionist article on the Battle of the Plains of Abraham, even Eccles devoted limited attention to the impact of the Conquest in his broader studies.[38] Stacey's account – which Eccles described as 'the best of a bad lot' – was still generally accepted as the definitive study of Wolfe and the battle, while English-Canadian military historians were attracted to other times and subjects.[39] The Conquest continued to be included in English-Canadian history texts, but it was increasingly interpreted as an internal Quebec issue, central to understanding the evolution of modern Quebec but not of modern Canada. The new scholarship is sympathetic to the conquered – Susan Mann Trofimenkoff in 1983 described the Conquest as like a 'rape'[40] – but much less sympathetic to the conquerors; indeed, much recent scholarship focuses less upon Wolfe's victory on the Plains of Abraham and more on the devastation his forces wrought upon the *Canadien* people.[41] 'Brave' Wolfe has become 'cruel' Wolfe.

Yet a trace of the earlier interpretation lingers on in the popular memory of English Canadians. Benjamin West's 1769 portrait of the death of Wolfe, given to Canada by the British government in gratitude for Canada's contribution during the First World War, remains one of the most popular pieces in the collection of the National Art Gallery in Ottawa.[42] Another version of the painting, dating from 1776, was recently chosen by the Royal Ontario Museum as one of its '15 Iconic Objects,'[43] while James Barry's painting of the 'Death of General Wolfe,' also from 1776, remains a prized possession of the New Brunswick Museum in Saint John. But for most English Canadians, particularly younger ones, Wolfe remains a shadowy figure and the significance of the Battle of the Plains of Abraham, if not forgotten, is only dimly remembered.

Indeed, except for the controversy over the proposed re-enactment of the battle by visiting American history buffs, it seems likely that its two hundred and fiftieth anniversary would have attracted little comment outside Quebec. There were, however, isolated outposts of resistance to the death of what can best be described as a form of British-Canadian nationalism.[44] In Calgary, for example, it was decided to refurbish the bronze statue of Wolfe that originally had come from New York and had stood in front of the Planetarium until it was removed in 2000 to a military museum, where it had lain covered in cobwebs for eight years. Thanks to private donations, on 13 September 2009, it was installed in South Mount Park on Wolfe Street, at a special ceremony in which wreaths were laid for the French and British who had died in the battle. The crowd of Calgarians who gathered in the park that Sunday included eighty-year-old Dennis Merritt, who had emigrated from England in the 1950s. Clutching 'a miniature Union Jack,' Merritt declared that he felt Wolfe 'symbolizes Canada.'[45]

Merritt's seems to have been a minority opinion, for few other commemorations were held elsewhere. In Quebec it was decided to read one hundred and forty poems and historical documents at an event called the *Moulin à paroles*, but the decision to include a reading of the controversial 1970 manifesto of the Front de libération du Québec, *Nous vaincrons!*, deprived the event of any support from federalists and angered public opinion outside Quebec – though, ironically, one of Wolfe's descendants agreed to participate. The saddest commemoration took place on Wolfe Island, Ontario, where for four years the local historical society had been planning a special tribute to the island's namesake. The event was cancelled at the last minute, however, when Victoria Stewart, the society's vice-president, referring to the proposed reading of the FLQ manifesto, said on a radio show that she hoped people would attend the society's tribute 'to show separatists the English aren't afraid to celebrate their own heritage.' In response, the mayor of Frontenac Islands, the township that includes Wolfe Island, decided that the township should not support a partisan event, and refused permission for it to be held on municipal property. Stewart then resigned from her position and listed her Wolfe Island home for sale – 'Another victim of politics and history,' declared Brian Johnson, the historical society's president.[46] In December 2009, before 'a small but enthusiastic audience,' the panel memorializing Wolfe was finally unveiled on the property of the Wolfe Island library. A brief ceremony ended with the singing of 'The Maple Leaf Forever.'[47] It is, of course, all too easy to parody the events at Calgary and Wolfe Island, and one suspects that the average age of the participants was on the far side of sixty. Nonetheless they represented the last gasp of a British-Canadian identity that still has meaning for a good many English-speaking Canadians even if their numbers are in decline.

For the descendants and cultural heirs of those who fought on the losing side in 1759 – the French, the *Canadiens*, and their aboriginal allies – the Battle of the Plains of Abraham has always occupied an ambiguous place in historical memory. For France, the loss of Canada was an embarrassment, but one with which it quickly came to terms. Even during the American Revolution, France made no effort to gain back what it had lost, and Napoleon's ambitions lay primarily in Europe, not in acquiring overseas possessions. In the nineteenth century, France would again acquire an extensive overseas empire, but despite Napoleon III's intervention in Mexico, the new French Empire would be based not in the Americas but in North and West Africa and Indochina. There was an attempt in the late nineteenth century to rehabilitate the memory of Montcalm, but Republican France's ties with Quebec were never all that strong. Only in the aftermath of the Second World War, when France was forced to accept the loss of its nineteenth-century empire, did it attempt to reassert real influence over its long-lost colony in Canada. As David Meren points out in his chapter, Charles de Gaulle accepted 'the idea of *abandon*' – the notion that France had abandoned New France during the Seven Years' War – and his actions were partly 'a bid for redemption.' But de Gaulle was primarily motivated by dissatisfaction with the emergence of the United States as a superpower and with 'the hegemony of the Anglo-Saxons.' As Meren argues, '[i]f de Gaulle did not expect to reverse Montcalm's defeat, he did hope to mitigate its geopolitical legacy as much as possible for the francophone populations on both sides of the Atlantic.' Because de Gaulle viewed French Canadians as an overseas branch of the French nation, Quebec neo-nationalism 'found an enthusiastic partner across the Atlantic' and his famous *cri de balcon* in Montreal in July 1967, 'Vive le Québec libre,' has come to be seen as one of the defining moments in modern Quebec history. Yet, as Meren points out, '1967 was not 1759.' De Gaulle's tendency to treat French Canada as an extension of the French nation ignored the reality that, after two hundred years' separation from France, Quebec had evolved its own distinctive North American identity. There was no going back – a reality not lost upon de Gaulle's successors, who have generally avoided direct interference in Canada-Quebec relations and have come to accept that the Conquest of Canada cannot be undone.

France's aboriginal allies in 1759 realized even more quickly than did France itself or the *Canadien* colonists that they had to adapt to a new reality. Their reactions to the Conquest varied, of course, since they were divided into a number of groups whose interests did not always coincide and sometimes directly conflicted. In a strict sense, the indigenous allies of the French in the Ohio region already had signed a separate peace with the British in 1758, but when it became clear that Britain intended to impose its authority over the region, many decided to resist and joined Pontiac's coalition in 1763. This option, however, was not particularly appealing to those who lived in mission villages in New France, who faced far more immediately the implications of the Conquest, and who sought to negotiate a ceasefire with the British army of occupation. There had been a string of earlier diplomatic encounters between the 'French praying Indians' and Anglo-American officials, but, as Jean-François Lozier points out in his contribution to this collection, the treaties of neutrality negotiated in 1760 eventually would become 'the foundation blocks of the relationship between the inhabitants of the mission villages and the British Crown.' Yet, for over two centuries, British, Canadian, and Quebec governments ignored these treaties as they gradually extended their control over the indigenous peoples of Quebec. Only in the aftermath of the constitutional crisis over the patriation of the Constitution in 1982 were the treaties of 1760 rediscovered, mainly as 'a result of mounting indigenous advocacy,' and, after a series of judicial appeals, the Supreme Court of Canada recognized their validity. Debate continues among historians and Quebec nationalists about the historical accuracy of the Supreme Court's decision, but in this case, a historical memory, temporarily lost, has been recovered.

For French Canadians, as *Canadiens* came to redefine themselves in the nineteenth century, the events of 1759 could hardly be forgotten, but they could be reinterpreted and the public memory of them used for different purposes. Not surprisingly, most of the chapters in this collection focus on this theme. In the evolving historiography of Quebec, the two hundred and fiftieth anniversary of the Conquest came at an intriguing moment. The twentieth century had seen a number of intense debates over such issues as the intellectual legacy of Abbé Lionel Groulx, the socio-economic effect of the ending of the French regime, and the degree to which Quebec is distinctive as a national society or shares strong similarities with other parts of North America. By the turn of the twenty-first century, authors such as Jean-Marie Fecteau, Yvan Lamonde, and Ronald Rudin were prompting historiographical reflection and stock-taking on the link between history and nation.[48] One point on which Fecteau and Rudin agree is that, in Fecteau's words, 'since the advent of the democratic ideal, the prevailing point of reference for defining identities has been the nation.'[49] And, as Jocelyn Létourneau notes, definition of identity is a matter for collective memory as much as for history as such. 'Indeed,' he asks pointedly, 'for what future do we remember?'[50]

The question is worth posing. Indeed, as Michel Ducharme points out in his chapter, even during the nineteenth century the different interpretations developed by French-Canadian political, intellectual, and cultural elites 'were not interested so much in the past as in the present and the future.' They were interested in discovering what historians today would call a 'usable past' that could legitimate their cultural, economic, and political goals. Ducharme shows that, until the 1840s, the Conquest was rarely mentioned in French-Canadian debates and then more likely to be referred to as a beneficial act that had protected the population of Lower Canada from the horrors of the French Revolution and given them the benefit of parliamentary institutions. But this interpretation did not survive the failed rebellions of 1837–8 and the reframing of the Lower Canadian struggle in ethnic, rather than political-constitutional, terms. Faced with the threat of assimilation, the French-Canadian elites came to see the Conquest as 'a pivotal and foundational moment in French-Canadian history,' and they developed a series of rhetorical strategies to explain the significance of the defeat of 1759 in a way that held out hope for the future survival of the French-Canadian nation. Thus, they argued, it was the French – not the *Canadiens* – who had been responsible for the defeat on the Plains of Abraham; the *Canadiens* had redeemed that defeat at the Battle of Ste-Foy in 1760 – and, in their honour, *Le monument des Braves* was inaugurated in 1863. In effect, France had abandoned New France. Ironically, this negative view of France did not extend to the marquis de Montcalm, whose reputation was restored at the end of the century. Montcalm's courage, Thomas Chapais proclaimed, 'crowned the destruction of New France with a glorious halo.'[51] Ducharme contends that, even if French Canadians 'chose a defeat as a founding moment of their national existence, they were not *defeatists*,' for they sought 'to transform this defeat into a victory, or at least into a positive source of inspiration.' As late as 1890, when Louis-Philippe Hébert produced sculptures of Wolfe and Montcalm for the facade of the Quebec legislature – now the Assemblée nationale – where they still sit, and even in 1901, when Louis Jobin carved a wooden statue of Wolfe for display by a resident of Quebec City – which was moved in 1964 to the safety of a museum – this *bonne-entente* tradition was the dominant one.[52]

Chapais's rather optimistic vision of the Conquest increasingly came under attack in the aftermath of the First World War by nationalist intellectuals in Quebec, particularly Abbé Groulx. In his chapter in this collection, Michel Bock notes that Groulx was 'the first prominent intellectual and historian in Quebec to place the British Conquest of New France squarely at the centre of both his ideology and his work as a scholar.' He saw the Conquest 'literally as a national "catastrophe,"' and he doggedly set out to discredit the theory held by Chapais that the Conquest had been ordained by Providence to shield New France from the horrors of the French Revolution. Nor did Groulx believe that the survival of French-Canadian culture owed much to British generosity; if French Canada had survived it was because of the determination of French Canadians. Groulx is often described as a separatist, but Bock argues that it was not Confederation to which Groulx was opposed but English Canada's failure to live up to the Confederation agreement and its attempt 'to limit French-Canadian influence to what he ironically called the "Quebec reservation."' Groulx called for French Canadians to live up to their responsibility to defend French culture and to spread the Catholic faith across North America, while firmly rejecting any attempt at 'la fusion des races.' Yet even this position proved too moderate for the new generation of Quebec nationalist historians that emerged after the Second World War. Members of the so-called Montreal school – principally Maurice Séguin, Guy Frégault, and Michel Brunet – were, Bock points out, disciples of Groulx and shared his interpretation of the Conquest. Unlike Groulx, however, they believed that the Conquest had been an economic and social catastrophe from which French Canadians could never recover so long as they lacked 'the ability to control their own economic and political structures and, in the end, their own destiny.'

Groulx's views on the catastrophic consequences of the Conquest continued to influence nationalist thought in Quebec, but in ways he did not intend. Indeed, while the *Québécois* nationalists of the 1960s accepted that the Conquest had been a calamity, Alexis Lachaine argues in his chapter that they believed it was time 'to move beyond the Conquest,' which 'had little place in the revolutionary discourse of emancipation.' Nationalists such as Hubert Aquin, Pierre Vadeboncoeur, and Jacques Ferron preferred to focus on another seminal event in French-Canadian history – the rebellions of 1837–8 – in order, Ferron noted in an interview in 1968, to relate 'our liberation struggle to all the other liberation struggles in the world.' Similarly, Pierre Vallières, in one of the most famous political tracts of the period, *Nègres blancs d'Amérique*, saw the Conquest as an event of only minor importance. These nationalists did not deny that the Conquest lay at the root of French-Canadian inferiority, but 'for a great number of *Québécois* nationalists of the 1960s, [the Conquest] ultimately had to be surpassed, and could only be surpassed, through action – revolutionary or otherwise.' So long as nationalist intellectuals in Quebec could believe in the dream of achieving an independent state, they could focus on the future, not the past. But as that dream waned after the loss of two referendums on sovereignty, the significance of the Conquest and the Battle of the Plains of Abraham, Lachaine believes, began to be reasserted as 'a nightmare' from which Quebec still has not awoken, which explains the vigorous nationalist reaction to the proposal to re-enact the battle in September 2009.

The 'nightmare' has been kept alive, Brian Young argues in his chapter, not so much by professional historians in Quebec as by several gifted popular historians. Young seeks to explain the contrast between the academic discourse surrounding the Conquest, which tends to emphasize the persistence of French institutions and French-Canadian culture, and the popular vision that emphasizes the centrality of the Conquest in Quebec history and its devastating impact. A large part of the answer, Young feels, lies in the work of popular historian Denis Vaugeois, who, with his collaborator Jacques Lacoursière, has 'easily eclipsed university historians' in purveying his interpretation of Quebec history. In 1962 Vaugeois and Lacoursière helped to create *Le Boréal Express*, a Canadian history tabloid with a wide readership in Quebec. They also began to produce teachers' guides and history texts for use in Quebec's Catholic schools. In 1968 they established one of Quebec's major publishing houses, Les Éditions du Boréal Express. Through these and other media activities, they have reached out to present a simple message, which focuses on the Conquest as 'a deep line in the sand, an irretrievable moment of Before and After.' This was not an original message – indeed, Vaugeois imbibed it at the feet of Maurice Séguin at the Université de Montréal. But Vaugeois and Lacoursière ensured that the message reached virtually every youth coming of age in francophone Quebec in the 1960s and 1970s, and their books continue to outsell all of the competition. From 1978 to 1981, as minister of culture in the first Parti Québécois government, Vaugeois was also able not only to influence what was taught in the schools of Quebec, but also to direct funds to libraries and museums to encourage them to promote the message. No one has done more to contribute 'to the construction of the post-1960 Quebec identity' and to ensure that the Conquest continues to occupy a central place in the Quebec historical imagination.

It is not surprising, therefore, that the plan of the National Battlefields Commission to re-enact the Battle of the Plains of Abraham on the site of the battle in the summer of 2009 unleashed such passion in Quebec, including threats of violence if the re-enactment took place. In the end it was cancelled, but even in Quebec, as Nicole Neatby points out in her chapter, the public was divided over the issue. There were those who defended the Commission's initial decision as 'a sign of maturity, a ca-

pacity to come to terms with the past and get beyond old resentments.'
But for most francophone Quebecers, as a *Le Devoir* columnist noted,
1759 marked the beginning of 'colonial domination.' Inevitably the debate over the re-enactment became politicized. The Parti Québécois,
languishing in opposition, attacked the Commission's decision, while
federalist politicians defended it, though somewhat lukewarmly. Partly
because the whole debate became so partisan and polemical, Neatby
notes that professional historians both inside and outside Quebec 'kept
a remarkably low profile.' So vehement was the reaction of those who
opposed the Commission's plan, however, that Neatby wonders if francophone Quebecers will ever be willing to countenance a re-enactment
of the defeat. She notes that, in the United States in contrast, Civil War
battles are frequently re-enacted without arousing controversy. But
Americans have come 'to share a consensual memory of the Civil War,'
which ended in the creation of a stronger nation that ultimately brought
prosperity to the South as well as the North. 'Today,' she points out,
'few and far between are those who advocate the South's separation
from the North, and it goes without saying that no one is promoting the
reinstitution of slavery.' In Quebec, however, a high percentage of those
of French ancestry regret the Conquest's outcome and wish to 'undo it'
through independence. So long as this attitude persists in Quebec, there
can never be 'a new shared memory of 1759.'

Jocelyn Létourneau, in his contribution to this volume, sees the possibility of a shift in historical memory, but only if one takes the long
view. Létourneau accepts that a specific interpretation of the Conquest
has now become firmly entrenched in Quebec – a grand narrative that
is central to the historical consciousness of the *Québécois* and is strongly
reflected in the worlds of politics and the arts. 'Over the years,' he notes,
'through a potent cocktail of abridgment, reductionism, and emotion,
[ideologues] have commandeered a complex event and turned it to the
service of a simplistic and one-dimensional view of the past in which
good and evil are easy to identify and an intractable foe – the English – is constantly landing hammer blows.' This form of national consciousness in Quebec 'is founded on a belief in destiny usurped and
progress thwarted.' But, Létourneau argues, this is not the only possible interpretation of 1759 nor even the most plausible. The Conquest
can be seen as a turbulent era of transition that led 'to the creation of
a distinctive society today known as *québécois*.' Such an interpretation
would see the conflict between the *Canadiens* and the English-speaking
population as just one of many social, economic, and political antago-

nisms within Quebec and not necessarily the most important. Although 'there was a disconnect between anglophone and francophone worlds ... there was also a degree of cooperation,' for the Conquest 'brought neither dislocation nor paralysis.' This interpretation depicts 'a society that, from the admittedly complex and paradoxical legacy of the Conquest, went on to a phase of economic and political development that was advantageous for some (not all of them anglophones) and disadvantageous for others (not all of them francophones).' This, Létourneau admits, is an interpretation to which powerful interests in Quebec are bound to be opposed, because they fear that 'the defeat of 1759 would be repackaged as a victory, opening the door to the idea of a conquest that was beneficial and even profitable for the *Canadiens* of the day, then to the notion that the *Québécois* of today are a hybrid people, drawing strength from both French and British heritages.' Nonetheless, there are signs, Létourneau believes, that Quebecers are ready to embrace this reinterpretation. If they do, 2034 – the two hundred and seventy-fifth anniversary of the Battle of the Plains of Abraham – 'might well signal the entire emancipation of the *Québécois* vis-à-vis 1759.'

In 1882 the French historian Ernest Renan wrote that 'the essence of a nation is that all its members have many things in common and also that they have forgotten many things.'[53] It is unlikely that English Canadians and French Canadians will ever come to share a common understanding of the Conquest. At best they might be able to agree to try to forget it ever happened. Certainly this process is well under way in English Canada. The whole thrust of modern English-Canadian scholarship is to be suspicious of national history and of official commemorations that attempt to emphasize collective national identities.[54] As Daniel Francis has declared, 'the myth of postmodernity seems to be challenging the myth of unity as a way of conceptualizing Canada.'[55] Indeed, in post-imperial, multicultural Canada, the emphasis is on oppositional histories, on those who challenged the status quo and fought for minority rights. Thus, Louis Riel – demonized in English Canada after the failed rebellion of 1885 – increasingly is seen by many Canadians as a more appropriate 'national' symbol than General James Wolfe. Ramsay Cook once declared that '[t]he Conquest is the burden of Canadian history.'[56] It is a burden that a majority of English Canadians would prefer to lay down. If the Battle of the Plains of Abraham hinders reconciliation between Quebec and the rest of Canada, then most English Canadians are happy to forget their imperial past and to focus their history on events other than a battle fought a quarter of a millennium ago between British and French troops – though it is also true that other events, particularly Canada's participation in the two world wars, remain extremely divisive. But, as the chapters in this collection indicate, in Quebec both the remembering and the forgetting of the Conquest travel on a distinct trajectory. The Battle of the Plains of Abraham might already be largely forgotten – at least in the popular memory – in Britain, France, the United States, and even in much of English Canada, but it continues to be indispensable in defining the collective identity of the *Québécois*. The fact that the battle was largely ignored in Quebec on the two hundred and fiftieth anniversary of Wolfe's victory was not a sign that it had been forgotten, but a silent protest against its celebration.

NOTES

1 Dan Snow, 'A flutter of protest, and some dog-walkers,' *BBC History Magazine*, 14 September 2009, http://www.bbchistorymagazine.com/blog/how-commemorate-battle. Snow was in Quebec City preparing a one-hour documentary for the BBC on the Battle of the Plains of Abraham. Entitled 'The Battle for North America,' it was eventually aired on BBC Two on 16 March 2010.

2 Jean Provencher, 'The Park of Memories,' in *The Plains of Abraham: The Search for an Ideal*, ed. Jacques Mathieu and Eugene Kedl (Sillery, QC: Septentrion, 1993), 241.

3 H.V. Nelles, *The Art of Nation-Building: Pageantry and Spectacle at Quebec's Tercentenary* (Toronto: University of Toronto Press, 1999), 78.

4 'The past is a foreign country,' is how L.P Hartley begins his novel *The Go-Between* (London: Hamish Hamilton, 1953).

5 W. Fitzhugh Brundage, 'Introduction,' in *Where These Memories Grow: History, Memory, and Southern Identity*, ed. W. Fitzhugh Brundage (Chapel Hill: University of North Carolina Press, 2000), 17.

6 Michael E. Geisler, 'Introduction: What Are National Symbols – and What Do They Do to Us?' in *National Symbols, Fractured Identities: Contesting the National Narrative* (Middlebury, VT: Middlebury College Press, 2005), xviii. See also Alice Fah and Joan Waugh, eds., *The Memory of the Civil War in American Culture* (Chapel Hill: University of North Carolina Press, 2004); and David W. Blight, *Beyond the Battlefield: Race, Memory, and the American Civil War* (Amherst, MA; Boston: University of Massachusetts Press, 2002).

7 There is a growing literature on commemoration and historical memory in Canada. See, in particular, Jonathan F. Vance, *Death So Noble: Memory,*

Meaning, and the First World War (Vancouver: UBC Press, 1997); Patrice Groulx, *Pièges de mémoire: Dollard des Ormeaux, les Amérindiens et nous* (Hull, QC: Éditions Vent d'ouest, 1998); Alan Gordon, *Making Public Pasts: The Contested Terrain of Montreal's Public Memories, 1891–1930* (Montreal; Kingston, ON: McGill-Queen's University Press, 2001); idem, *The Hero and the Historian: Historiography and the Uses of Jacques Cartier* (Vancouver: UBC Press, 2010); Colin Coates and Cecilia Morgan, *Heroines and History: Representations of Madeleine de Verchères and Laura Secord* (Toronto: University of Toronto Press, 2002); Ronald Rudin, *Founding Fathers: Champlain and Laval on the Streets of Quebec* (Toronto: University of Toronto Press, 2003); and idem, *Remembering and Forgetting in Acadie: A Historian's Journey through Public Memory* (Toronto: University of Toronto Press, 2009). Of course, none of these studies focuses upon commemoration and memories of the 1759 Conquest. Nelles touches upon this issue in *The Art of Nation-Building*, but only in the context of the 1908 Quebec tercentenary celebrations.

8 Stephen Brumwell, *Paths of Glory: The Life and Death of General James Wolfe* (London: Hambledon Continuum, 2006), xviii.

9 Ibid., xvi.

10 For the official report on the 'Westerham Wolfe Weekend,' see http:// www.visitwesterham.org.UK/pdf/ WWWReport-5.pdf.

11 'Wolfe Saved,' National Army Museum announcement, http://www .national-army-museum.ac.uk/pages/ wolfe.shtml.

12 Brumwell, *Paths of Glory*; and Matthew C. Ward, *The Battle for Quebec, 1759* (Stroud, UK: Tempus Publishing, 2005).

13 Sarah J. Purcell, *Sealed with Blood: War, Sacrifice, and Memory in Revolutionary America* (Pittsburgh: University of Pennsylvania Press, 2002), 21–33; and Alan McNairn, *Behold the Hero: General Wolfe and the Arts in the Eighteenth Century* (Montreal; Kingston, ON: McGill-Queen's University Press, 1997), 213–23.

14 Edith Fowke, 'Brave Wolfe,' *The Canadian Encyclopedia of Music*, http:// thecanadianencyclopedia.com.

15 Lorenzo Sabine, 'An Address before the New England Historic-Genealogical Society' (Boston: A. Williams, 1859), 98, 12.

16 Francis Parkman, *The Old Regime in Canada* (1874; rev. ed. Boston: Little, Brown, 1895), 256.

17 'STREETSCAPES/Readers' Questions,' *New York Times*, 1 April 2007, http://query.nytimes.com/gst/fullpage.html?res=9C01E3d801030F932A3 575COA9619C8B63.

18 Ibid.

19 See Richard R. Johnson, 'Charles McLean Andrews and the Invention of

American Colonial History,' *William and Mary Quarterly*, 3rd series, 43 (1986): 528–41; Jackson Turner Main, 'Lawrence Henry Gipson: Historian,' in *Revisioning the British Empire in the Eighteenth* Century, ed. William G. Shade (Cranbury, NJ: Associate University Presses, 1998); and Fred Anderson and Andrew Cayton, 'The Problem of Authority in the Writing of Early American History,' *William and Mary Quarterly*, 3rd series, 66 (2009): 467–94.

20 Fred Anderson, *Crucible of War: The Seven Years' War and the Fate of Empire in North America* (New York: Alfred A. Knopf, 2000), 365, 746.

21 Warren R. Hofstra, 'Preface,' in *Cultures in Conflict: The Seven Year' War in North America*, ed. Warren R. Hofstra (Lanham, MD: Rowman & Littlefield, 2007), vii.

22 Anderson, *Crucible of War*, 742.

23 Fowke, 'Brave Wolfe.'

24 Composed in 1867, the lyrics can be found at http://www.torontohistory .org/Pages_ABC/Alexander_Muir.html.

25 McNairn, *Behold the Hero*, 237.

26 Andrew Bell, *British-Canadian Centennium, 1759–1859. General James Wolfe, His Life and Death: A Lecture, Delivered in the Mechanics' Institute Hall, Montreal, on Tuesday, September 13, 1859* (Quebec City: John Lovell, 1859), 7, 9.

27 Nelles, *Art of Nation-Building*, 132.

28 Quoted by Little, in this volume.

29 Daniel Francis, *National Dreams: Myth, Memory and Canadian History* (Vancouver: Arsenal Press, 1997), 95–6.

30 Catherine Desbarats and Allan Greer, 'The Seven Years' War in Canadian History and Memory,' in *Cultures in Conflict* (see note 21), 152.

31 Berkeley Rhodes, 'On the Plains of Abraham,' *Globe and Mail* (Toronto), 12 September 1959, 6.

32 Donald E. Graves, 'Charles P. Stacey and the Siege of Quebec, 1759,' in C.P. Stacey, *Quebec, 1759: The Siege and the Battle*, ed. with new material by Donald E. Graves (Toronto: Robin Brass Studio, 2002), 10.

33 Ibid., 15.

34 Although the Union flag that had appeared on the Red Ensign prior to its replacement in 1965 was not, of course, exactly the same as the version that existed in 1759.

35 For some comparative studies, see Kate Darien-Smith and Paula Hamilton, eds., *Memory and History in Twentieth-Century Australia* (Melbourne: Oxford University Press, 1994); Sarah Nuttall and Carli Coetzee, eds., *Negotiating the Past: The Making of Memory in South Africa* (Cape Town: Oxford University Press, 1998); Annie E. Coombes, ed., *Rethinking Settler Colonialism:*

History and Memory in Australia, Canada, Aotearoa New Zealand and South Africa (Manchester: Manchester University Press, 2006); Marilyn Lake, ed., *Memory, Monuments and Museums: The Past in the Present* (Melbourne: Melbourne University Press, 2006); and Daniel J. Walkowitz and Lisa Maya Knauer, eds., *Contested Histories in Public Space: Memory, Race and Nation* (Durham, NC: Duke University Press, 2009). Of course, the ways in which the British populations in the former Dominions sought to readjust their memories of their imperial past varied from place to place since their pasts were rooted in very different social and historical contexts.

36 Tom MacGregor, 'Tribute Proposed for Canada's Military Valiant,' *Legion Magazine*, 1 January 2001.

37 'The Valiants Memorial,' http:/www.valiants.ca.

38 See W.J. Eccles, 'The Battle of Quebec: A Reappraisal,' in *Essays on New France* (Toronto: Oxford University Press, 1987). In his study of France in America, even in the second edition, Eccles deals only briefly with the impact of the Conquest in a few pages in the 'Epilogue,' stressing French Canada's survival; see *France in America*, rev. ed. (Markham, ON: Fitzhenry & Whiteside, 1990), 257–60.

39 W.J. Eccles, 'Bibliographical Essay,' in *The French in North America, 1500–1785*, 3rd ed. (Markham, ON: Fitzhenry & Whiteside, 1998), 314.

40 Susan Mann Trofimenkoff, *The Dream of Nation* (Toronto: Gage, 1983), 20.

41 See, for example, D. Peter MacLeod, *Northern Armageddon: The Battle of the Plains of Abraham* (Vancouver: Douglas & McIntyre, 2008).

42 Ruth B. Phillips, 'Settler Monuments, Indigenous Memory: Dis-membring and Re-membering Canadian Art History,' in *Monuments and Memory, Made and Unmade*, ed. Robert S. Nelson and Margaret Olin (Chicago: University of Chicago Press, 2003), 288. Phillips points out that the gallery has tried to add balance to West's depiction by commissioning aboriginal art that challenges the aboriginal image in the painting.

43 Royal Ontario Museum, News Release, 30 March 2009; the news release also acknowledged the donation of a nineteenth-century painting and a 1911 statuette of Wolfe to the museum's collection.

44 See Phillip Buckner, 'Canada and the End of Empire,' in *Canada and the British Empire*, ed. Phillip Buckner (Oxford: Oxford University Press, 2008); and C.P. Champion, *The Strange Demise of British Canada: The Liberals and Canadian Nationalism, 1964–1968* (Montreal; Kingston, ON: McGill-Queen's University Press, 2010).

45 Jamie Komarnicki, 'James Wolfe statue wins over Calgary,' *National Post*, 14 September 2009.

46 Brian Johnson,'Wolfe celebration: what happened?' undated, but from
    the archives of the *Kingston Whig Standard*, http://www.thewhig
    .com,ArticleDisplay.apex?e=1760395&archive=true.

47 Margaret Knott, 'Historic Panel Honouring Wolfe Island's Name-
    sake, "General James Wolfe" Unveiled,' *Kingston EMC*, 10 December
    2009, http:/www.emckingston.ca/20091210/News/Historic+Panel+
    Honouring+Wolfe+Island.

48 See Ronald Rudin, *Making History in Twentieth-Century Quebec* (Toronto:
    University of Toronto Press, 1997); Jean-Marie Fecteau, 'Between Scientific
    Enquiry and the Search for a Nation: Quebec Historiography as Seen by
    Ronald Rudin,' *Canadian Historical Review* 80 (1999): 641–66; Ronald Rudin,
    'On Difference and National Identity in Quebec Historical Writing: A Re-
    sponse to Jean-Marie Fecteau,' *Canadian Historical Review* 80 (1999): 666–76;
    and Yvan Lamonde, *Trajectoires de l'histoire du Québec* (Montréal: Fides,
    2001).

49 Fecteau, 'Between Scientific Enquiry,' 650; and Rudin, 'On Difference and
    National Identity,' 670.

50 Jocelyn Létourneau, *A History for the Future: Rewriting Memory and Identity
    in Quebec*, trans. Phyllis Aronoff and Howard Scott (Montreal; Kingston,
    ON: McGill-Queen's University Press, 2004; French-language edition,
    2000), 29.

51 Quoted in Ducharme, in this volume.

52 McNairn, *Behold the Hero*, 239–40.

53 Quoted in Michael Kammen, *Mystic Chords of Memory: The Transformation
    of Tradition in American Culture* (New York: Alfred A. Knopf, 1991), 694.

54 See Veronica Strong-Boag, 'Experts on Our Own Lives,' *Public Historian* 35,
    no. 1 (2009): 66.

55 Francis, *National Dreams*, 108.

56 Ramsay Cook, *Canada and the French-Canadian Question* (Toronto: Macmil-
    lan, 1967), 146.

2

'The Immortal Wolfe'?
Monuments, Memory, and the Battle of Quebec

JOAN COUTU AND JOHN McALEER

In 1769, on the tenth anniversary of the Battle of Quebec, Captain John Knox, an officer who had served with the 43rd Regiment, published his memoirs. For Knox and his readers, there was no question about the importance of the taking of the city. Yet Knox was writing as much for future generations as he was for his contemporaries: 'The end proposed, at least professedly, by all publications, is Instruction, or Entertainment. That I have the prospect of affording either, by a recital of facts, so recent as to be universally known, may possibly be a question with many. But the answer is ready. Though the facts, here recited, are known now, how long will that knowledge continue, if they are trusted meerly [sic] to memory?'[1] Knox recognized that 'meer' memory is indeed slippery – a dynamic, active force that shapes the past but that is itself shaped, as Raphael Samuel reminds us, by historical circumstances that change and respond to the specific political and social exigencies of the moment. It is altered and alterable from generation to generation, leaving the 'impress of experience' and bearing the marks of being 'stamped with the ruling passions of the time.'[2]

The historical understandings and interpretations of the Battle of Quebec for different groups were structured by the prevailing political exigencies of the time in which they were created. The ways that Major-General James Wolfe was celebrated, commemorated, memorialized, and sometimes vilified, by diverse communities at different times and in various locations gives an insight into how these groups related to the historical personalities and events of 1759. Monuments, which function as the visual vehicles for these memories, are equally subject to the conditions of 'successive presents,' to use Pierre Nora's words.[3] This chapter explores the different uses to which Wolfe's memory has been put over the course of two and a half centuries, and how this has been expressed in monuments in Britain and Quebec. It examines how Wolfe and the battle that made him famous have been remembered and commemorated in public forums during that period, mainly through the medium of figural monuments.

As with memory, monuments also purport to be unchanging and permanent. Furthermore, monuments are historically linked with empire, another concept that is imbued with apparent permanence. By focusing on monuments that commemorate James Wolfe, this chapter explores the paradox of the illusion of permanence inherent in memory, monuments, and empire. Initially, it focuses on the monument to Wolfe in Westminster Abbey and the construction of the memory of Wolfe in the months immediately following the Battle of Quebec. What Knox did not recognize was that the 'facts,' as he called them, had already passed through the filter of memory. The discussion then examines how Wolfe lived on in the nineteenth and twentieth centuries – how his memory was constructed and reconstructed by various constituencies for whom the importance of Wolfe and the British victory at Quebec continued to resonate.

The monument to Wolfe in Westminster Abbey was meant to be at once a permanent reminder for posterity of Wolfe's heroic and selfless actions and an anchor of sorts amid the contemporary euphoria surrounding the glorious victory (see Figure 2.1). William Pitt the elder, the architect of the British Empire that emerged during the *annus mirabilis* of 1759, was responsible for commissioning the monument that was ultimately erected. Having been reared in the political gardens of Stowe, Pitt recognized the persuasive properties of monuments and understood that a monument could articulate and lend legitimacy to his empire-building tendencies.[4] He was equally well aware, however, that both empires and monuments were historically tainted with autocracy, an evil that the liberty-loving British found especially odious. Consequently, although anxious to celebrate the empire that he had fostered, he was also careful to present it as something different from empires that had come before. To this end, he turned once again to the public, the key ingredient in his earlier drive to political prominence. Not that he actually ever consulted the public; rather, as the 'Great Commoner,' he used the amorphous, indistinct, and largely silent body of the public in his efforts to overturn the old order of the natural aristocracy.[5] In 1759–60, the new British Empire was to be an empire of the people.[6]

Regimes often seek to appropriate national memory – what Maurice

Figure 2.1. Joseph Wilton, detail of the monument to Major-General
James Wolfe, marble with lead bas-relief, conceived 1759, unveiled 1773.
Westminster Abbey, London.

Dean and Chapter of Westminster

Halbwachs has defined as the all-embracing collective memories of a
people[7] – and subvert it into official (that is, state) memory to serve the
agenda of the regime. As Avner Ben-Amos, who writes on state funerals, has observed, the 'aim of a regime is to make the official and the
national memories identical in order to reduce the potential threat to
its rule.'[8] Furthermore, as many scholars of memory have emphasized,
memory that is imposed upon a people requires, and is dependent
upon, outward supports, symbols, and signs because it is not 'lived in.'
What is interesting in the case of Wolfe and his victory at Quebec is that
there was no national memory. As Horace Walpole observed, it was at
Wolfe's death that 'his fame began.'[9] Consistent with the idea of the
empire as being of the people, Pitt was quick off the mark after news
of Wolfe's death reached Britain to manufacture a memory that would
become both the official and national memory.

When the bittersweet news of Wolfe's death in victory reached Britain in the middle of October 1759, it sparked an outpouring of patriotic euphoria on a scale never seen before.[10] Much of that euphoria was whipped up by Pitt and his administration. The day before Wolfe's death became known, Pitt had released to the press a mournful but patriotic letter, which Wolfe had written to him, claiming that 'Quebec is impregnable; it is flinging away the lives of brave men to attempt it,' but that he would nonetheless launch the offensive 'persuaded [as he was] that a victorious army finds no difficulties.'[11] When the news of Wolfe's death broke the following day, 'the Park and Tower guns were fired, flags every where were displayed from the steeples, and the greatest illuminations were made throughout the city and suburbs that were ever known,' which in turn prompted a cacophony of less dignified and unofficial squibs, firecrackers, and general rabble rousing.[12] Horace Walpole recounted that he saw 'joy, curiosity, astonishment ... painted in every countenance.'[13] Oliver Goldsmith used the occasion to attack the excesses of the mob, although his satirical comments were no doubt exacerbated by the fact that a firecracker had exploded in his wig.[14] An unprecedented spate of eulogies, sermons, epitaphs, and other panegyrics soon followed, further insinuating the significance of Wolfe's victory into the popular mindset. By 21 November 1759, when Wolfe's elaborate state-sponsored funeral cortège wound its way through slews of adoring crowds from Portsmouth to Greenwich (where his body was to be interred), the cult of Wolfe had become entrenched.[15]

Several calls for a monument to Wolfe were issued in the heat of the moment amid the fireworks and panegyrics, with little or no thought of bringing it to fruition. The aging George II, however, reportedly proposed to pay for a monument in Westminster Abbey as early as 1 November 1759.[16] Yet three weeks later, on the day after Wolfe's funeral procession (22 November), Pitt stood up in the House of Commons and called for a monument 'to be erected in the Collegiate Church of St. Peter, Westminster, to the memory of the ever-lamented, late Commander-in-Chief of his Majesty's Land Forces on an Expedition against Quebec, Major-General Wolfe, who, surmounting by Ability and Valour, all Obstacles of Art and Nature, was slain in the arduous and decisive Battle against the French Army, near Quebec, fighting for their Capital of Canada, in the Year 1759, and to assure his Majesty, this House will make good the Expence of erecting the said Monument.'[17] Walpole recorded that it was the 'worst harangue [Pitt] had ever uttered.'[18] Paid for by the House of Commons, Pitt essentially had stolen the king's monument and it had now, ostensibly, become a monument sponsored by the public, as represented by the House.

Westminster Abbey was the obvious choice for a monument to the young hero. By 1759 it had become a Valhalla of sorts, filled with monuments not only to monarchs and their families but also to statesmen, heroes, and anyone who had enough money to pay the fines to the dean and chapter to be commemorated in stone. People of all levels of society toured the Abbey, often with a guide who would explain the monuments to them; Pierre-Jean Grosley, a Frenchman who published a commentary of his visit to London in 1765, remarked with admiration that he would see guides explaining the monuments in the Abbey to even the lowliest herb- and milk-women.[19] Wolfe would thus join this great pantheon, and his monument would address the wide and varied populace that constituted Pitt's public.

One of the primary challenges of any public monument is to keep the monument in the public eye during the frequently long period between commission and completion. In the case of the Wolfe monument, some of this was offset by making it the subject of a competition, and Britain's most prominent sculptors, both young and old, submitted designs.[20] The competition was won by Joseph Wilton, fresh from his Grand Tour and full of promise, an appropriate parallel to the youthful general whose victory was thought to have ensured the future prosperity of Britain. The duke of Devonshire, who was also the lord chamberlain and an old political crony of Pitt's, ostensibly oversaw the competition and selected the winner.[21] An exchange of private letters between the duke and Richard, Earl Temple, Pitt's brother-in-law and comrade-in-arms in the Privy Council, reveals, however, that Pitt was very much involved in the selection process and preferred Wilton's design over all the others.[22] Temple, incidentally, was actively engaged in his own commemoration of Wolfe at Stowe, as part of his narrative program in the Grecian Valley, a self-laudatory celebration of his and Pitt's accomplishments. Erected in a private garden accessible to a circumscribed public conversant with esoteric classical allusions, Temple's indulgences at Stowe offer an instructive parallel to Pitt's far more public endeavour in London.[23]

For the Westminster Abbey commission, all seven of the designs that have survived – drawings each by John Michael Rysbrack, Peter Scheemakers, Louis-François Roubiliac, Robert Adam, and probably William Chambers, a written description of Agostino Carlini's no longer extant drawing, and Wilton's design as executed – are remarkably similar, suggesting that certain design conditions were laid down for the competition. Wolfe had to be presented dying, a personification of either Victory or Fame had to be included, and there had to be some indication of where the battle took place.[24] In other words, the design had to be a narrative that could be easily read by a wide range of people. As such, the design perpetuated the popular image of Wolfe constructed in the press reports following his death: only upon hearing the news that the French had been defeated did he lie back and utter his last words, 'Alas I die in peace.'[25] Wolfe was not cast as the conquering hero or the stoic military general. Rather, the conceit presented him as Everyman; he was portrayed as the sensitive commander, the man who left behind his widowed mother and fiancée to give his life for his country, quoting Thomas Gray's *Elegy* the night before his death: 'The paths of glory lead but to the grave.'[26]

Wilton's final design for the monument is easy to read. Wolfe lies back in the arms of a Highland soldier while a second soldier runs up to tell him that the French have been defeated. Peace/Victory descends to crown him with laurels and to present him with the palm branch of peace. The location of the battle is indicated by the scalping knife and axe entwined in the oak tree to the right of the tent as well as a portrayal of the battle in a lead relief at the base of the monument and in the simple forthright English inscription. The latter, incidentally, is taken from Pitt's initial call for the monument, thereby implicitly strengthening the link between Pitt and Wolfe.[27]

In its accessibility, the Wolfe monument differs significantly from the single previous monument to be commissioned by the House of Commons, that to Captain James Cornewall in Westminster Abbey.[28] The commission for the Cornewall monument, given to Robert Taylor, had been forced through the House by the Grenville Cousinhood, of which Pitt was a member, in the late 1740s following the politically contentious inquiry into the behaviour of admirals Lestock and Mathews in the battle off the coast of Toulon in 1743, in which Cornewall was killed. The Grenville Cousinhood used the commission to give further credence to their claim that the inquiry had been stacked against Mathews, who was ultimately court-martialled. The design of the Cornewall monument consists of esoteric allegory shrouded in classicism, which, combined with its lengthy Latin inscription, would have been too remote for many of those who frequented the Abbey. The Grenvilles, however, were not concerned with addressing a wide-ranging public, for the public, in Pitt's sense, did not figure in the socio-political realm of the 1740s. Rather, the design of the Cornewall monument was meant to be understood by those politicians caught up in the controversy, men who also recognized that a monument implied truth.

In contrast, the Wolfe monument is so easily understood that at times it descends into downright jingoistic propaganda for a contemporary audience. Wolfe grinds the *fleur-de-lys* underfoot, something that Jean-Pierre Grosley was quick to note when he saw the monument in Wilton's studio in 1765, and the axe and scalping knife hint at the contemporaneous voyeuristic popular stereotypes of North American aboriginal peoples.[29] Furthermore, the inclusion of the Highland soldiers is also firmly aimed at a contemporary audience, validating the renewed political embrace of the Scottish regiments, largely spearheaded by Pitt and his cronies in their drive towards empire, after a period of alienation and marginalization following the Jacobite Uprising of '45.

Yet for all the contemporary references and the unabashed pandering to even the lowliest herb- and milk-women, the figure of Wolfe is draped in a classical toga and lies back on an antique couch that seems miraculously to have appeared on the battlefield. This combination of classical and contemporary, of naturalism, symbol, and narrative in allegory, has offended many scholars and connoisseurs. Margaret Whinney, the author of the relevant volume on sculpture in the Pelican History of Art series, describes the monument as 'bordering on the grotesque,' while more charitable authors have referred to it as 'transitional' in design, caught between the Baroque and the Neoclassical.[30] Pitt and Wilton, after all, were of their time and, as such, were saturated in the classics.[31] Classical allusions imparted timelessness, universality, nobility, and, most importantly for Pitt, legitimacy. Pitt himself was often cast as Cicero.[32]

Yet, in contrast to the first half of the eighteenth century, when temporal distance between the past and the present was often elided – the recasting of Lord Pembroke as Carvilius Magnus and Wilton House as the Villa Carviliana by the antiquarian William Stukeley is a particularly potent example – by the time of the Seven Years' War a decidedly sharp wedge divided past from present.[33] This accentuated distinction came about as the result of myriad reasons, one of which was the heightened engagement with the public, especially through the press, and the unprecedented involvement of the public in so many aspects of the war. Pitt was not a reincarnation of Cicero but rather a new Cicero for a new age that was grounded in a classical education. Likewise, his empire was not a reincarnation of the Roman Empire but a new empire for this

Figure 2.2. James Athenian Stuart and Peter Scheemakers, monument to
Vice-Admiral Charles Watson, marble, designed 1759, unveiled 1763.
Westminster Abbey, London.

Dean and Chapter of Westminster

new age. Thus, the classical operates in conjunction with the contemporary and, to this end, the monument to Wolfe offers a new style for a new
empire. It is, in effect, a facet of rememoration, of 'the overall structure
of the past within the present,' to use Pierre Nora's words.[34]

Another monument, commissioned shortly after the Wolfe monument by the East India Company with the approbation of William Pitt,
is comparable in its union of classical and contemporary. This is the
monument to Vice-Admiral Charles Watson, also in Westminster Abbey and designed by James 'Athenian' Stuart, who had been the runner-
up for the Wolfe monument (see Figure 2.2). The discontinuity between
classical and contemporary is visually less jarring in the Watson monument because the Hindu is portrayed almost in the nude and the figure
of Calcutta is swathed in a sari, not unlike an ancient toga. Wilton, to
his credit, seems to have tried to smooth over the clash in the Wolfe
monument by portraying Wolfe nearly nude, rather than in a toga or

ancient armour; however, the inconsistency between the undressed Wolfe and the uniformed grenadiers remains awkward.[35]

When official memory fails to coincide with national memory, it is active only as long as the power exists that supports it.[36] Pitt resigned as prime minister in 1761 when he could not find support for further prosecuting the war by drawing Spain into the conflict, and his empire was irrevocably altered with the independence of the American colonies in 1783. Yet Wolfe and the victory at Quebec, a battle ironically pursued for the protection of those American colonies, became entrenched in the fabled popular history of British imperial might. The equally fabled image of the gallant young general lying back to die in peace became iconic, although ironically cast not so much by the Wilton monument as by Benjamin West's painting of *The Death of Wolfe*, exhibited at the Royal Academy in 1771, a full two years before the monument was unveiled in Westminster Abbey. The painting is entirely more cohesive, showing Wolfe and his comrades in contemporary dress. After initial consternation among artists and connoisseurs – the king initially refused to buy the painting because the figures were wearing 'coats, breeches, and cock'd hats' – West successfully argued for the relevance of contemporary dress for the portrayal of such a noble contemporary British event in painting.[37] As for sculpture, the president of the Royal Academy, Sir Joshua Reynolds, who had led the assault on West's painting, would continue to advocate the primacy of the classical style, citing the permanence of the stone medium.[38]

The success of West's painting of Wolfe was not conditioned solely by the aesthetic battle regarding contemporary versus classical dress. Indeed, the painting struck a popular nerve, for when it was exhibited in 1771 the fledgling British Empire, based on trade and the supposed perpetuation of British liberty, had been dealt a body blow by the American colonists' increasingly belligerent calls for adequate representation in Parliament, and the painting rode on a wave of anxiety about the future of the empire. A corresponding flurry of interest in Wilton's monument also arose in response to an unauthorized competition announced in mid-1772 by Almack's Assembly Rooms for an inscription for the monument; the saccharine tones of the epitaphs of the 1760s were now almost screechingly nostalgic.[39] In contrast, when the Wolfe monument was finally unveiled in November 1773, there was no official fanfare. Lord North certainly would have been reluctant to celebrate the achievements of Pitt at any time, and especially when relations with the American colonies were particularly strained; no doubt he would have preferred to see Wolfe recede rapidly into the annals of British history.[40] Yet the juggernaut of national memory had been set in motion, and the memorialization of Wolfe continued unabated in the popular mindset in the latter part of the eighteenth century and throughout the nineteenth century.[41] For the British government, after the departure of the thirteen colonies and the subsequent transformation of the empire, dwelling on Wolfe's victory and what might have been was not particularly efficacious, although invoking Wolfe's gallant patriotism at times had its place. Subsequent monuments to men who built the empire consisted of a range of types, effecting dying young officers in the manner of Wolfe, stern yet benevolent statesmen, and equestrian commanders.[42] For the colonial governments in British North America, however, Wolfe – as well as Montcalm – had much more immediate resonance. When such figures were commemorated, such as with Lord Dalhousie's obelisk in the governor's garden in Quebec, the French-English divide was carefully negotiated.

The commemoration of Wolfe took on new import in 1909 on the one hundred and fiftieth anniversary of the Battle of the Plains of Abraham. Anniversaries themselves are especially potent memorial moments, often prompting a reconstitution of the person or thing commemorated to enhance the relevance to the time and place. In the case of Wolfe and his victory, the sesquicentennial served as something of a catalyst for both Britain and the now self-governing Canada to rearticulate their identity within both a commonwealth and international framework.

Pointedly, the initial stimulus came from the people, not from government. Greenwich, one of the places most closely associated with Wolfe in both life and death, became a site for expressing the importance of his memory to Britons and Canadians alike. On 18 September 1908, an article by Miss Edith Harper on 'The Hero of Quebec' appeared in the *Kentish Mercury*. She set out the case for considering historic Greenwich as a shrine of the British nation. For her, the place evoked 'memories of Henry the Eighth; of "Good Queen Bess"; of pleasure-loving Anne of Denmark, and her dream-palace, the "House of Delight"; of Charles the Second and his Observatory (which gives time to the world); of the great Elizabethan heroes, Drake, Frobisher and Hawkins – names that thrill the blood; of Sir John Franklin; of the immortal Nelson.'[43] When Wolfe was a boy, his parents had moved to Greenwich as his father sought closer proximity to the sources of patronage that distributed military commissions in the eighteenth century. Situated near important naval and military bases to the southeast of London, Greenwich seemed a suitable location.[44] The family lived first in a house in Greenwich town centre before moving to a house in Blackheath giving on to Greenwich Park. When she visited St Alfege's, the church in which 'lies the sacred dust of the gallant soldier, General Wolfe, who gave his life in winning Canada for England,' Harper was surprised to find very little acknowledgment of the connection with Wolfe. There was a stained-glass window, high up in the gallery, but 'nothing says "siste, viator" [stop, traveller], to the chance stranger. Nothing speaks to him of the illustrious dead.'[45]

Possibly inspired by Harper's article, the vicar and churchwardens of the parish of St Alfege applied to the Diocese of Southwark for an omnibus faculty – a special licence authorizing them to carry out work in the church building. They sought permission to place a 'mural tablet' to the memory of Wolfe, and appended a drawing of how it would appear.[46] After some debate about the text, the motto was changed from what were reputed to be Wolfe's last words to a quotation from Thomas Gray's *Elegy*: 'Heart once pregnant with celestial fire.'[47] Adolphus E. Rost of Oxford prepared the tablet for St Alfege's, which was unveiled on 20 November 1909, one hundred and fifty years after Wolfe's burial there.[48]

A month before this event, a blue memorial tablet was affixed to the house in Blackheath where Wolfe's parents had lived.[49] Known today as 'Blue Plaques,' these tablets were conceived as a means of acknowledging famous London residents.[50] G.L. Gomme, the clerk of London County Council (LCC), explained it to one interested party: 'As you are perhaps aware, the Council is engaged in the work of indicating, by means of memorial tablets, houses in London which are notable as having been the residence of celebrated individuals.'[51] Interestingly, the tablet dedicated to Wolfe seems to have been part of a larger campaign mounted around this time by the LCC to commemorate 'eminent military men' by 'memorial tablets.' On 13 January 1908, Gomme wrote a memorandum to the Historical Records and Library Sub-Committee of the Council submitting 'the names of eminent military men for the Sub-Committee to select certain [of them] with a view to detailed investigation as to their residences (if any) in London being made.'[52] The names considered provide an interesting example of the politics of selection, and how notions of perceived national historical relevance informed such decisions. Of the twelve men chosen (and they were all men), five were connected with the Revolutionary and Napoleonic Wars, five with the British Empire in India, and one (Baron Raglan) with the Crimean

War; only Wolfe was associated with anything or anywhere else. Indeed, apart from Clive of India, Wolfe is the only figure associated with
the eighteenth-century British Empire. There was also the matter of the
inscription. An early report suggested that, together with the requisite
dates, Wolfe might be referred to simply as 'Major-general,' which implies a general knowledge of Wolfe's exploits among the public in the
early twentieth century. However, the qualification 'Victor of Quebec'
seems quickly to have been settled upon.[53] Extracts from the minutes
(and every subsequent reference thereafter) note that the inscription
will read 'Victor of Quebec,' thereby reiterating the perceived importance of Wolfe's actions: victory at Quebec, possession of Canada, and
the consolidation of empire.[54]

The sesquicentennial of his death was a busy year in the commemoration of Wolfe. In Westerham, his birthplace, plans were under way to
erect a statue in his honour. Indeed, this small Kentish village was one of
the first to honour Wolfe's memory with the placing of a tablet over the
door of the local parish church, apparently 'by Wolfe's old friends and
neighbours in the year after his death.'[55] The sesquicentennial statue,
eventually unveiled in 1911, would reaffirm Wolfe's relationship with
the village of his birth (see Figure 2.3), but it would also highlight wider
themes relating to Britain's perceived place in the world at the dawning
of the twentieth century and the future of its empire. The dedication
of the statue and the accompanying comments made by Field Marshal
Lord Roberts were deeply indicative of the ways in which Wolfe's memory was harnessed and represented in the early years of the twentieth
century. The work of Mr F. Derwent Wood, the statue was paid for by
public subscription, including contributions 'from all classes – from the
Royal Family to the patriotic artisan who sent his shilling.'[56] The report
of the unveiling in the *Times* describes Wolfe 'with his sword uplifted
and in the act of moving forward, just before he received the bullet from
which he died in the moment of victory on the Heights of Abraham.' In
speaking before the gathered dignitaries, however, Lord Roberts chose
to focus not so much on an individual act of courage and leadership as
on the interdependence of the empire: 'It is only on the assured welfare
and security of the whole that the prosperity of each component depends. In other words, we cannot now do without the help of our great
oversea [*sic*] Dominions any more than the oversea Dominions can do
without our help. (Cheers.)'[57] The early years of the twentieth century
saw Britain's global hegemony increasingly challenged as the United
States, Germany, and Japan all began to flex their economic, political,

Figure 2.3. F. Derwent Wood, statue of Major-General James Wolfe, unveiled 1911. Westerham, Kent.

John McAleer

and military muscles. As a response to this, the essential connectedness and interdependent nature of the British Empire as a 'family' of like-minded polities was a powerful and widely disseminated message. James Wolfe's legacy as one who had contributed to bringing Canada into the British imperial orbit clearly advertised him (and his memorialization) as particularly fitted for this purpose.

At around the same time this activity was taking place in Greenwich and Westerham, a campaign was getting under way in Canada to raise money to fund another monument. Mr F.C. Wade, the agent general of British Columbia in London, first called for a public subscription to erect such a monument in 1906 in Winnipeg.[58] The Great War interrupted the process, but the plan was eventually brought to fruition in 1930, when Robert Tait Mackenzie's statue was unveiled, not in Winnipeg, but at the top of Observatory Hill in Greenwich Park, London (see Figure 2.4).[59] This was not the first time the site had been proposed for a monument to celebrate a hero of the British Empire and the part he played in a crucial victory over the French. In 1799, Parliament invited artists and architects to submit anonymous designs for a public monument to celebrate Horatio Nelson's victory at the Battle of the Nile the previous year. Presumably as a riposte to the prevailing idea that the monument be architectural rather than sculptural, John Flaxman put forward both a drawing and a model for a 230-foot statue of Britannia that would stand atop Greenwich Hill (see Figure 2.5).[60] It seems Flaxman never intended to see his design come to fruition, as he disqualified himself from the competition by attaching his name to the design, which he then published, accompanied by a long description that emphasized why he chose to place it at 'the point from which the world would be measured.'[61] Ultimately, the entire competition came to naught as the Battle of the Nile was shortly overshadowed by the Battle of Trafalgar. Although it would be another three decades before Trafalgar Square was completed, it is worth noting that by 1799 the British Empire was a fact, far more firmly grounded than forty years before when Wolfe won the day at Quebec. Flushed once again with victory over the French, Parliament was happy to engage in bombastic displays of might and superiority.

In contrast, by the 1920s, Britain's position as a global power was under increasing strain. The imperial 'family' evoked by Lord Roberts only twenty years previously would shortly morph into a commonwealth of loosely connected autonomous states. Mackenzie's altogether more modest statue of Wolfe – the pedestal and statue together rising

Figure 2.4. R. Tait Mackenzie, statue of Major-General James Wolfe, bronze, designed 1927, unveiled 1930. Greenwich, London.

John McAleer

Figure 2.5. William Blake, *View of Greenwich, with the proposed statue of Britannia in Greenwich Park, near the Observatory.* Plate in John Flaxman's *Letter to the Committee for Raising the Naval Pillar, or Monument, under the Patronage of His Royal Highness the Duke of Clarence*, engraving, December 1799.

© Victoria and Albert Museum, London

no more than thirty feet – had much more to do with Canadian identities than British ones. According to John Clarence Webster, the foremost collector of Canadiana at the time, the statue was a 'gift to the motherland' by a group of eminent colonials.[62] Its funding was part of a trend towards using art and history to instil cultural pride in Canadians, a trend most clearly exemplified in the paintings of the Group of Seven. Webster's own collections clearly illustrate this phenomenon. Consisting of paintings, sculpture, maps and plans, photographs, medals, and documents, the collection was donated to the New Brunswick Museum in Saint John in 1934 to foster greater knowledge of Canadian history, evoke pride in the country's achievements, and point to a unified and united future.[63]

Much consideration had been taken with regard to the placement of Mackenzie's monument. There was nowhere, Wolfe himself had written, where the air blew 'cleaner or purer than upon Shuter's Hill [*sic*] or in the Park.'[64] The bronze effigy of Wolfe was subject to the inevitable disagreements over location, site, and the like; Mackenzie wanted the work to be seen at the viewer's eye level, while the authorities wanted to elevate Wolfe on a thirty-foot-high pedestal. In the end, a rather unsatisfactory compromise was reached, with a nine-foot-tall Wolfe standing some eighteen feet off the ground. Nevertheless, Webster chose to be positive about the eventual installation of a statue to Wolfe in the park that he loved so dearly: '[S]tanding at such an elevation, its outlook as a monument will have a wider sweep, and it will be easily seen by the myriad vessels, half a mile away, which move up and down the river of liquid history, that link in the long lines of communication which extend to the uttermost parts of the earth, nearest the great heart of the Empire of which Wolfe was one of the mighty builders.'[65] In the context of this monument, however, the British identity that it expressed was alloyed with recognition of the multiplicity of twentieth-century Canadian identities and their origins in both British and French antecedents.[66] Far from being mutually exclusive, these dual identities were often used in support of each other, a fact illustrated by the example of the Greenwich statue. This statue of one of the British Empire's 'greatest sons' was unveiled by the marquis de Montcalm, the descendant of Wolfe's aristocratic adversary on the Plains of Abraham in 1759, whose reputation had been rehabilitated during the late nineteenth century and who was now being presented in some circles as a great hero of French Canada. The tenor of the ceremony, as reported in the *Times*, was one of unity and shared collective purpose, apparently confirming that, 'out of that mingling of British and French blood' on the battlefield, there 'arose the united Canada which has given this monument to Britain.'[67]

In Canada itself, the formulation, consolidation, and re-evaluation of Canadian identities had been at the core of scholarly discussion for some time.[68] It continues unabated, in both academic and popular forums,[69] and has filtered into the ways in which Canadians relate to the complex historical factors that created the society in which they live today.[70] Material commemorations of the Battle of Quebec at the very site where it took place reflect this. In comparison with events in Britain in the decades after Wolfe's death, things were entirely different in Quebec City. It was 1790 before a simple cairn was erected on Wolfe's Hill.[71] Here, the commemoration of Wolfe had to compete with that of French-Canadian heroes such as Samuel de Champlain, the founder of the city and first governor of the colony, and François de Laval, the first bishop of Quebec.[72] As the tercentenary of the founding of Quebec approached in 1908, the governor general, Earl Grey, was annoyed that the column marking the site of Wolfe's death, one of the holiest shrines of British imperialism, was besmirched by the presence of a jail in the near vicinity: 'A hero so illustrious in the Annals of Empire, and associated at all times with the early history of Quebec, is surely deserving of something better than this insignificant and mutilated memorial.' He aimed to redeem these hallowed grounds, writing to the king: 'You can imagine the shock felt by the visitor ... when he looks up to the Plains of Abraham, where the destiny of North America was decided, and the foundations of Your Majesty's Self-Governing Dominion across the sea was laid, and sees no inspiring monument ... but only a great frowning ugly and abominable gaol! And this gaol stands on the very ground over which Wolfe was carried after he had received his third and fatal shot to the spot where he died happy.'[73]

The story of the commemoration of Wolfe and the Battle of Quebec in Quebec continues to be fraught with difficulties and differences of opinion even up to the present day. The Doric column identifying the spot where Wolfe expired – the fifth to be erected there – now simply states, 'here died Wolfe,' the qualification 'victorious' having been expunged.[74] The first project for a Wolfe memorial in Quebec City was proposed for the Anglican Cathedral; it foundered, but not before it had elicited the suggestion of incorporating the marquis de Montcalm into the monument, too.[75] This was to become a recurring strategy. Later, in 1828, Lord Dalhousie, the governor general, unveiled an obelisk in the garden of the Château St-Louis (today, Dufferin Terrace) that included the name not only of Wolfe but also of Montcalm (see Figure 2.6).[76] As Edward Salmon remarked, 'The Wolfe-Montcalm monument which stands on Dufferin Terrace, Quebec, is surely an unique memorial to rival heroes: Mortem virtus communem/ Famam historia/Monumentum posteritas/dedit.'[77] A.G. Bradley considered that 'of all the tributes to his memory, the one which surely strikes the most stirring note is the stately column on the heights of Quebec which he shares with his gallant but vanquished foe. For here Frenchmen and Englishmen have combined to honour the memory of the two illustrious chiefs by whose blood the prosperity of their common country was established.'[78] This is not an isolated incident: Quebec's Assemblée nationale building has a bronze statue of Wolfe executed by Louis-Philippe Hébert, again standing beside Montcalm.[79] The use of these two historical personalities was interpreted as symbolically bringing together the two nations that they supposedly represented. On 29 July 1895, an editorial in the *Toronto Globe* remarked: 'On the heights of Abraham [*sic*], the monument to Wolfe and Montcalm stands, a lesson in reconciliation to all the world.'[80]

Figure 2.6. Wolfe-Montcalm monument, limestone and marble, 1828–69. Dufferin Terrace, Quebec.

John McAleer

Two anniversaries, 1908–9 and 1959, witnessed important changes in how Canadians understood and interpreted the Battle of Quebec and Wolfe's role in the formation of a Canadian identity or identities. They were the first major 1759-related anniversaries to be commemorated since Confederation in 1867. These two dates, therefore, reflect the political compromises reached over cultural affiliations and loyalties. The appearance of monuments and memorials to the battle in this context is illustrative as much of the historical legacy of 1759 as it is of the actual taking of the city. In these instances, the monuments to Wolfe were presented less in marble than in the interpretation of events. Static depictions of the general gave way to commemorations that ordained the entire battlefield as a memorial or designated the unique and complex cultural legacy of all Canadians as the ultimate testimony to Wolfe's (and Montcalm's) sacrifice.

In 1908, Canadians celebrated the tercentenary of the founding of Quebec – in effect, the establishment of French Canada.[81] As Lyn Spillman has remarked, 'organized public festivals have long been seen as important representations of collective identity.'[82] What part should a battle that, essentially, heralded the death of French Canada play in such commemorations? The answer might be somewhat surprising: in that year, a number of streets in Quebec were named after Wolfe, and the federal government was persuaded to designate the Plains of Abraham a 'National Battlefield.'[83] On 24 July 1908, the prince of Wales presented Lord Grey with a cheque for $450,000 and the title deeds to the Plains. This was to herald a new appreciation of the area, the prince claimed, as somewhere that would be preserved 'as a perpetual memorial, by English and French Canadians, of the great deeds in which both people feel an equal pride.' The new spirit of cooperation was, according to the prince, one of the greatest tributes to 'the political genius of England's rule.'[84] The Plains might have become a place of memory for all Canadians, but they remained a site of contestation over who had access to that memory and controlled its interpretation.

One of the most significant points is that of when and in what context the battle was remembered: the tercentenary of the founding of Quebec, not the sesquicentennial of the battle. The battle of 1759 became part of a three-hundred-year continuum of history, marked as a significant year but not necessarily the defining one. Similarly, Wolfe and the battle were pressed into service as part of a wider interpretation of the events of the Seven Years' War. In preparing for the tercentenary celebrations, Lord Grey promoted the idea of giving equal weight to the British victory on the Plains of Abraham and the Battle of Ste-Foy (1760), a French victory that was, however, ultimately unsuccessful in restoring the *status quo ante bellum*. Wolfe was no longer to be the only martial hero on display; now he was joined by the chevalier de Lévis, the victor at Ste-Foy. The historical message from 1759–60 was that two peoples could be fused together in the crucible of war. Grey hoped that the tercentenary celebrations would 'commemorate the two battles in which the two contending races were alternately victorious, and in both of which the vanquished were entitled to as great honour in battle as the victors.'[85] Lévis and Wolfe would become personifications of their respective 'peoples.'

Of course, Lévis is not Wolfe's most famous partner in the ark of historical representations. Wolfe and the marquis de Montcalm are, as Francis Parkman pointed out in his classic history of the Seven Years' War, 'two names [that] stand as representative of the two nations' who fought at Quebec.[86] And it would seem that, in creating monuments and sites of memory, it was believed that, by placing these two together, the Tweedle-dum and Tweedle-dee of the Seven Years' War, the peoples of Canada could also be brought together. At the tercentenary pageant on the Plains of Abraham, almost one hundred and fifty years after their first encounter, Wolfe and Montcalm did not engage their troops in battle but rather joined in procession, singing 'God Save the King' and, in its first outing as a national anthem, 'O Canada.'[87] Montcalm and Wolfe became stock figures to be wheeled out in support of a nation-building project that sought to yoke together former adversaries in bonds of mutual respect and admiration. The designation of the Plains of Abraham as a National Battlefield during the tercentenary in 1908 was to be interpreted in a similar way. In his speech, the prince of Wales regarded the designation as indicative of a desire to preserve forever as 'a shrine of union and peace these historic and hallowed battlefields [note the plural] where two contending races won equal and imperishable glory.'[88]

One of the people listening to the prince that day was Sir Campbell Stuart, who later went on to become the chairman of the Quebec House Permanent Advisory Committee, Quebec House being the residence at Westerham, Kent, where James Wolfe spent his childhood before the family moved to Greenwich. It was the first property purchased, rather than received as a donation, by the National Trust.[89] Some fifty years later, the approach of the bicentenary of the battle brought back memories for Sir Campbell. Looking back in 1959, and evincing a similar view as those Canadians who funded the Wolfe statue in Greenwich Park,

he remarked that, during the pageant, there was 'no French or English
Canada that day – we were all Canadians.' Stuart continued to promote
this view of Canada, its history and its peoples. He agitated for the establishment of a Société française d'histoire du Canada. At a banquet
held in the Palace of Versailles in 1924 to mark its founding, the prime
minister of France, Édouard Herriot, was moved to say that, in 1759,
'neither France nor England was victorious, neither France nor England was vanquished, the only victor was Canada, who owed so much
to her two motherlands.' Warming to his theme, Stuart also recalled
the words of Ramsay MacDonald, when he was British prime minister, that, in his view, 'the memory of Wolfe and Montcalm had done as
much as political sagacity to bind all Canadians in a common loyalty.'
All of this shaped Sir Campbell's bicentenary address as chairman of
Quebec House, delivered on 13 September 1959. His words spoke of
compromise and reconciliation and, again, the material evidence of a
monument was adduced as a symbol of this new dispensation of mutual respect: 'This is the two hundredth anniversary of the Battle of
the Plains of Abraham, a battle in which two of the greatest soldiers of
that time, Wolfe and Montcalm, died in their country's service. Nothing epitomizes that farewell sacrifice more than the joint monument
erected by the two races in the City of Quebec overlooking the St Lawrence River.'[90] For Stuart and the people he addressed, the history of
Quebec and the historical events that had shaped it spoke directly to
them about their present and pointed firmly towards a collective Canadian future.

In sum, the *annus mirabilis*, with the Battle of Quebec as a key incident,
was a year as much about catalytic as cataclysmic events. It created
consequences, rather than providing neat conclusions, and the ramifications of what happened in 1759 continued long after it had passed.
Nearly a century and half later, at the unveiling of the monument to
Wolfe in Westerham, Lord Roberts remarked on the critical perspective that historical distance apparently bestowed: 'We members of the
British Empire as it exists to-day are better able to understand the work
done in the past than were those who lived while the work was being
carried on, and it is with a full knowledge of what Wolfe's military
skill achieved for us, and a correct appreciation of the part he played
in our history, that we are assembled here to-day to do honour to his
memory.'[91] Every generation believes it has access to unalloyed historical truth. For William Pitt the elder, John Knox, the London County
Council in 1909, and the Quebec tercentenary committee in 1908, their

versions of the Battle of Quebec tell us more about the malleable nature of Wolfe's victory and his subsequent commemoration in marble and stone than about the event itself.

NOTES

1 John Knox, *An Historical Journal of the Campaigns in North-America for the Years 1757, 1758, 1759 and 1760* (London: Johnston and Dodsley, 1769), vi.

2 Raphael Samuel, *Theatres of Memory: Past and Present in Contemporary Culture* (London: Verso, 1996), x.

3 Pierre Nora, *Realms of Memory*, trans. Arthur Goldhammer and ed. Lawrence D. Kritzman (New York: Columbia University Press, 1996), xxiv.

4 The literature on Stowe landscape garden is substantial. For the political inferences, George Clark's essays in *The Stoic* are seminal, encapsulated in his 'The Gardens of Stowe,' *Apollo* 97 (1973): 558–65. See also John Martin Robinson, *Temples of Delight: Stowe Landscape Gardens* (London: National Trust, 1990); and Joan Coutu, *Persuasion and Propaganda: Monuments and the Eighteenth-Century British Empire* (Montreal; Kingston, ON: McGill-Queen's University Press, 2006), 147–78.

5 Pitt's administration ushered in one of the most politically contentious decades in British history when George III, the natural aristocracy, and the new men of politics each vied to preserve their hold on leadership. See John Brewer, *Party Ideology and Popular Politics at the Accession of George III* (Cambridge: Cambridge University Press, 1976); and Frank O'Gorman, *The Long Eighteenth Century* (London: Arnold, 1997), esp. 176–232.

6 Linda Colley, *Britons: Forging a Nation 1707–1837* (New Haven, CT; London: Yale University Press, 1992) has become the seminal work on the formation of a popular national identity, bound up with war and the beginnings of an empire in the eighteenth century.

7 Maurice Halbwachs, *On Collective Memory*, trans. and ed. Lewis A. Coser (Chicago; London: Chicago University Press, 1992).

8 Avner Ben-Amos, 'The Other World of Memory: State Funerals of the French Third Republic as Rites of Commemoration,' *History and Memory* 1 (1989): 88. See also idem, *Funerals, Politics and Memory in Modern France, 1789–1996* (Oxford: Oxford University Press, 2000); and Aleida Assmann and Jan Assmann, 'Das Gestern im Heute. Medien und soziales Gedächtnis,' in *Die Wirklichkeit der Medien: Eine Einführung in die Kommunikationswissenschaft*, ed. Klaus Merten, Siegfried J. Schmidt, and Siegfried Weichsenberg (Opladen, Germany: Der Westdeutsche Verlag, 1994).

9 Horace Walpole, *Memoirs of the Reign of King George the Second*, vol. 3, ed. John Brooke (New Haven, CT; London: Yale University Press, 1985), 80.

10 The celebrations at news of Wolfe's victory far surpassed those surrounding Admiral Vernon's victory at Portobello twenty years before. For an excellent account of the Vernon phenomenon, see Kathleen Wilson, *The Sense of the People: Politics, Culture and Imperialism in England, 1715–1785* (Cambridge: Cambridge University Press, 1998), 140–65.

11 *Gentleman's Magazine* 29 (1759): 469.

12 Ibid., 495.

13 Walpole, *Memoirs of the Reign of King George the Second*, vol. 3, 75.

14 Alan McNairn, *Behold the Hero: General Wolfe and the Arts in the Eighteenth Century* (Montreal; Kingston, ON: McGill-Queen's University Press, 1997), 10.

15 The funeral was recounted many times in the popular press. See, for example, *Royal Magazine* 1 (1759): 270; *London Magazine* 28 (1759): 580.

16 *Public Advertiser*, 1 November 1759.

17 Pitt's call for the monument is recorded in the *Journals of the House of Commons*, vol. 28, 643.

18 Walpole, *Memoirs of the Reign of King George the Second*, vol. 3, 80.

19 Pierre-Jean Grosley, *A Tour to London, or New Observations on England and its Inhabitants*, vol. 1 (London: Lockyer Davis, 1772), 205.

20 Designs were submitted by John Rysbrack, Peter Scheemakers, Louis-François Roubiliac, Robert Adam, William Chambers, Agostino Carlini, James 'Athenian' Stuart, and Joseph Wilton. The entries are discussed at length in Coutu, *Persuasion and Propaganda*, 120–35.

21 Horace Walpole to Horace Mann, 1 August 1760, in Horace Walpole, *Horace Walpole's Correspondence*, vol. 21, ed. W.S. Lewis (New Haven, CT; London: Yale University Press, 1937–83), 428.

22 Richard, Earl Temple to the duke of Devonshire, 16 March 1760, Chatsworth House, Correspondence of the 4th duke of Devonshire, 402.7. We are grateful to His Grace the Duke of Devonshire for permission to consult the 4th duke's correspondence in the Chatsworth Library.

23 For more on Temple's work at Stowe, see Coutu, *Persuasion and Propaganda*, especially 163–78.

24 Ibid., 117–20.

25 Even the visual memory of Wolfe was constructed: no lifetime portraits of Wolfe were known, and a death mask was not feasible since his facial features had so deteriorated by the time his body arrived in Portsmouth (apparently in a barrel of rum) in October 1759. The portrait for the monument, a bust, and several paintings was derived from a sketch by Wilton

of a servant of Lord Gower who apparently looked like Wolfe, with details
adjusted from memory by Lord Edgcumbe. See Horace Walpole, *Anecdotes
of Painting in England*, vol. 3, ed. J. Dalloway and R.N. Wornum (1762;
London: Swan Sonnenschein Lowrey, 1888), 156.

26 Wolfe's copy of Thomas Gray's *An Elegy Written in a Country Church Yard*
    (London: R. & J. Dodsley, 1754) is now in the collection of the Thomas
    Fischer Rare Book Library at the University of Toronto. Although such
    lines as 'The paths of glory lead but to the grave' and 'On some fond
    breast the parting soul relies' are underlined, there is nothing to suggest
    that Wolfe read the *Elegy* the night before he died. Indeed, his marginalia
    indicate that he was more concerned with such prosaic issues as advance-
    ment through patronage than with talent and wealth. At the bottom of
    page 7, he noted, 'How ineffectual are often our own unaided exertions
    – especially in early Life? How many shining Lights owe to Patronage &
    Affluence what their Talents would never procure them?' and at the bot-
    tom of page 8, he wrote, 'The Poet might have said with Truth that Penury
    forbids even the performance of Common Duty.'
27 The inscription was finalized in the early 1770s after a renewed spate of
    interest following the exhibition of Benjamin West's painting of *The Death
    of Wolfe* in 1771; see Coutu, *Persuasion and Propaganda*, 142–6.
28 Technically, there was one earlier monument commissioned by the House,
    to Admiral Cloudsley Shovell, but the commission was pushed through
    the House at the insistence of Queen Anne. Geoffrey Beard, *The Work of
    Grinling Gibbons* (London: John Murray, 1989), 78–9.
29 Grosley, *Tour to London*, vol. 1, 102–3.
30 Margaret Whinney, *Sculpture in Britain, 1530–1830* (1964; Harmondsworth,
    UK: Penguin, 1988), 266. See also Malcolm Baker, 'Rococo Styles in Eight-
    eenth-Century English Sculpture,' in *Rococo: Art and Design in Hogarth's
    England* (London: Victoria and Albert Museum, 1984), 306.
31 On classical education, see Viccy Coltman, *Fabricating the Antique: Neoclas-
    sicism in Britain, 1760–1800* (Chicago: University of Chicago Press, 2006).
32 The characterization of Pitt as Cicero was especially appealing to Ameri-
    can colonists concerned about perceived infringements of their liberty by
    George III and his political allies. See Bernard Bailyn, *The Ideological Ori-
    gins of the American Revolution* (Cambridge, MA: Harvard University Press,
    1967), 25; and *Boston Gazette*, 21 April 1766, cited in Paul Langford, 'British
    Correspondence in the Colonial Press, 1763–1775: A Study in Anglo-Amer-
    ican Misunderstanding before the American Revolution,' in *The Press and
    the American Revolution*, ed. Bernard Bailyn and John B. Hench (Worcester,
    MA: American Antiquarian Society, 1980), 286. See also the pamphlet enti-

tled, *The Trial of England's Cicero, on the Four Important Articles of His Being An Orator, a Patriot, An Author and A Briton* (London: J. Williams, 1767).

33 William Stukeley, *Itinerarium Curiosum*, 2nd ed. (London: The Author, 1726), 128.

34 Nora, *Realms of Memory*, xxiv.

35 For a fuller discussion of the iconography of the hero in British art, see Martin Myrone, *Bodybuilding* (New Haven, CT; London: Yale University Press, 2005), especially 23–46, 105–20.

36 As Aleida Assmann and Jan Assmann have stated, it is like a room that changes its furniture with each new tenant ('Das Gestern im Heute,' 125).

37 John Galt, *The Life of Benjamin West*, quoted in Helmut von Erffa and Allen Staley, *The Paintings of Benjamin West* (New Haven, CT; London: Yale University Press, 1986), 213. See also Myrone, *Bodybuilding*, 105–20.

38 Joshua Reynolds, 'Discourse X,' in *Discourses on Art*, ed. Robert R. Wark (New Haven, CT; London: Yale University Press, 1975), 187–8.

39 McNairn, *Behold the Hero*, 82–90.

40 North was quick to point out that Pitt was feathering his own hat with a call for a monument to Wolfe; see Walpole, *Memoirs of the Reign of King George the Second*, vol. 3, 80.

41 West's painting of Wolfe alone was inexhaustibly reproduced in paint, in print, on Toby jugs, in Wedgwood, and so on. McNairn, *Behold the Hero*, gives a strong sense of the persistence of Wolfe's fame in the popular mindset.

42 See, for example, the monuments erected in St Paul's Cathedral around the turn of the nineteenth century and the involvement of the Royal Academy through the Committee of Taste; Alison Yarrington, *The Commemoration of the Hero, 1800–1864* (New York; London: Garland, 1988); and Holger Hoock, *The King's Artists* (Oxford: Oxford University Press, 2003), 257–76. On the evolving masculine nature of the imperial hero, see Myrone, *Bodybuilding*.

43 Edith Harper, 'The Hero of Quebec,' *Kentish Mercury*, 18 September 1908, 5.

44 Clive Aslet, *The Story of Greenwich* (London: Fourth Estate, 1999), 172–3.

45 Harper, 'The Hero of Quebec,' 5.

46 Petition for Omnibus Faculty to the Diocese of Southwark, 18 November 1908, London Metropolitan Archives, DS/FO/1908/37/1.

47 Ibid., DS/FO/1908/37/2.

48 McNairn, *Behold the Hero*, 240.

49 See the website of English Heritage, http://www.english-heritage.org.uk.

50 See *Lived in London: Blue Plaques and the Stories Behind Them*, ed. Emily Cole (London: Yale University Press, 2009), 1, 26–7. The familiar circular blue format and nineteen-inch diameter of today's plaques became standardized only after the Second World War.

51 G.L. Gomme to Secretary, HM's Office of Works, 2 October 1908, English Heritage, Blue Plaque Archives (hereafter cited as EH), AR/HB/SG/BP.36.

52 Memorandum to the Historical Records and Library Sub-Committee of the London County Council, 13 January 1908, EH, AR/HB/SG/BP.36.

53 Extract from report by Gomme to the Historical Records and Library Sub-Committee, 17 July 1908, EH, AR/HB/SG/BP.36.

54 Extract from minutes of the Historical Records and Library Sub-Committee, 17 July 1908, EH, AR/HB/SG/BP.36.

55 A.G. Bradley, *Wolfe* (London: Macmillan, 1904), 211.

56 'The Wolfe Statue at Westerham: Lord Roberts's Tribute,' *Times* (London), 3 January 1911, 6.

57 Ibid.

58 John Clarence Webster, *Wolfe and the Artists: A Study of His Portraiture* (Toronto: Ryerson Press, 1930), foreword.

59 'The Wolfe Statue: Gift of United Canada,' *Times* (London), 6 June 1930, 5.

60 For a discussion of the competition, see Alison Yarrington, 'The Commemoration of the Hero, 1800–1864: Monuments to the British Victors of the Napoleonic Wars' (PhD thesis, University of Cambridge, 1980), 57–9, 338–44; Lynda Pratt, 'Naval Contemplation: Poetry, Patriotism and the Navy, 1797–99,' *Journal for Maritime Research* 2 (December 2000): 88; and Coutu, *Persuasion and Propaganda*, 322–8.

61 John Flaxman, *A Letter to the Committee for Raising the Naval Pillar, or Monument, under the Patronage of His Royal Highness the Duke of Clarence* (London, 1799).

62 Webster, *Wolfe and the Artists*, foreword.

63 See the website of the New Brunswick Museum, http://website.nbm-mnb.ca/Wolfe/Webster.html (accessed 29 October 2009).

64 Quoted in Robert Wright, *The Life of Major-General James Wolfe* (London: Chapman and Hall, 1864), 148.

65 Webster, *Wolfe and the Artists*, 58.

66 For a discussion of how another historical personage, central to Canadian debates about national identity, was employed by both English- and French-speaking Canadians, see Alan Gordon, *The Hero and the Historians: Historiography and the Uses of Jacques Cartier* (Vancouver: University of British Columbia Press, 2010).

67 'The Wolfe Statue: Gift of United Canada,' 5.

68 For an introduction to the complex issue of Canadian identities, see Phillip Buckner, 'Introduction,' in *Canada and the British Empire*, ed. Phillip Buckner (Oxford: Oxford University Press, 2008), 1–21.

69 See Eva Mackey, *The House of Difference: Cultural Politics and National Identity in Canada* (Toronto: University of Toronto Press, 2002). For a recent example, see David Keys, 'Canada's other nation,' *BBC History Magazine* 10, no. 8 (2009): 16–17.

70 See Lyle Dick, 'Public History in Canada: An Introduction,' *Public Historian* 31, no. 1 (2009): 8.

71 McNairn, *Behold the Hero*, 89.

72 See Ronald Rudin, *Founding Fathers: The Celebration of Champlain and Laval in the Streets of Quebec, 1878–1908* (Toronto: University of Toronto Press, 2003).

73 Quoted in H.V. Nelles, *The Art of Nation-Building: Pageantry and Spectacle at Quebec's Tercentenary* (Toronto: University of Toronto Press, 1999), 72, 86.

74 Stephen Brumwell, *Paths of Glory: The Life and Death of General James Wolfe* (London: Hambledon Continuum, 2007), xxi. For further details, see also the website of the National Battlefields Commission, http://www.ccbn-nbc.gc.ca/_en/site-rassembleur.php (accessed 13 August 2010).

75 McNairn, *Behold the Hero*, 237–8.

76 C.J. Taylor, *Negotiating the Past: The Making of Canada's National Historic Parks and Sites* (Montreal; Kingston, ON: McGill-Queen's University Press, 1990), 10; see also Alan Gordon, in this volume.

77 Edward Salmon, *General Wolfe* (London: Pitman, 1909), 221. The inscription translates as 'Valour gave them one death, history one fame, posterity one monument.'

78 Bradley, *Wolfe*, 212.

79 McNairn, *Behold the Hero*, 238.

80 Quoted in Taylor, *Negotiating the Past*, 6.

81 See J.I. Little, in this volume.

82 Lyn Spillman, *Nation and Commemoration: Creating National Identities in the United States and Australia* (Cambridge: Cambridge University Press, 1997), 6.

83 Taylor, *Negotiating the Past*, xiii–xiv.

84 Quoted in Nelles, *Art of Nation-Building*, 38, 24.

85 Ibid., 86.

86 Francis Parkman, *Montcalm and Wolfe: The French and Indian War* (London: Macmillan, 1884), vii.

87 Nelles, *Art of Nation-Building*, 36.

88 Quoted in ibid., 8.

89 *Quebec House, Kent* (London: National Trust, 1993), 9; see also Beckles Willson, 'Portraits and Relics of General Wolfe,' *The Connoisseur* 23, no. 89 (1909): 3.

90 *Wolfe: Portraiture and Genealogy* (Westerham, UK: Quebec House, 1959), 9, 10, 14.

91 'The Wolfe Statue at Westerham,' 6.

3

'Where Famous Heroes Fell': Tourism, History, and Liberalism in Old Quebec

ALAN GORDON

Enchanted by the view from the Quebec Citadel in September 1850, an American tourist struggled to address the majesty of nature contrasted with the historic memory of a sacred place. 'The view from Cape Diamond,' he mused, 'has been compared by European travellers with the most remarkable views of a similar kind in Europe, such as from Edinburgh Castle, Gibraltar, Cintra, and others.' As a poet of the Romantic era, his confirmed inclination was to associate 'the beauty of Quebec' with the wildflowers and the mystery of the landscape he saw all around him. 'Yet even I yielded,' he admitted 'in some degree to the influence of historical associations, and found it hard to attend to the geology of Cape Diamond or the botany of the Plains of Abraham.'[1] Although he finally chose nature over human history, Henry David Thoreau, the great American Romantic poet of the Victorian age, wrestled with a question many tourists would have quickly understood: how best to balance attention to nature's beauty with humanity's past. By the middle of the nineteenth century, when Thoreau took his trip to Canada, Quebec City had been the subject of close to a century of travel literature description that encouraged people to anticipate certain sentiments and emotions. But just what they were to anticipate, and what they actually felt, was subject to changing cultural and ideological beliefs.

This chapter presents a tourists' view of the Plains of Abraham and Quebec City, and evaluates the shifting role of the memory of the battle of 1759. Sociologist John Urry has commented that, on the surface, there could not be a more trivial subject for study than tourism, travel, and holiday-making. Yet, he says, the study of tourism, much like the study of deviance, can help us get at the construction of normalcy in mainstream society. Tourism is, in many senses, a form of departure from the everyday that helps reveal aspects of normal practices that might otherwise be left opaque.[2] Historians might push this sociologist's defence of the study of tourism further. Cultural historians recognize in the literature of tourism a record of how past societies expressed notions of collective identities and delineated expectations and norms of social conduct. Attention paid to local attractions at Quebec City helped strangers and English-speaking residents negotiate the character of the place. As Thoreau implied, tourism drew on, and helped cement, memories of the battle and the place of the battlefield in the local landscape. It did so, however, in ways that reflected an ambiguity about the nature of what might be termed 'historic,' or what associations of the past are selected and elevated as worthy of present-day attention. What drew travellers to Quebec, and what they hoped to gain from the experience, changed over the first half of the nineteenth century. Tourist literature at first reflected a fascination with the natural world typical of Romanticism. Over time, the literature shifted to include an appreciation of the town's human past, as locals and strangers worked out a dialogue setting the boundaries and meanings of Quebec City and the Plains of Abraham.

Over the first century following General Wolfe's victory on the Plains of Abraham, Quebec City and the battlefield site developed into a destination for tourists and travellers from the English-speaking world. They came at first as individual pilgrims to a sacred site and later following established itineraries. Some, such as Charles Dickens, Thoreau, and, to a lesser degree, Amelia Murray, were famous. Others were much less renowned. They were typically drawn from the middle and upper classes, with military officers, clergymen, authors, and lawyers prominent among their occupations. This chapter is informed by a reading of the travelogues, tourist guides, and emigrant guides that visitors and local residents produced from the cession of Canada to the 1870s. By the time of Lord Dufferin's 1870s 'preservation' of Quebec's built heritage as a walled, French-regime city, this cohort of writers had come to a consensus about Quebec's historic character.

In such an investigation, Urry's notion of the 'tourist gaze' is a useful tool for assessing how travelers visually framed and consumed the people, sights, and events they experienced on their travels. Although Urry's formulation has had its critics, notably over its privileging of white male perspectives and its insufficient attention to the ideological nature of the gaze, his insights remain helpful to historians. While the gaze is not in itself a historical model, it can provide historians with a lens for viewing travel literature in ways that help bring past perceptions into focus as long as it is tempered in ways that recognize the participation of locals in the construction of meaning. While strangers came to Quebec with certain perceptions, locals, as suggested in locally produced guides, helped them see Quebec City at new angles. Through the combined record of individual gazes on specific destinations or places, working together both strangers' views and local accounts, historians can use travel literature to contextualize developing world views and to chart, as John Mackenzie has argued, 'the development of the processes of imperial modernisation.'[3]

This notion of modernization is also connected to the ideological development that Ian McKay has termed the liberal order framework.[4] Through the progress of liberalism, and in particular through the project of its expansion undertaken by its main proponents, McKay sees the historical process that shaped the modern Canadian state unfolding. McKay's bold prospectus has not gone unchallenged, and yet it does provide a further perspective on the tourist gaze. At its simplest level, the gaze was predominantly white, male, and bourgeois – precisely the characteristics of the chief beneficiaries of the liberal order. Looking deeper, if one takes the liberal order as a defining feature of modernity, then acting as a tourist and thus participating in a leisure activity that presupposes its opposite of regulated and organized work, conforms to a defining characteristic of being 'modern.'[5] Tourism involves the packaging of a community, its social relations, and its physical environment as a product for leisure consumption. Tourist literature consists, in large part, of a series of descriptions of the spaces travellers can or should visit. As Henri Lefebvre has argued, space is the product of complex processes of social construction, so that the production of urban space is fundamental to the reproduction of capitalist society and of capitalism itself. For Lefebvre, the social production of space is organized as a hegemonic means to reproduce the ideology and material control of the dominant class.[6] Thus, ideology orders space, and the process that assigns meaning to space is a means to normalize specific ideological positions.

Seen in this light, tourist destinations are not merely sites or simple locations that people visit. Their very status as destinations marks them as deeply symbolized, valued, and layered places. Place itself is, in Tim Creswell's words, 'meaningful location.'[7] It is a concept that brings together meaning and the material world in a particular bounded location. It is a lived experience that is simultaneously material and abstract. Our 'sense of place' is similarly a concept that draws out the connection between the character or identity of locales and our own identities: it provides a sense of *knowing* to those places, which become 'imagined locations' in the sense often attributed by historical geographers to urban sites that are wrapped in heritage.[8] Heritage, with its associated historical memory, may, of course, be of recent construction. As R.J. Morris informs us, the 'historic' nature of even such an obvious site as the centre of Edinburgh is a recent social and physical construct.[9] A coupling of this insight with Lefebvre's reminder that place is ideological suggests how the process of creating a tourist place works. Accordingly, one should not anticipate that the tourists who gazed on old urban spaces, such as Quebec City, always saw them as historic or quaint in the guise in which so many twenty-first-century tourists see them.

Many scholars mark 1850 or thereabouts as a turning point in the development of modern tourism.[10] Usually this is related to technological or infrastructural developments, such as the expansion of steam travel and the development of service industries. Certainly by mid-century it was possible for Americans to satirize tourist literature, suggesting something of its penetration into middle-class consciousness. For instance, William Tappan Thompson's fictional Major Jones, a down-to-earth southern planter, made a trip to Quebec in 1845 following a standard tourist itinerary. The satire played on the presumed superiority of Thompson's readers to the naive tourist, but also on readers' familiarity with the form of travel and travel infrastructure.[11] Yet, although infrastructure developed first around urban networks, much of the historiography of early North American tourism has bypassed towns and cities for the delights of nature. Catherine Cocks, to take one example, reveals how anxieties about urban disorder made cities unworthy of tourist attention. Only after these anxieties gave birth to efforts to impose (liberal) order on public spaces did middle-class Americans come to appreciate the tourist attractions of urban space.[12] Until cities became orderly places, they were not attractions; they offered services, such as hotels, and formed transportation hubs for travellers making their way between phenomena of the natural world.

Patricia Jasen's trailblazing work on Ontario tourism connects the development of tourism at Niagara to Romanticism's obsession with sublime nature.[13] Much of the early literature guiding travellers to Quebec City reflects this interest in the sublime, the romantic, and nature's wonders. In the 1790s, Isaac Weld felt compelled to describe two scenes near Quebec 'more particularly deserving of attention than any others':[14] Montmorency Falls and the cataract on the Chaudière River. Through the nineteenth century, these romantic scenes continued to be the 'lions,' or highlights, of the tourist's itinerary at Quebec, and they figured in most visitors' accounts. For instance, Henry Tudor's comparison of the Chaudière and Montmorency Falls drew on language rich with Romanticism in praising the superiority of the former: 'the volume of water being much more copious – the falling sheet more extensive – the rocky masses lying on the descent of the stream being thrown into such singular and grotesque forms, – and the lonely grandeur of the forest inspiring a more impressive feeling of the sublime.'[15] As the modern scholar John Mackenzie has implied, the hinterland around Quebec City offered opportunities for brief forays into the wilds.[16]

Despite an obvious preference at Quebec for the wonders of the natural world, civilization also emerged as an attraction. As a tourist destination, the town had the advantage of being at the site of a celebrated battle. Battlefield tourism was a new feature of Victorian travel, as the romance of men dying bravely in defence of their country began to emerge. Almost immediately following the Battle of the Plains of Abraham there was a sense of its historic importance. After a decade of British political discourse in which fear of French global domination was prominent, victory at Quebec unleashed a sense of euphoric release. In Britain and its American colonies, people took to the streets to celebrate Wolfe's victory with rapt enthusiasm. Poems, songs, speeches, paintings, and engravings flooded the artistic markets.[17] London-based engravers especially began producing depictions of the battle accompanied by views of the town and surrounding landscape for a public hungry for visual confirmation of Britain's glory. Moreover, the victory played an enormous role in the consolidation of an emerging 'British' nationalism and imperialism.[18] The death of the victorious general in the battle only added to the romance of the story. Wolfe's death, most famously depicted in Benjamin West's painting and reproduced in various forms by dozens of followers, set the scene. Generations of middle-class British grew up hearing tales and seeing artists' depictions of the battle, making it one of the great symbols of British national conquest.[19] As Edward Allen Talbot informed his readers in 1824, 'every account of Quebec, how ample soever it may be, will be considered incomplete unless it comprise a description of the celebrated *Plains of Abraham*.'[20]

Indeed, with only a few exceptions, every guide or journal of a visit to Quebec City took time, however briefly, to describe these 'celebrated Plains.' Many also outlined the tropes of the battle and its key sites, already set by the first decade of the nineteenth century: Wolfe's cove, where the British force landed; the lines of the opposing armies when Montcalm left the fortifications to attack; the spot where Wolfe fell and died with news of victory fresh in his ears. In this process, the Plains were separated from the town site physically by its walls, but, more important, in the eye of the tourist. 'Issuing from the city' through the St Louis Gate, visitors were 'conducted by a beautiful road to the Plains of Abraham.'[21] The act of passing through the gate and city walls helped divide the sacred space of the battlefield from the town itself, even as suburban growth spread beyond the walls, obliterating the distinction.

Clearly, the Plains of Abraham were the first attraction at Quebec. The first mentions of a site known as the 'Plains of Abraham' are found in 1759 military sources, in both French and English. In July the chevalier de Lévis mentioned the Heights of Abraham in his diary, and a few months later the same term was noted in English officers' diaries as well. It is generally accepted that 'Abraham' refers to Abraham Martin *dit l'Écossais*, a fairly obscure settler who came to New France in 1617 and established a farm below the high ground a few miles northwest of the present-day National Battlefields Park. By 1734, a road running past Martin's farm that reached today's Grande Allée was known as the rue d'Abraham. It is likely that official military toponomy simply adopted vague, local place names and usage. Nevertheless, even after the celebrated battle, the definition of the place called the Plains of Abraham continued to be flexible. The battle itself ranged over a territory much wider than today's National Battlefields Park. Indeed, cartographers in the late eighteenth century usually marked the 'Heights of Abraham' in the area closer to Abraham Martin's farm, roughly between today's Grande Allée and chemin Ste-Foy. But the building of the Faubourg St-Jean starting in the 1820s caused the 'Plains' to shrink and slip westward on new maps. This period also saw the encroachment of housing and public institutions, including the new citadel and its defensive Martello towers. Suburban construction continued through the 1840s, and the name slid further south towards its present location at the Battlefields Park.[22] Thus, during the first half of the nineteenth century, as the tourist literature was developing, the Plains of Abraham was an ambiguously bounded place.

However, even if the precise boundaries of the battlefield were unclear, local people certainly knew the site. As Quebec City grew out
from its French walls, the open spaces of the Plains of Abraham and
their close proximity to the town quickly turned the battlefield into a
site of leisure, sport, and spectacle. Horse races were organized as early
as 1767, and the Quebec Turf Club was formed in 1789 for the purpose
of staging races there. In the summer of 1797, the Philadelphia-based
Ricketts Equestrian and Comedy Circus set up camp outside the St-
Louis Gate to put on three shows a week. And in May 1819, the Quebec
Agricultural Society held its first 'Cattle Shew, Exhibition, and Plough-
ing Match' on the Plains of Abraham.[23] Not all spectacles were pleasant diversions: at least ten executions took place there between 1763
and 1810, most famously that of 'La Corriveau,' who was hanged on 18
April 1763 and whose gibbet cage was left on the Plains for a few days
before being transferred to a crossroads in Lévis, on the other side of
the river. But as the nineteenth century progressed, Victorian pastimes,
such as cricket, lacrosse, and, in winter, snowshoeing and toboggan-
ing, became more common. Promenading, which involved being seen
fashionably in the right places, was also popular. Francis Hall, a visiting
army lieutenant, sneered that 'the fashionables of Quebec commonly
prefer making a kind of Rotten Row of the Plains of Abram,' oblivious
to its beautiful natural setting.[24]

The area was also steeped with memory. The first 'monument' on the
Plains was likely the rock against which General Wolfe had lain dying.
This was not unusual for battlefield commemoration. At Waterloo, the
'Wellington tree,' under which the Iron Duke had set up his command,
similarly became a site of pilgrimage. Only days after the battle, the
Wellington tree had been picked clean of grape and musket shot, and
covetous travellers had taken to cutting its branches for souvenirs.[25]
Similarly, Wolfe's stone was chipped away by visiting pilgrims seeking a memento of the famous battle. By 1823, it had been so smoothed
by the hands of souvenir-seekers that John Morison Duncan found it
impossible to cut his own piece. The American professor Benjamin Silliman, equipped with a rock hammer, had more success.[26] But it was
more than just souvenir-seeking that brought people to the spot where
the general died – it was a spiritual experience. In 1807, Hugh Gray
made sure to stand 'on the spot where Wolfe fell,' and was moved to
comment that 'the glory which we attach to the hero who falls in his
country's cause, sanctifies the grounds on which he fell.'[27]

The importance of locating the precise spot where Wolfe died is connected to what Dean MacCannell calls a process of 'site sacralization.' Through describing a sequential process of bounding and marking specific objects, MacCannell proposes a means by which mundane objects or sites are vested with deep emotional potency for tourists. As Gray implied, for many visitors to Quebec it was not Wolfe's body or grave (secured at St Alfege's Church, Greenwich) that was sacred, but the ground where he expired. However, there seems to have been some confusion in locating the stone that marked the spot. John Lambert, who visited Quebec about the same time as Hugh Gray, lamented its loss, claiming it had been removed by an unscrupulous property owner.[28] Yet later visitors, such as Duncan and Silliman, found it. It had at least deteriorated enough that, in 1832, the governor general, Lord Aylmer, had a small truncated column raised on or near the same spot. It too was chipped at by tourists and had to be replaced by a more elaborate, fenced monument in 1849. Later travellers sought other indications of the exact spot, with at least one settling for the exact well that had provided the dying Wolfe with water.[29]

Lambert had been even more incensed by the lack of a proper Wolfe memorial than by the apparent removal of his stone deathbed. When Silliman commented on this same curiosity, he was reminded that the sensibilities of the French inhabitants had to be considered.[30] This was not entirely accurate: one of the few points of interest in the town itself was a small wooden statue of Wolfe. It had been placed in a niche above the door of a house at the corner of rue St-Jean and rue du Palais early in the century. Opinions were mixed on the quality of this 'monument.' Yet Talbot found it a despicable insult to so great a British hero, and John Duncan called it 'a miserable attempt at sculpture.'[31] Later, in 1828, Lord Dalhousie unveiled in the garden of the Château St-Louis (the governor's official residence) an Egyptian-inspired obelisk to mark the memory of both Montcalm and Wolfe.[32] Invoking the glory of the ancients and erected within eyeshot of the modern citadel, it helped draw into the city the gaze of tourists in search of memories of 1759. This more dignified and sanctioned monument supplanted the wooden statue and was even believed by some to be the grave of both generals.

The rhetoric used to describe the Battle of the Plains of Abraham was full of the high diction of Romanticism. Lieutenant J.C. Morgan, upon reaching the Plains in 1812, sat 'near the stone on which that truly great man sat, when his gallant soul took flight ... I readily gave myself up to that elevation of soul, a portion of which even the coldest hearts must feel, when conscious they are upon ground sacred to valour.' For

Isaac Taylor, mere prose was insufficient. He committed his thoughts to verse:

> Tho' high the scale be heaped by pride;
> Death, death, the sinking balance fills;

> Yet we may love thee, and admire;
> When up the steep terrific heights
> Thou ledst the van; the hero's fire
> Delights us, while it half affrights.[33]

It was the romance of the victorious general's dying at the moment of victory that captured the imagination. But the accomplishment of conquest over nature was also worthy of admiration. Virtually every author noted the impressive *natural* defences of Quebec, its heights guarding the town from conventional siege. As John Duncan noted, 'except on the side adjoining to the plains, the position of Quebec is so strong, that the city has scarcely any need of fortification.'[34] Hugh Gray was probably most explicit in linking Wolfe's victory to a conquest of nature. 'Notwithstanding the difficulty of ascent,' he commented, leading an army to the heights astonished the French. No one had dreamed it possible to penetrate Quebec's natural defences and so lay siege to its man-made ones.[35] Scaling the heights was the true accomplishment of the battle, for in combat Wolfe quickly defeated the French army. Of course, there were other battles and other sieges in the city's history, but few, with the exception of American general Richard Montgomery's attack in 1775, received much notice. Indeed, Gray was the only British author to mention that James Murray lost to the French in April 1760, on nearly the same ground as Wolfe had won;[36] such a story would have spoiled the glory of the initial victory. Indeed, Montgomery's failure was a compelling reinforcement of the greatness of Wolfe's success for, despite Murray's loss, the French capitulated a few months later.

The focus on the natural world extended also to the surrounding countryside, especially to the farms and settlements of the hinterland. Like Thoreau, almost every visitor scaled Cape Diamond to take in the panorama of an impressive and beautiful landscape. Henry Tudor thought the 'unexcelled beauty' of the landscape made the town's position 'one of the most attractive in the world.'[37] John M'Gregor announced that, 'the grandeur of the view from the citadel of Cape Diamond has been extolled by all that ever beheld it.'[38] Early visitors to Quebec were almost as unanimous in their praise of the first view of the town. Whether the visitor approached Quebec from upriver or downriver, the sentiment was unanimous that the view was inspiring. Lambert, who sailed up the St Lawrence from the Atlantic, thought the view of Quebec and surrounding country was 'an assemblage of everything that is grand and beautiful.'[39] Lieutenant Frederick de Roos of the Royal Navy, who sailed from Montreal, observed that 'nothing could be more grand or striking than the first view of the city and its environs.'[40] As the years passed, writers of travel guides kept topping the hyperbole of the first view. In 1832 John M'Gregor swooned that 'the grandeur of the first view of this city is so irresistibly striking that few who have ever beheld it can, I think, ever forget the magically impressive picture it presents.'[41] J.C. Morgan of the Royal Marines put it most succinctly: 'There is not in nature a more beautiful scene.'[42]

On landing and entering the city itself, however, the tone often changed. While Martine Geronimi has claimed that, even in the eighteenth century, Quebec City was a much reputed town, this was not exactly the case.[43] Certainly its natural setting was widely known, as was its historic association with Wolfe, but early visitors were not much impressed with the town itself. Arthur Middleton, according to Priscilla Wakefield, described the Lower Town as a 'dirty, confined, disagreeable place,' and complained about the narrow, irregular streets of the Upper Town.[44] Francis Hall dismissed both the Upper and Lower Town, suggesting that 'neither has much to boast on the score, either of beauty, or convenience.'[45] Disgust with the Lower Town, which in the early nineteenth century consisted of one main, unpaved street and reeked of the stench of rotting fish and human waste that washed down from the Upper Town when it rained, was almost obligatory. Throughout the century, tourists quickly fled the Lower Town and braved the arduous trek up Mountain Street for the relatively more open spaces of the Upper Town. Even here, visitors complained that 'the ascent to the upper town is very bad' as the rutted, muddy passage or the rickety wooden steps took the visitor up a steep and slippery climb, ever conscious of the rocky cliffs above and increasingly below them.[46]

For decades after Hall, Wakefield, and Hugh Gray passed judgment, authors continued to find the town disagreeable or, at best, boring. A case in point is John Morison Duncan, an American who visited in 1819. Duncan, like most travellers, preferred the Upper Town, but, 'although the upper town is clean and airy in comparison of the lower ... yet there is not much in its appearance to interest a stranger, who has seen more

splendid cities of our native country.'[47] Although Duncan's haughty
dismissal might be passed off as simple chauvinism, it nevertheless
underscores the relative displeasure of visitors to Quebec. Not only
Americans looked down on Quebec's attractions. Tudor, an English
barrister, felt the town was simply 'not remarkable for much elegance,'
as did the Swedish traveller Carl David Arfwedson.[48] Sir George Head
went so far as to contrast Quebec City unfavourably to Kingston, in
Upper Canada.[49] This distaste for even the Upper Town, though, was
not unanimous – some visitors found its public spaces and buildings
pleasant enough – but general disappointment was pronounced and
represented a clear majority of opinion.

Visitors' distaste for Quebec's 'charms' was due in part to the poor
quality of the services available. Before mid-century, and despite its position on the northern tour, Quebec City had not developed a particularly sophisticated tourism infrastructure. The hotels, Adam Fergusson
commented in 1833, were not among the town's inducements.[50] Tales
of bedbugs and rats in the night, even at the better hotels, fill the pages
of travel narratives. The weakness of its tourism infrastructure might
reflect the nature of travel to Quebec City. Many travelogue writers
visited on business or as part of an official military of administrative
excursion, yet many others travelled for leisure. The weakness of the
infrastructure is more likely a reflection of the small scale of the town,
which, for tourist purposes, was rendered even smaller by the fact that
very few francophone *habitants* travelled overnight for pleasure, re-
stricting the number of hotels and visitors' options.

No doubt the improvement in services over the second half of the
century helped to improve travellers' impressions of the town. But another explanation for the poor reputation of the town itself was that
'old' was not always seen as 'historic.' The old houses and buildings
that modern tourists associate with Quebec's historic character were, to
many nineteenth-century visitors, just old. In 1817 the American Joseph
Sansom described 'wretched buildings,' and assessed the whole town
as 'antiquated.'[51] Old, to Alfred Pairpoint, was associated with ugly
and inconvenient.[52] John M'Gregor similarly deplored the 'confusion
of antiquity' that surrounded him in the Lower Town, but he was more
forgiving about the Upper Town: even though it was constructed 'in the
style of olden time,' he still glimpsed some respectability in its public
buildings.[53] This is, perhaps, not surprising – the nineteenth century,
at least for the middle class, was a century for 'improvements.' Civilization, by which the writers of travel guides meant modern, Anglo-

American ways of living, meant the necessary obliteration of all that was past and other. It was the same spirit that prompted the writer of one tourist guide to contrast Montreal, where the old French houses were being torn down, to Quebec City, where they remained.[54] And this same spirit led the Oxford chemist, Charles Daubeny, to express his preference for the newly built 'more genteel and respectable houses' he found in Toronto.[55] The tourist attraction at Quebec City that most captured this preference for the new over the old was the Citadel, built on the edge of the Plains of Abraham by the Royal Engineers between 1820 and 1831. Every visitor following the mid-1820s asked to enter its walls and inspect this formidable advance in modern defences. It was the modern fortress, not the old French walls or public buildings, that drew visitors' attention. Early visitors were interested in what was modern about the town's amenities. Certainly there were exceptions. Yale's Professor Silliman felt it required only a little imagination to pretend he was entering a 'fortress of the dark ages.'[56] But this was a fantasy past, not a historic one.

Improvements and advances return us to the rhetoric of the liberal order. The clutter and confusion that characterized the Lower Town and the narrow, irregular streets of the Upper Town did not correspond to emerging notions of respectability and social order. Many historians have commented on the Anglo-American middle class's efforts to establish social distance from the rabble below and the corrupt aristocracy above.[57] The spaces they saw at Quebec City corresponded more clearly to those 'olden styles' best left behind. And indeed, this rhetoric was racialized. James Dixon was sharpest in his disdain for French Canadians: 'theirs is a primitive race, remaining in much the same state as they were in the time of their ancestors' coming to the colony. British rule causes no innovation in their manners and habits.'[58] Dixon continued to grumble about the strange French language and 'superstitious' religious beliefs. 'Popery, that great antidote to social progress,' wrote Isabella Bishop some years later, meant that, 'generally, the only building with any pretensions is a Romish church.'[59] Another author found the people 'obstinately adverse to any and every change.'[60] This was not an improving people, as their wretched homes and use of urban spaces attested. Indeed, 'improvements are intolerable to them,' Arfwedson mused. Combining anti-Semitism with his contempt for the French population, who lived 'unrivaled in filth,' James Logan compared them to Jews he had encountered in Prague.[61] Even the better class of the French citizens were subject to scorn for their old-fashioned ways. M'Gregor lampooned the 'folly and inconsistency' of those obsessed with rank, and noted that families that ascribed to high social position 'have frequently been reduced to poverty.'[62] Pairpoint similarly deplored the 'strong tendency to extravagance among the upper classes of the French.'[63] Neither the upper nor the lower classes of French Canadians represented the rational, disciplined individuals of liberal theory. It is no surprise that the urban environment they bequeathed to the British after 1759 was subject to similar scorn.

To be fair, many writers quite liked the rustic *habitants* they encountered in the countryside. Even so, they tended to depict to themselves a primitive, pastoral folk – a people happy with their simple way of life. J.C. Myers found them 'a contented, gay, harmless people ... but very ignorant.'[64] A common refrain was the attractiveness of the women: 'the female French peasants are generally very pretty,' noted Arthur Middleton, adding that the tastefulness of their summer clothes improved their beauty.[65] 'The very picture of cheerfulness,' another observer remarked of French-Canadian women.[66] Even the nuns were the subject of comment about their attractiveness, although Hugh Gray could not believe they were happy living 'so contrary to human nature.'[67]

Gradually, however, visitors began to see more of value than pretty girls and natural wonders. As local authors began to produce tourist guides and influence perceptions, the features of the town and its history figured more and more prominently in travel literature. As well as being characterized by a political awakening in Lower Canada that McKay has interpreted as the first moment in the emerging liberal order,[68] the 1820s and 1830s also marked a time of cultural and intellectual quickening. The Quebec Literary and Historical Society, established in 1824 under the patronage of Lord Dalhousie, was only one of many middle-class associations organized in an effort to improve society. It was not devoted to local history, but some members of the Society attempted to commemorate Jacques Cartier's 'discovery' of the city with a memorial cross in 1835. Although exact dates are impossible to establish in cultural movements, many more people developed an interest in Canadian history in the years that straddled the rebellions of 1837–8. This interest certainly accelerated afterwards.

Visitors at first contrasted their own activities while in town to the lives of the locals. Basil Hall wrote at length of the dinner parties and learned conversations he attended.[69] By the start of the 1830s, some visitors were also taking note of the intellectual and cultural developments in the provincial capital. Among the most interesting diversions for many was to attend the sessions of the legislative assembly or the court. Duncan thought the assembly was more interesting than any other site in the city, and many, such as Arfwedson, recorded their own opinions of Canadian politics.[70] M'Gregor noted growth in education, and believed he saw, at least among some citizens, a 'spirit for improving.'[71] British and American visitors were impressed by these modern developments, which they contrasted with the French institutions of the *ancien régime*. How they imagined space and place thus reflected what they understood to be valuable and improving. However, as they learned from local informants, there was also historic value to these old spaces put to new uses. Charles Roger, a Scottish immigrant who lived and wrote in Quebec in the 1850s, responded to visitors' complaints about the town by pointing out the harmonious commingling of French and English peoples and architectural styles. The public and religious buildings of the old regime offered a visual contrast to more recent constructions, but both were functional.[72]

Interest in the 'historic' character of the town, as opposed to just the battlefield or Wolfe's sacrifice, began to rise in the 1830s. The battlefield was not supplanted by the sites of the *ancien régime*; instead, the travel literature recast the battle as one of many events in a more robust reading of local history. Perhaps the catalyst for this interest was the destruction of the Château St-Louis, lost to fire on 23 January 1834. The site occupied by the Château had long been the seat of government at Quebec – Champlain seems to have built forts on the site, as did Governor Montmagny after him – but the foundation of the Château was the fortified building Frontenac had constructed in 1694. After Canada fell to the British, Governor Haldimand constructed a new Château nearby. In 1811 Governor Craig renovated the old one, so that there was a common misappropriation of old for new. Craig's remodelled building was the one destroyed in the fire.

Among the first visitors to comment on the ruins of the Château was the Irish actor Tyrone Power, who visited Quebec in the spring of 1834. Power was much taken by the loss of the old building and by the moonlight streaming through its open roof and playing across its blackened walls. Perhaps, with his thespian gaze, he saw a setting for a romantic tale of loss. He certainly described his vision of the moonlit scene in such terms. Nevertheless, in the next breath he called on the people of Quebec to seize this 'opportunity' to construct a new and better building on the site.[73] Similarly, David Wilkie found the human history of Quebec compelling and recounted it in some detail. He even placed the destruction of the Château in its own historical context, and told the story of saving a bust of General Wolfe from its flames.[74]

Wilkie and Power helped mark the beginning of a growing interest in the historic value of the townscape of Quebec and in other historical events besides the celebrated battle. Tourists continued to visit the Plains of Abraham, but growing interest in the town's other historic attractions diluted the centrality of the battlefield in the imagination. With more history to see, the Plains saw a relative decline in importance, becoming one of many major attractions rather than the only one. For instance, beginning in the mid-1830s, some visitors began to imagine Quebec's narrow, irregular streets as something picturesque and romantic, and saw the beginnings of history unfolding in its public places. When Charles Dickens visited in 1842, he commented that 'the impression made upon the visitor by this Gibraltar of America: its giddy heights; its citadel suspended, as it were, in the air; its picturesque steep streets and frowning gateways; and the splendid views which burst upon the eye at every turn: is at once unique and lasting.' Here was a description that brought together elements to construct a sense of place familiar to modern viewers: 'Apart from the realities of this most picturesque city, there are associations clustering about it which would make a desert rich in interest.'[75] This change of heart, however, was neither abrupt nor universal. As late as 1860, *Moore's Handbook of Montreal, Quebec and Ottawa* could still complain of the irregularity of the streets and the foreign look of the city: 'The streets are steep and tortuous, twisting about, here and there, in the attempt to secure a passage through the French-looking houses, which, on their part, seem to manifest a strong desire to throw every obstacle in the way, they possibly can.'[76]

Dickens had the advantage of a local guide in the person of John Charlton Fisher, a founding member of the Literary and Historical Society who no doubt could reveal the charms of the town to his guest. Others, such as David Wilkie, relied on another type of local guide provided by Alfred Hawkins. Hawkins was a businessman and later shipping master for the busy Port of Quebec. He appears to have arrived at Quebec in early 1817 to establish a trade as a wine merchant. He was active in the social and business life of the town, serving on a number of social committees as well as a director of the Quebec Bank. Later, during the political turmoil of 1837, he established a newspaper, the *Morning Herald*. Although his associations with John Charlton Fisher and Joseph Hamel suggest a supporter of the government in a time of rebellion, the *Herald* was mostly a commercial paper largely free of political news.[77] Hawkins was also active in historical research: his map of the military operations of the siege of Quebec in 1759 was published in London in 1841 to considerable praise for its detail and accuracy.[78]

The publication of Hawkins's *A Picture of Quebec* in 1834 coincided with the destruction of the Château St-Louis. Together they marked a turning point in the historic imagination of locals and strangers at Quebec. Hawkins's was not the first locally produced guide to the city. In 1829, George Bourne published a guide and directory that included sample itineraries for walking tours of the town and its environs,[79] and Bourne seems to have plagiarized sections of a work by James Pattison Cockburn, an American-born, English army officer who spent a decade in Quebec.[80] But Hawkins's guide was the most detailed and influential. In his 1836 narrative, Wilkie cited Hawkins as grounds for not delving even deeper into the town's interesting history, and urged his readers to secure a copy. Many writers obliged, and carried a copy of Hawkins with them on their trips.[81]

A Picture of Quebec opened with six chapters of local history, and continued, over five hundred pages, to outline the historical significance of the town's major public buildings, streets, and squares, providing context, culled from primary source evidence, for the description of the town at stages of development in the seventeenth and eighteenth centuries.[82] Reading Hawkins allowed visitors to imagine the full press of history as they walked the streets of the walled town. Here was a recasting of the city's past as worthy of notice, juxtaposed with the development of modern and liberal institutions, much as he mixed the rhetoric of science with that of romance in his own prose: 'The capital of the Province of Lower Canada and the principal seat of British dominion in America cannot be approached without emotions of respect and admiration. It is situated on the north-west side of the great River of St. Lawrence, in latitude 46 59' 15', and longitude 71 13' ... There stands QUEBEC, formerly the seat of the French empire in the west – purchased for England by the blood of the heroic Wolfe.'[83]

In this passage, Hawkins mixed romantic high diction – 'the blood of the heroic Wolfe' – with the precision of geographical science. He continued to mix ideas of history and progress as he spun stories of the great events of the past, and described the modern buildings that British dominion had produced. His tenth chapter, for instance, described ancient and modern religious institutions, including a description of courses in science taught under the roof of the old Seminary, itself steeped in history.[84] Or, in describing the Place d'Armes, one of the city's old public squares, Hawkins noted that it housed the offices of the Commissariat Office, 'where the business of that efficient department is conducted.'[85] Efficiency and modernity, touchstones of a liberal order, could exist in an ancient urban space.

In subsequent decades, more guidebooks followed Hawkins's lead and began to treat the public space of Quebec City as historical and worthy of comment. Charles Roger claimed to have written his own guide to serve as a replacement for Hawkins, copies of which had become rare in the late 1850s.[86] And so Dickens was neither the first nor the last foreign visitor to accept the historic character of the place. Isabella Bishop considered Quebec the 'goal' of her trip to America in 1856, for she had read so much of its natural beauty. Although she was much disgusted with the French and Irish working people she saw in the Lower Town, and especially the chaos of its streets and squares, she was not disappointed with the Upper Town, citadel, and Plains, all 'celebrated in history.'[87]

By this time, tourist guides regularly included walking itineraries of the town that drew on the sense of history to be found in its streets and lost French buildings. Many of these, such as Godfrey O'Brien's, the various Holiwell *Guides*, or the American-produced *Tunis's Guide*, mixed old and new as Hawkins had done.[88] The great fires of the 1840s and 1850s destroyed much of the built environment of the city and reconstructions created a more modern townscape, so that guides turned instead to invoking a lost past to develop a sense of the historic. This was a romantic or nostalgic history that invoked what had been lost in the century's quest for improvements. Yet, at the same time, it helped develop a sense of the past that could coexist with improvement. It is worthy of note that the first efforts to rehabilitate the town's public buildings and spaces came from residents of Quebec. American and British visitors were the harshest critics of Quebec City as a town and most dismissive of its streets, public buildings, and squares. But, as more guides began to be produced locally, the town came to be seen as more historic. The history they saw drew on Romanticism for its value and helped guide visitors around the town. But they also helped reveal how its modern residents adapted urban spaces to liberal ends. Paradoxically, local authors emphasized the historic in an attempt to counter strangers' perceptions of a backward and unappealingly old town. The historic value of the Plains of Abraham or the spot of Wolfe's death was immediately recognized as speaking to British anxieties and honour; a similar historic value for the town's urban history leaned on the importance of the emerging liberal ideology. In this particular instance, liberalism was a partner of Romanticism in changing the focus of the tourists' gaze.

Today's tourists gaze on Quebec in a much different light than did those of the first decades of the nineteenth century. Indeed, much of what today is considered historic was new to nineteenth-century visitors, as Lord Dufferin, governor general from 1872 to 1878, led a massive reconstruction project to save the city's historic charms. Observers generally refer to this moment of historic restoration as the birth of a historic 'sense of place' about Quebec. As a result of Dufferin's initiative, people began to recognize the historical value of the French-regime past, even as they tore down its physical remains in the pursuit of improvement.

However, this interpretation glosses over a more complex interplay between local people and strangers who, in a dialogue over the first half of the nineteenth century, worked out a kind of understanding about Quebec City and its sense of place. In the century that followed Wolfe's famous victory, the historical memory of the battle naturally receded. The passage of time – what Walter Benjamin famously described as the 'Angel of History' – softens memories and combines events, as subsequent generations view the past through their own eyes.[89] Waterloo and Sevastopol, romanticized by the likes of Walter Scott and Alfred Tennyson, joined Wolfe and Quebec in the pantheon of British engagements. Locally, in Quebec City, the mnemonic landscape became crowded as locals and visitors cast their gaze on a wider field. Using the language of liberalism, even if only briefly, English-speaking residents brokered a new understanding of Quebec City's urban space, one that at once promoted their vision of a progressive city and paradoxically shifted attention away from the Plains of Abraham and memories of 1759. Romanticism encouraged visitors to reflect on the lost past of the *ancien régime*, while residents drew on the rhetoric of liberalism to validate the urban environment that provided the setting of that history. Together, they helped construct a local context for an episode of imperial, or global, history. This new sense of place was not constructed by the tourists' gaze, but the gaze reveals much of its process of construction. Through tourist literature, historians can see the ideological and cultural underpinnings of memory in the place 'where famous heroes fell.'[90]

NOTES

1 Henry David Thoreau, *A Yankee in Canada with Anti-Slavery and Reform Papers* (Boston: Tickner and Fields, 1866), 81–2.

2 John Urry, *The Tourist Gaze: Theory, Culture and Society*, 2nd ed. (London: Sage, 2002), 2.

3 John Mackenzie, 'Empires of Travel,' in *Histories of Tourism*, ed. John Walton (Clevedon, UK; Buffalo, NY: Channel View Publications, 2005), 34.

4 Ian McKay, 'The Liberal Order Framework: A Prospectus for a Reconnaissance of Canadian History,' *Canadian Historical Review* 81, no. 3 (2000): 617–45. See also idem, 'Canada as a Long Liberal Revolution: On Writing the History of Actually Existing Canadian Liberalisms, 1840s–1940s,' in *Liberalism and Hegemony: Debating the Canadian Liberal Revolution*, ed. Jean-François Constant and Michel Ducharme (Toronto: University of Toronto Press, 2009).

5 Urry, *Tourist Gaze*, 2.

6 Henri Lefebvre, *The Production of Space*, trans. Donald Nicholson-Smith (1974; London: Blackwell, 1991).

7 Tim Creswell, *Place: A Short Introduction* (Oxford: Blackwell, 2003), 7–11.

8 Jeff Malpas, 'New Media, Cultural Heritage and the Sense of Place: Mapping the Conceptual Ground,' *International Journal of Heritage Studies* 14, no. 3 (2008): 199–200. See also Tim Creswell and Gareth Hoskins, 'Place, Persistence, and Practice: Evaluating Historical Significance at Angel Island, San Francisco, and Maxwell Street, Chicago,' *Annals of the Association of American Geographers* 98, no. 2 (2008): 393–4.

9 Robert J. Morris, 'The Capitalist, the Professor and the Soldier: The Remaking of Edinburgh Castle, 1850–1900,' *Planning Perspectives* 22, no. 1 (2007): 55–78.

10 See Catherine Cocks, *Doing the Town: The Rise of Urban Tourism in the United States, 1850–1915* (Berkeley: University of California Press, 2001); Donna Garvin, *Consuming Views: Art and Tourism in the White Mountains, 1850–1900* (Concord: New Hampshire Historical Society, 2006); and Stephen Ward, *Selling Places: The Marketing and Promotion of Towns and Cities, 1850–2000* (London: Routledge, 1998).

11 W.T. Thompson, *Major Jones's Sketches of Travel comprising the Scenes, Incidents, and Adventures in his tour from Georgia to Canada* (Philadelphia: T.B. Peterson, 1848).

12 Cocks, *Doing the Town*. For Michael Broadway, the development of tourism in Canadian cities flowed from improvements in transportation technology and industrialization in the 1880s; see Michael J. Broadway, 'Urban

Tourist Development in the Nineteenth Century Canadian City,' *American Review of Canadian Studies* 26, no. 1 (1996): 83–99.

13 Patricia Jasen, *Wild Things: Nature, Culture, and Tourism in Ontario, 1790–1914* (Toronto: University of Toronto Press, 1995).

14 Isaac Weld, *Travels through the States of North America and the Provinces of Upper and Lower Canada during the Years 1795, 1796, and 1797* (London: John Stockdale, 1799), 205.

15 Henry Tudor, *Narrative of a Tour in North America* (London: James Duncan, 1834), 319–20.

16 Mackenzie, 'Empires of Travel,' 34. Another key attraction was the Huron village at Lorette. Nearly every visitor to Quebec made a day trip to Lorette and many combined a picnic there with a visit to Montmorency Falls. Visitors' observations of aboriginal peoples could encompass an entire paper in itself and are beyond the scope of this investigation.

17 Fred Anderson, *Crucible of War: The Seven Years' War and the Fate of Empire in North America, 1754–1766* (New York: Alfred A. Knopf, 2000), 373–6. See also John Crowley, '"Taken on the Spot": The Visual Appropriation of New France for the Global British Landscape,' *Canadian Historical Review* 86, no. 1 (2005): 1–28.

18 Kathleen Wilson, *The Sense of the People: Politics, Culture and Imperialism in England, 1715–1785* (Cambridge: Cambridge University Press 1995), 193–4.

19 On the depiction of Wolfe's death, see Alan McNairn, *Behold the Hero: General Wolfe and the Arts in the 18th Century* (Montreal; Kingston, ON: McGill-Queen's University Press, 1997).

20 Edward Allen Talbot, *Five Years Residence in the Canadas including a Tour through part of the United States in the Year 1823*, vol.1 (London: Longman, Hurst, Rees, Orme, Brown, and Green, 1824), 47.

21 John Duncan, *Travels through part of the United States and Canada in 1818 and 1819*, vol. 2 (New York: Gilley, 1823), 211; and G.M. Davison , *The Traveller's Guide through the Middle and Northern States and the Provinces of Canada*, 6th ed. (Saratoga Springs: Duncan, 1834), 305.

22 Jacques Mathieu and Eugen Kedl, *The Plains of Abraham: The Search for the Ideal* (Sillery, QC: Septentrion, 1993), 25–7, 32.

23 *Journal of the House of Assembly of the Province of Lower Canada*, 3rd session, Appendix D.

24 Francis Hall, *Travels in Canada and the United States in 1816 and 1817* (London: Longman, Hurst, Rees,Orme & Brown, 1818), 88.

25 Stuart Semmell, 'Reading the Tangible Past: British Tourism, Collecting, and Memory after Waterloo,' *Representations* 69 (Winter 2000): 21. See also

A.V. Seaton, 'War and Thanatourism: Waterloo 1815–1914,' *Annals of Tourism Research* 26, no. 1 (1999): 134–5.

26 Duncan, *Travels through part of the United States and Canada*, 212; and Benjamin Silliman, *A Tour to Quebec in the Autumn of 1819* (London: Richard Phillips, 1822), 97.

27 Hugh Gray, *Letters from Canada: written during a residence there in the years 1806, 1807 and 1808* (London: Longman, Hurst, Rees, and Orme, 1809), 64–5.

28 John Lambert, *Travels through Canada, and the United States of North America, in the years 1806, 1807, & 1808 to which are added, biographical notices and anecdotes of some of the leading characters in the United States* (London: C. Cradock and W. Joy, 1813), 43–5.

29 William Chambers, *Things as they Are in America* (London: William and Robert Chambers, 1854), 84.

30 Silliman, *Tour to Quebec*, 97.

31 Talbot, *Five Years Residence in the Canadas*, 49; and Duncan, *Travels through part of the United States and Canada*, 212.

32 The date for this obelisk is often given as 1827. Its cornerstone was laid in 1827, but construction was completed in 1828 and it was inaugurated on 8 September that year; see Joseph Bouchette, *The British Dominions in North America* (London: Longman, Rees, Orme, Brown, Green, and Longman, 1832), 243–4.

33 Isaac Taylor, *Scenes in America: For the Amusement and Instruction of Little Tarry-at-home Travelers* (London: Harris and Son, 1821), 97–8.

34 Duncan, *Travels through part of the United States and Canada*, 181.

35 Gray, *Letters from Canada*, 62–5.

36 Ibid.

37 Tudor, *Narrative of a Tour in North America*, 307.

38 John M'Gregor, *British America*, vol. 2 (Edinburgh: William Blackwood, 1832), 489.

39 Lambert, *Travels through Canada*, 13.

40 F.F. De Roos, *Personal Narrative of Travels in the United States and Canada in 1826* (London: Harrison, 1827), 111.

41 M'Gregor, *British America*, 474.

42 J.C. Morgan, *The Emigrant's Note Book and Guide* (London: Longman, Hurst, Rees, Orme, and Brown, 1824), 93.

43 Martine Geronimi, 'Québec dans les discours des guides touristiques, 1830–1930,' *Folklore canadien* 18, no. 2 (1996): 69–91.

44 Quoted in Priscilla Wakefield, *Excursions in North America described in letters from a Gentleman and his Young Companion to their Friends in England* (London: Darton and Harvey, 1806), 291.

45 Hall, *Travels in Canada and the United States*, 75.

46 James Logan, *Notes of a Journey through Canada, the United States of America and the West Indies* (Edinburgh: Fraser, 1838), 21.

47 Duncan, *Travels through part of the United States and Canada*, 186.

48 Tudor, *Narrative of a Tour in North America*, 306; and C.D. Arfwedson, *The United States and Canada in 1832, 1833, and 1834*, vol. 2. (London: Richard Bentley, 1834.), 343.

49 George Head, *Forest Scenes and Incidents in the Wilds of North America* (London: John Murray, 1829), 166.

50 Adam Fergusson, *Practical Notes Made During a Tour in Canada and a Portion of the United States in MDCCCXXXI* (Edinburgh: William Blackwell, 1833), 75.

51 Joseph Sansom, *Sketches of Lower Canada, Historical and Descriptive With the Author's Recollections of ... That Isolated Country, During a Tour to Quebec in the Month of July, 1817* (New York: Kirk & Mercein, 1817), 66–8.

52 Alfred J. Pairpoint, *Uncle Sam and His Country, or, Sketches of America, in 1854-55-56* (London: Simpkin, Marshall, 1857), 97.

53 M'Gregor, *British America*, 475–6, 486.

54 *Moore's Hand-Book of Montreal, Quebec and Ottawa* (Montreal: British American Advertising, 1860), 13, 44.

55 Charles Daubeny, *Journal of a Tour through the United States and Canada Made During the Years 1837–38* (Oxford: T. Combe, 1843), 38–9.

56 Silliman, *Tour to Quebec*, 92.

57 This practice was established by the 1980s literature on Victorian professionalization and moral reform. For a more recent representational interpretation of class identity, see Dror Wahrman, *Imagining the Middle Class: The Political Representation of Class in Britain, c. 1780–1840* (Cambridge: Cambridge University Press, 1995).

58 James Dixon, *Personal Narrative of a Tour through a Part of the United States and Canada* (New York: Lane and Scott, 1849), 151.

59 Isabella Bishop, *The Englishwoman in America*, 2nd ed. (London: John Murray, 1856), 283.

60 Henry Beaufoy, *Tour through Parts of the United States and Canada by a British Subject* (London: Longman, Rees, Orme, Brown, and Green, 1828), 121–2.

61 Logan, *Notes of a Journey through Canada*, 20–1. Beginning in the 1840s, the working-class Irish population of the town was viewed in a similar light.

62 M'Gregor, *British America*, 485.

63 Pairpoint, *Uncle Sam and His Country*, 99.

64 J.C. Myers, *Sketches on a Tour through the Northern and Eastern States, the Canadas, and Nova Scotia* (Harrisonburg, VA: Wartman and Brothers, 1849), 224.

65 Wakefield, *Excursions in North America*, 297.

66 Logan, *Notes of a Journey through Canada*, 25.

67 Gray, *Letters from Canada*, 58–9; and M'Gregor, *British America*, 479.

68 McKay, 'Liberal Order Framework,' 632.

69 Basil Hall, *Travels in North America in the Years 1827 and 1828*, vol. 1 (Edinburgh: Cadell and Co.; London: Simpkin and Marshal, 1829), 391.

70 Duncan, *Travels through part of the United States and Canada*, 186–89; and Arfwedson, *United States and Canada*, 347–50.

71 M'Gregor, *British America*, 485.

72 Charles Roger, *Stadacona Depicta; or Quebec and its Environs Historically, Panoramically, and Locally Exhibited* (Quebec: Carey, 1857), 58–9.

73 Tyrone Power, *Impressions of America; During the Years 1833, 1834, and 1835*, vol. 1 (Philadelphia: Carey, Lea, & Blanchard, 1836), 199.

74 David Wilkie, *Sketches of a Summer Trip to New York and the Canadas* (Edinburgh: Sherwood, Gilbert, and Piper, 1837), 261.

75 Charles Dickens, *American Notes for General Circulation* (London: Chapman and Hall, 1842), 167.

76 *Moore's Hand-Book*, 44.

77 Dorothy E. Ryder, 'Alfred Hawkins,' in *Dictionary of Canadian Biography*, http://www.biographi.ca.

78 James Wyld, *Plan of the Military and Naval Operations under the Command of the Immortal Wolfe and Vice Admiral Saunders* (London: James Wyld for Alfred Hawkins Esq., 1841).

79 George Bourne, *The Picture of Quebec* (Quebec: Smillie, 1829, 1831).

80 See Didier Prioul, 'James Pattison Cockburn,' in *Dictionary of Canadian Biography*, http://www.biographi.ca; and James Pattison Cockburn, *Quebec and its environs; Being a picturesque guide to the stranger* (Quebec, 1831).

81 See, for instance, Davison, *Traveller's Guide*; Godfrey O'Brien, *The Tourist Guide to Quebec* (Quebec: Hunter, Rose, 1864); and William James Anderson, *Holiwell's Tourist Guide to Quebec* (Quebec: C.E. Holiwell, 1872). James Logan had the benefit of a personal tour with Hawkins himself.

82 Alfred Hawkins, *Hawkins's Picture of Quebec: With Historical Recollections* (Quebec: Neilson and Cowan, 1834).

83 Ibid., 154.

84 Ibid., 214–15.

85 Ibid., 171.

86 Roger, *Stadacona Depicta*, iv.

87 Bishop, *Englishwoman in America*, 257.

88 O'Brien, *Tourist Guide to Quebec*; Anderson, *Holiwell's Tourist Guide to Quebec*; *Tunis's Guide Book: Niagara, Montreal, Quebec, &c* (Detroit: Tunis, 1871);

and Thomas J. Oliver, *Holiwell's New Guide to the City of Quebec and Environs* (Quebec: C.E. Holiwell, 1888).

89 Benjamin's ninth thesis on the philosophy of history was a reaction to Paul Klee's 1920 watercolour *Angelus Novus*. See Howard Eiland and Michael Jennings, eds., *Walter Benjamin: Selected Writings*, vol. 4, *1939–1940* (Cambridge, MA: Belknap Press of Harvard University Press, 2006), 392.

90 See Canadian Pacific Railway, *The Ancient City of Quebec: Where Famous Heroes Fell* (Quebec: Canadian Pacific Railway Company, 1894).

4

In Search of the Plains of Abraham: British, American, and Canadian Views of a Symbolic Landscape, 1793–1913

J.I. LITTLE[1]

According to geographer Donald Meinig, '[e]very mature nation has its symbolic landscapes. They are part of the iconography of nation-hood, part of the shared set of ideas and memories and feelings which bind a people together.'[2] Meinig's examples are from the United States, but A.R.M. Lower's *Colony to Nation* had expressed a similar idea for Canada in 1946: 'If the Canadian people are to find their soul, they must seek for it ... in the little ports of the Atlantic provinces, in the flaming autumn maples of the St. Lawrence Valley, in the portages and lakes of the Canadian Shield, in the sunsets and relentless cold of the Canadian prairies, in the foothill, mountain and sea of the west and in the uncon-querable vastness of the north. From the land, Canada, must come the soul of Canada.'[3] Others, however, have sought symbolic landscapes with long-standing historical associations,[4] as illustrated by the follow-ing passage from the first report of the Quebec Landmarks Commis-sion, published in 1907:

> So it is no idle sentiment, but a scientific fact, that most of the national energy now displayed in bridging the St Lawrence at Cap Rouge, build-ing new transcontinental railways and transoceanic steamers, prospecting and surveying and pioneering far and wide, repatriating French-Canadi-ans in the Quebec hinterland, or directing towards the waiting prairie the full flood tide of human life that surges so eagerly through Winnipeg Sta-tion – it is a scientific fact that most of this transmuted energy is inherited from the national heroes of the Plains of Abraham.[5]

The heroes referred to in all such flights of rhetoric about the Plains of Abraham are the two generals who lost their lives in the battle, Wolfe and Montcalm. Problematic as was the attempt to convert the defeat of one of the two founding European nations into a victory for its descendants, the site of the British victory in 1759 was powerfully symbolic long before Canadian Confederation. In fact, the published memoirs of travellers from Britain and the United States played a significant role in shaping that particular space as a *lieu de mémoire*, to use Pierre Nora's phrase.[6] This chapter, based on comprehensive research in more than seventy-five travel narratives and tourist guidebooks, examines how the Plains of Abraham were viewed by British and American visitors, as well as how Canadian tourist promoters presented the landscape in the promotional literature they produced before the First World War.[7] The focus is largely on English-language sources because French travellers, who have been examined elsewhere, obviously did not share the same enthusiasm for the Plains of Abraham, and French Canadians were not targeted as tourists in their own province.[8]

Unlike Waterloo, which immediately became a major site of battlefield tourism,[9] the Plains of Abraham were relatively inaccessible to all but the wealthier British travellers, or those stationed in Quebec as soldiers, before the age of steam facilitated the rise of middle-class tourism. Furthermore, the American War of Independence soon weakened the significance of the British victory over the French, and colonial authorities tended to neglect the site rather than offend French-Canadian sensibilities with tangible reminders of the Conquest. As a result, travellers' accounts and tourist guidebooks focused on the expansive view from the cliff-top Citadel and on the Old-World appearance of Quebec City, rather than on the Plains of Abraham as a physical space. But they also described the famous battle that had taken place just beyond the walls of the town in the fall of 1759. In fact, it was the history of Quebec City that was its most powerful attracting force, and that history was largely encapsulated in the heroic encounter between Wolfe and Montcalm.

Judging from two of the earliest memoirs, British travellers were not particularly interested in the Plains of Abraham during the late eighteenth century. Patrick Campbell, whose account was published in 1793, mentioned only that he had paid a brief visit to Wolfe's Cove and the site of the famous battle.[10] Six years later, the young Irish travel writer Isaac Weld did include a brief description of the military engagement, noting that the spot where Wolfe died 'is marked by a large stone, on which a true meridional line is drawn,'[11] but otherwise he ignored the Plains of Abraham. The tone began to change after the turn of the

century. The English traveller and painter John Lambert claimed in
1810 that Wolfe's death 'was a national loss, and as greatly lamented as
that of Nelson.' He also complained that the only monument to Wolfe,
a large rock where he was said to have 'received the mortal wound,'
had been removed by 'a certain Commissary-general, who had erected
what he called a pavilion, and would, probably, have soon planted po-
tatoes and cabbages in the redoubt, had he not been discharged from
his office by 'the present Governor-general, for a *trifling* deficiency in
his accounts.' Referring to the wooden statue that had been carved by
the Chaulette (or Cholette) brothers for a local merchant in the 1770s,[12]
Lambert added caustically that, to their shame, 'the only mark of respect' that the English in Canada had bestowed upon Wolfe was 'a
paltry wooden statue, about four feet high, stuck up at the corner of
a house in St. John-street. This *humble*, (or I should rather say *elegant*),
specimen of Canadian carving, represents the General in the uniform
of a common soldier, with his musket, belts, cartouch-box, and bayonet,
a little three-cornered hat, and a long-skirted coat reaching half-way
down his legs' (see Figure 4.1).[13]

Hugh Gray, who visited Quebec around the same time as Lambert,
noted of the Plains of Abraham that '[o]ne cannot help feeling a good
deal interested in traversing a field of battle; – the glory which we attach to the death of the hero who falls in his country's cause, sanctions
the ground on which he fell.'[14] The pseudonymous 'Jeremy Cockloft'
expressed a very different opinion in 1811. In his *Cursory Observations
Made in Quebec*, Cockloft claimed that the remaining colonies should
simply be given to the Americans. His sole comment on the Plains of
Abraham was, 'I do not believe the Patriarch of old ever saw them; if
he had, he never would have pitched a tent there to graze sheep.' As
for the battle of 1759, Cockloft's only observation concerned the memorial stone (or a replacement) that presumably had been made accessible
to the public once again. He wrote that British visitors had purloined
so many fragments from it 'that I would advise every man or woman
desirous of obtaining a piece, to make haste, and perform a pilgrimage
to Quebec, before it is all destroyed; it is as much thought of here, as a
small chip of our saviour's cross ... was in ancient times, and will be of
just as much utility to the fortunate possessor.'[15]

Cockloft's anticolonial stance was unique among British travel writers, although Lieutenant Francis Hall's travel memoir published in
1819 made little reference to the battle of 1759 or to the Plains of Abraham other than to note that 'traces of field-works are still visible on

Figure 4.1. General Wolfe's Corner, St John's Place and Palace Streets, Quebec City, about 1865. James George Parks.

British officer John Knox remarked on the life-size statues of Catholic saints occupying Quebec's corner niches in 1759. The wooden statue of Wolfe was still occupying the same niche in 1865 as it had been when viewed by John Lambert in 1809, but the new building shown here meant that it was now far out of reach of passersby.

McCord Museum

the turf, and the stone is pointed out on which the hero expired.' Far
from being considered sacred ground, Hall added, the 'fashionables of
Quebec commonly prefer making a kind of Rotten Row of the Plains of
Abraham, round which they parade with the periodical uniformity of
blind horses in a mill.'[16] In 1818, John Palmer was less judgmental, simply commenting that a race track stood on 'the very ground on which
the battle was fought which decided the fate of Quebec,' and that it was
'a fine situation for the purpose.'[17]

John Morison Duncan's *Travels through Part of the United States and
Canada in 1818 and 1819* was more detailed. He offered a brief factual
account of the British victory and a description of the Plains, noting
that 'an oval block of granite, three or four feet long, has been sunk into
the ground, to mark the spot where tradition says that Wolfe breathed
his last.' Duncan also observed that, if Weld was right in reporting that
a meridional line had been cut into the stone, 'it has long since disappeared under the dilapidating attacks of relic-hunters; who have so
rounded away every projection that I found it totally impossible to chip
off the smallest fragment.' Stuart Semmel claims that the British relic
hunters who flooded the battlefield of Waterloo around this time were
'straining to reach the past through the medium of its tangible remains'
because people had become aware of 'the elusiveness of the past, the
fragmented quality of history.'[18] This would explain the eagerness with
which British visitors chipped away at Wolfe's rock and their anger at
not finding a suitable monument to Wolfe on the Plains of Abraham.
Duncan, for example, echoed Lambert's dismissive comments about
the 'small wooden figure' standing in a street-corner niche that 'would
hardly be allowed to pass as a figure-head for a collier.' In his rather
presumptuous opinion, past British concerns about French-Canadian
sensitivities no longer posed an obstacle to erecting a proper monument because they no longer felt that the Conquest was 'either a humiliation or a misfortune' due to the 'inestimable advantages of a free
constitution.'[19]

In the following year, 1824, the Irish-born inventor, settler, and emigration proponent Edward Talbot expressed still greater umbrage about
the wooden carving. After stating that the Plains of Abraham 'presents
no remarkable natural features to distinguish it from the bold scenery
in its neighbourhood,' Talbot declared of Wolfe's statue that '[t]he utmost stretch of human thought would be inadequate to the conception
of anything more beggarly and insignificant.' Referring to it as 'a block
of wood, about four feet and a half long, rudely cut and scraped with

a view to make it convey some semblance of a human body,' Talbot added that, '[i]f I had not every reason to believe, from my personal knowledge of the Canadians, that they are a loyal people, and exceedingly well-pleased with the British Government, I should be ready to draw the inference, that, instead of erecting this memorial in HONOUR of General Wolfe, they had employed some French puppet-carver to furnish them with such a *caricature* of the great and gallant conqueror, as might convince posterity, that the only sentiments which they felt towards him were those of supreme contempt and implacable abhorrence.' Talbot suggested that the inhabitants of Quebec should 'either consign to the fiery element this wooden memento of the conquest of their country' or 'make a liberal bequest of it to some signless tobacco-twister, and thus create a vacancy for an erection more worthy of themselves, and of the hero whose fame they wish to perpetuate.'[20]

Like Duncan, Talbot was engaging in wishful thinking as far as French-Canadian attitudes to the Conquest were concerned, but judging from J.C. Morgan's *The Emigrant's Notebook and Guide*, which also appeared in 1824, the cult of Wolfe was on the ascendant in Britain at this time. Like those who were then promoting tours to Waterloo, Morgan implied that actually viewing the Plains of Abraham would enable one to 'envision the historical battle far more meaningfully than one could through encountering a work of human pen or brush.'[21] Morgan described how, '[s]eated near the stone on which the truly great man sat, when his gallant soul took its flight for the realms of eternity ... I beheld in imagination the gallant Wolfe, struggling with the innumerable difficulties he had to encounter previous to the action, which immortalized him for ever, and enrolled his name amongst the departed heroes.'[22] The accomplished Scottish artist David Wilkie, who had purloined a souvenir branch of the famous Wellington tree at Waterloo,[23] was also carried away by 'many thick-coming fancies, real, unreal, romantic, traditionary, and historical' as his steamer approached Quebec a decade later. Unlike most travellers who depicted the Plains of Abraham as a somewhat desolate site, Wilkie found it to be 'attractive,' covered as it was 'with fertile gardens, villas, and pasture fields.'[24]

A year earlier, in 1833, Edward Thomas Coke's *A Subaltern's Furlough* noted that the plains upon which Wolfe and Montcalm had fallen 'lie a mile to the west of the citadel' and that 'the field of action is yet open,' but reiterated the old complaint that 'the rock against which the British general reclined, when dying (near a redoubt which may be even now traced out on the borders of the plains), was destroyed by blasting with gunpowder' by 'the Vandalic proprietor of the garden in which it was situated.' Coke was intrigued, however, by the wooden figure of Wolfe. Unlike other British observers, Coke claimed that it 'has always been considered an excellent likeness,' and even though he felt that the general appeared 'in a rather strange costume for a warrior: a double breasted red coat with yellow facings, cocked hat, yellow top-boots, white breeches, and white shoulder-belt for his sword,' he added approvingly that one arm was 'extended as in the attitude of giving orders.'[25] Sir James Edward Alexander, visiting Quebec City the same year, was even told by his two officer-guides that the wooden statue marked 'the spot to which the conqueror of Quebec penetrated as a spy previous to his victory.'[26] The increasingly romantic British travellers were now allowing their imaginations to compensate for the lack of tangible or suitably grandiose reminders of the historic event. Observing in 1834 that the Plains of Abraham 'afforded, to the contending generals, a noble arena for military conflict,' the much-travelled Henry Tudor noted approvingly that the site was now used as a horse-race track where British officers and Canadian residents 'annually divert themselves with this truly English amusement.' This practice suggested to the imaginative Tudor that, 'in imitation of the funeral games of ancient Greece,' the participants 'were paying posthumous honours to the memory of the departed chief.'[27]

Due to the efforts of Governor General Lord Aylmer, a small memorial to Wolfe was finally erected on the Plains of Abraham in 1832, and, three years later, the popular Irish actor Tyrone Power recorded how he had stopped by 'a little potato-field, memorable as the spot where the gallant Wolfe fell' and gazed upon a 'broken column of black marble ... a tribute honourable to the taste of the gallant soldier living, and which will henceforth worthily mark the spot where the young victor died' (see Figure 4.2).[28] But even finding this site appears to have required an effort on the part of visitors. James Logan wrote in 1838 that he had employed a French-Canadian guide to visit the Plains of Abraham, and army engineer Sir Richard Bonnycastle complained in 1841 that the battleground was difficult to locate 'without a competent guide.' He himself appears not to have found one, for – apparently unaware of the column erected by Lord Aylmer – he worried that the site where Wolfe had fallen 'will be forgotten, if some patriot does not start up to eternize it by an adequate memorial.'[29] Three years later, self-styled mercantile man James Lumsden simply observed that the Plains of Abraham were a 'sterile waste' with no monument and only the slightest trace of the redoubt where Wolfe was said to have received

Figure 4.2. 'The Plains of Abraham near Quebec (The spot where General
Wolfe fell).' William Henry Bartlett.

This romantic engraving from a painting by the widely travelled English artist
W.H. Bartlett depicts the Plains of Abraham as a barren landscape.

From Michel Brunet and J. Russell Harper, eds., *Quebec 1800: W.H. Bartlett*
(Montreal: Les Éditions de l'Homme, 1968), 31

his fatal wound.[30] In 1849, however, a touring Methodist minister, Dr
James Dixon, reported being conducted through the entire battle scene,
including an ascent up the path 'which tradition has marked as the
identical line which was trodden by the immortal hero.' Dixon was un-
impressed by the broken column erected by Aylmer, for he complained
that the spot where Wolfe expired 'is marked by a mean and paltry
monumental stone,' but, he added feelingly, 'I clung to the place where
the destinies of a mighty country were fixed, by the decrees of God, in
the death-throes of the successful instrument. There are events in history which turn the tide of national interests; form the epochs of time;
raise the monuments of great destinies; pillars written upon by the fin-
ger of God, in the annals of the world, as the *data* of nationalities; and
that little monumental stone on the summit of the Plains of Abraham is
one of these mementos.'[31]

In a similar vein, William Chambers, the Scottish publisher whose

Things As They Are in America appeared in 1854, declared that none of Quebec's public buildings 'was of sufficient note to detain me any length of time from the scenes associated with Wolfe's victory; these, in reality, imparting to Quebec the chief interest which is attached to it in England.' Chambers had a more advanced geographical sensibility than the other travel writers, describing the ground as he walked it while recounting the familiar narrative of Wolfe's campaign. In summary, he asked, '[c]ould the scene of this memorable engagement be visited without emotion? Some slight changes have taken place, as I have said, on the field of battle; but, on the whole, it remains pretty much what it was a century ago – a piece of bare and open pasture-land adjoining the public thoroughfare, which runs westward from the town.' Chambers noted that the rock where Wolfe had expired had been removed, but 'within an enclosure further down, the well is pointed out from which water was brought to him in his last moments.' Despite the Christ-like imagery, Chambers hinted that Wolfe's strategy might have been reckless, though he concluded that the British general probably 'reckoned on circumstances of which we have now no precise knowledge.'[32]

The only British travel writer to question Wolfe's greatness as a general was Thomas Hamilton, who observed in *Men and Manners in America*, published in 1833, that '[h]is first attempt was a failure, and the second was successful only from the blunder of his opponent.'[33] It was fortunate for Wolfe's reputation, then, that Montcalm's earlier successes and his death also qualified him to be a romantic hero. Thus, John Morgan described the French general in 1824 as 'scarcely his [Wolfe's] inferior,'[34] and three years later Governor General Dalhousie included Montcalm's name with that of Wolfe on a monument erected in the governor's garden (see Figure 4.3). On viewing the column in 1831, Henry Tudor wrote approvingly that there was 'something noble and high-minded in thus associating the memory of the conquered general with that of his victorious opponent; as one to whom the tribute of bravery was equally due, though the fortune of war had snatched the laurel from his brow.'[35] And even though his visit was in 1842, during the era of post-rebellion political repression, Charles Dickens referred to 'the fortress, so chivalrously defended by Montcalm; and his soldier's grave, dug for him while yet alive, by the bursting of a shell.'[36] Robert Baird's *Impressions and Experiences of the West Indies and North America in 1849* asked the rhetorical question concerning the Dalhousie monument to Wolfe and Montcalm: 'what can be more noble, or more proper, than

Figure 4.3. 'Monument to Wolfe and Montcalm, Quebec.' William Henry Bartlett.

The white monument reaching to the sky, the lush foliage in the foreground, and the numerous sailboats in the background of this Bartlett engraving convey a very different emotion from the one depicting the broken column erected where Wolfe died.

From Brunet and Harper, eds., *Quebec 1800*, 37

that the differences and contests of this world should not [*sic*] overleap the grave?'[37] A year later, the English army surgeon and geologist John J. Bigsby referred to 'the battle-plain of Abraham, now a stony pasture and race-course, but for ever memorable as the spot where died Wolfe and Montcalm, – men of views, and aims, and qualities far in advance of their age.'[38] Finally, in *A Glimpse at the United States and the Northern States of America, with the Canadas*, which appeared in 1853, Edmund Patten wrote that Montcalm 'endeavoured to retrieve the day, and was killed in the attempt – what could a brave man do more?' Patten also claimed, inaccurately, that '[t]hese two warriors now lie side by side, under a column erected to their memory in the public walks.'[39]

By mid-century, however, the interest of British travel writers in Quebec was on the wane, perhaps due to its familiarity in an era of rapidly growing British emigration through the port city. Imperial expansion was shifting westward, and the few writers who did mention Quebec City paid less attention to its history. The adventurous young Isabella Bishop's *The Englishwoman in America*, published in 1856, focused largely on the social scene and on what she described as the impoverished and demoralized population of the Lower Town.[40] Alfred Pairpoint did mention Quebec City in his *Uncle Sam and His Country*, published in 1857, but he paid little attention to the famous battle or its site,[41] and the topic largely disappears in British travel narratives thereafter. One significant exception is *On the Cars and Off*, written by Douglas Brooke Wheeton Sladen to promote Canadian railway tourism after the completion of the Canadian Pacific Railway to the West coast. Appealing to the renewed sense of British imperialism during the 1890s, Sladen declared that, to an Englishman, Quebec City 'brings back so much – the brilliant conquest of Canada, the proud day when England won an empire as large as the United States, and the banner of St. George's waved from Oglethorpe's colony of Georgia to Rupert's Land and Hudson's Bay.'[42] Sladen described the Plains of Abraham only from the Citadel, but he did mention 'the turf outworks of the French fortress that held out against Wolfe's bombardment so long,' as well as 'the column built over the ruins of the monument that marked the place where Wolfe died with the shouts of victory in his ears.'[43]

American travel writing about Quebec followed a similar trajectory. Americans could claim a share in the glory of the Conquest, and they generally saw Wolfe as a hero, as was the case for Joseph Sansom, who claimed that his *Sketches of Lower Canada, Historical and Descriptive*, published in 1817, was the first account of Canada to be written by an American.[44] Sansom described the Plains of Abraham as the scene of 'the decisive action which for ever separated Canada from the dominion of France,' a spot commemorated by Benjamin West as the birthplace of American independence. The uncultivated plain had little to distinguish it, however, apart from the stone that marked where Wolfe had fallen. Even this marker, Sansom claimed, was only identifiable by 'the repeated efforts of British visitors to possess themselves of the minutest specimen of this monument of national prowess.'[45] Dr Benjamin Silliman of Yale College was more enthusiastic, indeed sufficiently so that his *A Tour to Quebec in the Autumn of 1819* was published in London rather than in the United States. Because the British victory had paved the way for American independence, Silliman wrote, '[n]o American can ... contemplate with indifference the spot where Wolfe fell, and so much gallant blood was spilt.' As a scientist, he went into consider-able detail about the stone where Wolfe had died, reporting that it was of red granite, 'four or five feet by two or three in diameter,' and that it was one of the four 'arranged in a meridian line by the surveyor-general of Canada, in 1790, for the purpose of adjusting the instruments used in the public surveys of land.' Like the British visitors referred to by Sansom, Silliman ('with the utmost difficulty') knocked off a small piece of the now rounded stone as a relic. But he also wrote that 'Mont-calm deserved as much commendation as Wolfe,' for 'in talent, military skill, and personal courage, and devotion to his king and country, he was in no way inferior to his rival.'[46]

Quebec had become part of the American tourist circuit by 1828 when it received considerable attention in G.M. Davison's *The Fash-ionable Tour*. Describing the Plains of Abraham as 'an extensive plain, which the progress of improvement or military prudence has rid of its forests,' Davison declared that '[n]ever did the glory of the soldier shine with greater lustre, or his heroism command a greater tribute of ap-plause, than did that of Wolfe on the memorable plains of Abraham.'[47] Two years later, Theodore Dwight's *The Northern Traveller* was one of the first publications to comment on any remaining physical reminder of the battle, noting that a little east of the spot where Wolfe fell was 'the remnant of a breastwork, with several angles, marked out by bushes, and commanding a fine view.'[48]

Given that the aim of guidebooks was to promote tourism, one would hardly expect Davison or Dwight to adopt a critical perspec-tive, but William Tappan Thompson was less restrained. Assuming the character of 'Cracker' plantation owner Major Jones, he noted in 1848 that he and his travelling companion 'tuck a calash and went out to the Plains of Abraham ... whar we had a quiet view of that place whar so much gallantry was displayed, and so much blood spilled on the 14th of September, 1759.' Rather than evoking the theme of French-English brotherhood that had come to characterize British publications, Jones declared: 'It was a hard piece of bisness, that contest, in which France lost her General and her cause; and though the English may try til dooms-day to make the French Canadians forgit the injustice they have suffered, by givin ther Catholic churches all sorts of priviliges, and by bildin monuments, like they have in the Palace Gardin with Wolf's name on one side and Montcalm's on the other, tryin to make the honors of that day *easy* between em – they never can make loyal, contented subjects out of em as long as Cape Diamond stands whar it does.' Thompson/Jones also noted that the monument to Wolfe erected on the Plains of Abraham in 1832 illustrated the depth of French-Canadian resentment, for the words 'HERE DIED WOLFE VICTORIOUS' were now illegible: 'Every countryman that crosses over the Plains with a basket of eggs for the market, gives it a pelt with a stone, til the whole side of the monument is almost nocked off.'[49]

It is more likely that the monument was the victim of souvenir seekers, for in 1849 J.C. Myers wrote that the iron railing that had protected it had been broken down and corners of the granite shaft 'knocked off no doubt by travellers, and the pieces carried away.' Myers himself managed to chip off a small piece, and yet claimed to have felt it strange 'to find so handsome a monument as this must have been, in such a ruinous and disfigured condition.'[50] No doubt embarrassed by such reports, the government erected a more impressive monument to Wolfe that same year. It would be overshadowed, however, by the construction of a large prison nearby in 1867, much to the disapproval of genteel tourists such as Henry James, who visited Quebec City shortly afterward. In the distinguished American novelist's opinion, 'a battlefield remains a battlefield, whatever may be done to it; but the scene of Wolfe's victory has been profaned by the erection of a vulgar prison, and this memento of human infirmities does much to efface the meagre column which, with its neat inscription, "Here died Wolfe, victorious," stands there as a symbol of exceptional virtue' (see Figure 4.4).[51]

Like their British counterparts, American travel writers did not pay much attention to Quebec City in the later nineteenth century, but Eleanor Gertrude Farrell's *Among the Blue Laurentians*, published in 1912, did not allow the prison or the more recently constructed munitions factory to break the spell of the Plains of Abraham. Like the earlier romantic British writers, she described how 'fancy' called forth the famous battle and assured visitors that they would see in their minds 'the brave Wolfe anchor his fleet in the harbor, cannonading the city for months; see him take his army a few miles up the St. Lawrence river, to feign abandoning the struggle,' and so on, until the two armies met in battle and both generals were mortally wounded: 'All this, fancy vividly portrays, and down the long century and more of years the dying words of Wolfe and Montcalm are wafted to the ear as we, wrapt in thought, are overpowered with admiration for the conquered and the conqueror.'[52]

British North Americans themselves did not publish travel narratives about Quebec City, but local residents were well placed to produce the

Figure 4.4. 'Wolfe's monument and jail under construction, Quebec City, about 1875.' Anonymous.

This photograph provides a good illustration of the impact that the construction of the Quebec jail had on the view of the monument to Wolfe erected in 1849.

McCord Museum

tourist guidebooks that increasingly outnumbered the more personal travel narratives as the century progressed. Though aimed largely at the American market, these guidebooks often followed the example of the British memoirs by referring to Montcalm as a hero nearly equal to Wolfe, thereby promoting what Daniel Francis refers to as the 'myth of unity.'[53] But American tourists were also interested in the spot where General Montgomery had fallen in his failed attempt to take Quebec from Britain in 1775, and in 1829 the first Canadian-produced guidebook to describe Quebec City, George Bourne's *The Picture of Quebec*, noted that visitors who wished 'to trace the precise spots where Wolfe and Montgomery fell, must procure a guide to designate them.'[54] *Que-*

bec and Its Environs; Being a Picturesque Guide to the Stranger, produced anonymously two years later by the British army officer and landscape artist Lieutenant-Colonel James Patterson Cockburn, consisted largely of illustrations. It described the route to the Plains of Abraham, but skipped over the battle, claiming that the details were 'too familiar in the recollection to require any mention.'[55]

The first guidebook to devote many pages to the city's history was *Hawkins's Picture of Quebec with Historical Recollections*, published in 1834.[56] Of the Plains of Abraham, the English-born Alfred Hawkins claimed that '[t]o either race the ground is sacred,' adding that the French-Canadian population, 'fostered by the strength and generosity of British protection, has grown from seventy thousand to half a million of souls, enjoying a degree of rational liberty and happiness unequalled on the surface of the globe.'[57] Hawkins's aim, clearly, was to nurture a unifying myth during a period of political crisis. After describing in detail the 1827 ceremonial unveiling in the governor general's garden of the twenty-metre-high obelisk in memory of the two generals, he noted that 'there is nothing more lasting and perennial than the fame, which is handed down by such monuments.' Dalhousie had included Montcalm's name in a conciliatory gesture towards the French Canadians, and Hawkins explained that the words were in Latin because 'to have adopted an inscription in either French or English might have been dissatisfactory to one portion of the inhabitants.' On the north side of the monument, facing 'to the country,' was the word 'Montcalm;' on the opposite side, the word 'Wolfe' faced the river by which he had 'reached the scene of his glorious victory and death.'[58] Alain Parent claims that the obelisk design was a symbol of British imperialism and that Montcalm's name faced away from the river because the monument was essentially to Wolfe and not the French general,[59] but Hawkins wrote that Montcalm was also worthy of fame and had made all the right military decisions. The British had won, however, because Wolfe was 'a HERO,' and therefore too much for opponents even as gallant as the French and French Canadians. What made Wolfe the greater hero, apparently, was the fact that '[t]he French sought dominion in military power – the English cherished the spirit and enjoyed the blessings of freedom.'[60]

The city directory for 1844–5, which adopted the title of the *Stranger's Guide*, echoed Hawkins with phrases such as '[t]he capture of the City and Fortress of Quebec was an achievement of so romantic a character, so distinguished by chivalrous enterprise, and so fraught with singular adventure, that the interest attending it still remains undiminished and its glorious recollections unfaded.'[61] Similarly, *Quebec As It Was and As It Is*, published in 1867 by Scottish emigrant Charles Roger, claimed that the city's 'greatness' was 'purchased by England with the blood of Wolfe' so that the Anglo-Saxon and Celtic races could spread their laws, customs, and institutions 'modified by place and circumstances.'[62] He did not forget Montcalm, however, noting that he was buried in the chapel of the Ursuline convent, and that Lord Aylmer had placed a marble slab there declaring in French, 'Honour to Montcalm. Destiny denied him victory, but rewarded him with a glorious death.'[63] Roger also informed his readers that Montcalm's skull had recently been put on display in a glass case, 'where the curious in relics may see it by applying to the Chaplain of the convent.'[64] A year later, in 1868, the *Quebec and Montreal Travellers' Free Guide* described how Wolfe and Montcalm had fallen, 'each a bitter loss to his country, each a living name in the annals of their military glory, and both a brilliant evidence of French and British valor.'[65] And the romantic sensibility became still more intense in 1876 with the appearance of *The Tourists' Notebook*, published by the Quebec City naturalist, folklorist, and historian James MacPherson LeMoine.[66] LeMoine wrote that 'the visitor may uninterruptedly meditate whatever emotion he will for the scene of Wolfe's death,' but his 'loftiest emotion will want the noble height of that heroic soul, who must always stand forth in history a figure of beautiful and singular distinction, admirable alike for the sensibility and daring, the poetic pensiveness, and the martial ardour that mingled in him, and taxed his feeble frame with tasks greater than it could bear.'[67]

As Alan Gordon notes in this volume, tourism is generally viewed as a quintessentially 'modern' activity because it is based on the highly regulated consumption of leisure. The fact remains, however, that the dramatic rhetoric of the Quebec tourism promoters not only echoed that of the earlier British travel writers but also paralleled the turn in the United States during the 1870s towards what Michael Kammen refers to as an enhanced 'retrospective vision.' This same vision took a material form in Quebec at this time due to the campaign led by LeMoine and Governor General Lord Dufferin to preserve the city's fortifications and add medieval embellishments.[68] Not yet threatened by development, however, the Plains of Abraham continued to receive relatively little attention as a physical space. For example, Agnes Maule Machar's contribution to *Picturesque Canada*, published in 1882, simply described the site as a 'barren and neglected-looking ground on which stands Wolfe's monument.'[69] Six years later the battleground was barely mentioned in the sixth edition of *Holiwell's New Guide to the City of Quebec and Environs.*[70] Finally, in 1895, a competing guidebook by E.T.D. Chambers did devote considerable attention to the Plains of Abraham as a geographic site, noting, for example, that it now served 'as a pasturage for the cattle of city milkmen.'[71]

By this time the threat of subdivision was beginning to spur a campaign to preserve what remained of the battlefield, reflected in the controversy concerning the main location of the fighting in 1759.[72] A pamphlet written by an unknown author in 1899 declared, however, that 'the whole neighborhood is consecrated by the bravery and devotion of the French and English generals alike, so that to-day their names are linked together, not as if they were enemies, but as if they had gone down to death in an imperishable friendship to be known forever as Wolfe and Montcalm.' Far from being a reminder of British superiority and French humiliation, then, the Plains of Abraham were a symbol of national unity, 'sanctified by the blood of the heroes of two great nations.'[73]

While French-Canadian nationalists resented and feared the growth of imperialist sentiment, which threatened to involve them in Britain's wars, the ultramontane Conservative judge Adolphe-Basile Routhier produced a publication that drew a positive lesson from the Battle of the Plains of Abraham.[74] In his *Quebec: A Quaint Mediaeval French City in America*, which appeared around 1904, Routhier claimed that Montcalm should be forgiven for his flawed strategy because he was a 'noble hearted and brilliant soldier, so prompt in action so dauntless and already covered with glory.' Furthermore, the French race did not die upon the Plains of Abraham, but, rather, 'France alone died, in the person of Montcalm. The sword of Albion cut the umbilical cord which joined the mother to the child; but the child was born to live, and will live and retain the ties of filial love which bind him to his mother.' Shielded by Britain, the French race had made great intellectual and religious progress, and French Canadians were gradually acquiring their share of the city's industrial growth. The monument to Wolfe and Montcalm symbolized their immortality and unity in death, as well as the 'the union of the two races forming the Canadian Nation!'[75]

The theme of national unity became more pronounced than ever with the approach of the city's tercentenary in 1908. A year earlier, the Toronto author Emily P. Weaver declared in her *Old Quebec: The City of Champlain* that 'two rival races, under two rival leaders, unconsciously joined hands on the Plains of Abraham,'[76] thereby converting a bloody battle into a sort of picnic. In more dramatic language, the *Canadian Trade Review's* illustrated volume on the city noted of the monument to Wolfe and Montcalm that the 'conqueror and the conquered are equally commemorated. If the ponderous weight of the granite shaft crushes out the divisions and enmities of the past, its summit, like an index, points to the regions where the souls of the heroes are united.'[77] In 1909 a promotional booklet stated that what had perished 'was the Bourbon monarchy and the narrow absolutism which fettered the life of New France throughout the Old Regime. What survives to this day is the vigour of two great races, striving to make Canada strong and free and reverent of law.'[78]

After protracted negotiations and delays, the Laurier government finally appointed the National Battlefields Commission in 1908 with the mandate to acquire the land on which the battle had taken place, remove structures such as the prison and more recently built rifle factory, erect a museum and various monuments, and embellish the grounds. Laurier was under pressure from Governor General Earl Grey, who wanted to promote national unity as well as stronger ties with the mother country by making the city's tricentennial celebration a national and even imperial event. Grey described the Plains of Abraham as the birthplace of the nation, and even though his campaign to raise funds to establish the park was largely a failure, this setback did not prevent the adoption in 1911 of a plan drafted by landscape architect Frederick Todd in the style of the great urban parks of New York, Montreal, and other major cities.[79]

In *The King's Book of Quebec*, the most lavish of the publications related to the tercentenary, Lieutenant-Colonel William Wood declared in 1911 that the park gardens should not 'spoil the essential character of the fields of battle.'[80] Two years later, Wood published *In the Heart of Old Canada*, with the declared aim of augmenting the battlefield fund and increasing the 'glory' of Montcalm, Lévis, and Wolfe, so that Canadians would become more patriotic. These were not tourist guidebooks, and the colonel felt that it was his duty to prevent Quebec from becoming 'a mere "show place," devoted to the prettier kinds of touristry and dilettante antiquarian delights,' but they did aim to attract visitors to Quebec and to shape their view of the Plains of Abraham. They also reveal how the battlefield had become what Wood referred to as Quebec City's greatest landmark, a term that he defined as 'anything preservable which is essentially connected with great acts or persons that once stirred our life and still stir our memory.'[81] Wood argued that the site

was unique because it had been 'the one scene of so many mighty conflicts, which changed the destinies of empires, but ever maintained the
honour of all who met in arms. Here Americans shared the triumph of
one victory, British-born of two, French of three, the French-Canadians
of no less than four.' No one had ever been disgraced in these battles,
the causes of which were no longer relevant – only the 'chivalry' remained. Wood was clear about which was the most important victory, however, for he added that 'the top of the promontory was a giant
stage,' a 'stupendous amphitheatre in the midst of which Wolfe was
waiting to play the hero's part.'[82]

* * * *

Prime Minister William Lyon Mackenzie King famously declared that
Canada had too much geography and too little history, a challenge that
the Canadian state responded to by nurturing what historical geographer Brian Osborne has referred to as 'a collective memory and social
cohesion through the representation of national narratives in symbolic
places.'[83] But the Plains of Abraham were a symbolic place long before Canada existed as a country, reminding us that, in Simon Schama's
words, '[l]andscapes are culture before they are nature: constructs of
the imagination projected onto wood and water and rock.'[84] British
travellers viewed this particular landscape as the site of a great imperial victory, Americans claimed that victory as a preliminary step in the
founding of their nation, and English Canadians adopted Wolfe and
Montcalm as symbols of national unity. In short, travel literature was
a powerful instrument in the multi-step process described by tourism
scholar Dean MacCannell as site sacralization.[85]

But the problem, as far as national unity was concerned, was that
French Canadians did not share the same vision of the Conquest. Following the rebellions of 1837–8, French-Canadian spokesmen developed a myth that emphasized their struggle for national survival and
celebrated the French victory at the Battle of Ste-Foy in 1760.[86] From
this perspective, the French Canadians had not been conquered by the
British, they had been abandoned by the French, and they therefore had
a legitimate claim to equality with English Canadians. This redemptive
interpretation was supported by colonial authorities, beginning with
Governor General Lord Elgin in the early 1850s, but the Battle of Ste-Foy
was largely ignored in the English-language travel literature, as was the
Monument des Braves, slowly constructed by the Société St-Jean-Baptiste
between 1855 and 1863 to honour the soldiers killed in that battle.[87]

Despite exceptions such as Judge Routhier's optimistic interpretation of the Conquest, which was aimed at English-speaking tourists, and despite the rehabilitation of Montcalm's reputation by French-language historians in the late nineteenth century, French Canadians and English Canadians clearly perceived two distinct symbolic landscapes as far as the Plains of Abraham were concerned.[88]

These conflicting views help to explain why state authorities paid little attention to the site as a physical space (making it a symbolic landscape in a rather literal sense) until late in the nineteenth century, when it was threatened by development. In the interests of national unity, the Plains of Abraham were fashioned after 1910 as a modern urban park, one that, as the historian of Canada's national parks has observed, has 'little didactic meaning.'[89] As we have seen, the lack of historical signposts did not prevent Quebec City's visitors and tourist promoters from imagining or describing the famous battle, but long before the park was completed the perception of war as a chivalrous exercise in which heroic generals willingly laid down their lives had dissolved in the muddy fields of northern France. As a result, the Plains of Abraham lost much of their remaining potency as a symbolic landscape, or what W.J.T. Mitchell refers to as 'an instrument of cultural power.'[90] But a group of military history re-enactors from the United States who proposed to mark the two hundred and fiftieth anniversary of the famous battle did learn that the Plains of Abraham still have the power to stir up nationalist controversy. In short, as Nora has said of France, from the standpoint of memory, Canada is more division than diversity.[91]

NOTES

1 I wish to thank Donald Fyson and Brian Young, as well as the editors of this volume, for their very helpful advice, Michael Olson and Sean Wilkinson for their research assistance, and the Social Sciences and Humanities Research Council of Canada for the funding that made their employment possible.

2 D.W. Meinig, 'Symbolic Landscapes: Models of American Community,' in D.W. Meinig, ed., *The Interpretation of Ordinary Landscapes: Geographical Essays* (Oxford; New York: Oxford University Press, 1979), 164.

3 A.R.M. Lower, *Colony to Nation: A History of Canada* (Toronto: Longmans, Green, 1946), 560.

4 On this theme, see Brian S. Osborne, 'Landscapes, Memory, Monuments, and Commemoration: Putting Identity in its Place,' *Canadian Ethnic Studies* 33, no. 3 (2001): 3–4, 10 (Proquest online version).

5 Quoted in H.V. Nelles, *The Art of Nation-Building: Pageantry and Spectacle at Quebec's Tercentenary* (Toronto: University of Toronto Press, 1999), 307.

6 See Pierre Nora, 'From *Lieux de mémoire* to *Realms of Memory*,' in *Realms of Memory: Rethinking the French Past*, vol. 1, *Conflicts and Divisions*, dir. by Pierre Nora (New York: Columbia University Press, 1996). On the reification of Wolfe, see Alan McNairn, *Behold the Hero: General Wolfe and the Arts in the 18th Century* (Montreal; Kingston, ON: McGill-Queen's University Press, 1997).

7 Most of these are available on microfiche in the series produced by the Canadian Institute for Microhistorical Reproductions.

8 During the nineteenth century, French Canadians were more drawn to religious pilgrimage sites than to secular ones. See Roger Brière, 'Les grands traits de l'évolution du tourisme au Québec,' *Bulletin de l'association des géographes de l'Amérique française* 11 (September 1967): 93; and Christine Hudon, 'La sociabilité religieuse à l'ère du vapeur du rail,' *Journal of the Canadian Historical Association* 10, no. 1 (1999): 129–47. The only French-language guidebook I found was Eugène Gingras, *Guide de Québec* (Québec: L.J. Demers, 1880). On French views of Quebec City, see Sylvain Simard, *Mythe et reflet de la France: l'image du Canada en France, 1850–1914* (Ottawa: Les Presses de l'Université d'Ottawa, 1987), 121–33.

9 See A.V. Seaton, 'War and Thanatourism: Waterloo 1815–1914,' *Annals of Tourism Research* 26, no. 1 (1998): 130–58; and Stuart Semmel, 'Reading the Tangible Past: British Tourism, Collecting and Memory After Waterloo,' *Representations* 69 (Winter 2000): 9–37.

10 Patrick Campbell, *Travels in the Interior Inhabited Parts of North America. In the Years 1791 and 1792* (Edinburgh: n.p., 1793), 124–7, 131.

11 Isaac Weld, *Travels through the States of North America, and the Provinces of Upper and Lower Canada, During the Years 1795, 1796, and 1797* (London: John Stockdale, 1799), 197–204; and 'Weld, Isaac,' in *Oxford Dictionary of National Biography Online*, http://www.oxforddnb.com.

12 McNairn, *Behold the Hero*, 190. According to a guidebook published in 1888, the statue had been carved for a local butcher in 1771. Thomas J. Oliver, *Holiwell's New Guide to the City of Quebec and Environs* (Quebec: C.E. Holiwell, 1888), 31–2.

13 John Lambert, *Travels through Lower Canada, and the United States of North America, in the Years 1806, 1807, and 1808* (London: Richard Phillips, 1810), 44–6. For a brief biography, see Jacqueline Roy, 'John Lambert,' in *Dictionary of Canadian Biography*, http://www.biographi.ca.

14 Hugh Gray, *Letters from Canada, written during a residence there in the Years 1806, 1807, and 1808* (London: Longman, Hurst, Rees, and Orme, 1809), 64–7.

15 Jeremy Cockloft, *Cursory Observations Made in Quebec Province of Lower Canada in the Year 1811* (Bermuda, n.d.; reprinted Toronto: Oxford University Press, 1960), 15, 30, 36–7. On the still-unsolved question of Cockloft's identity, see Donald Fyson, 'Jeremy Cockloft's Cursory Observations,' *Society Pages* (Quebec Literary and Historical Society) 20 (Summer 2008): 3–5.

16 Francis Hall, *Travels in Canada and the United States, in 1816 and 1817*, 2nd ed. (London: Longman, Hurst, Rees, Orme, and Browne, 1819), 58–9, 67–8.

17 John Palmer, *Journal of Travels in the United States of North America, and in Lower Canada, Performed in the Year 1817* (London: Sherwood, Nelly, and Jones, 1818), 226; and 'Palmer, John,' in *Oxford Dictionary of National Biography Online*, http://www.oxforddnb.com. In his *Description of a View of the City of Quebec, now exhibiting at the Panorama, Leicester Square* (London: J. and C. Adlard, 1830), Robert Burford noted that the Plains of Abraham were the 'Hyde Park of the fashionables of Quebec, round which they parade on foot, and in every description of carriage' (11). On other uses for this site, see Alan Gordon, in this volume.

18 Semmel, 'Reading the Tangible Past,' 11.

19 John Morison Duncan, *Travels through Part of the United States and Canada in 1818 and 1819*, vol. 2 (New York: W.B. Gilley; New Haven, CT: Howe and Spalding, 1823), 181, 211–13.

20 Edward Allen Talbot, *Five Years' Residence in the Canadas*, vol. 1 (London: Longman, Hurst, Rees, Orme, Brown and Green, 1824; reprint Toronto, 1968), 48–54;. and Daniel J. Brock, 'Edward Allen Talbot,' in *Dictionary of Canadian Biography*, http://www.biographi.ca. After the house at 'Wolfe's corner' was demolished in 1846, the wooden statue was placed in a new third-storey niche where it was more secure from being pulled from its perch by indignant French Canadians and drunken British sailors. It was retired in 1898 and, three years later, replaced by a new wooden Wolfe, which was removed to a museum in 1964 after the owner of the building was threatened with arson. McNairn, *Behold the Hero*, 234–5, 239.

21 Semmel, 'Reading the Tangible Past,' 20.

22 J.C. Morgan, *The Emigrant's Notebook and Guide* (London: Longman, Hurst, Rees, Orme, and Brown, 1824), 95–101.

23 Semmel, 'Reading the Tangible Past,' 12, 21, 22, 29.

24 David Wilkie, *Sketches of a Summer Trip to New York and the Canadas* (London: Berwick, 1837), 248, 250, 269.

25 E.T. Coke, *A Subaltern's Furlough: Descriptive Scenes in Various Parts of the*

United States, Upper and Lower Canada, New Brunswick, and Nova Scotia During the Summer and Autumn of 1832 (London: Saunders and Otley, 1833), 69–70.

26 James Edward Alexander, *Transatlantic Sketches Comprising Visits to the Most Interesting Scenes in North and South America, and the West Indies* (London: R. Bentley, 1833), 202.

27 Henry Tudor, *Narrative of a Tour in North America*, vol. 1 (London: James Duncan, 1834), 1, 3.

28 Tyrone Power, *Impressions of America, During the Years 1833, 1834, and 1835*, vol. 2 (1836; reprint New York: Benjamin Blom, 1971), 316; and 'Power, Tyrone,' in *Oxford Dictionary of National Biography Online*, http://www.oxforddnb.com.

29 Donald Guay, 'Sports, Culture, and Leisure, 1800–1900,' in *The Plains of Abraham: The Search for the Ideal*, ed. Jacques Mathieu and Eugen Kedl (Sillery, QC: Septentrion, 1993), 140; Richard H. Bonnycastle, *The Canadas in 1841* (1841; New York: Johnson Reprint, 1968), 48–9; and 'Bonnycastle, Sir Richard Henry,' in *Oxford Dictionary of National Biography Online*, http://www.oxforddnb.com. According to De Roos in 1827, the field's owner 'had the barbarous selfishness to sink the stony pillow twenty feet below the surface of the ground, and the plough has now gone over it'; F.F. DeRoos, *Personal Narrative of Travels in the United States and Canada* (London: William H. Ainsworth, 1827), 121. In 1838, Logan claimed that the granite that supported the 'small circular stone ... has already been chipped by visitors'; Logan, *Notes of a Journey*, 28–9.

30 James Lumsden, *American Memoranda by a Mercantile Man, During a Short Tour in the Summer of 1843* (Glasgow: Bell and Bain, 1844), 18.

31 James Dixon, *Personal Narrative of a Tour through a Part of the United States and Canada* (New York: Land and Scott, 1849), 148–9.

32 William Chambers, *Things As They Are in America* (1854; reprint New York: Negro Universities Press, 1968), 81–4; and 'Chambers, William,' in *Oxford Dictionary of National Biography Online*, http://www.oxforddnb.com.

33 Thomas Hamilton, *Men and Manners in America*, new ed. (Edinburgh: William Blackwood and Sons, 1843), 426.

34 Morgan, *Emigrant's Notebook*, 100–1.

35 Tudor, *Narrative of a Tour*, 328.

36 Charles Dickens, *American Notes for General Circulation*, vol. 2 (London: Chapman and Hall, 1842), 201–2.

37 Robert Baird, *Impressions and Experiences of the West Indies and North America in 1849* (Philadelphia: Lea and Blanchard, 1850), 238.

38 John J. Bigsby, *The Shoe and Canoe or Pictures of Travel in the Canadas*, vol. 1

(1850; New York: Paladin Press, 1969), 1, 12, 24; and 'Bigsby, John Jeremiah,' in *Oxford Dictionary of National Biography*, http://www.oxforddnb.com.

39 Edmund Patten, *A Glimpse at the United States and the Northern States of America, with the Canadas, Comprising Their Rivers, Lakes, and Falls During the Autumn of 1852* (London: Effingham Wilson, 1853), 79.

40 Isabella Bishop, *The Englishwoman in America* (London: John Murray, 1856), 257–71; and 'Bishop [née Bird], Isabella Lucy,' in *Oxford Dictionary of National Biography Online*, http://www.oxforddnb.com.

41 Alfred Pairpoint, *Uncle Sam and His Country; or Sketches of America in 1854-55-56* (London: Simpkin, Marshall, 1857), 94–9.

42 Douglas Brooke Wheeton Sladen, *On the Cars and Off: Being a Pilgrimage Along the Queen's Highway, From Halifax in Nova Scotia to Victoria in Vancouver Island* (London and New York: Ward Lock, 189_?), 35, 51–8.

43 Ibid., 49.

44 Joseph Sansom, *Sketches of Lower Canada, Historical and Descriptive* (New York: Kirk and Mercein, 1817), 5–6.

45 Joseph Sansom, 'Travels in Lower Canada, 1820,' in *Yankees in Canada: A Collection of Nineteenth-Century Travel Narratives*, ed. James Doyle (Toronto: University of Toronto Press, 1980), 50–2.

46 Benjamin Silliman, *A Tour to Quebec in the Autumn of 1819* (London: Sir Richard Phillips and Co., 1822), 97–8.

47 G.M. Davison, *The Fashionable Tour; An Excursion to the Springs, Niagara, Quebec, and through the New England States* (Saratoga Springs, NY: G.M. Davison, 1828), 206.

48 Theodore Dwight, *The Northern Traveller, and Northern Tour, With the Routes to the Springs, Niagara & Quebec, and the Coal Mines of Pennsylvania* (New York: J. and J. Harper, 1830), 227–9.

49 *Major Jones's Sketches of Travel: Comprising the Scenes, Incidents, and Adventures, in his Tour from Georgia to Canada* (1848), in *Yankees in Canada* (see note 44), 53, 61–2. On public monuments as contested terrains, see Osborne, 'Landscapes, Memory, Monuments,' 15.

50 J.C. Myers, *Sketches on a Tour through the Northern and Eastern States, the Canadas and Nova Scotia* (Harrisonburg, VA: J.H. Wartmann and Brothers, 1849), 214.

51 Henry James, 'Quebec,' in *Yankees in Canada* (see note 45), 125, 128–9.

52 Eleanor Gertrude Farrell, *Among the Blue Laurentians, Queenly Montreal, Quaint Quebec, Peerless Ste. Anne de Beaupré* (New York: P.J. Kenedy, 1912), 25–6, 32. My thanks to Nicolas Kenny for bringing this book to my attention. See also Katherine Haldane Grenier, *Tourism and Identity in Scotland, 1770-1914* (Burlington, VT: Ashgate, 2005), 152–3.

53 Daniel Francis, *National Dreams: Myth, Memory, and Canadian History* (Vancouver: Arsenal Pulp Press, 1997), 95–6.

54 George Bourne, *The Picture of Quebec* (Quebec: D. and J. Smillie, 1829), 34, 39.

55 *Quebec and Its Environs; Being a Picturesque Guide to the Stranger* ([Quebec]: Thomas Cary, 1831), 5, 9–10, 33–42; Didier Prioul, 'James Pattison Cockburn,' in *Dictionary of Canadian Biography*, http://www.biographi.ca; and Martine Geronimi, 'Québec dans les discours des guides touristiques, 1830-1930,' *Folklore canadien* 18, no. 2 (1996): 72.

56 This guidebook was republished by Charles Roger as *Stadacona Depicta; or Quebec and its Environs Historically, Panoramically, and Locally Exhibited* (Quebec: Carey, 1857).

57 *Hawkins's Picture of Quebec with Historical Recollections* (Quebec: Neilson and Cowan, 1834), 1–3, 7. On Hawkins, see Dorothy E. Rider, 'Alfred Hawkins,' in *Dictionary of Canadian Biography*, http://www.biographi.ca.

58 *Hawkins's Picture*, 266, 276–9. Only the contrarian Thomas Hamilton objected that there was 'nonsense and pedantry' in using a language that ninety-nine out of a hundred could not read; Hamilton, *Men and Manners*, 427.

59 Alain Parent, *Entre empire et nation: les représentations de la ville de Québec et de ses environs, 1760–1833* (Québec: Les Presses de l'Université Laval, 2005), 226–34.

60 *Hawkins's Picture*, 299, 329, 359, 365.

61 *The Quebec Directory and Stranger's Guide to the City and Environs, 1844–5* (Quebec: W. Cowan for A. Hawkins, 1844), 27, 185, 189–91, 231.

62 Charles Roger, *Quebec As It Was and As It Is, or, a Brief History of the Oldest City in Canada* (Quebec: P. Lamoureux, 1867), 21, 27.

63 The original citation was 'Honneur à Montcalm. Le Destin en lui dérobant la Victoire, L'a récompensé par une mort glorieuse.'

64 Roger, *Quebec As It Was*, 38. A guidebook published in 1868 stated that Americans had been denied access to the Ursuline convent ever since the destruction of its sister institution in Charlestown, Massachusetts; see *The American House Traveller's Guide for River St. Lawrence, and the Cities of Montreal, Quebec & Ottawa* (Montreal: Daniel Rose, 1868), 26–30, 32.

65 *Quebec and Montreal Travellers' Free Guide: Containing General Information for Tourists* (Montreal?: s.n., 1872), 82–3.

66 Carol W. Fullerton, 'LeMoine, Sir James MacPherson,' in *The Canadian Encyclopedia Online*, http://www.thecanadianencyclopedia.com; Guy Mercier and Yves Melançon, 'A Park in the City, 1830–1910,' in *Plains of Abraham* (see note 28), 181, 187–8.

67 J.M. LeMoine, *The Tourists' Notebook* (Quebec: F.X. Garant, 1876), 32.

68 Michael Kammen, *Mystic Chords of Memory: The Transformation of Tradition in American Culture* (New York: Alfred A. Knopf, 1991), 93. On Dufferin's campaign, see Martine Geronimi, *Québec et la Nouvelle-Orléans: paysages imaginaires français en Amérique du Nord* (Paris: Éditions Belin, 2003); Christina Cameron, 'Lord Dufferin contre les gothes et les vandales,' *Cap-aux-Diamants* 2, no. 2 (1986): 39–41; R.G. Moyles and Doug Owram, *Imperial Dreams and Colonial Realities: British Views of Canada, 1880–1914* (Toronto: University of Toronto Press, 1988), 103–6; and Mercier and Melançon, 'Park in the City,' 188–9.

69 A.M. Machar, 'Quebec, Picturesque and Descriptive,' in *Picturesque Canada; The Country As It Was and Is*, ed. George Monro Grant (Toronto: Belden, [1882]), 46, 59. See also *American House Traveller's Guide;* and *Chisholm's All Round Route and Panoramic Guide of the St Lawrence* (Montreal: C.R. Chisholm, 1880).

70 Oliver, *Holiwell's New Guide*, 31–2.

71 E.T.D. Chambers, *The Guide to Quebec* ([Quebec]: Quebec Morning Chronicle, [1895]), 93.

72 The prevailing view, ultimately, was that the main battle site was north of the rue Ste-Foy in the area that had already been developed; see John Murdoch Harper, *The Battle of the Plains* (Quebec: Published for the author, 1895); Arthur G. Doughty, *The Probable Site of the Battle of the Plains of Abraham* (Ottawa: J. Hope, 1899); P.-B. Casgrain, *Les Plaines d'Abraham, Endroit Historique à Conserver* (Québec?: s.n., 1900?); and Arthur G. Doughty, *The Siege of Quebec and the Battle of the Plains of Abraham* (Quebec: Dussault and Proulx, 1901–2).

73 *The Plains of Abraham, 1759: A Spot Sacred to the Memory of Wolfe and Montcalm* (Quebec: s.n., 1899), 6. See also W.H. Withrow, *Our Own Country Canada, Scenic and Descriptive* (Toronto: William Briggs, 1889), 192.

74 On Routhier, see Andrée Désilets, *Hector-Louis Langevin: un père de la Confédération canadienne (1826–1906)* (Québec: Les Presses de l'Université Laval, 1969), 217, 219, 220, 400; Ronald Rudin, *Founding Fathers: The Celebration of Champlain and Laval in the Streets of Quebec, 1878-1908* (Toronto: University of Toronto Press, 2003), 78–9; and Michel Ducharme, in this volume.

75 A.B. Routhier, *Quebec: A Quaint Mediaeval French City in America at the Dawn of the XXth Century* (Montreal: Montreal Printing and Publishing, 1904), 213, 231, 232, 234, 246.

76 Francis, *National Dreams*, 106; and Emily P. Weaver, *Old Quebec: The City of Champlain* (Toronto: William Briggs, 1907), 41.

77 *The Canadian Trade Review: An Illustrated Descriptive Edition of the City of Quebec* (Montreal?: s.n., 1908?), 2.

78 *Quebec Ancient and Modern* (Montreal; Quebec: Cambridge Corporation, 1909), 15–16.

79 Francis, *National Dreams*, 95; Rudin, *Founding Fathers*, 169–73; Claude Paulette and Jacques Mathieu, 'The Natural Park: A Romantic Garden,' in *Plains of Abraham* (see note 28), 212–13; and Nelles, *Art of Nation-Building*, 80–1, 83–4, 86–101, 303–12.

80 William Wood, *The King's Book* (Ottawa: Montmorency, 1911), 157; and Nelles, *Art of Nation-Building*, 308.

81 William Wood, *In the Heart of Old Canada* (Toronto: William Briggs, 1913), 2, 28.

82 Ibid., 3, 20, 23, 26, 77.

83 Osborne, 'Landscapes, Memory, Monuments,' 3, 8.

84 Simon Schama, *Landscape and Memory* (New York: Knopff, 1995), 61.

85 Travel literature falls into MacCannell's 'mechanical reproduction' category. Other steps, such as the erection of monuments as 'framing and elevating devices,' were clearly less effective. See Seaton, 'War and Thanatourism,' 140–55; and Dean MacCannell, *The Tourist* (London: Macmillan, 1976).

86 See Ducharme, 'Interpreting the Past.' According to Gordon ('Where Famous Heroes Fell'), Hugh Gray was the only English author to mention this French victory.

87 See Patrice Groulx, 'La commemoration de la bataille de Sainte-Foy: du discours de la loyauté à la "fusion des races,"' *Revue d'histoire de l'Amérique française* 55, no. 1 (2001): 45–83.

88 Ducharme ('Interpreting the Past') claims that, in rehabilitating Montcalm, French-Canadian nationalists were looking for great men to inspire their nation, as well as reaffirming their cultural ties with France. This did not prevent the liberal P.B. Casgrain, who was president of the Quebec Literary and Historical Society, from attempting to stir up support in 1904 for a new Wolfe monument. He declared that '[a] hero so illustrious in the Annals of the Empire, and associated at all times with the early history of Quebec, is surely deserving of something better than this insignificant and mutilated memorial, utterly dwarfed by the huge jail at its side, and not easily found, owing to the site selected being a side lane'; P.B. Casgrain, *The Monument to Wolfe on the Plains of Abraham: and the Old Statue at 'Wolfe's Corner'* (Ottawa?: s.n., 1904), 213. For references to Casgrain, see Robert Rumilly, *Honoré Mercier et son temps*, vol. 2 (Montréal: Fides, 1975), 288, 296, 303, 321.

89 Paulette and Mathieu, 'The Natural Park,' 208; Nelles, *Art of Nation-Building*, 306; and C.J. Taylor, *Negotiating the Past: The Making of Canada's National Historic Parks and Sites* (Montreal; Kingston, ON: McGill-Queen's University Press, 1990), xiv. Like the Gettysburg National Military Park, which Wood had visited as a member of the Quebec Landmarks Commission in 1907, the aim was to evoke a sense of the sublime in nature by 'an expression of grandeur'; see J.S. Patterson, 'A Patriotic Landscape: Gettysburg, 1863–1913,' *Prospects* 7 (1982): 321, 324.

90 W.J.T. Mitchell, *Landscape and Power* (Chicago: University of Chicago Press, 1994), 1–2.

91 Nora, 'Conflicts and Divisions,' in *Realms of Memory* (see note 5), vol. 1, 21. For a useful journalistic account of the re-enactment controversy, see Ian Brown, 'In Wolfe's clothing,' *Globe and Mail*, 31 July 2009; see also the relevant chapters in this volume.

5

History, Historiography, and the Courts: The St Lawrence Mission Villages and the Fall of New France

JEAN-FRANÇOIS LOZIER

Aboriginal peoples did not feature prominently in the narratives wrought by the first several generations of historians of the Conquest or *la Conquête*, whose extensive scholarship and heated debates, as the other contributions to this collection make abundantly clear, revolved above all around the meaning and legacy of this event for French-Canadian society. The Iroquois, Huron, and Montagnais could act as convenient foils in the early, seventeenth-century chapters of the story of the *nation*. In later chapters, though, they invariably receded to the background as the English became the dominant adversary and most resonant 'other.'[1] Conversely, the first generation of Canadian scholars to view aboriginals as more than accessories in the story of European settlement and Euro-American nation building trained their attention solidly on the initial, seventeenth-century phase of commercial, military, and spiritual contact between natives and newcomers.[2] It was only in the late 1980s and early 1990s that interest arose in how aboriginal peoples had experienced the military fall of New France and the transition from the French to the British regime. In these past three decades, inquiries into the meaning of this moment for the inhabitants of the mission villages of the St Lawrence valley – the Iroquois, Huron, Abenaki, Algonquin, and Nipissing who were known to the French as *domiciliés*, and to the British as 'French Praying Indians' or 'Canada Indians,' and eventually as the 'Seven Nations'[3] – have been particularly copious and contested. While the treaties that were concluded in 1760 – notably the 'Murray Treaty' – served as crucial points of reference in the relationship between aboriginals and the Crown during the first few decades of integration within the British Empire, they have more recently been remembered as much for legal as for historical reasons.

Thus, consideration of the events surrounding the Conquest itself leads also to reflection on the complex interrelationship of historiography, historical memory, and indigenous rights.

France's Iroquois, Abenaki, and Huron allies, though residents of similar mission villages, experienced the Seven Years' War and the British Conquest of Canada in rather different ways. Peter MacLeod's *The Canadian Iroquois and the Seven Years' War* offers the most detailed chronicle and analysis of the involvement of the people of Kahnawake (Sault St-Louis, or Caughnawaga), Kanehsatake (Deux-Montagnes), Akwesasne (St-Régis), and Oswegatchie (La Présentation) in the military operations of 1759 and 1760. It was as allies of the French, rather than as enemies of the British, that these Canadian Iroquois entered the conflict. And it was the fact that the security and integrity of their communities were not threatened for most of the conflict's duration that made it possible for them to honour their alliance while pursuing traditional wartime opportunities: the search for individual achievement, for prisoners, scalps, and loot. The fall of Carillon/Ticonderoga and Niagara in 1759 became the turning point of the war for the Canadian Iroquois. Their priorities shifted to ensuring the safety of their villages, and neutrality became an increasingly desirable prospect.[4]

As they closed in on the St Lawrence Valley, the British went to great lengths to neutralize the Franco-aboriginal alliance. It was a time of innovation, for the Indian Department had existed only since 1755. The negotiation of treaties, which for a long time had been the purview of colonial governors, was centralized under the authority of the British commander-in-chief, General Jeffery Amherst by the end of the war, and then of the superintendent of the northern department, Sir William Johnson.[5] Amherst's and Johnson's efforts to neutralize the Franco-aboriginal alliance were nonetheless in keeping with a long diplomatic tradition. On many occasions since the 1680s, the New Yorkers and the Iroquois of the Five (and later Six) Nations had adopted a conciliatory but forceful stance towards the *domiciliés*, cycling between sympathetic warnings, angry threats, and ultimatums to secure their neutrality if not their relocation away from French lands.[6] Given the increasing likelihood of a British invasion in 1759 and 1760, the latest round of overtures made by Sir William Johnson and the Six Nations had unparalleled resonance. In April and May 1759, Johnson's threats were answered by the news that the councils of Oswegatchie, Kahnawake, and Kanehsatake had resolved to cease their military activity. Similar assurances were reiterated in October. Yet consensus was elusive in these communities. Many of their warriors continued to fight alongside the French on the Quebec, Lake Champlain, and Lake Ontario fronts until well into the summer of 1760.[7]

While Johnson focused on the Canadian Iroquois, Amherst made corresponding attempts to secure the neutrality of the Abenaki. During the summer of 1759, he dispatched British and Mahican emissaries led by Quinton Kennedy and Jacob Cheeksaunkun, *alias* Captain Jacob, to make contact with the people of Odanak (St-François). Hostility towards the British ran unmistakably deeper here than in the Iroquois mission villages. For the Abenaki, the outbreak of the Seven Years' War had represented the welcomed formalization and intensification of an enduring conflict with New England. The detention and mistreatment of Amherst's emissaries in August prompted the commander-in-chief to allow a retaliatory strike. Much has been written on the resulting 'St Francis Raid' or 'Rogers' Raid' of 4 October 1759, the most balanced treatment to date being Stephen Brumwell's *White Devil*. It is now clear that, notwithstanding Major Robert Rogers' exaggerated impressions of success, the destruction of the village did not entail the extermination of its inhabitants. That only about thirty of them were killed is explained by Abenaki oral traditions, first scrutinized by Gordon Day in the 1960s, according to which the community had been forewarned of the attack. While some of the survivors joined French forces near Quebec and others withdrew to remote hunting grounds, a significant core soon found refuge among the Iroquois of Akwesasne.[8]

The Abenaki of Odanak were the only *domiciliés* to experience the destruction of their village. Yet the recently rediscovered recollections of the Huron chief Ondiaraété, or Petit Étienne, reveal that the people of Wendake (Lorette) were as dramatically, if less violently, uprooted. Published in *The Star and Commercial Advertiser* in 1828 but brought to the attention of the historical community only in 2000 by the historian Alain Beaulieu, this first-hand account sheds more light than any other single document on how the Huron experienced the last year of the conflict. Shortly after the Battle of the Plains of Abraham, in which their warriors took part alongside more numerous Abenaki and men from the Great Lakes nations, the inhabitants of Lorette abandoned their village and began a protracted withdrawal towards Montreal.[9]

The threat of retaliation gave teeth to the British policy of conciliation. There is no doubt that the destruction of St-François sent a clear message to the other *domiciliés* – that those who persisted in their opposition to the British could expect to see their homes destroyed and their population killed, captured, or exiled. As British and, significantly, Six Nations Iroquois forces closed in on Montreal during the summer of 1760, they continued to court the inhabitants of the mission villages, whom they judged could still field some eight hundred warriors. Faced with the apparent inevitability of a French defeat, deputies from the mission villages responded with pragmatism and accepted the overtures made by Johnson in early August with the aim of 'bring[ing] them to a neutrality.'[10] A crucial conference was held at Oswegatchie on 30 August during which men from Oswegatchie, Akwesasne, Kahnawake, and probably Kanehsatake, as well as displaced Abenaki, representing in all 'nine Severall Nations and Tribes of Indians Inhabiting the Country about Montreal,' met with Sir William Johnson. Neither minutes nor detailed accounts of the event have survived, and its significance is not readily apparent. On the basis of contemporary allusions and oral traditions fixed after 1769, however, scholars have demonstrated that a treaty of neutrality was formalized on this occasion, whereby, in exchange for their non-intervention in the conflict, the inhabitants of the mission villages received pledges that they would not be subjected to reprisals and that the rights and privileges that they had enjoyed under the French regime, notably with regards to religion and land occupancy, would be maintained.[11]

The neutrality of the *domiciliés* allowed the British army to advance unmolested through the difficult rapids and portages of the upper St Lawrence. On 2 September, Governor Vaudreuil, 'believing the Natives to be in more favourable dispositions'[12] than they turned out to be, had them assembled at La Prairie, on the south shore of the St Lawrence opposite Montreal and a short distance from Kahnawake. There he invited them to march with his army to attack the enemy with aplomb. News of what had occurred at Oswegatchie arrived at that moment, however, and the warriors abandoned the camp. By 5 September, the three British armies had converged on Montreal. The Huron of Lorette sent representatives of their own to General James Murray at Longueuil, just east of La Prairie, and secured guarantees analogous to those of Oswegatchie.[13] As we will see, the precise nature of the guarantees proffered on that day would give rise to a polemic two centuries later.

Montreal capitulated on 8 September. The Articles of Capitulation of Montreal negotiated on that occasion by Vaudreuil and Amherst touched lightly on the inhabitants of the missions. Vaudreuil obtained for his allies guarantees analogous to those of Oswegatchie, perhaps unaware that they had already done so on their own, perhaps unwilling to recognize formally their diplomatic independence from the French.[14] In any case, at Kahnawake on 15 and 16 September, Sir William Johnson again met in conference with representatives of the 'Eight nations of Canada' on whose behalf spoke local headmen, as well as with representatives of the Six Nations. The parties proceeded to confirm the terms of the agreement made at Oswegatchie, to renew and strengthen the Covenant Chain that had united them before the war. The former allies of the French buried 'the French hatchet we have made use of, in the bottomless pit,' and pledged to maintain a 'firm peace with the English and the 6 Nations.' Johnson's request for the release of their prisoners of war was accepted, and his clearing of obstacles along the 'road' that linked Canada to New York, a metaphorical promise of free circulation and trade, was met with enthusiasm. It was agreed that the regime change would not alter the fundamental bases of the relationship between the inhabitants of the mission villages and the colonial government: that the former would be allowed to retain the Catholic religion, that priests, blacksmiths, and interpreters would continue to be provided to them, that trade and the sale of alcohol would be carefully regulated, and that while the British were now in 'possession of this country,' they would retain 'peaceable possession of the spot of ground we live now upon.'[15]

The value of the promises made at Oswegatchie, Longueuil, and Kahnawake in August and September 1760 was challenged in the months that followed. As Peter MacLeod and Jean-Pierre Sawaya have each demonstrated, for all the rhetoric of peace, friendship, and harmony that was deployed on these occasions, relations between the new neighbours and allies were turbulent. The Kahnawake, in particular, complained of abuse at the hands of British troops who provoked, assaulted, and robbed them with apparent impunity. The generals, too, continued to treat the former allies of the French with suspicion. Disregarding assurances given at Oswegatchie and Kahnawake, Amherst refused government funding to their missionaries and blacksmiths, and ordered that the distribution of presents be kept to a strict minimum, while Thomas Gage placed strict restrictions on circulation and commerce with Albany. The Mahican, old allies of the British, for their part made ominous threats of vengeance against the Abenaki of St-François who in August 1759 had killed one of their ambassadors. Sir William Johnson and his new deputy in Canada, Daniel Claus, were left to defuse these crises, and to advocate the importance of handling Britain's new allies with care.[16]

The Kahnawake and Abenaki momentarily considered the idea of taking part in an insurgency – a 'General Indian War' – in 1761.[17] After failing to elicit the sympathy of the Six Nations, however, the Kahnawake opted decisively for the British alliance, convincing the more bellicose Abenaki to desist and in June 1761 and May 1762 renewing the treaty of September 1760. In 1763, following the news of the Treaty of Paris and of the uprising in the interior, the inhabitants of the mission villages again reiterated their allegiance to the British, and assisted them by formulating an ultimatum to their 'Brethren of Towaganha, or Western Indians.' In 1764–5, Canadian Iroquois warriors took part, alongside those of the Six Nations and *Canadien* volunteers, in the campaign against the Shawnee and Delaware of the Ohio Valley.[18]

The rallying of the inhabitants of the mission villages to the British Crown was a matter of pragmatism. Military resistance, alluringly feasible in the remote Great Lakes and Ohio, was not a viable alternative in the densely occupied St Lawrence Valley. Besides – though historians, who have been above all attentive to contrasts in colonial models and indigenous policies, have not emphasized this – the frustrations of the new regime were arguably little worse than those of the old. French officials, too, had treated the *domiciliés* with suspicion, held a sometimes fickle rein on the distribution of presents and material assistance, and striven to restrict the contraband trade with Albany.[19] In the same way, much of the attractions of the colonial partnership remained unchanged. The administrative novelty of an Indian Department, extremely rudimentary at this time, grafted itself naturally on the informal, nebulous arrangements that had been the administration of indigenous relations under the French regime. Despite the altered relationship of church and state, Jesuit and Sulpician missionaries remained at their posts at the spiritual head of the communities. Justice continued to be administered in a parallel and accommodating fashion, as it had been under the French regime, exceptional treatment being accorded to aboriginals until the early nineteenth century.[20] The British pledges of 1760, soon joined by those of the Royal Proclamation of 1763, stood as assurance that, once the difficulties of transition had been resolved, the new colonial regime would be no harsher than the old. Collaboration with the British Crown flowed logically from a long tradition of collaboration with that of France.

For the Kahnawake at least, beyond a degree of status quo, the transition from one colonial regime to another in fact offered opportunities. For one, they were able successfully to challenge their place within the

seigneurial order, a previously unthinkable achievement. In 1762, represented by Daniel Claus, they approached the military tribunal pre-
sided by Thomas Gage to contest the legal status of the seigneury of
Sault St-Louis on which they were established. Referring to the guarantees of 1760 to the effect that the inhabitants of the missions would
maintain possession of their lands, they complained that the Jesuit *seigneurs* had for some time been illegally conceding parcels to *habitants*,
to the detriment of the Iroquois community, and made the case that it,
in fact, was the rightful *seigneur*. On the basis of the evidence presented
to him, Gage judged that the French monarch's intention had been to
grant the land for the express use of the Iroquois and ruled in their
favour, thereby dispossessing the Jesuits and appointing a receiver of
rents on the behalf of the aboriginal community. This reading of the evidence, to be sure, was at least partly influenced by political motives: a
long-standing British suspicion of the Jesuits coupled with the desire to
cultivate a new alliance.[21] For the Huron of Lorette, an opportunity to
make claims over seigneurial lands presented itself four decades later
with the liquidation of Jesuit estates – a late result of the British decision, taken in the 1760s, to let the missionary order die out in Canada.[22]

The Kahnawake exploited another opportunity with the institutionalization of the Seven Nations Confederacy. The precise nature of this
political entity has caused a lot of scholarly ink to flow in recent years,
partly the result of the judicial scrutiny of the treaties of 1760 – a process
to which the last part of this chapter is devoted. The treaty concluded
at Oswegatchie, after all, had been negotiated with representatives of
'nine Severall Nations and Tribes of Indians Inhabiting the Country
about Montreal' and that concluded at Kahnawake with those of 'Eight
nations of Canada,' regrettably unnamed. Afterward, references to
'Seven Fires' or 'Seven Nations' appear with increasing frequency in Indian Department records.[23] Spotting a potentially significant lacuna in
the scholarship, Denys Delâge and his student Jean-Pierre Sawaya, the
latter of whom went on to devote his graduate studies to the subject,
began to probe the origins and development of this forgotten political
organization. Through the 1990s, they initially and prolifically argued
that, between 1660 and 1860, the Huron of Wendake, the Algonquin
of Pointe-du-Lac, the Abenaki of Wôlinak and Odanak, the Iroquois of
Kahnawake and Akwesasne, and the Iroquois, Algonquin, and Nipissing of Kanehsatake were politically united in a *confédération* or *fédération*.[24] Though critics pointed to the lack of evidence supporting such
ancient roots, the notion of the 'Seven Nations' came into fashion as

both a means of conceptualizing collectively the inhabitants of the mission villages of the St Lawrence Valley and of elucidating the transition between the French and British regimes.[25] The notion that the *domiciliés* had been politically united throughout the period, it can be argued, had the marked advantage of suggesting a tantalizing compatibility of *Québécois* and aboriginal ambitions for political autonomy on a territorial basis.

In a cluster of publications in 2001–2, the result of a decade-long investigation, Delâge and Sawaya corrected their initial position. The formation and institutionalization of the Seven Nations as a political organization, it is now clear, was a direct consequence of the Conquest. Borrowing the notions of *direct* and *indirect* rule from scholars working on the British Empire in Asia, Delâge and Sawaya now argue that, whereas the French had interposed themselves between their allies and negotiated with each nation on an individual basis, the British had instead preferred to elevate one nation above the others and to use it as broker between the Crown and the others.[26] In the St Lawrence Valley this meant giving pre-eminence to the Kahnawake, whose friendship the British had been cultivating since the turn of the century, and fostering the formation of a confederacy, with the familiar Six Nations Confederacy offering, if not a true model, at least a label. Kahnawake was to serve as the site of the general council fire, and its headmen were to act as representatives of the whole. In fact, as Sawaya has argued in his later work, this new 'confederacy' was not founded on the equality and consensus of its members. It appears instead to have furthered above all the specific ambitions of the Kahnawake, who among other things used its authority to further their own claims over hunting territories.[27] Since then, a few authors have nevertheless continued to use the term 'Seven Nations' as a dubious shorthand for the inhabitants of the mission villages at the time of the Conquest, in an anachronistic overstatement of their political unity.[28]

The Conquest was far from a disaster for the Kahnawake, which is not to say that it was without new challenges. The extension of British trade networks to the St Lawrence Valley, for one, spelled the end of the contraband trade that had become a cornerstone of the economy of Kahnawake and Kanehsatake. Within a few decades it would push the men of these villages to find employment with the emerging fur-trading companies, the greatest leap perhaps in their gradual integration into the wage economy.[29] For the Abenaki of Odanak and Wôlinak, however, the Conquest was a very real disaster. After the raid of 1759, they were scattered, angered, and disempowered. Though some of their number were already back at Odanak by 1760, it was not until 1768 that they managed to 'collect themselves' there and metaphorically light their fire anew. The elimination of the 'French and Indian' threat allowed a new phase of rapid and relentless expansion to begin in the century-long progress of Anglo-American encroachment on traditional Abenaki homelands and hunting grounds. The cession of lands claimed by the Abenaki of Missisquoi and St-François in 1766, by Kahnawake headmen dubiously speaking on behalf of the Seven Nations, contributed to their formal dispossession.[30]

What to make of the treaties concluded at Oswegatchie, Longueuil, and Kahnawake in 1760? They occupy the tail end of a long series of diplomatic encounters between 'French Praying Indians' and Anglo-American officials, a frequent occurrence since the turn of the century. Delâge and Sawaya have situated the treaties of 1760 in the wake of three others concluded between the sachems of Kahnawake and the commissioners of Albany in 1735, 1742, and 1753.[31] To this list we should add a string of earlier diplomatic encounters that occurred in 1705, 1708, 1710, 1723, and 1724. On these occasions, a consistent rhetoric of peace, friendship, and commerce was deployed, as Canadian Iroquois and occasionally Abenaki headmen laid down with great solemnity the metaphorical hatchet of war and buried it forever, often promising to use their influence to convince others to do the same. Their British interlocutors for their part cleared the obstacles that stood on the path to Albany, thereby renewing commercial relations.[32] Thus, already in 1735, the Kahnawake orators spoke of strengthening 'antient peace, friendship & intercourse'; in 1753, they spoke of renewing the Covenant Chain.[33] The strength of the French alliance, however, coupled with the diffuse and non-coercive nature of authority within the *domicilié* communities, made the periodical digging up of the war hatchet unavoidable. To the individuals and communities who opted to negotiate peace in 1760, it was not at all obvious that this pattern would not again repeat itself.

In light of Britain's continued occupation of the St Lawrence Valley, however, the hatchet would remain buried, and these latest treaties became the foundation blocks of the relationship between the inhabitants of the mission villages and the British Crown. Contrary to earlier treaties, those of 1760 – and most obviously that of Kahnawake – were negotiated within the context of a destabilized balance of power. Having eliminated its imperial competitor, Britain secured the military and

commercial means to increasingly impose its will on aboriginal populations, beginning with those who lived along the shores of the St Lawrence. Alain Beaulieu has thus interpreted these treaties as ushering a
shift between two different colonial logics, from one based on the con-
vergence of French and aboriginal interests and on French ambitions
of diplomatic hegemony, to another based on British protection and
aboriginal vulnerability. 'By their form,' explains Beaulieu, 'the treaties of the Conquest seem to recognize the autonomy or independence
of aboriginals; in fact, they instituted a relationship characterized by a
form of subjugation.'[34]

Still, to the aboriginal inhabitants of the St Lawrence Valley, the treaties of Oswegatchie and Kahnawake must have seemed like the antidote to their newfound vulnerability, rather than a factor contributing
to it. As Daniel Claus put it in 1761, 'they ... look upon, and expect to be
supported by said promises as much as the people here [the *Canadiens*]
by the Capitulation.'[35] On many occasions during the few decades
that followed, representatives of the mission villages brought up these
promises when dealing with colonial officials and the courts. In 1765, an
orator from Kahnawake came to Johnson Hall to meet with Sir William
Johnson 'on behalf of all the Nations in Canada, to repeat to you our
former Engagements, and to refresh your Memory Concerning what
then passed.' Johnson responded that he had 'every thing that passed
between us fresh in my memory... I expect you will all be careful, and
keep it in remembrance.'[36] It was not long, however, before memories
faded. Though the inhabitants of the mission villages-turned-reserves
continued to voice claims concerning territorial, financial, and administrative matters well into the nineteenth and twentieth centuries, for
all intents and purposes they ceased to evoke 1760. That the events and
engagements of that year escaped the recognition of officials, jurists,
and historians alike for over two centuries can best be explained by a
shift in treaty-making practices. With the rapid expansion of colonial
settlement and the correspondingly sharp decline in the strategic and
economic weight of aboriginal peoples in and beyond the St Lawrence
Valley, 'peace, commerce, and friendship' treaties of the type that had
been concluded there and in the Maritimes lost their relevance. From
the 1780s onward, the only treaties that mattered to the Crown were
those that hinged on the surrender of lands and closely defined mutual
obligations.[37]

This state of affairs changed radically in the final decades of the
twentieth century. The rediscovery of the treaties of 1760 was a re-

sult of mounting indigenous advocacy and recognition of indigenous rights on the Canadian and international stages. More narrowly, it was a consequence of section 35 of the Constitution Act of 1982, which declares that '[t]he existing aboriginal and treaty rights of the aboriginal peoples of Canada are hereby recognized and affirmed.'[38] The Constitution Act left to aboriginal individuals and communities the onus of identifying and reclaiming the rights in question, and to the courts the responsibility of interpreting exactly to what extent such rights could hold precedence over existing laws. In Quebec and the Maritimes, this development generated an unprecedented enthusiasm for eighteenth-century indigenous diplomacy. Certain aboriginal individuals faced with penal charges began to invoke long-forgotten promises, forcing the courts, and ultimately historians, to revisit the eighteenth century. With respect to the Maritimes, a series of 'peace and friendship treaties' negotiated with the Mi'kmaq, Maliseet, and Passamaquoddy between 1725 and 1779 were rediscovered.[39] As far as the St Lawrence Valley was concerned, it became clear that the crucial year had been 1760.

In Quebec, the most protracted, legally significant, and historically contested case was *R. v. Sioui*. In May 1982, a group of Huron-Wendat from Wendake was intercepted in the Parc de la Jacques-Cartier, a provincial park north of Quebec City. Four brothers, Régent, Konrad, Georges, and Hugh Sioui, were summarily charged with cutting down trees, encamping, and making fire outside designated areas contrary to the regulations of the Quebec Parks Act. Promptly convicted by the Court of Sessions of the Peace, they filed an appeal on the grounds that their treaty rights had not been taken into account. Before the Superior Court, in 1984, they presented as evidence a copy of the document given by General James Murray to a band of Huron at Longueuil on 5 September 1760. In a few sentences only, Murray acknowledged that the Huron chief had surrendered and made peace with the British Crown on behalf of his nation, and guaranteed that the Huron would benefit from the same concessions as the *Canadiens* – that they would not be molested, and that they could freely exercise their religion, customs, and commerce.

Until then, neither historians nor jurists had paid much attention to this document or to the diplomatic encounter that it documented. Could it legitimately be considered a treaty? Justice Desjardins of the Superior Court judged that Murray had neither the authority nor the intention to enter into such a serious engagement, that the document was accordingly only a *certificate*, and dismissed the Siouis' appeal in

1985. Three years later, however, Justices Bisson and Paré of the Court of Appeal for Quebec found that the document's wording was such that it did indeed qualify as a treaty under the terms of the Indian Act, and proceeded to reverse the judgment. Having examined the matter, the Supreme Court of Canada confirmed this ruling in 1990, concluding unanimously that the document was indeed a treaty, that it was still in effect, and that the park regulations were accordingly unenforceable with respect to Huron-Wendat. The *Sioui* decision, which clarified several points of law and provided guidelines for the future interpretation of treaties, was hailed as a landmark victory for aboriginal rights. It gave the broadest interpretation yet of the notion of a 'treaty' with reference to agreements between aboriginals and non-aboriginals.[40] To what extent the right to exercise religion and customs granted by the 'Murray Treaty' might serve as the basis for a form of governmental autonomy remained undetermined.

There were a number of other trials, none as drawn out or as significant as that of the Sioui brothers, during which aboriginal individuals accused of breaking the law invoked in their defence, among a variety of legal arguments, promises made at the time of the Conquest – from Huron-Wendat from Wendake accused of smuggling tobacco over the international border or of failing to collect sales tax on the reserve, to Mohawk from Kanehsatake accused of organizing bingo games without permit, to Algonquin from Kitigan Zibi accused of entering and fishing without a permit in a restricted zone. Revisiting 1760 in light of the Constitution Act of 1982, Canadian courts thus rediscovered a number of treaties deemed valid: besides the treaty concluded at Longueuil between Murray and the Huron, which was recognized by the Quebec Court of Appeal (1987) and affirmed by the Supreme Court in *R. v. Sioui* (1990), this was also the case of the treaties of 'Swegatchy' and 'Caughnawaga' (Oswegatchie and Kahnawake), recognized by the Quebec Provincial Court (1988) and by the Supreme Court in *R. v. Côté* (1996).[41]

A great deal of historical evidence having to do with political, military, and economic relations among aboriginals, French, and British at the time of the Conquest was reviewed and subjected to textual and contextual analysis by the courts. In marked contrast with the *Delgamuukw v. British Columbia* proceedings, where oral traditions and anthropological evidence were extensively and effectively deployed, documentary evidence reigned supreme during these trials.[42] In another contrast, no professional historian testified during the Sioui trials – with the arguable exception of one of the plaintiffs, Georges Sioui, then historian-in-training, who obtained his MA and PhD at Laval in 1987 and 1991 respectively. The academic and consulting historians who served as expert witnesses for the Crown or defence during the flurry of parallel and subsequent trials, however, included deans of early Canadian history (Marcel Trudel, William Eccles, Cornelius Jaenen, and Denys Delâge) and up-and-coming scholars (such as Alain Beaulieu and D. Peter MacLeod). Subsequently, historians were also mobilized to prepare reports for governments and communities eager to negotiate claims, formulate new policies, and establish new relationships. It was out of this judicial and political process that emerged the core of monographs, edited volumes, and articles that have shed light on how the inhabitants of the mission villages experienced the Conquest and the transition from the French to the British regime.[43] Which is not to say that scholarship on the subject was not also influenced by parallel societal developments (the armed standoff at Oka in 1990 played its part in increasing the visibility of aboriginal issues) and unrelated scholarly currents (notably a recent burst of interest in colonial warfare).

There was little disagreement among the above-noted historians regarding the treaties of Oswegatchie and Kahnawake. Yet, whereas the Supreme Court had adopted 'a broad and generous interpretation of what constitutes a treaty' and opted to resolve uncertainties in favour of aboriginals, scholarly divergences persisted as to what had really occurred at Longueuil. For some, such as Delâge and Jaenen, there was little doubt that Murray and the Huron had negotiated an agreement that deserved to be considered a treaty, given the well-documented policy of conciliation that characterized the years of the Conquest. Others, including Marcel Trudel, Alain Beaulieu, and soon Denis Vaugeois, countered each in his own way that the evidence did not substantiate this view. They argued that the key document, signed by Murray alone, was more accurately interpreted as a mere certificate of safe-conduct. In their view the lack of evidence that there had been any negotiation or solemn exchange of ritual 'words' and wampum effectively countered the argument, retained by the Supreme Court, that this document represented the embodiment of an oral agreement.[44]

With the entry into the fray of the publisher and popular historian Denis Vaugeois – the subject of Brian Young's chapter in this volume – scholarly disagreement morphed into polemic. His interest in the Murray Treaty was sparked shortly after the publication of his book *L'Indien généreux* (1992), a sympathetic survey of the contributions of aboriginals to European and Euro-American ways of life. During the promotional storm that accompanied its publication, Vaugeois was prompted for his thoughts on the newly recognized treaty, of which he in fact knew nothing. The silence of the secondary literature on the place of aboriginals in the events surrounding the Conquest had the effect of stoking his curiosity. In parallel, the increasingly conspicuous invocations of this treaty to support Huron-Wendat claims of immunity from various regulations pertaining to land access, hunting and fishing, and commerce, fuelled his frustration. In 1993, he made his first public intervention in the pages of the Quebec daily *Le Devoir* regarding what he derisively dubbed the 'traité Murray-Lamer,' in reference to the Supreme Court Justice who had penned the majority opinion.[45] He soon established himself as the most persistent and prolific defender of the view that, in its careless reconstruction of the events of 1759 and 1760 and in its acceptance of an inaccurate version of the document issued by Murray, the Supreme Court had committed a travesty of justice and of the historical craft. The author of *L'Indien généreux*, as it turns out, was unwilling to subscribe to the Supreme Court's self-described 'liberal and generous attitude' towards the interpretation of treaties. Besides a few opinion pieces and interviews with the media, Vaugeois went on to publish the revealingly titled *La fin des alliances franco-indiennes: enquête sur un sauf-conduit de 1760 devenu un traité en 1990* (1995), translated as *The Last French and Indian War: An Inquiry into a Safe-Conduct Issued in 1760 that Acquired the Value of a Treaty in 1990* (2002), as well as to edit a collection of papers under the title *Les Hurons de Lorette* (1996). Unpublished research reports that would otherwise have lain dormant, by Delâge, Jaenen, Trudel, and Beaulieu, were thus made available to a broader audience.[46]

At the root of the controversy surrounding the Murray Treaty lay, among other things, the uneasy intersection of history, a reasoned reconstruction of the past rooted in research, and memory – the narratives and meanings that form the heritage, the identity, of a community. In both the emotions that were stirred and its nationalist undertones, this new polemic carried faint echoes of older controversies regarding the impact of *la Conquête* on French-Canadian society. In his seminal *Pour une auto-histoire amérindienne* (1991), published just a year after the Supreme Court's ruling, Georges Sioui summed up the importance of the Murray Treaty for the Wendat: 'both then and now' it 'constitutes recognition of a sovereignty they have never ceded or sold.'[47] Responding to Vaugeois' initial intervention in the pages of *Le Devoir*, Jocelyne Gros-Louis and Michel Bastien, respectively grand chief and lawyer for the Huron-Wendat Nation, stated that '[t]he Québécois want their ambitions of self-determination to be understood, that is fair; Aboriginals do not want anything less for themselves.'[48] The treaty, indeed, has emerged as a key symbol for the people of Wendake, as well as a potent instrument in their struggle for greater self-determination. A press release from the Conseil de la Nation huronne-wendat, concerning the commemoration of the Battle of the Plains of Abraham in 2009, aptly made reference to 'our national treaty.'[49]

Vaugeois' interest in the events of 1759 and 1760 was equally rooted in national sentiment, though of a different stamp. A former member of the Assemblée nationale for the sovereigntist Parti Québécois and minister of cultural affairs during the premiership of René Lévesque, he anchors his historical inquiry in *La fin des alliances franco-indiennes* to contemporary political developments, from Pierre Elliott Trudeau's and Jean Chrétien's White Paper of 1969 to the failed ratification of the Meech Lake Accord in 1990. He concludes it with a nostalgic note on the unfulfilled efforts of the government of Quebec to foster a rapprochement with its aboriginal peoples in 1985. From this perspective, the *Sioui* decision was yet another federal-aboriginal attack on Quebec. The author's qualms regarding the Supreme Court's historical reconstruction and interpretation are tied inextricably to his contention that the misguided legal recognition of this safe conduct as a treaty has dangerous political implications, undermining as it does the principle of equality between all citizens that he perceives as the foundation of *québécois* society, to say nothing of Quebec's pursuit of political autonomy.[50]

Clashing nationalisms were paralleled by clashing approaches and methodologies. Vaugeois' historical scholarship, especially in approaching the question of the Murray Treaty, is of the popular (his analysis is based mainly on secondary and published primary sources) and positivist vein (his preoccupation with historical 'truth' is less nuanced than that of most contemporary academics). Moreover, in discussing the subject, Vaugeois and a few others after him have purposefully steered away from what he flippantly described as 'political correctness.' In so doing he has attracted sharp criticism from many in the academic community, where it is now generally admitted that cultural sensitivity is vital to any discussion of aboriginal history and issues. Needless to say, the Huron-Wendat leadership has been equally vehement.[51]

Legal historians and scholars for their part have generally agreed with the Supreme Court's ruling, and denounced the marked lack of appreciation displayed by its detractors for the divergent logics, methods, and objectives of Law and History. They have pointed, for example, to the fact that the role of an appellate court such as the Supreme Court of Canada is normally to review the application of the law, not the facts of the case as they have already been determined. Vaugeois' faulting of the Supreme Court for not bothering to ascertain the Murray document's authenticity, and his belief that it erred in accepting copies instead of the original, was thus misguided. His lament that the courts failed to conduct a rigorous investigation falls flat given the fact that, in the adversarial system, courts must reach their decisions based on the evidence submitted by the litigating parties. Several of Vaugeois' reproaches might thus more persuasively have been directed at the Crown prosecutors (and defence team).[52]

As it happens, the unearthing of new documents has vindicated both the proponents of the Murray-Treaty-as-treaty (Delâge, Jaenen) and those of the Murray-Treaty-as-certificate (Vaugeois, Beaulieu). When the original manuscript was discovered in the collection of notary B. Faribault, Jr, at the Archives nationales du Québec in 1996, it was indeed found that its text differed from the version accepted by the Supreme Court six years earlier: whereas the latter recognized 'liberty of trading with the English,' the original document alludes more narrowly to trade 'with the English Garrison.'[53] Similarly, the chronicle of Huron movements recollected by Ondiaraété, or Petit Étienne, brought to the attention of historians in 2000, appears to confirm that no negotiations or solemnities occurred between Murray and the Huron. At the same time, however, it demonstrates that the Huron did maintain the memory of their meeting with Murray well into the 1820s, an indication of the great importance they attributed to it.[54] All of this said, as legal experts have been wont to point out, such discoveries in no way call into question the Supreme Court's ruling in *R. v. Sioui* or in subsequent cases, given its decision to adopt a broad understanding of what constitutes a valid treaty. Moreover, neither Denis Vaugeois nor Alain Beaulieu has ever hesitated to recognize the treaties of Oswegatchie and Kahnawake as such.[55] Given what historians now know about what occurred in 1760, it is likely that these two treaties will be cited increasingly in court – and to much less polemical effect.

Almost a decade ago, a few specialists of the eighteenth-century mission villages expressed worries that Canadian courts might, in the case of the Murray Treaty and other instances, establish a historical dogma and impose an end to debates on the nature of historical phenomena.[56] The context of the promulgation of 'memory laws' in Europe, which have sought to impose the official point of view of states on historical events (notably in France, concerning negationism and slavery), coupled with a superficial understanding of the powers and aims of Canadian courts and legislators, was no doubt at the root of this unwarranted apprehension.[57] Judicial and political interest in the significance of the Conquest in aboriginal history has, on the contrary, acted as an unparalleled catalyst to scholarship and debate. It has provided historians incentives – both intellectual and financial – to dig deep into the sources to rediscover forgotten historical actors, events, and processes; it has provided them the opportunity to explore divergent interpretations and to develop a more complex understanding of the period. The importance that the events of 1760 have reacquired in the minds of those who wish to rethink the relationship between aboriginal peoples and the Canadian state – though the challenges of bridging history and memory may seem daunting – is only fitting. The peacemakers, after all, intended their work to serve as a point of reference. The exchange that occurred at Johnson Hall in 1765 regarding what had taken place five years earlier illustrates this well. To the Kahnawake orator's exhortation 'to refresh your memory concerning what then passed,' Sir William Johnson answered that indeed he had 'every thing that passed between us fresh in my memory.' 'I expect,' Johnson echoed, that 'you will all … keep it in remembrance.'[58]

NOTES

1 For a sampling, see Guy Frégault, *La guerre de la Conquête* (Montréal: Fides, 1955); and Michel Brunet, *Les Canadiens après la Conquête, 1759–1775, de la Révolution canadienne à la Révolution américaine* (Montréal: Fides, 1969). In *Histoire du Canada par les textes*, Frégault cited large swaths of the Articles of Capitulation of Montreal but did not bother including articles 8 and 40, which concern France's aboriginal allies, noting dismissively, 'L'article 40 se rapporte aux sauvages.' See Guy Frégault, Marcel Trudel, and Michel Brunet, *Histoire du Canada par les textes*, vol. 1 (Montréal: Fides, 1963), 106–14. See also C.P. Stacey, *Quebec, 1759: The Siege and the Battle* (1959; Toronto: Robin Brass Studio, 2002).

2 On the place of aboriginals in Canadian and *québécois* historiography, see Bruce G. Trigger, 'The Historian's Indian: Native Americans in Canadian Historical Writing from Charlevoix to the Present,' *Canadian Historical Review* 67 (1986): 315–42; and Allan Greer, 'Comparisons: New France,' in *A*

Companion to Colonial America, ed. Daniel Vickers (Oxford: Oxford University Press, 2003), 474–7.

3   On the formation and development of the mission villages, see G.F.G. Stanley, 'The First Indian "Reserves" in Canada,' *Revue d'histoire de l'Amérique française* 4, no. 2 (1950): 178–210; Marc Jetten, *Enclaves amérindiennes: les 'réductions' du Canada, 1637–1701* (Sillery, QC: Septentrion, 1994); Denys Delâge, 'Les Iroquois chrétiens des réductions, 1667–1770: 1, Migration et rapports avec les Français,' *Recherches amérindiennes au Québec* 19, nos. 1-2 (1990): 59–70; idem, 'Les Iroquois chrétiens des réductions, 1667–1770: 2, Rapports avec la Ligue Iroquoise, les Britanniques et les autres nations autochtones,' *Recherches amérindiennes au Québec* 19, no. 3 (1990): 39–50; and Thomas M. Charland, *Histoire des Abénakis d'Odanak, 1675–1937* (Montréal: Éditions du Lévrier, 1964).

4   D. Peter MacLeod, *The Canadian Iroquois and the Seven Years' War* (Ottawa; Toronto: Dundurn Press, 1996), chaps. 8–9.

5   Julian Gwyn, 'Sir William Johnson,' in *Dictionary of Canadian Biography*, vol. 4 (Toronto: University of Toronto Press, 1979), 394–8, http://www.biographi.ca; and Fintan O'Toole, *White Savage: William Johnson and the Invention of America* (New York: Farrar, Straus and Giroux, 2005).

6   This diplomatic history is partially narrated by Gretchen Lynn Green, 'A New People in an Age of War: The Kahnawake Iroquois, 1667–1760' (PhD thesis, College of William and Mary, 1991); and Jon Parmenter, 'At the Wood's Edge: Iroquois Foreign Relations, 1727–1768' (PhD thesis, University of Michigan, 1999).

7   MacLeod, *Canadian Iroquois*, chaps. 8–9; J.-P. Sawaya, 'Les Sept-Nations du Canada et les Britanniques, 1759–1774: alliance et dépendance' (PhD thesis, Université Laval, 2001), chap. 2; and Denys Delâge and J.-P. Sawaya, *Les traités des Sept-Feux avec les Britanniques: droits et pièges d'un héritage colonial au Québec* (Sillery, QC: Septentrion, 2001), chap. 2.

8   Stephen Brumwell, *White Devil: A True Story of War, Savagery, and Vengeance in Colonial America* (Cambridge, MA: Da Capo Press, 2005). See also Colin G. Calloway, *The Western Abenakis of Vermont, 1600–1800: War, Migration, and the Survival of an Indian people* (Norman: University of Oklahoma Press, 1990), chap. 9; and Gordon Day, 'Rogers' Raid in Indian Tradition,' *Historical New Hampshire* 27 (June 1962): 3–17. Marge Bruchac's *Malian's Song* (Middlebury, VT: August House, 2006), which retells the St Francis Raid from an Abenaki perspective, is a wonderful example of children's literature informed by historical scholarship.

9   Anonymous, 'Indian Lorette,' *Star and Commercial Advertiser / L'Étoile et Journal du commerce* 11 (13 February 1828), 12 (20 February 1828), and 13

(27 February 1828); Alain Beaulieu, 'Les Hurons et la conquête: un nouvel éclairage sur le "Traité Murray,"' *Recherches amérindiennes au Québec* 30, no. 3 (2000): 53–63. See also Serge Goudreau, 'Étienne Ondiaraété 1742–1830, chef huron du village de Lorette,' *Cahiers de la Société généalogique canadienne-française* 54, no. 4 (2003): 269–88.

10 James Sullivan et al., eds., *The Papers of Sir William Johnson*, vol. 3 (Albany: University of the State of New York, 1921–65), 272–3.

11 Alain Beaulieu, 'Les garanties d'un traité disparu: le traité d'Oswegatchie, 30 août 1760,' *Revue juridique Thémis* 34 (2000): 369–408; Delâge and Sawaya, *Traités des Sept-Feux avec les Britanniques*, chap. 3; and Pierre Grégoire, 'Le traité de Swegatchy: un traité sans texte. Côté c. R. (C.A.) [1993] R.J.Q.,' *Recherches amérindiennes au Québec* 24, nos. 1-2 (1994): 159–62.

12 '[C]royant les sauvages dans des dispositions plus favorables'; Henri-Raymond Casgrain, ed., *Collection des manuscrits du maréchal de Lévis*, vol. 11 (Montréal: C.O. Beauchemin & fils, 1889–95), 256.

13 See Beaulieu, 'Hurons et la conquête.' The original document bearing the certification of James Murray, 5 September 1760, was deposited on 4 August 1810 in the records of notary Barthélémy Faribault fils, Archives nationales du Québec, Quebec, CN301 S99.

14 Of the fifty-five articles that make up the Articles of Capitulation of Montreal, two are directly concerned with the welfare of France's traditional allies. Article 8 specifies that the British would provide medical care to the injured and sick native warriors, while article 40 stipulates that '[t]he Savage or Indian allies of his most Christian Majesty [the king of France], shall be maintained in the Lands they inhabit; if they choose to remain there; they shall not be disturbed on any pretense whatsoever, for having taken arms, and served his most Christian Majesty,' adding that they would also be allowed to retain their Catholic religion and missionaries. See *Documents Relating to the Constitutional History of Canada, 1759–1791*, part 1, ed. Arthur G. Doughty and Adam Shortt (Ottawa: J. de L. Taché, 1918), 1–37; see also Delâge and Sawaya, *Traités des Sept-Feux avec les Britanniques*, chap. 5.

15 The text of the treaty is found in the Journal of Jelles Fonda, in the Miscellaneous Manuscripts of the New York Historical Society, *Papers of Sir William Johnson* (see note 10), vol. 13, 163–6. See also Sawaya, 'Sept-Nations du Canada et les Britanniques,' 109–32; Delâge and Sawaya, *Traités des Sept-Feux avec les Britanniques*, chap. 6; MacLeod, *Canadian Iroquois*, 177–9; and Beaulieu, 'Garanties d'un traité disparu,' 402–5.

16 MacLeod, *Canadian Iroquois*, 181–9; J.-P. Sawaya, *Alliance et dépendance: comment la couronne britannique a obtenu la collaboration des Indiens de la vallée*

du Saint-Laurent entre 1760 et 1774 (Sillery, QC: Septentrion, 2002), 25–9; and idem, 'Sept-Nations du Canada et les Britanniques,' 124–32. On Claus, see Douglas Leighton, 'Christian Daniel Claus,' in *Dictionary of Canadian Biography*, vol. 4, 154–5, http://www.biographi.ca.

17 Sawaya, *Alliance et dépendance*, 29–37; and idem, 'Sept-Nations du Canada et les Britanniques,' chap. 4.

18 Sawaya, *Alliance et dépendance*, chap. 2; and idem, 'Sept-Nations du Canada et les Britanniques,' chap. 5.

19 On the tensions in the relationship of the French and *domiciliés*, in particular the Canadian Iroquois, see Green, 'New People in an Age of War'; and Delâge, 'Iroquois chrétiens des réductions, 1667–1770: 1, Migration et rapports avec les Français.'

20 On the integration of aboriginals within the British colonial justice system, see Denys Delâge and Étienne Gilbert, 'La justice coloniale britannique et les Amérindiens au Québec 1760-1820, I: En terres amérindiennes,' *Recherches amérindiennes au Québec* 32, no. 1 (2002): 63–82; and idem, 'La justice coloniale britannique et les Amérindiens au Québec 1760-1820, II: En territoire colonial,' *Recherches amérindiennes au Québec* 32, no. 2 (2002): 107–17.

21 See Arnaud Decroix, 'Le conflit juridique entre les Jésuites et les Iroquois au sujet de la seigneurie du Sault Saint-Louis: analyse de la décision de Thomas Gage (1762),' in *Revue juridique Thémis* 41, no. 1 (2007): 279–97; and idem, 'Nos Seigneurs les Iroquois: contestations juridiques autour de la propriété de la seigneurie du Sault Saint-Louis,' *Cahiers aixois d'histoire des droits de l'Outre-Mer français* 3 (2006): 77–105.

22 Michel Lavoie, *C'est ma seigneurie que je réclame: la lutte des Hurons de Lorette pour la seigneurie de Sillery, 1658–1890* (Montréal: Boréal, 2009).

23 For early allusions to the Seven Nations and scholarship on its activity during the late eighteenth century, see Georges Boiteau, 'Les chasseurs hurons de Lorette' (MA thesis, Université Laval, 1954), 29; David S. Blanchard, *Seven Generations: A History of Kanienkehaka* (Kahnawake, QC: Kahnawake Survival School, 1980), 275–82; idem, 'The Seven Nations of Canada: An Alliance and a Treaty,' *American Indian Culture and Research Journal* 7 (1983): 3–23; Lawrence Ostola, 'The Seven Nations of Canada and the American Revolution 1774–1783' (MA thesis, Université de Montréal, 1989); Calloway, *Western Abenakis*, 194–5; and idem, *The American Revolution in Indian Country: Crisis and Diversity in Native American Communities* (Cambridge: Cambridge University Press, 1995), 26–84.

24 Delâge, 'Iroquois chrétiens des réductions, 1667–1770: 2, Rapports avec la Ligue iroquoise,' 46–9. Sawaya's 'Les Sept-Nations du Canada: traditions

d'alliance dans le Nord-Est, XVIIIe–XIXe siècles' (MA thesis, Université Laval, 1994) was revised and published as *La Fédération des Sept Feux de la vallée du Saint-Laurent: XVIIe–XIXe siècle* (Sillery, QC: Septentrion, 1998). Delâge's submission to the Royal Commission on Aboriginal Peoples, prepared in collaboration with Sawaya, Marc Jetten, and Régent Sioui, 'Les Sept Feux, les alliances et les traités autochtones du Québec dans l'histoire' (Ottawa, 1996), was published in digital format by Delâge and Sawaya as 'Les Sept-Feux et les traités avec les Britanniques,' in *Pour Sept Générations* (Ottawa: Libraxus, 1997), and revised and published in book form as *Les traités des Sept-Feux avec les Britanniques* (see note 7).

25 For misgivings regarding the early interpretation of the origins of the Seven Nations, see John A. Dickinson's review of Sawaya's *La Fédération des Sept Feux* in *American Historical Review* 105 (2000): 202–3; and Normand Clermont's review in *Revue d'histoire de l'Amérique française* 52 (1999): 590–1. It was not long after the publication of *La Fédération des Sept Feux* that Sawaya attempted to work out some of the ambiguities. See his article with Alain Beaulieu, 'Qui sont les Sept Nations du Canada? Quelques observations sur une appellation ambiguë,' *Recherches amérindiennes au Québec* 27, no. 2 (1997): 43–51.

26 Sawaya footnotes Rupert Emerson's study of Malaysia and C.A. Bayly's and Philip D. Morgan's more recent reflections on the British Empire. See Rupert Emerson, *Malaysia: A Study in Direct and Indirect Rule* (New York: Macmillan, 1937); C.A. Bayly, 'The British and Indigenous Peoples, 1760–1860: Power, Perception and Identity,' in *Empire and Others: British Encounters with Indigenous Peoples, 1600–1850*, ed. Martin Daunton and Rick Halpern (Philadelphia: University of Pennsylvania Press, 1999); and Philip D. Morgan, 'Encounters between British and "Indigeneous" peoples, c. 1500–1800,' in ibid. For Delâge's reflections on colonial models, and direct and indirect rule with regards to Canada under the French and British regimes, see 'Modèles coloniaux, métaphores familiales et changements de régime en Amérique du Nord aux XVIIe et XIXe siècles,' *Les Cahiers des Dix* 60 (2006): 19–78; see also Delâge and Sawaya, *Traités des Sept-Feux avec les Britanniques*, 37–42.

27 See Denys Delâge and J.-P. Sawaya, 'Les origines de la Fédération des Sept-Feux,' *Recherches amérindiennes au Québec* 31, no. 2 (2001): 43–54; and idem, *Traités des Sept-Feux avec les Britanniques*. Sawaya's PhD thesis, *Les Sept-Nations du Canada et les Britanniques, 1759-1774: alliance et dépendance* (Université Laval, 2001) was published in much condensed form as *Alliance et dependence: comment la couronne britannique a obtenu la collaboration des Indiens de la vallée du Saint-Laurent entre 1760 et 1774* (Sillery, QC: Septentrion, 2002).

28 See, for example, Alain Beaulieu, 'Les traités avec les Autochtones du
Canada: de l'alliance à l'assujettissement (1760–1876),' in *Être Indien dans
les Amériques: spoliations et résistance, mobilisations ethniques et politiques du
multiculturalisme*, ed. Christian Gros and Marie-Claude Strigler (Paris: Éditions de l'Institut des Amériques, 2006), 20.

29 On Iroquois voyageurs, see Jan Grabowski and Nicole St-Onge, 'Montreal
Iroquois *engagés* in the Western Fur Trade,' in *From Rupert's Land to Canada*,
ed. Theodore Binnema, Gerhard J. Ens, and R.C. Macleod (Edmonton:
University of Alberta Press, 2001); and Trudy Nicks, 'The Iroquois and the
Fur Trade in Western Canada,' in *Old Trails & New Directions: Papers of the
Third North American Fur Trade Conference*, ed. Carol M. Judd and Arthur J.
Ray (Toronto: University of Toronto Press, 1978).

30 Calloway, *Western Abenakis*, chap. 10; Gordon Day, 'The Identity of the St.
Francis Indians,' Canadian Ethnology Service, Paper 71 (Ottawa: National
Museum of Man Mercury Series, 1981); Jack A. Frisch, 'The Abenakis
among the St Regis Mohawks,' *Indian Historian* 4, no. 1 (1971): 27–9; and
Sawaya, 'Sept-Nations du Canada et les Britanniques,' 227–42.

31 Delâge and Sawaya, *Traités des Sept-Feux avec les Britanniques*, 24–9.

32 See, for example, Peter Wraxall and Charles Howard McIlwain, eds., *An
Abridgement of the Records of Indian Affairs: Contained in Four Folio Volumes,
Transacted in the Colony of New York, from the Year 1678 to the Year 1751*
(Cambridge, MA: Harvard University Press, 1915), 44, 53, 80, 146, 151,
193–6.

33 Ibid., 193; and Delâge and Sawaya, *Traités des Sept-Feux avec les Britanniques*, 28. The claim that the inhabitants of the missions entered the Covenant Chain in 1760 thus deserves to be nuanced. See, by way of comparison, Beaulieu, 'Garanties d'un traité disparu,' 384.

34 Beaulieu, 'Traités avec les autochtones,' 20–1; see also idem, 'Garanties
d'un traité disparu,' 408.

35 Daniel Claus to Major Beckwith, 30 March 1761, Claus Papers, Library and
Archives Canada (hereafter cited as LAC), MG 19 F1, vol. 1, f. 39.

36 *Papers of Sir William Johnson* (see note 10), vol. 11, 872–5. For references to
the treaties of the Conquest during diplomatic encounters and in the context of grievances, see ibid., vol. 3, 394; ibid., vol. 10, 269, 558–9, 724–5, 766;
ibid., vol. 11, 354–5, 502, 872–3; ibid., vol. 12, 109–11, 1027; ibid., vol. 13,
237–8, 622–33; LAC, RG10, vol. 1833, 235–8; and LAC, RG 8, vol. 267, 287.

37 On this shift from peace and friendship treaties to territorial treaties, see
Delâge and Sawaya, *Traités des Sept-Feux avec les Britanniques*, chap. 12; and
Canada, *Indian Treaties and Surrenders From 1680 to 1890*, 2 vols. (Ottawa:
Queen's/King's Printer, 1891, 1912).

38 The distinction between aboriginal and treaty rights is that, while the latter

stem from agreements between an aboriginal community and a non-aboriginal government, the former stem from an aboriginal community's occupation of the land from time immemorial.

39 On these eighteenth-century Atlantic treaties and their modern legal ramifications, see William C. Wicken, *Mi'kmaq Treaties on Trial: History, Land, and Donald Marshall Junior* (Toronto: University of Toronto Press, 2002); Stephen Patterson, 'Eighteenth-Century Treaties: The Mi'kmaq, Maliseet, and Passamaquoddy Experience,' *Native Studies Review* 18, no. 1 (2009): 25–52; Ken S. Coates, *The Marshall Decision and Native Rights* (Montreal; Kingston, ON: McGill-Queen's University Press, 2000); and Thomas Isaac, *Aboriginal and Treaty Rights in the Maritimes: The Marshall Decision and Beyond* (Saskatoon, SK: Purich, 2001).

40 For abstracts of the Sioui trials, see *Jurisprudence Express* 83 (1983): 722; *Jurisprudence Express* 85 (1985): 947; *Recueils de Jurisprudence du Quebec* (1987), 1722; and *Supreme Court Reports*, vol. 1 (1990), 1025. See also Franklin S. Gertler and Peter W. Hutchins, 'Introduction: The Marriage of History and Law in R. v. Sioui,' *Native Studies Review* 6, no. 2 (1990): 115–30, and reproduced documents, 131–93; and Pierre Grégoire, 'L'arrêt Le procureur general du Québec c. Régent Sioui et al.,' *Recherches amérindiennes au Québec* 20, nos. 3–4 (1990): 73–5.

41 For the trials of Franck Côté et al. see *Recueils de Jurisprudence du Quebec* (1989), 1969; *Recueils de Jurisprudence du Quebec* (1991), 1893; *Recueils de Jurisprudence du Quebec* (1994), 1350; *Supreme Court Reports*, vol. 3 (1996), 139; Grégoire, 'Traité de Swegatchy'; and Renée Dupuis, *Tribus, peuples et nations: les enjeux des revendications autochtones au Canada* (Montréal: Boréal, 1997), 59–63. For *Gabriel Sioui v. Sous-ministre du Revenu du Québec*, see *Recueils de Jurisprudence du Québec* (1995), 2105; and *Recueils de Jurisprudence du Québec* (1997), 16. For *R. v. Elizabeth Vincent*, see *Ontario Reports*, 3rd series (1993), 427. These cases, as well as others, are summarized in Denis Vaugeois, *La fin des alliances franco-indiennes: enquête sur un sauf-conduit de 1760 devenu un traité en 1990* (Montréal: Boréal, 1995), 144–8.

42 On the *Delgamuukw* trials, see Adele Perry, 'The Colonial Archive on Trial: Possession, Dispossession, and History in *Delgamuukw v. British Columbia*,' in *Archive Stories: Facts, Fictions, and the Writing of History*, ed. Antoinette Burton (Durham, NC: Duke University Press, 2005); and Richard Daly, *Our Box Was Full: An Ethnography for the Delgamuukw Plaintiffs* (Vancouver: University of British Columbia Press, 2005).

43 Denys Delâge, 'Les Hurons de Lorette dans leur contexte historique en 1760'; Marcel Trudel, 'Les Hurons et Murray en 1760: un traité qui n'est qu'un laissez-passer'; Cornelius Jaenen, 'Rapport historique sur la na-

tion huronne-wendat'; Alain Beaulieu, 'Les Hurons de Lorette, le "traité Murray" et la liberté de commerce,' all in *Les Hurons de Lorette*, ed. Denis Vaugeois (Sillery, QC: Septentrion, 1996); D. Peter MacLeod, 'The Huron of Lorette and the Murray Treaty of 1760' (unpublished, 1990); Donald E. Graves, 'The Huron of Lorette, the General Murray Treaty of 1760, the Jay Treaty and the Treaty of Ghent: Historical Analysis and Opinion,' vol. 1 (unpublished, 1990); Helen Stone, 'Assessment of Murray Treaty report by C. Jaenen, jointly for the Huron-Wendat Nation and the Department of Indian and Northern Affairs Canada and Discussion on Legal-Historical Issues and Sources for Their Clarification; Interim Report' (unpublished, 1995); and idem, 'Report on the Murray Treaty of 1760 Affecting the Huron-Wendat of Jeune Lorette, Quebec' (unpublished, 1995). Copies of these unpublished reports can be found in the departmental library of Indian and Northern Affairs in Ottawa. See also Vaugeois, *Fin des alliances*, pt. 2; and André Münch, *L'expertise en écritures et en signatures* (Sillery, QC: Septentrion, 2000), chap. 14.

44 See note 42.

45 For a sampling of newspaper articles chronicling these early claims, see 'Maison longue,' *Le Soleil*, 15 February 1992; 'Les Hurons devront respecter la loi pour la protection de la faune,' *La Presse*, 12 September 1992; Roger Bellefeuille, 'Pour Québec, les Hurons n'ont aucun droit de chasser ou de pêcher,' *Le Soleil*, 12 September 1992; 'Les Hurons refusent de limiter leurs droits de chasse,' *Le Soleil*, 2 December 1992; and Louis-Gilles Francoeur, 'Les Hurons émettent des directives aux chasseurs,' *Le Devoir*, 31 August 1993. The pages of *Le Soleil*, *Le Journal de Québec*, *La Presse*, and *Le Devoir* abound with references to subsequent claims and counterclaims.

46 Denis Vaugeois, 'Les Hurons: faux traité, faux espoirs ... ou la tentation de réécrire l'histoire,' *Le Devoir*, 8 September 1993; idem, *Fin des alliances*; idem, *Hurons de Lorette* (see note 44); idem, 'Les Indiens et la Conquête,' *Cap-aux-Diamants* 41 (Spring 1995): 22–6; idem, 'Réplique à une recension de D. Vaugeois, *La fin des alliances franco-indiennes: enquête sur un sauf-conduit de 1760 devenu un traité en 1990*,' *McGill Law Journal* 43 (1998): 969; idem, 'Traité de Murray: simple laissez-passer?' *Le Devoir*, 7 July 1999; and idem, 'Les alliances franco-indiennes,' *Le Devoir*, 20 August 2001.

47 Georges E. Sioui, *For an Amerindian Autohistory* (Montreal; Kingston, ON: McGill-Queen's University Press, 1992), 94; originally published in French as *Pour une auto-histoire amérindienne* (Québec: Presses de l'Université Laval, 1991), 126. While Georges went on to become an eminent academic, it is also worth noting that his brother and co-plaintiff Konrad Sioui, who was already involved with the Assembly of First Nations at the time of

the trial, was elected grand chief of Wendake in 2008. For another early examination of the political possibilities of the Murray Treaty, see René Boudreault, 'Réflexion sur une réalité moderne à "incarner": le traité préconfédératif de la Nation Huronne-Wendat,' *Recherches amérindiennes au Québec* 23, no. 1 (1993): 5–16.

48 'Les Québécois désirent que leurs ambitions d'autodétermination soient comprises, soit; les autochtones n'en désirent pas moins pour eux-mêmes'; Michel-René Bastien and Jocelyne Gros-Louis, 'Le mur du mépris,' *Le Devoir*, 22 September 1993.

49 Or 'notre traité national,' cited in Claude Vaillancourt, 'Les Hurons désirent être présents,' *Le Soleil*, 12 February 2009.

50 Vaugeois, *Last French and Indian War*, intro. and concl., quotation on 13. As one reviewer, the anthropologist René Savard, pointed out, the linkage of Trudeau with the recognition of the Murray Treaty does not hold water. Speaking to an assembly of First Nations chiefs in Vancouver in 1969, Trudeau declared, 'It's inconceivable, I think, that in a given society one section of the society have a treaty with the other section of the society.' Cited in Rémi Savard, 'Commentaire sur *La fin des alliances franco-indiennes: enquête sur un sauf-conduit de 1760 devenu un traité en 1990*,' *Recherches amérindiennes au Québec* 26, no. 1 (1996): 80.

51 Rémi Savard went as far as to level at Vaugeois the thinly veiled accusation that '[r]acism is sometimes like alcoholism: the less you believe you are affected by it, the higher the odds that you are'; Savard, 'Commentaire.' See also Stéphane Paquet, 'Alliances et traités de 1760: réflexions sur le débat historiographique,' *Recherches amérindiennes au Québec* 27, no. 2 (1997): 32–42. For an even less 'politically correct' intervention in the debate than that of Vaugeois, see Nelson-Martin Dawson and Éric Tremblay, 'Du "traité Murray" aux "orphelins de Duplessis": quand l'histoire manipule la justice,' *Le Devoir*, 29 May 1999; and idem, 'La preuve historique dans le cadre des procès relatifs au droit autochtone et aux crimes contre l'humanité,' *Revue de droit de l'Université de Sherbrooke* 30 (2000): 377–406.

52 David Schulze, 'Book Review: Denis Vaugeois, *La fin des alliances franco-indiennes: enquête sur un sauf-conduit de 1760 devenu un traité en 1990*,' *McGill Law Journal* 42 (1997): 1045–53; Michel Morin, 'Les insuffisances d'une analyse purement historique des droits des peuples autochtones,' *Revue d'histoire de l'Amérique française* 57 (2003): 241–3; and idem, 'Quelques réflexions sur le rôle de l'histoire dans la détermination des droits ancestraux et issus de traités,' *Revue juridique Thémis* 34 (2000): 349–56. On the intersection of law and history in Quebec more broadly, see also Donald Fyson, 'Les historiens du Québec face au droit,' *Revue juridique Thémis*

34 (2000): 295–328; and Alain Beaulieu, 'Les pièges de la judiciarisation de l'histoire autochtones,' *Revue d'histoire de l'Amérique française* 53, no. 4 (2000): 541–51; For a sense of the broader Canadian context, see W.J. Eccles, 'Sovereignty-Association, 1500–1783,' *Canadian Historical Review* 65, no. 4 (1984): 475–510; Donald J. Bourgeois, 'The Role of the Historian in the Litigation Process,' *Canadian Historical Review* 67, no. 2 (1986): 195–205; G.M. Dickinson and R.D. Gidney, 'History and Advocacy: Some Reflections on the Historian's Role in Litigation,' *Canadian Historical Review* 68, no. 4 (1987): 576–85; Arthur J. Ray, 'Creating the Image of the Savage in Defence of the Crown: The Ethnohistorian in Court,' *Native Studies Review* 6, no. 2 (1990): 13–29; John G. Reid, William C. Wicken, Stephen E. Patterson, and D.G. Bell, 'History, Native Issues and the Courts: A Forum,' *Acadiensis* 28 (1998): 3–26; Stephen Patterson, 'Historians and the Courts,' *Acadiensis* 28 (1998): 21; A.J. Ray, 'Native History on Trial: Confessions of an Expert Witness,' *Canadian Historical Review* 84, no. 2 (2003): 253–73; and Perry, 'Colonial Archive on Trial,' 325–50.

53 The document was discovered during a search made for the lawyer David Schulze, of Hutchins Caron & Associés. See David Schulze, 'The Murray Treaty of 1760: The Original Document Discovered,' *Canadian Native Law Reporter* 1 (1998): 1–13.

54 Alain Beaulieu, 'Hurons et la conquête.'

55 Vaugeois, 'Traité de Murray'; idem, 'Alliances franco-indiennes'; and Beaulieu, 'Garanties d'un traité disparu.'

56 See Beaulieu, 'Pièges de la judiciarisation'; and Jan Grabowski, 'L'historiographie des Amérindiens au Canada: quelques données et commentaires portant sur les directions de la recherche et sur les travaux en cours,' *Revue d'histoire de l'Amérique française* 53 (2000): 560.

57 For a sense of recent developments in the French context, see Pascal Blanchard and Isabelle Veyrat-Masson, eds., *Les guerres de mémoires: la France et son histoire, enjeux politiques, controverses historiques, stratégies médiatiques* (Paris: La Découverte, 2008); Patrick Fraisseix, 'Le droit mémoriel,' *Revue française de droit constitutionnel* 67 (2006–09): 483–508; and Gert Oostindie, 'Public Memories of the Atlantic Slave Trade and Slavery in Contemporary Europe,' *European Review* 17 (2009): 611–26.

58 *Papers of Sir William Johnson* (see note 10), vol. 11, 872–5.

6

Interpreting the Past, Shaping the Present, and Envisioning the Future: Remembering the Conquest in Nineteenth-Century Quebec[1]

MICHEL DUCHARME

In 1911, Louis-Joseph, marquis de Montcalm, the French general who died defending Quebec City in September 1759, could at last rest in peace. After a fifty-year rehabilitation campaign in France and Canada, his reputation was restored on both sides of the Atlantic. On 16 October 1911, a monument dedicated to his memory was inaugurated on the prestigious Grande Allée in Quebec City. Montcalm was represented courageously fighting, swinging his sword in the air even while fatally wounded, and supported by an allegorical representation of *Glory*. The monument was a replica of another that had been inaugurated the previous year (on 17 July 1910) in Vestric-Candiac, France, where Montcalm was born in 1712. The monument had been placed first near the family castle, but was moved in 1994 to a public square.[2] The only difference between the two monuments was their pedestal: the French one was made of limestone from Caen (the same stone that had served to build the White Tower in London) while the Quebec one was made of New Brunswick granite.[3] That same year, Thomas Chapais, a conservative French-Canadian politician and historian, published the first heroic biography of Montcalm in French Canada. Chapais presented the French general as the embodiment of patriotism, a courageous hero ready to sacrifice his life for king and country.[4]

By celebrating Montcalm's courage and patriotism in 1911, French Canadians were not so much talking about the past as commenting on the present and envisioning the future; their concerns were immediate and practical. They were trying to imbue their fellow countrymen with a deep sense of patriotism, and were also creating a model that French Canadians could imitate in the context of a deteriorating relationship with English Canadians. By redeeming Montcalm's memory, French-

Canadian nationalists were encouraging their fellow countrymen to resist English Canadians' encroachments on their rights in Canada, and ultimately to fight for their nation's survival.

Over the past decade or so the relationship between public memory and politics in Canada has been studied extensively.[5] Historians have shown that, by interpreting, commemorating, and representing the past according to certain values, public memory has been a very useful political tool in orienting and manipulating public opinion. Among the different perspectives adopted by Canadian historians interested in this issue, one has been especially popular: the study of how individuals have been remembered over time. The public memory of figures such Jacques Cartier, Samuel de Champlain, Dollard des Ormeaux, Monsignor François Montmorency de Laval, Madeleine de Verchères, Laura Secord, and Louis Riel have been extensively studied. These works have demonstrated how historical figures have been used and reused in different circumstances to justify different purposes.[6] The same argument can be made for the memory surrounding the marquis de Montcalm or James Wolfe, the Battle of the Plains of Abraham, and the Conquest of New France more broadly. But while the Conquest and its consequences have been studied thoroughly by historians over the past century, the public memory created around it has not received much attention. With the exception of some historiographical surveys, Ramsay Cook's 1966 article, Maurice Lemire's analysis of nationalist themes in French-Canadian literature, and Patrice Groulx's excellent analysis of the commemoration of the Battle of Ste-Foy (April 1760), very little has been said about the topic.[7]

This chapter examines the development of the public memory created in nineteenth-century Quebec around Montcalm, the Battle of the Plains of Abraham, and the Conquest of Quebec. It focuses primarily on the meaning ascribed to the Conquest in political discourses, literary works, and historical studies in French Canada during the long nineteenth century (1791–1911). By exploring the different interpretations developed by politicians, novelists, poets, intellectuals, and priests, I show that these leaders were not interested so much in the past as in the present and the future. These individuals were looking forward, not backward; they were projecting their contemporary political program into the past. Their interpretations of the Conquest therefore were dependent on a specific political context, and evolved over the century. The public memory of the Conquest was used successively to promote French-Canadian loyalty to the British Crown, celebrate the advent of freedom or democracy in Lower Canada, justify the preservation of French culture in Canada, strengthen the relationship between French Canada and France, and encourage French Canadians to fight for their rights.

Despite its importance for the French inhabitants of the St Lawrence Valley, the Conquest was not discussed seriously in the colony until the 1840s.[8] Between the publication of Pierre-François-Xavier de Charlevois' *Histoire et description générale de la Nouvelle-France* in 1744 and that of François-Xavier Garneau's *Histoire du Canada depuis sa découverte jusqu'à nos jours* a century later in 1845, not one serious historical work on the subject was written in Lower Canada. Michel Bibaud and Joseph-François Perrault published a few articles and books about Lower-Canadian history between 1831 and 1837, but neither added anything to Charlevoix's book or William Smith's collection of documents that had appeared in the colony in 1826.[9] It is fair to say that, until the 1840s, French Canadians did not study their past. Their preoccupations and concerns were rooted in the present. When they appealed to the past, they generally preferred to refer to Greek or Roman Antiquity, or even to English constitutional evolution, than to local history.[10] When a local historical event was mentioned in the newspapers or in literary works (mainly poems[11]), this was always done to highlight a contemporary issue. There was no dialogue between the past and the present. Current views of the world were simply imposed on the past. In this context, it seems that Lord Durham was not totally wrong when he said in his *Report on the Affairs of British North America* (1839) that French Canadians were 'a people with no history,' even if this is not at all what he meant.[12]

The Conquest of New France was mentioned in Lower Canada before 1837, but only rarely. Two political arguments about the Conquest were developed before 1828, and both tried to prove how beneficial British sovereignty had turned out to be for the colony. No regrets were ever expressed about the Conquest, and not once was the 1759 defeat referred to as a disaster or a cataclysm. During the 1790s, one French-Canadian interpretation of the Conquest ended up being very similar to the interpretation proposed by William Smith, the chief justice of Quebec.[13] Between 1789 and 1793, Smith repeated many times that the Conquest had been a blessing for the colony – indeed, an act of God – as it had protected Quebec from the destruction engendered by the French Revolution. His interpretation was taken up in 1792 by the colonial legislative councillors of Lower Canada (who included both French Canadians and British immigrants). Smith and the political colonial elite were not the only ones to adhere to this interpretation of the Conquest. On 27 June 1794, in the midst of the French Revolutionary Terror, Joseph-Octave Plessis, a Roman Catholic priest, adopted the same interpretation and made it his own in his *Funeral Oration* for Monsignor Jean-Olivier Briand, the seventh bishop of Quebec and the first bishop to serve under the British Crown. According to Plessis, not only had the British government been more generous than one would have expected from a conqueror, but the Conquest had also protected French Canadians from the throes of the French Revolution. Plessis repeated his claims, especially in his *Thanksgiving Sermon for the Victory of Great Britain at the Battle of the Nile*, delivered in 1799.[14] In all these cases, the past itself was not at stake. Neither Smith, the legislative councillors, Plessis, nor anyone else who promoted this *providential* interpretation was really interested in what had happened in 1759. Rather, they were all preoccupied with the political state of the colony in the context of the French Revolution. By portraying the Conquest as an act of God, they were trying to convince French Canadians to remain loyal to the British Crown.[15] The past merely served to illustrate the benefits of British sovereignty in Canada.

The second argument that developed in Lower Canada concerning the Conquest rested on the French Canadians' gratitude for the creation of parliamentary institutions in the colony. Since its foundation, the colony had been governed by appointees from the metropolis (France until 1760 and Britain thereafter). In 1791, the British government granted a new constitution to the Province of Quebec (the Constitutional or Canada Act) that included parliamentary institutions. The creation of these institutions convinced French-Canadian leaders of Britain's goodwill and benevolence towards the colony, even if the institutions had been granted mainly to prevent republicanism from becoming a real threat in Quebec. It is not that French-Canadian politicians failed to see the flaws in their new constitution. On the contrary, they lobbied the metropolitan government to obtain important constitutional reforms from 1806 onward. Their demands focused on giving the assembly genuine control over the executive power through a kind of ministerial responsibility, impeachment trials, or budgetary management. Even when they were demanding reforms, however, French-Canadian leaders did not question Britain's goodwill towards the colony, British sovereignty over Canada, or the value of the British constitution itself, at least until 1828. In this context, they steadily argued that the British Conquest had been politically beneficial to the colony.

This is how Pierre Bédard, the reformers' leader and the editor of *Le Canadien* (1806–10), portrayed the Conquest in 1809. He emphasized the differences between the state of the colony under French and British rule to promote the advantages of the latter. Under the French regime, the colony went through 'unhappy times': according to Bédard, 'a man, indeed the people, were nothing, or even less than nothing.' The colonial state was ruled by a 'despotic' governor under whose leadership the colony was languishing and facing famine and penury of all sorts. According to Bédard, the Conquest had prevented the colony from 'dying of misery.' It was also followed by the imposition of the rule of law, which tremendously improved the political situation of the colonists.[16]

The same argument was also used by the reform leader Louis-Joseph Papineau. In a speech delivered on 1 July 1820 in honour of the late George III, Papineau also contrasted the 'arbitrary and oppressive nature' of French rule to the benevolent British one. He presented a long list of advantages that the Conquest supposedly had brought to French Canadians. It included the rule of law, an efficient defence of the colony, the protection of the language and institutions of the French Canadians, a free constitution, real religious toleration, trial by jury, and *habeas corpus*.[17] The same rhetoric was also presented by another reformer, Jacques Labrie, in his analysis of the British and Lower-Canadian constitutions in 1827.[18]

Bédard, Papineau, and Labrie may have been sincerely loyal to Britain, but their allegiance to the British Crown was not the main motivation behind their interpretation of the Conquest. These men were reformers. They demanded political reforms. Even if they always framed such demands within the context of the British constitution,[19] they were accused by their opponents of being disloyal. By reinterpreting the Conquest as having been politically beneficial for them, French-Canadian reformers were reasserting their loyalty to the British Empire, restating their admiration for the British political system, and undermining those who accused them of being anti-British.

Positive allusions to the Conquest progressively disappeared from French-Canadian discourse at the end of the 1820s, along with admiration for the British constitution. In 1828, after more than twenty years of political struggle in the colony, the reformers had come to realize that their faith in the British government had not served them well. No fundamental reforms had been brought to the colonial institutions – or seemed likely to take place anytime soon – even after the submission in 1828 of a report from a Special Committee on Canadian Affairs to the House of Commons recognizing the validity of the reformers' complaints. From 1828 onward, the reformers began to question their political institutions and progressively lost faith in the British Crown. Britain was becoming part of the problem, not of the solution. In the 1830s, Lower-Canadian reformers progressively rediscovered republicanism as an oppositional ideology and discourse, and began to call themselves the *Patriotes*.[20] In this context, neither the French nor the British regime could really provide precedents to justify the *Patriotes'* claims. The *Patriotes* had to content themselves with references to the American Revolution, advocating a radical departure from the institutions inherited from the past and a decisive rupture with the current political culture. For the first time, French Canadians were imagining a future that would be very different from the past. Accordingly, references to the Conquest disappeared almost entirely from French-Canadian discourse until the 1840s.

At the same time, British colonial authorities and British colonists used the Conquest to promote their own political goals. First, after 1827, British governors actively commemorated the Battle of the Plains of Abraham. Trying not to antagonize French Canadians more than they had already done, they celebrated both Wolfe and Montcalm as heroes. In 1827, Lord Dalhousie, governor general of Lower Canada, commissioned the erection of a monument in honour of both generals.[21] A dedication in honour of Dalhousie was engraved on the base, along with a few words in Latin about the two gallant heroes from John Charlton Fisher, editor of the *Quebec Gazette*, translated by a later American visitor, Henry David Thoreau, as 'Valor gave them one death; history, one fame; posterity, one monument.'[22] In 1831, Dalhousie's successor, Matthew Aylmer, had a plaque installed in the Ursulines Chapel where Montcalm was buried, with a few words (in French) in honour of the French general: 'Honour to Montcalm. Destiny denied him victory, but rewarded him with a glorious death.'[23] A year later, Aylmer commissioned a new monument to replace the deteriorating one that indicated where Wolfe had died. A small plaque mentioned the fate of the conqueror of Quebec: 'Here Died Wolfe Victorious September the 13th, 1759.'[24] If the British authorities took great care to celebrate Montcalm as well as Wolfe, British colonists thought that the outcome of the battle should not be forgotten. Reinterpreting their political struggle with the *Patriotes* through the lens of the Battle of the Plains of Abraham, they refused to see Wolfe's victory as a Pyrrhic one. As the editor of the *Montreal Gazette* wrote in June 1836 (and he was not the only one to say this), '[t]he sons of those who conquered on the Plains of Abraham will not allow the laurels so gloriously won by Wolfe to be tarnished, by permitting a tricolour to float upon the wall of Quebec, or the king's authority to be superseded by that of Louis-Joseph Papineau, as Dictator of Canada.'[25]

The failure of the 1837–8 rebellions initiated major changes in French-Canadian society. Republicanism was progressively marginalized between 1837 and 1848 and replaced by another dominant political ideology: French-Canadian nationalism.[26] Lord Durham helped to strengthen this new ideology, probably more than he would have liked. In his *Report*, he interpreted the 1837 Lower-Canadian rebellion as a struggle between two *nations*: the British and the French. In order to restore peace, the French *nation* had to be assimilated into the British one. By reframing the Lower-Canadian political struggle of the 1830s in ethnic terms, Durham helped to orient French Canadians towards a program aimed at preserving their cultural inheritance. The British government united Upper and Lower Canada into the Province of Canada in 1841, and Charles Poulett Thomson, Durham's successor as governor general, sought to rally English Canadians and promote the assimilation of the French Canadians, who became very concerned (in a way that they had not been since 1791) about their future as an ethnic group and as a cultural community. These perceived threats encouraged them to adopt an ethnic nationalism aimed primarily at preserving their cultural distinctiveness within the British imperial framework. This program was not entirely new since people such as Étienne Parent had begun to articulate it in the 1830s. However, it had remained marginal in the colony until the following decade. As this new ideology rested on the preservation of French-Canadian cultural inheritance, it established a close connection between the past, the present, and the future. By looking back into the past, French Canadians were in fact projecting themselves into the future. In opposition to the statesmen who were imagining a future without a French-Canadian community, French Canadians saw a future in which their community would exist and thrive.

Because French-Canadian nationalists hoped to preserve a cultural distinctiveness inherited from previous generations, they participated in the development of French-Canadian history and public memory. It is nowadays normal to make a distinction between history and memory. History is seen as a scientific activity performed by trained professionals: based on primary sources, it is a rational discourse about the past resulting from a dialogue between the past and the present.

Public memory, however, rests on a people's own experiences and heritage, and is not so much a dialogue between the past and the present as a contemporary discourse legitimized by references to the past.[27] But this distinction was not so clear in nineteenth-century French Canada. The development of the discipline of history contributed openly to the creation of public memory. Nineteenth-century French-Canadian historians had very well-known political objectives, which were often mentioned in the prefaces of their works. In turn, their works aimed to legitimize the emerging French-Canadian nation.

François-Xavier Garneau was the first French Canadian to study seriously the history of his colony. His *Histoire du Canada*, published between 1845 and 1852, consciously aimed at creating a national public memory. Conceiving of his nationality as a 'sacred inheritance' that could not be abandoned, he wanted to defend its right to survive by giving it a past.[28] Adopting a Romantic perspective, Garneau structured his narrative of French-Canadian history as an everlasting struggle for the nation's survival. [29] He transformed the Conquest into a key event in this history. Indeed, he framed it as the nation's founding moment. By doing so, he was able to project the roots of this new French-Canadian nationalist order into the past, giving legitimacy to the whole nationalist project. Jean-Baptiste-Antoine Ferland, although more conservative than Garneau, followed his predecessor's model by ending his *Histoire du Canada* in 1763, as if that year was an obvious break in Canadian history.

Even if Garneau and, to a lesser extent, Ferland were essential to the advent of a new understanding of the Conquest, they were not alone in reflecting on this historical event. They were part of a broader movement that was using the Conquest of French Canada as a pivotal moment in the nation's history. For instance, the first French-Canadian tragic play, published in 1844, addressed the issue, albeit in an indirect fashion. In *Le jeune Latour*, Antoine Gérin-Lajoie discussed an event that had happened in Acadia following its conquest by the English army in 1630.[30] It is not difficult to see that, by talking about Acadia in 1630, Gérin-Lajoie was alluding to the 1760 Conquest of New France and the 1840 Act of Union. By subtly projecting the present of French Canada into the seventeenth century, Gérin-Lajoie was encouraging his fellow countrymen to follow Roger Latour's patriotic example and refuse to acknowledge the British military victories. He was asking them to remain faithful to their *patrie*. Twenty years later, Napoléon Bourassa also conflated the calamity Acadians endured in 1755 and French Canadians in 1759. His novel *Jacques et Marie* (1866) was set mainly in Acadia during the *Grand dérangement*. By celebrating the loyalty of Marie to her nation – she refused to marry a British soldier even if such a union would have prevented her family's deportation – Bourassa was promoting the French-Canadian struggle for survival. To make sure the reader would make the connection between Acadia and Canada, Bourassa ended his novel on the Plains of Abraham by celebrating the courage shown by French Canadians in 1759. The Conquest also more directly provided the backdrop in other works of historical fiction, such as *Les Anciens Canadiens* (Philippe Aubert de Gaspé, 1863); *L'intendant Bigot* (Jacques Marmette, 1872), *Le Château de Beaumanoir* (Émile Rousseau, 1886), and *Un épisode dans la guerre de Conquête* (Adèle Bibeau, 1905).

Around the same time, the Conquest began to attract the interest of poets. In a poem published in 1843, Thomas-Jean-Jacques Loranger praised the French heroes of the colonial period, among them Cartier, Champlain, Roberval, Latour, Verchères, Maisonneuve, and Montcalm. He ended his poem with the Conquest of New France, as if it were the end of something. Adolphe-Basile Routhier also used the Conquest as a pivotal moment in a poem entitled 'Les dates historiques 1760–1867,' published in 1867, but he portrayed the Conquest not as an ending, but as the beginning of something new. The difference between Loranger's and Routhier's interpretations might be explained in part by the different contexts in which their poems evolved. The former wrote his piece in the early 1840s, when Lower Canada had just been forced into the union with Upper Canada. The poem reflected the prevailing pessimism in the colony. Conversely, the latter wrote his poem in 1867, following the creation of the new province of Quebec, which would have a French-Canadian majority.

It did not require much imagination to present the Conquest as a turning point, a pivotal and foundational moment in French-Canadian history. After all, the Conquest was in part responsible for the political questions that French Canadians had to face in the nineteenth century. The challenge was to transform a defeat into a national founding moment without depriving the nation of a glorious future. But could one make sure that this defeat did not prefigure the ultimate subjugation of the nation? Between 1845 and 1911, at least five rhetorical strategies were developed to solve this problem.

The first strategy was to go back to the ahistorical interpretations that had been developed prior to the 1830s. It was in this context that the idea of a providential conquest re-emerged in the colony. Like Monsignor Plessis before him, Monsignor Louis Laflèche argued in 1866 that the Conquest had been a blessing since it had prevented the spread of the immoral principles of Voltaire and Rousseau into the colony: thanks to the Conquest, French Canadians had survived as a Roman Catholic nation. Laflèche even added a proselytizing touch to his argument; according to him, French Canadians had to understand that their national mission was to spread the Roman Catholic faith in North America.[31] Also revived was the discourse about the political advantages brought by the Conquest, developed before 1828 by Bédard, Papineau, and Labrie, among others. This strategy was used as much by conservatives as by liberals in the province. For instance, in 1905, Benjamin Sulte, a conservative, wrote that, thanks to the Conquest, French Canadians '[had] passed from a reign of absolute subjection under the Bourbons to the free and untrammelled life of a constitutional government.'[32] Wilfrid Laurier also talked about the Conquest in his famous 1877 discourse concerning liberalism. In a speech full of historical inaccuracies, Laurier acknowledged the Conquest but argued that, 'if we are a conquered race, we have also made a conquest, the conquest of liberty.'[33] While the previous reformers had said that the Conquest had brought more freedom to the colony, Laurier argued that freedom was obtained *despite* the Conquest. The freedom Laurier referred to in his discourse, however, was a 'British' freedom, implicitly acknowledging that the Conquest had made freedom possible in Canada.

The second strategy was to focus on the French victories during the Seven Years' War (1756–63) instead of concentrating on the French defeat on the Plains of Abraham.[34] François-Xavier Garneau was among the first to do so in his 1840 poem 'Louise: Une légende canadienne,' set around the 1755 Battle of the Monongahela, in which the French defeated British troops led by General Edward Braddock[35] – interestingly, this battle happened prior to the arrival in the colony of the marquis de Montcalm, for whom Garneau did not have much sympathy. In 'Le drapeau de Carillon' (1855), Octave Crémazie chose to discuss the battle at Carillon (1758), the last French victory before the 1759 defeat. Marc-Aurèle Plamondon, Adolphe de Puisbusque, Louis-Honoré Fréchette, Alfred Garneau, and Émile Rousseau were also inspired by this victory.[36] None of the French victories, however, was as celebrated as that at Ste-Foy in April 1760, which, for many, redeemed the defeat on the Plains of Abraham. Not only was the Battle of Ste-Foy celebrated by French-Canadian poets,[37] but a monument to it, *Le monument des Braves*, was constructed between 1855 and 1863.

Even if, by celebrating French victories, French Canadians could celebrate implicitly their own future, they could not pretend that the French
had not lost the Battle of the Plains of Abraham in 1759. They therefore
adopted a third strategy: accusing the mother country of having abandoned them or finding scapegoats for the military disaster – by presenting their ancestors not as losers, but as victims. They began by accusing
France of having abandoned the colony. This accusation, which was not
new, was frequently repeated after 1845.[38] By the end of the 1850s, such
recriminations did not seem sufficient. At this point, direct accusations
were made against the king, the court, and Madame de Pompadour.[39]
When French Canadians focused on the colony itself, they made a clear
distinction between French Canadians (led by Governor Vaudreuil)
and the French troops (led by General de Montcalm) in order to blame
the latter for the defeat. The main villain, however, was the *intendant*,
François Bigot, who was accused of being responsible for the defeat,
whether as a result of simple corruption or of outright treason. One
of Bigot's protégés, Louis Du Pont de Chambon, sieur de Vergor, was
also blamed. Vergor had gained a bad reputation in 1755 by abandoning Fort Beauséjour in Acadia without putting up much of a fight. His
surrender eventually led to the deportation of the Acadians, a historical
event that was being rediscovered in the 1840s and 1850s. Vergor was
also accused of not having defended his position at the Anse au Foulon
on 13 September 1759, allowing Wolfe to disembark at this place.[40] By
emphasizing the metropolitan wrong-doing in the defeat or by accusing local Frenchmen of corruption or treason, French Canadians were
absolving their ancestors of any responsibility; 1759 was portrayed as a
French defeat, rather than a French-Canadian one.

A fourth strategy was also employed. Instead of putting emphasis
on the British Conquest of New France, some French Canadians used
it, especially before Confederation, to promote good relationships between French and English Canadians. This strategy was appealing
because French-Canadian nationalism initially rested on the idea that
collaboration and friendship between French and English Canadians
in the colony were possible and desirable. Politically, this idea was
embodied in the collaboration between Louis-Hippolyte La Fontaine
and Robert Baldwin, Augustin-Norbert Morin and Francis Hincks, and
George-Étienne Cartier and John A. Macdonald. This attitude briefly
shaped the meaning attributed to the Conquest. As Patrice Groulx has
explained, the *monument des Braves*, inaugurated in 1863, celebrated the
soldiers on both sides who had made possible the creation of a new nation in which French and English Canadians were able to collaborate.[41]

Ultimately, this Franco-English friendship was limited: it had to contribute to the preservation of the French-Canadian *cultural* nation, not to its assimilation. As Chauveau, the future superintendent of public education in Lower Canada and the first premier of Quebec after Confederation, said in his 1846 novel *Charles Guérin*, 'I am not in favour of fusion. Different peoples, like different metals, cannot be joined together without heat. For such an event to occur, there must be great tremors, great changes.'[42] This friendship and its limits were nowhere better exposed than in *Les Anciens Canadiens*, a novel by Philippe Aubert de Gaspé (1863). Here, the Conquest served as the backdrop of the novel, which was structured around the friendship of Jules d'Haberville, a French Canadian, and Archibald Cameron de Locheill, a Scot. Even their involvement in the war on opposite sides did not undermine their friendship. Yet, despite this friendship, a matrimonial union between Archie and Jules' sister was deemed unacceptable, even though the fact that Jules was involved with an English woman was not considered a problem. Blanche explained to her brother that 'what [he] could do without the slightest impropriety, it would be cowardly [for her] to do.' While her brother had 'nobly acquitted [himself] of [his] debt to [his] country' on the battlefield, she had not done so. 'Shall a d'Haberville be the first to give the example of a double yoke [as a French Canadian under the British rule and as a wife under the bond of matrimony] to the noble daughters of Canada?' she asked. Her answer was unambiguous: 'Oh! Never! Never!'[43] This was an original way of presenting the proper boundaries that existed at the heart of relationships between French and English Canadians. The subordination of French Canada, personified by a woman, to English Canada, represented by a man, was denounced as a crime against the nation. The same argument is also present in *Charles Guérin* and *Jacques et Marie*.

This thesis of sincere, if limited, friendship was characteristic of a short period of nation building when French Canadians were still optimistic about their relationship with English Canadians. This attitude and its interpretation of the Conquest were progressively abandoned after Confederation, in the midst of different national crises that swept through Canada. The Northwest rebellion of 1885 and the subsequent hanging of the Métis leader Louis Riel in November 1885 was interpreted by French-Canadian nationalists as an English-Canadian affront. At the same time, French Canadians were losing their rights to a French and Roman Catholic public education in New Brunswick (in the 1870s) and Manitoba (in the 1890s), and they were about to lose them in Ontario as well (in 1912). As if these problems were not enough, French and English Canadians disagreed over Canadian participation in British imperial wars. In this context, French-Canadian nationalists resurrected Garneau's argument presenting Canadian history after 1759 as a French struggle against the British threat. In *La légende d'un peuple* (1877), Louis Fréchette explicitly interpreted the Conquest in this way. Indeed, by the beginning of the twentieth century, the friendship thesis had no resonance among most French Canadians. As J.I. Little shows in his contribution to this volume, it was English Canadians who then promoted such an interpretation, focusing on the union of French and English Canadians into one nation (country). Governor General Lord Grey also used it to frame the celebrations surrounding the tercentenary of Quebec City in 1908.[44] As for French Canadians, they were by then developing a fifth strategy to deal with the Conquest.

Even if the Conquest had been transformed into a founding moment in French-Canadian history at the time of Confederation, there was still one major problem to solve: that of Montcalm's role in the fall of New France. As the general in charge of the defence of Canada, he could not easily be portrayed as a hero. The first French-Canadian historians, Garneau and Ferland, did not have a very high opinion of Montcalm. Even if they acknowledged that the marquis had been brilliant, brave, and courageous, they concluded that he had also been arrogant, full of contempt for the colonists, and a poor general: 'His genius was shown more by his richly-educated mind than it was by his ability in the art of war; brave but lacking initiative, he neglected troop discipline and never recommended any significant plan or strategy.'[45] Furthermore, he did not want to collaborate with the governor of the colony, the marquis de Vaudreuil, while his lack of confidence in the ability of the French to resist the invaders in 1759 contaminated his subordinates and prepared them to capitulate after the Battle of the Plains of Abraham.[46]

Nonetheless, in the last decades of the nineteenth century, Montcalm was progressively transformed from an arrogant French general into a hero symbolizing patriotism. The tense relationship between French and English Canadians at the end of the nineteenth century encouraged French-Canadian nationalists to look for great men who could inspire their nation, heroes who had not been afraid to fight for it even if the odds were not in their favour. This desire to find or even create heroes encouraged the reinterpretation of Montcalm's endeavours in New France. The French general's redemption was also made possible by French Canadians' rediscovery of their *Frenchness* during the second half of the century. Until then, French Canadians had talked about their cultural inheritance without putting too much emphasis on their French origins. Doing otherwise would have made them vulnerable to accusations of disloyalty. Things began to change in the 1850s. From the establishment of a new alliance between France and Britain at the time of the Crimean war (1853–6) to the *Entente cordiale* of 1904, the relationship between France and Great Britain became friendlier, allowing French Canadians to celebrate their French roots without questioning their membership in the British Empire. The visit of *La Capricieuse*, a French vessel, to Quebec City in 1855 and the opening of a French commercial office there four years later signified the re-establishment of an official relationship between the former colony and the former *mère-patrie*.[47] At the same time, the French were rediscovering French Canada, trying to highlight the links that united the two nations. In this context, the distinction Garneau made in 1848 between French and French Canadians at the time of the Conquest progressively lost its relevance.

One of the first manifestations of this positive attitude towards the French general in Quebec can be found in the reprinting of a eulogy to Montcalm – initially published in the *Mercure de France* in 1760 – in 1855, the same year that *La Capricieuse* visited Quebec.[48] Then, on 14 September 1859, Montcalm's ultimate sacrifice was commemorated by the unveiling of a funeral monument in the Chapel of the Ursulines in Quebec, where Montcalm had been buried a century earlier. The ceremony had been organized by Georges Barthélemi Faribault, the former assistant secretary of the Canadian Legislative Assembly. Faribault was then fulfilling the wishes of Louis-Antoine de Bougainville and other French officers who had fought with Montcalm, and who had lobbied the British government for the right to place a plaque on Montcalm's grave in 1761. Their plaque had included a Latin inscription written by the French Académie des Inscriptions et Belles-Lettres; unfortunately, the plaque was lost en route to Quebec. The monument unveiled in 1859, however, included the 1761 inscription.[49] In 1867, Adolphe-Basile Routhier wrote in a poem that 'The immortal hero of a great epic / Montcalm had fallen before his enemies / All gazes were fixed on his valiant sword / He had said: I died, defeated but unbroken.'[50] Already the myth could be seen in embryonic form: Montcalm was an immortal hero who had died courageously.

This myth was encouraged and sustained by the development of an international literature on Montcalm in the last decades of the nineteenth century. In France, nationalist authors restored Montcalm's reputation in the wake of the French defeat at the hands of the Prussians and their German allies in 1871. They were eager to promote patriotism among their youth, and nothing seemed more fitting than the celebration of heroes who had sacrificed their lives for the fatherland. On 14 September 1859 Félix Martin, SJ, gave a funeral oration commemorating the centenary of the general's death in Quebec; a few years later, he published a hagiographic biography of Montcalm. Accusing François-Xavier Garneau of having been partial and unfair towards the fallen French general, Martin wrote of Montcalm as a true patriotic hero – in his account, it was Governor Vaudreuil and the corrupt officials surrounding him who were responsible for the conquest of the colony, not Montcalm.[51] Martin was followed by many other French nationalists who celebrated the general's patriotism and sacrifice in the following years.[52] The inauguration of the Vestric-Candiac monument in 1910 can be seen as the culmination of this redeeming campaign in France.

Even more influential was American historian Francis Parkman. In *Montcalm and Wolfe* (1884), the last of his seven-volume study of the struggle between France and Britain in North America, Parkman focused on the last few years of New France. His analysis was, to say the least, not sympathetic to the French colony: he depicted New France as the embodiment of absolutism and popery.[53] For Parkman, the struggle between France and Britain could be reduced to a conflict of 'the past against the future; of the old against the new; of moral and intellectual torpor against moral and intellectual life; of barren absolutism against a liberty, crude, incoherent, and chaotic, yet full of prolific vitality.'[54] Despite his antipathy towards New France, Parkman portrayed Montcalm in a favourable light, presenting him as the alter ego of James Wolfe. The real villains in Parkman's version of the Conquest were the French authorities in Versailles, the egoistic, incompetent, and indecisive Vaudreuil, and the Roman Catholic clergy.

In *Guerre du Canada, 1756–1760: Montcalm et Lévis*, published in 1891, Henri-Raymond Casgrain tried to find middle ground between Garneau's and Parkman's interpretations. Like Garneau, Casgrain refused to blame Vaudreuil, the good *Canadien* governor, for the fall of New France – though he certainly found fault with Vaudreuil's character. At the same time, Casgrain acknowledged recent French historiography and Parkman's work. Unlike his French-Canadian predecessors, he was not afraid to acknowledge the qualities and courage Montcalm had shown between 1756 and 1759. In the end, he blamed the French general only for having launched the attack against Wolfe's troops too hastily on the fatal morning of 13 September 1759 (supposedly against

Vaudreuil's instructions). In order to blame neither Vaudreuil nor Montcalm for the defeat on the Plains of Abraham, Casgrain finally pinned the blame on Bougainville and Vergor. The former was guilty of not having sent more men to the Anse au Foulon on the fateful night (as requested by Vaudreuil) and for not having warned the sentry that the convoy that was supposed to bring supplies that night had been countermanded. As for the latter, he was accused of having allowed most of his soldiers to go back home in order to bring in the harvest. These decisions allowed the British to reach the Plains on 13 September 1759.[55]

Casgrain's mild accusation against Montcalm was to be the last one published in French Canada. By the end of the century, French Canadians had stopped blaming Montcalm for the fall of New France, preferring to remember him for his courage and his heroic death. By focusing on his courage and sacrifice, Montcalm could become an example to follow. In 1894, Montcalm's place in Quebec history had been sufficiently redressed to allow the erection of a statue in his honour on the Legislative Assembly's facade in Quebec City, beside one of James Wolfe; one of Lévis, was added in 1896. In 1907, Louis Guyon wrote a play, *Montcalm: drame historique,* that embodied most of the strategies developed since 1845 by highlighting Louis XV's debauchery, Madame de Pompadour's poor political judgment, Vaudreuil's deficiencies as leader, Bigot's corruption and treacherous endeavours, Montcalm's patriotism, and French-Canadian courage.[56]

By 1911, Montcalm's reputation could be officially vindicated. Nobody did more for the marquis than Thomas Chapais. Chapais's work was based on the assumption that the Conquest had been both a cataclysm that divided Canadian history into two segments and a providential event that prevented French Canada from suffering even more traumatic events (that is, the French Revolution). Participating in the debate over the merits of Vaudreuil and Montcalm, Chapais unambiguously sided with the general. Even if he did not deny Vaudreuil's dedication to the *Canadiens'* cause, he portrayed him as weak, vain, and authoritarian. Conversely, if Montcalm was not without faults, his courage, his patriotism, and his sacrifice were exemplary. According to Chapais, 'Montcalm was the most outstanding and appealing individual among the military men and administrator who held the destiny of New France in their hands ... Thanks to his cultured manner, his erudition, his experience on the battlefields of Germany and Italy, his spontaneity, his alertness, his warm eloquence – in a word, thanks to the many gifts that were his – he dominated and eclipsed the dull and mediocre

Vaudreuil.'[57] In the end, Chapais considered that Montcalm's courage 'crowned the destruction of New France with a glorious halo.'[58] With this assessment, the memory of Montcalm had been redeemed and that of the Battle of the Plains of Abraham and the Conquest reconstructed so that it could now serve to inspire a new generation.

Although Chapais' pro-British interpretation of the Conquest gave way to more critical appraisals in the following decades, as demonstrated by Michel Bock, Alexis Lachaine, and Brian Young in their contributions to this volume, the centrality of the Conquest in Quebec history remained generally unchallenged in the province during the twentieth century. After a debate that lasted almost two hundred years, the Conquest is now seen by most French Quebecers as a cataclysm that prevented the nation that once thrived on the St Lawrence from achieving its full potential and independence. This interpretation is so entrenched in Quebec public memory that any alternative discourse is deemed unacceptable, as demonstrated by the passionate debates over the Conquest's importance in the high school history curriculum (2008) and its two hundred and fiftieth anniversary re-enactment (2009), which Nicole Neatby and Jocelyn Létourneau discuss in this volume. Even if this version of history, focusing on the defeat of 1759–60, seems like a self-evident truth today, we should not forget that it is one of many interpretations that have been articulated over the past two hundred and fifty years.

It is now a truism to say that French-Canadian leaders were discouraged after the failure of the 1837–8 rebellions, and that they adopted a pessimistic political program called *la survivance* out of despair during the 1840s. It is undeniable that these French-Canadian leaders were concerned about their future in the second half of the nineteenth century and that their main objective was to preserve their national existence. But they were neither discouraged nor looking constantly to the past out of nostalgia. Their nationalist program was in tune with what was going on elsewhere in the Western world. The diversity of interpretations ascribed to the key event in French-Canadian history attests to the existence of a vibrant intellectual life in French Canada in the nineteenth century rather than a sclerotic one. And even if French Canadians chose a defeat as a founding moment of their national existence, they were not *defeatists*. They never stopped trying to transform this defeat into a victory, or at least into a positive source of inspiration. In the end, these pessimistic elites were able to do one thing that contemporary Quebecers seem unable to do: use the Conquest to foster hope for the future. They could remember what Pierre Corneille said in *The Cid*: 'Triumph without peril brings no glory.'[59]

NOTES

1 I would like to express my gratitude to Michèle Dagenais and Robert A.J. McDonald for their thoughtful comments. My thanks also go to Dzavid Dzanic and Michael Lanthier for the assistance they offered in the preparation and writing of this chapter, and to the Social Sciences and Humanities Research Council of Canada for its support.

2 On the French monument, see the website of the town of Vestric-et-Candiac, http://vestricetcandiac.24hactus.com/tag/statue+de+montcalm (accessed on 20 August 2009).

3 On these two monuments, see Georges Bellerive, *Œuvre des deux monuments à Montcalm à Vestric-Candiac, France, et Québec, Canada, 1910–1911* (Québec: Compagnie de publication Le Soleil, 1911).

4 Thomas Chapais, *Le marquis de Montcalm (1712–1759)* (Québec: J.P. Garneau, 1911).

5 See, for instance, Jonathan F. Vance, *Death So Noble: Memory, Meaning, and the First World War* (Vancouver: UBC Press, 1997); H.V. Nelles, *The Art of Nation-Building: Pageantry and Spectacle at Quebec's Tercentenary* (Toronto: University of Toronto Press, 1999); Alan Gordon, *Making Public Pasts: The Contested Terrain of Montreal's Public Memories, 1891–1930* (Montreal; Kingston, ON: McGill-Queen's University Press, 2001); Christian Labrèche, 'De l'utilisation politique de la mémoire des patriotes de 1837-1838 au Québec depuis la Révolution tranquille,' *Bulletin d'histoire politique* 10 (2001): 150–62; Béatrice Richard, *La mémoire de Dieppe: radioscopie d'un mythe* (Montréal: vlb éditeur, 2002); and Mourad Djebabla-Brun, *Se souvenir de la Grande Guerre: la mémoire plurielle de 14-18 au Québec* (Montréal: vlb éditeur, 2004). See also Jocelyn Létourneau, *Passer à l'avenir: histoire, mémoire, identité dans le Québec d'aujourd'hui* (Montréal: Boréal, 2000).

6 Douglas Owram, 'The Myth of Louis Riel,' *Canadian Historical Review* 63 (1982): 315–33; Patrice Groulx, *Pièges de la mémoire: Dollard des Ormeaux, les Amérindiens et nous* (Hull: Éditions Vents d'Ouest, 1998); Colin Coates and Cecilia Morgan, *Heroines and History: Representations of Madeleine de Verchères and Laura Secord* (Toronto: University of Toronto Press, 2002); Albert Braz, *The False Traitor: Louis Riel in Canadian Culture* (Toronto: University of Toronto Press, 2003); Ronald Rudin, *Founding Fathers: The Celebration of Champlain and Laval in the Streets of Quebec, 1878–1908* (Toronto: University

of Toronto Press, 2003); Jennifer Reid, *Louis Riel and the Creation of Modern Canada* (Albuquerque: University of New Mexico Press, 2008); Mathieu d'Avignon, *Champlain et les fondateurs oubliés: les figures du père et le mythe de la fondation* (Quebec: Presses de l'Université Laval, 2008); and Alan Gordon, *The Hero and the Historians: Historiography and the Uses of Jacques Cartier* (Vancouver: UBC Press, 2009).

7 See Georges Robitaille, *Montcalm et ses historiens: étude critique* (Montréal: Granger frères, 1936); Ramsay Cook, 'Some French-Canadian Interpretations of the British Conquest: Une quatrième dominante de la pensée canadienne-française,' Canadian Historical Association, *Historical Papers* (1966); Maurice Lemire, *Les grands thèmes nationalistes du roman historique canadien-français* (Québec: Presses de l'Université Laval, 1970); and Patrice Groulx, 'La commémoration de la bataille de Sainte-Foy: du discours de la loyauté à la fusion des races,' *Revue d'histoire de l'Amérique française* 55 (2001): 45–83.

8 These French inhabitants called themselves *Canadiens* until the 1840s. They then began to use the term 'French Canadians.' For the sake of consistency, I use only the latter term.

9 See Michel Bibaud, *Histoire du Canada sous la domination française* (Montréal: John Jones, 1837); and idem, *Histoire du Canada, et des Canadiens, sous la domination anglaise* (Montréal: Lovell & Gibson, 1844). Joseph-François Perrault published an *Abrégé de l'histoire du Canada* in four volumes (Québec: P. & W. Ruthven, 1831–6) for the provincial elementary schools. On the work of Jacques Labrie, a medical doctor and politician who wrote during the 1820s a lengthy but unpublished book about the colony, see Jonathan Lemire, *Jacques Labrie: écrits et correspondence, suivi de ses Notes sur l'histoire du Canada* (Québec: Septentrion, 2009), 110–27, 285–329. See also William Smith, *History of Canada*, 2 vols. (Quebec: J. Neilson, 1815); and J.M. Bumsted, 'William Smith,' in *Dictionary of Canadian Biography*, vol. 7 (Toronto: University of Toronto Press, 1988), 816–19, http://www.biographi.ca.

10 See, for instance, Denis Benjamin Viger, *Considération sur les effets qu'ont produit en Canada, la conservation des établissements du pays, les mœurs, l'éducation, etc. de ses habitants et leurs conséquences qu'entraîneraient leur décadence par rapport aux intérêts de la Grande-Bretagne* (Montréal: James Brown, 1809); idem, *Analyse de l'entretien sur la conservation des établissemens du Bas-Canada, des lois, des usages, etc. de ses habitants* (Montréal: James Lane, 1826); and Jacques Labrie, *Les premiers rudimens de la constitution britannique; traduits de l'anglais de M. Brooke; précédé d'un précis historique, et suivis d'observations sur la constitution du bas-canada, pour en donner l'histoire et en indiquer les principaux vices, avec un aperçu de quelques-uns des moyens probables d'y remédier* (Montréal: James Lane, 1827).

11 A team of researchers under the direction of Jeanne Lortie and Yolande
    Grisé has collected all the poems published in the colony between 1606
    and 1867: *Les textes poétiques du Canada français, 1606–1867*, 12 vols. (Mon-
    tréal: Fides, 1987–2000). All the poems mentioned in this chapter were
    drawn from this collection.

12 John George Lambton, 1st earl of Durham, *Report on the Affairs of Brit-
    ish North America*, vol. 2, ed. Sir Charles Lucas (Oxford: Clarendon Press,
    1912), 294. Even if Durham's statement was, and still is, sometimes under-
    stood as a derogatory comment about the lack of literary and historical
    publications in the colony (or even worse, as a comment about the inglori-
    ous past of French Canadians), it can also be interpreted as a statement
    about the kind of society that existed in Lower Canada in 1837–8. When
    Durham said that French Canadians had 'no history and no literature,' he
    did not mean that they had no past (glorious or not). In fact, he accused
    French Canadians of being enslaved to their past because of their French
    language and the survival of their social institutions, and he wanted to free
    them from the yoke of their cultural inheritance through assimilation. See
    Michel Ducharme, 'L'État selon lord Durham: liberté et nationalité dans
    l'Empire britannique,' *Cahiers d'histoire* 18 (1998): 55–7; Jean-Paul Bernard,
    'La réplique de Garneau à Lord Durham: un peuple "sans histoire" ou
    sans avenir?' in *François-Xavier Garneau, une figure nationale*, ed. Gilles
    Gallichan, Kenneth Landry, and Denis St-Jacques (Québec: Éditions Nota
    Bene, 1998).

13 On William Smith, see L.F.S. Upton, *The Loyal Whig: William Smith of New
    York and Quebec* (Toronto: University of Toronto Press, 1969).

14 On the first appearance of the providential interpretation of the Conquest,
    see Claude Galarneau, *La France devant l'opinion canadienne (1760–1815)*
    (Québec: Presses de l'Université Laval, 1970), 336–9; and David M. Hayne,
    'Conquête providentielle et Révolution diabolique: une constante dans la
    littérature québécoise du XIXe siècle,' in *La Révolution française au Canada
    français*, ed. Sylvain Simard (Ottawa: Presses de l'Université d'Ottawa,
    1991). See also Joseph-Octave Plessis, *Oraison funèbre de Mgr Jean-Olivier
    Briand, ancien évêque de Québec: prononcée dans la cathédrale de Québec le
    27 juin 1794* (Québec: Bulletin de recherche historique, 1906); and idem,
    *Discours à l'occasion de la victoire remportée par les forces navales de Sa Majesté
    britannique dans la Méditerranée le 1 et 2 août 1798 sur la flotte française, pro-
    noncé dans l'Église cathédrale de Québec le 10 janvier 1799* (Québec: Imprimé
    au profit des pauvres de la paroisse, 1799).

15 On the political context in Quebec in the 1790s, see F. Murray Greenwood,
    Legacies of Fear: Law and Politics in Quebec in the Era of the French Revolution
    (Toronto: University of Toronto Press, 1993).

16 Pierre Bédard, *Le Canadien*, 4 November 1809.

17 Louis-Joseph Papineau, 'France et Angleterre. Discours électoral, 1er juillet 1820,' reproduced in *Un demi-siècle de combats: interventions publiques*, ed. Yvan Lamonde and Claude Larin (Montréal: Fides, 1998), 42–4.

18 Labrie, *Premiers rudimens de la constitution britannique.*

19 Michel Ducharme, *Le concept de liberté au Canada à l'époque des Révolutions atlantiques (1776–1838)* (Montréal; Kingston, ON: McGill-Queen's University Press, 2010).

20 On republicanism in Lower Canada, see Louis-Georges Harvey, *Le Printemps de l'Amérique française: américanité, anticolonialisme et républicanisme dans le discours politique québécois, 1805–1837* (Montréal: Boréal, 2005); Allan Greer, *The Patriots and the People: The Rebellion of 1837 in Rural Lower Canada* (Toronto: University of Toronto Press, 1993), 120–52, 219–57; and Ducharme, *Concept de liberté*, chap. 4.

21 It seems that Dalhousie wanted to commemorate only Wolfe's victory, but was 'forced' to mention Montcalm on the monument; see Alain Parent, *Entre empire et nation: les représentations de la ville de Québec et de ses environs, 1760–1833* (Québec: Presses de l'Université Laval, 2005). I am grateful to Normand Legault of the Royal Military College of Canada for this reference.

22 The Latin sentence was 'Mortem virtus communem, famam historia, monumentum posteritas.' For the monument, see Pierre-Georges Roy, *Les monuments commémoratifs de la Province de Québec* (Québec: Ls-A. Proulx, imprimeur du Roi, 1923), 11–14. For Thoreau's translation, see *A Yankee in Canada* (Boston: Ticknor and Fields, 1866), 68.

23 'Honneur à Montcalm. Le Destin en lui dérobant la Victoire, L'a récompensé par une mort glorieuse'; Chapais, *Marquis de Montcalm*, 684.

24 James MacPherson Le Moine, *Picturesque Quebec: A Sequel to Quebec, Past and Present* (Montreal: Dawson Brothers, 1882), 310.

25 *Montreal Gazette*, 18 June 1836.

26 On the difference between patriotism and nationalism in the French-Canadian context, see Ducharme, *Concept de liberté*, 155–60.

27 This distinction between history and public memory was inspired by Jacques Le Goff, *Histoire et mémoire* (Paris: Gallimard, 1988), 9–10; Olivier Mongin, 'Les discordances de l'histoire et de la mémoire,' *Esprit* 266–7 (2000): 7; Pierre Nora, 'Entre mémoire et histoire: la problématique des lieux,' in *Les lieux de mémoire*, vol. 1 (Paris: Gallimard, 1984–92), xix–xx; and Tzvetan Todorov, 'La mémoire devant l'histoire,' *Terrain* 25 (1995): 101–12.

28 François-Xavier Garneau, *Histoire du Canada depuis sa découverte jusqu'à nos jours*, vol. 1 (Québec: N. Aubin, 1845), 20.

29 Allan Smith, 'Seven Narratives in North American History: Thinking the Nation in Canada, Quebec and the United States,' in *Writing the Nation: A Global Perspective*, ed. Stefan Berger (Basingstoke, UK: Palgrave Macmillan, 2007).

30 This play was based on a historical event described by Michel Bibaud in *Histoire du Canada*, vol. 1, 57–8. As has been pointed out to me by the editors of this volume, the story is historically inaccurate: those who settled at Port-Royal were Scots, not English, they did so in 1629, and they did not have to use any armed force.

31 Louis Laflèche, *Quelques considérations sur les rapports de la société civile avec la religion et la famille* (Montréal: Eusèbe Sénécal, 1866), 47–74. These two concepts, providential conquest and providential mission, evolved independently from each other. For instance, Monsignor Louis-Adolphe Pâquet talked about the French Canadian providential mission in 1902 without mentioning the Conquest; see 'Sermon sur la vocation de la race française en Amérique' (1902), in *MENS: Revue d'histoire intellectuelle de l'Amérique française* 3 (2002): 77–95.

32 Benjamin Sulte, 'The French Canadians and the Empire,' in *The Empire and the Century*, ed. C.S. Goldman (1905), quoted in Cook, *Maple Leaf Forever*, 102.

33 Wilfrid Laurier, *Lecture on Political Liberalism* (Quebec: Printed at the 'Morning Chronicle' Office, 1877), 4.

34 For some poems using this strategy, see Marc-Aurèle Plamondon, 'Aux abonnés du *Journal de Québec*,' *Journal de Québec*, 1 January 1847; and Un écolier du collège de Ste-Thérèse, 'Adieux: d'un vieil officier canadien à son fils qui part pour la guerre en 1813,' *L'Ordre*, 27 July 1860.

35 François-Xavier Garneau, 'Louise: une légende canadienne,' *Le Canadien*, 17 February 1840.

36 See, for instance, Marc-Aurèle Plamondon, 'La Saint Jean-Baptiste, 24 June 1852: au Peuple,' *Le Moniteur canadien*, 1 July 1852; Adolphe de Puisbusque, 'Les couleurs du Canada,' *La Minerve*, 23 June 1858; Octave Crémazie, 'Fête nationale,' *La littérature canadienne de 1850 à 1860*, vol. 2 (Québec: G. et G.-E. Desbarats, 1864), 86–8; Louis-Honoré Fréchette, 'Le héros de 1760,' *Journal de Québec*, 26 June 1860; and Alfred Garneau, 'Le porte-drapeau,' *Poésies* 1906 (1866).

37 François-Xavier Garneau, 'Le vieux chêne,' *Le Canadien*, 29 September 1841; Adolphe Marsais, 'Aux braves morts dans les plaines d'Abraham,' *Journal de Québec*, 21 July 1855; idem, 'Ste-Foy, près de Québec,' *Le Canadien*, 12 October 1859; Octave Crémazie, 'Un soldat de l'empire,' *Journal de Québec*, 10 March 1859; Arthur Cassegrain, 'À mon ami Édouard Sempé,

compatriote du général de Lévis: le héros de Sainte-Foy,' *Courrier du Canada*, 30 April 1860; Louis-Honoré Fréchette, 'Le héros de 1760,' *Journal de Québec*, 26 June 1860; Édouard Sempé, 'À mon ami Arthur Cassegrain, "Digne enfant de Champlain,"' *L'Ordre*, 4 May 1860; Léon-Pamphile Lemay, 'Souvenir des braves de 1760,' *Journal de Québec*, 17 October 1863; and Louis-Honoré Fréchette, 'Les braves de 1760,' *Le Canadien*, 21 October 1863.

38 François-Xavier Garneau, 'À lord Durham,' *Le Canadien*, 8 June 1838; idem, *Histoire du Canada*, vol. 3, 79, 107, 142, 231, 263; Pierre-Joseph-Olivier Chauveau, *Charles Guérin: roman de mœurs canadiennes* (Montréal: John Lovell, 1853 (1846)), 349; Octave Crémazie, 'Le vieux soldat canadien,' *Journal de Québec*, 21 August 1855; idem, 'Le drapeau de Carillon,' *Journal de Québec*, 1 January 1858; and Marsais, 'Ste-Foy, près de Québec.' This accusation was not new: François-Xavier Garneau was already articulating such an idea in the 1830s (see 'Le Canadien en France,' *Le Canadien*, 12 August 1833). It also had a lasting influence on Quebec historiography; see, for instance, Henri-Raymond Casgrain, *Guerre du Canada, 1756–1760: Montcalm et Lévis*, vol. 1 (Québec: J.-L. Demers, 1891), 18–19.

39 Adolphe Marsais, 'Le trappeur canadien: esquisse locale, en 1759,' *Le Canadien*, 18 October 1858; idem, 'Le Château Bigot,' *Le Canadien*, 15 October 1858; Louis-Joseph-Cyprien Fiset, 'Montcalm. Poème,' *La Ruche littéraire*, June 1859; and F.D.L., 'Montcalm,' *Le Courrier des États-Unis*, 19 September 1859.

40 On the idea of treason, see Louis-Michel Darveau, 'Le vingt-quatre juin,' *L'Observateur*, 30 June 1858. On François Bigot's corruption and treason, see, among others, Jacques Marmette, *L'intendant Bigot* (Montréal: G.-E. Desbarats, 1872); J. Eugène Corriveau, *Le secret des Plaines d'Abraham: grand drame historique canadien. Drame en 4 actes* (Québec: Imprimerie de la 'Parole libre,' 1909). As for the accusations against Vergor, they were not new: see Anonyme, '[Quand Georges III, prit l'Canada]' (1763), in *Les textes poétiques du Canada français* (see note 11), vol. 1, 191.

41 On this monument, see Groulx, 'Commémoration de la bataille de Ste-Foy.' See also Marsais, 'Aux braves morts dans les plaines d'Abraham'; and idem, 'Romance: adieux des Canadiens aux marins de La Capricieuse,' *La Minerve*, 16 August 1855.

42 'Je ne suis pas pour les fusions. Les peuples comme les métaux ne se fondent pas à froid. Il faut pour cela, de grandes secousses, une grande fermentation'; Chauveau, *Charles Guérin*, 56.

43 Philippe Aubert de Gaspé, *Les Anciens Canadiens* (Québec: Desbarats and Derbishire, 1863), 337; published in English as *Canadians of Old*, trans.

Georgiana M. Pennée (Québec: G. & G.-E. Desbarats, 1864), 278–9. The original French text was as follows:

Si tu épousais une Anglaise, mon cher Jules, je la recevrais dans mes bras avec toute l'affection d'une sœur chérie; mais ce que tu peux faire, toi, sans inconvenance, serait une lâcheté de la part de ta sœur. Tu as payé, noblement, ta dette à la patrie. Ton cri de guerre 'à moi grenadiers!' électrisait tes soldats dans les mêlées les plus terribles [...]. Oui, mon frère chéri, tu as payé noblement ta dette à la patrie, et tu peux te passer la fantaisie d'épouser une fille d'Albion! Mais, moi faible femme, qu'ai-je fait pour cette terre asservie et maintenant silencieuse; pour cette terre qui a pourtant retenti tant de fois des cris de triomphe de mes compatriotes? Est-ce une d'Haberville qui sera la première à donner l'exemple d'un double joug aux nobles filles du Canada?

44 On this issue, see H.V. Nelles, 'Historical Pageantry and the "Fusion of the Races" at the Tercentenary of Quebec, 1908,' *Histoire sociale/Social History* 29 (1996): 391–415; and idem, *Art of Nation-Building*, chap. 3.

45 'Il était plus brillant par les avantages d'une mémoire bien ornée que profond dans l'art de la guerre; brave mais peu entreprenant, il négligea la discipline des troupes et ne proposa jamais aucune entreprise importante'; Garneau, *Histoire du Canada*, vol. 3, 213. This assessment was repeated in J.B.A. Ferland, *Cours d'histoire du Canada*, vol. 2 (Québec: Augustin Côté, 1865), 587.

46 Garneau, *Histoire du Canada*, vol. 3, 211–12.

47 Yvan Lamonde and Didier Poton, eds., *La Capricieuse (1855): poupe et proue. Les relations France-Québec (1760–1914)* (Québec: Presses de l'Université Laval, 2006).

48 *Éloge historique de monsieur le marquis de Montcalm (extrait du 'Mercure de France' de 1760)* (Quebec: A. Côté, 1855).

49 On this commemoration, see Henri-Raymond Casgrain, *Faribault et la famille De Sales Laterrière* (Montréal: Beauchemin, 1912), chap. 3.

50 'Le héros immortel d'une grande épopée,/ Montcalm, était tombé devant les ennemis;/ Et les regards fixes sur sa vaillante épée/ Il avait dit: je meurs, vaincu mais insoumis.' This poem was written in 1867, but published in 1879: 'Dates historiques. 1760–1867,' *Le Foyer domestique*, 1 October 1879. See also A.-B. Routhier, *Quebec: A Quaint Mediaeval French City in America at the Dawn of the XXth Century* (Montreal: Montreal Printing and Publishing, 1904), 195–235; *Montcalm et Lévis: Drame historique* (Québec: Imprimerie franciscaine missionnaire, 1918).

51 Un ancien missionnaire, *De Montcalm en Canada ou Les dernières années de la colonie française (1756–60)* (Tournai, Belgium: H. Casterman , 1867). The book was later republished under the name of its author, Félix Martin, S.J., as *Le marquis de Montcalm et les dernières années de la colonie française au Canada (1756–1760)* (Paris: G. Téqui, 1879).

52 For political discourses and/or historical works, see Charles de Bonnechose, *Montcalm et le Canada français* (Paris: Hachette, 1877); Edmond Falgairolle, *Montcalm devant la postérité: étude historique* (Paris: Challamel, 1886); Christophe Allard, *La conquête et la perte de la Nouvelle France* (Rouen, France, 1888); Émile Lonchampt, *Pourquoi l'Amérique du Nord n'est-elle pas française?* (Paris: Challabel Aîné, 1888); Alexander Héron, *Montcalm et la défense du Canada: réponse au discours de réception de N. Christophe Allard* (Rouen, France: E. Cagniard, 1888); and Eugène Guénin, *Montcalm* (Paris: A. Challabel, 1898). See also the discourses delivered by French officials at the 1910 inauguration of the Montcalm monument in France: Bellerive, *Œuvre des deux monuments*, 22–42. For a novel on the same theme, see Henri Cauvain, *Le grand vaincu: dernière campagne du marquis de Montcalm au Canada* (Paris: J. Hetzel, 1878); Cauvain reprinted excerpts of Martin's biography in an appendix to his novel, 322–6.

53 Francis Parkman, 'Canadian Absolutism,' in *The Old Régime in Canada* (Boston: Little, Brown, 1874), 394–401.

54 Francis Parkman, *Montcalm and Wolfe*, vol. 1 (Boston: Little, Brown, 1884), 35.

55 Casgrain, *Guerre du Canada, 1756–1760*, 2 vols. This work was later translated in English and published as *Wolfe and Montcalm* (Toronto: Morang, 1905). Some sentences in this book are clearly plagiarized from Parkman.

56 Louis Guyon, *Montcalm: drame historique* (Montréal: Imprimerie mercantile, 1907).

57 'Montcalm était la plus brillante et la plus attachante figure du groupe militaire et administratif auquel étaient liées à ce moment les destinées de la Nouvelle-France. [...] Par sa culture intellectuelle, son érudition, son expérience acquise dans les campagnes d'Italie et d'Allemagne, par son esprit primesautier, son style alerte, sa chaude éloquence, en un mot, par la variété de talents qui le distinguait, il dominait et éclipsait la terne et médiocre personnalité de Vaudreuil'; Chapais, *Marquis de Montcalm*, 488–9.

58 Ibid., xi–xii.

59 'À vaincre sans péril on triomphe sans gloire'; Pierre Corneille, *Le Cid* (II.2 V:435). Translation from Patrice Pavis, *Dictionary of the Theatre: Terms, Concepts, and Analysis* (Toronto: University of Toronto Press, 1998), 205.

7

Overcoming a National 'Catastrophe': The British Conquest in the Historical and Polemical Thought of Abbé Lionel Groulx

MICHEL BOCK

Abbé Lionel Groulx was arguably the most influential nationalist thinker in twentieth-century French Canada, at least prior to Quebec's Quiet Revolution of the 1960s. Born to a modest peasant family in 1878 and ordained to the priesthood in 1903, Groulx would make a remarkable and varied contribution to the institutionalization of the historical discipline in Quebec. In 1915, he became the first academic to hold a Canadian history chair in a French-Canadian university.[1] In 1946, he would launch the Institut d'histoire de l'Amérique française, the first full-fledged professional organization for French-speaking historians across the country. The following year, he would go on to publish the *Revue d'histoire de l'Amérique française*, the first scholarly historical journal ever to be published in French Canada. Groulx was not only a historian; he was equally a fearsome polemicist who gained a considerable following during the inter-war years, especially as editor of the monthly journal *L'Action française*, which came to be regarded as the leading and most radical voice for French-Canadian nationalism during the 1920s. The following decade saw him rise to even greater prominence, as the nationalist and often separatist youth movements of the Great Depression would come to revere and see him as their unquestioned intellectual leader.[2] Even after the Second World War, though his influence was in decline, he continued to be viewed as the *maître à penser* of the French-Canadian and eventually *Québécois* nationalist movement.

Through his historical and polemical writings, as well as his teachings, Abbé Groulx developed a traditionalist and messianic conception of the French-Canadian nation based on language, culture, faith, and historical 'consciousness.' He was also the first prominent intellectual

and historian in Quebec to place the British Conquest of New France
squarely at the centre of both his ideology and his work as a scholar.
Whereas many of his predecessors and contemporaries had lauded the
passing of the colony from French to British rule, inasmuch as it had
prevented it from succumbing to what they viewed as the horrors of the
French Revolution, Groulx instead saw the Conquest literally as a national 'catastrophe,' and mercilessly vilified the theory that it had been
ordained by none other than Divine Providence to protect New France
from such evils as French republicanism, anti-clericalism, and godless-
ness. In his view, the British conquerors' ultimate aim was to suppress
the young *Canadien* nation, perhaps not individually, but certainly collectively, a prospect that was entirely unacceptable to an organic and
not entirely unromantic nationalist such as himself.

Although Abbé Groulx saw the Conquest as an event of catastrophic
proportions, this is not to say that, in his view, all hope had left the
banks of the St Lawrence along with the French in 1760 – quite the contrary. Although Providence might not have predetermined the victory
of the British over the French in the Seven Years' War, Providence did
have a plan for French Canadians, a plan that would guarantee their
collective survival as a nation for as long as they chose to do their part
in its accomplishment. It is the messianic and voluntarist aspects of this
interpretation that would provoke a serious intellectual rift between
Groulx and the younger generation of nationalist historians who would
rise to prominence after the Second World War and during the years
leading up to and including the Quiet Revolution.

The idea that the British Conquest of New France had been a god-
send, as opposed to a trauma, for French Canada was not, in fact, new
to the twentieth century. As early as 1793, immediately following the
decapitation of Louis XVI, the *Canadien* clergy condemned the Revolution and professed its undisputed loyalty to the British Crown and
its colonial representatives. The throne and the altar, in the eyes of the
bishop of Quebec, Monsignor Jean-François Hubert, were ultimately
meant to remain united.[3] Given that the British had demanded nothing
from the *Canadiens* that might have been contrary to their conscience
and faith, loyalty was the only responsible attitude to espouse. The first
to suggest explicitly that Divine Providence had played a decisive role
in the Conquest of New France, however, was the coadjutor bishop of
Quebec, Monsignor Joseph-Octave Plessis, as early as 1794. In a speech
given five years later at the request of Governor Prescott to celebrate
the British victory over the Napoleonic fleet off Aboukir, Egypt, Ples-

sis would reiterate his belief in the Providential Conquest theory in no uncertain terms: 'What a joy it was for us that Providence separated us from France before she abandoned herself to such deplorable blindness [the Revolution] and submitted us, through a sense of goodness we had hardly deserved, to the liberal and salutary government of His Majesty the King of Great Britain ... This generous Empire understood right from the beginning of the French Revolution the grievous consequences that would flow from the principles of anarchy and misunderstood liberty that constituted its base.'[4]

This theme of providential intervention in the course of French-Canadian history was not to obtain unanimous consent, however, following its formulation by the clerical elite at the turn of the nineteenth century. French Canada's first so-called national historian, François-Xavier Garneau, who would publish the four volumes of his monumental *Histoire du Canada depuis sa découverte jusqu'à nos jours* between 1845 and 1852, was certainly no admirer of the ultramontane clergy or of the British colonial power.[5] Indeed, he had written his *Histoire du Canada* in order to challenge Lord Durham's assertion that French Canadians were a people deprived of history and literature. Even in the later editions of his work, in which he considerably toned down his apparent liberalism and anticlericalism, he squarely rejected the Providential Conquest theory. On the other hand, Abbé Jean-Baptiste-Antoine Ferland's view of the Conquest was more consistent with the ideas Plessis had expressed decades earlier:[6] in his *Cours d'histoire du Canada*, published in 1861 and 1865, Ferland would support the idea that the British victory during the Seven Years' War had shielded French Canadians from the French Revolution, while allowing them to maintain their religious and national integrity.[7]

Among Groulx's contemporaries – and intellectual adversaries – none, however, had the clout of Thomas Chapais. The son of Jean-Charles Chapais, one of the Fathers of Confederation, Thomas, who was also a journalist, a member of Quebec's Legislative Council, a minister in Maurice Duplessis' first government, a senator, and a professor of history at Quebec City's Université Laval, was certainly someone to be reckoned with. As a historian, Chapais published a great many studies on the history of New France and of the British regime and gave much historical credibility to the Providential Conquest theory. In 1911, he produced a substantial biography of the marquis de Montcalm in which he portrayed the leader of the French army in New France as a hero tragically defeated on the Plains of Abraham, to the great sorrow of the French and *Canadiens* alike. Such hero-worshipping, however, did not keep him from criticizing the upper echelons of New France society, who had become, in his opinion, frivolous and decadent. Much like their metropolitan counterparts, the leaders of the colony had lost their sense of duty, which in turn led them to lose the colony itself. Montcalm's sacrifice, in Chapais' view, had been necessary in order to purify New France:

> The upper spheres of our *Canadien* society had to be tried and purged, and they were. The cataclysm that divided our history into two parts, though it may have appeared disastrous to our fathers, saved us from many evils. And, mercifully, God, who had cradled us into existence, had wanted that at the very moment He sent us war, invasion and all of their sinister consequences, our defeat and downfall would be illuminated by a reflection of glory that would shine upon our future. Montcalm was the soldier God had chosen to this end, and his exploits, his triumphs, as much as his death on the battlefield crowned the passing of New France with a halo that continues to glow over French Canada, now embarked upon its new destiny.[8]

Chapais' principal work was his *Cours d'histoire du Canada*, a study of the British regime (from the Conquest to Confederation) in eight volumes published between 1919 and 1933. In it, he strived to demonstrate that the ordeal of 1760 was not as great as it could have been, thanks in large part to the generosity and liberal attitude the British Crown had quickly adopted towards its new subjects. Though his description of the dilemma the *Canadiens* had faced after the Treaty of Paris may have been poignant, the rest of the story was proof that the Conquest had not meant the death of French Canada:

> One thing had died: the French regime. Another thing was threatened with death: the French nationality. The French regime had passed. The situation in which Europe found itself at the outset of the Seven Years' War forbade anyone from hoping it might be resurrected. Our destiny had been irrevocably altered. Providence, which governs all things according to its own mysterious designs, had decreed this change in sovereignty against which it was useless to struggle. There was nothing to do but adapt to the new regime. Did such an adaptation represent for us a very difficult task? No, gentlemen, we must recognize such a truth if we carefully study the reality of the situation.[9]

Chapais' interpretation of French-Canadian history after 1760 was indeed quite reassuring. He found evidence of Britain's reasonable and enlightened attitude in many places, including the Quebec Act of 1774, which guaranteed religious freedom in the colony, and the Constitutional Act of 1791, which bestowed upon French Canadians their first parliamentary institutions. Their political situation had never ceased to improve, at least until the unfortunate uprisings of 1837–8. Chapais' condemnation of the rebellions was unequivocal: not only had the rebel leaders repudiated the Church's authority, they had acted without the support of the vast majority of the population and thrown the country into chaos. Though their desire to grant Lower Canada's Legislative Assembly more autonomy vis-à-vis the Executive and Legislative Councils was justifiable, their impatience and especially their revolutionary methods were not. Political change would have come – as indeed it did merely a few years later. No self-respecting French-Canadian and Catholic historian could bring himself to pardon the *Patriotes*.[10] Yet, even the Act of Union, which the rebels had thoughtlessly and needlessly brought upon their entire people, had not sealed the fate of French Canadians, whose greatest causes for rejoicing still lay ahead of them. Responsible government became a reality in 1849, thanks to the wisdom and serenity of the great Baldwin–La Fontaine ministry, which gave proof, in Chapais' narrative, that when English and French Canadians chose to unite their efforts for the common good, progress was never very far behind.[11] The British North America Act of 1867, for its part, represented no less than the culmination of French-Canadian political autonomy. Chapais took no small measure of delight in the 'spectacle of the inauguration, in 1867, of a French legislature, created by an act of the Parliament of England, in order to freely govern a French province, covering the entire territory that had formerly constituted the main part of old New France.'[12] The road travelled since 1760 had been long, but not nearly as arduous as it might have been.

Chapais' interpretation of the Conquest was formulated at a time when relations between English and French Canadians had come under considerable stress. His particular brand of loyalism and *bonne ententisme* would be severely critiqued and deconstructed among the growing ranks of French-Canadian nationalist intellectuals. The leader of this movement in both the academic and polemical spheres would be Lionel Groulx, a secular priest who, while Chapais was establishing himself as the leading voice of French-Canadian historiography, had been working as a relatively unknown professor of history in Valleyfield. In 1915, Groulx would leave his small-town classical college and head for the metropolis in order to take on the first chair of Canadian history at the Université Laval de Montréal. Quebec's intellectual life would never be the same.

Ronald Rudin correctly points out in his study of French-Canadian historiography that Lionel Groulx's dogged attempts to discredit the Providential Conquest theory were essentially aimed at Chapais, who, though twenty years his senior, was nonetheless his principal adversary in the historical arena, at least at the beginning of his career. Despite some fundamental differences in interpretation between the two schol-ars, there did exist, however, a mutual respect, even a kinship, born of a common quest for historical truth.[13] In his memoirs, Groulx would later write that he had maintained excellent relations with Chapais, at least until 1937, when a speech given during the second Congrès de la langue française in Quebec City famously – but perhaps too hastily – caused him to be labelled the leader of the 'separatist' movement by both pro-moters and critics of French-Canadian separatism, an ideological option that had gained a considerable amount of weight during the 1930s, espe-cially among Quebec's nationalist youth organizations.[14] Chapais had even endorsed Groulx's candidacy for a fellowship from the Carnegie Foundation a few years earlier, lauding the younger historian's tremen-dous talent, which placed him among the country's very best research-ers.[15] Upon Chapais' death in 1946 at the more than venerable age of eighty-eight, Groulx was handed what might have seemed the unlikely task of writing his obituary for *Liaison*, a journal recently founded by lit-erary critic Victor Barbeau. The published text is quite remarkable in the way it pays homage to Chapais, while producing some rather scathing criticism of both his political and academic careers. The senator, wrote Groulx, had been a true gentleman, and had on more than one occasion proven his ability to tolerate dissent and respect opinions contrary to his own. The only significant exception was in the area of politics, where he had suffered, like many men of his generation, from the most damaging disease ever to have stricken the French-Canadian elite: political parti-sanship. *Bleu* to the core, Chapais had reduced himself to a despicable and sectarian form of *torysme* that had driven him to adopt a centraliz-ing position in matters pertaining to internal politics, to the detriment of Quebec's provincial autonomy vis-à-vis Ottawa, and an imperialist one in matters of external politics, to the detriment, this time, of Canada's autonomy vis-à-vis Britain. Even in 1931, he had remained unwavering in his imperialist convictions, to the point of deploring the passing of the

Statute of Westminster, which had finally granted Canada the right to determine its own foreign policy.[16]

As a historian, however, Groulx believed that Chapais had been capable of a much greater degree of open-mindedness. In the world of academia, he wrote, 'where dogmatism belongs only to the self-important, he was not so sure of his opinions that he believed them infallible.'[17] This was not to say that his historical *œuvre* was free of any shortcomings. On the contrary, Groulx judged Chapais' practice of the historian's craft completely outdated from a strictly methodological point of view. His complete and utter submission to the minutiae of chronology made his writing superficial and more the stuff of chronicle than of serious historical analysis. Second, and more important, Groulx believed Chapais to have been devoid of the objectivity and critical distance that were essential to any historian more concerned with historical truth than with political propaganda. Chapais' greatest failing, in Groulx's view, was that he had not come first to history before entering politics. As a result, his historical research bore the unmistakable imprint of his *bleu* and loyalist partisan beliefs. This was especially true of his *Cours d'histoire du Canada*, his crowning achievement: 'Shall we say of it that it is heavy with the deformations the author suffered by way of his political activities? Let us say it again: [Chapais] is of the era following Confederation, an era when our politicians turned their backs on the old ideal of *Canadien* independence and succumbed to the offensive return of English imperialism. Nowhere more than in Quebec were there such professions of loyalism, aimed, for our part, at obtaining forgiveness for our French origins. Mr. Thomas Chapais, as a politician, was unable to write anything but a loyalist history.'[18] Groulx viewed Chapais as the embodiment of the great faults of the post-1867 generation: political partisanship, loyalism, imperialism, and antinationalism (whether French-Canadian or simply Canadian). In the political as well as in the historical arena, he had cast over French Canada's problems a 'smoke screen' and through his sectarian ideology contributed, sadly, in returning his compatriots to their 'political infancy.'[19]

Groulx's judgment of Chapais was severe, to say the least. In his memoirs, he would hint at his own feelings of remorse for perhaps having taken something of a malicious tone in assessing the senator's legacy.[20] The article did raise some controversy among Quebec's political elite and even provoked the anger of Premier Maurice Duplessis, who was said to be a great admirer of Chapais'.[21] Yet, despite the tone of the paper, it does enable the reader to understand the intellectual

chasm that separated the two historians' interpretations of Canadian
history since 1760. Indeed, Abbé Groulx could not share Chapais' loyalist views on the providential nature of the British Conquest, in the
same way that he was utterly unable to conclude that the expansion
of French-Canadian religious and political autonomy after 1760 had
primarily been the result of British generosity and good-heartedness.
In a sense, one might even view Groulx as the first true 'revisionist' in
French-Canadian historiography.

If Groulx saw Chapais as the unfortunate embodiment of his generation's shortcomings, it is safe to say that his own views on Canadian
history can be better understood by analysing them in relation to the
context during which he himself came of age. The idea that French Canadians had received in the early days of New France a providential
mission that made them agents for the growth of Catholicism in North
America had in fact been in circulation since the 1840s.[22] It is only after Confederation, however, that the notion became more heavily intertwined with the rising French-Canadian nationalist movement. The
acceleration of the industrialization and urbanization processes underscored the growing threat of materialism for French Canadians and its
deconstructive effects on their society and way of life. The repeated
assaults against Catholic and French minority schooling rights in New
Brunswick (1871), Manitoba (1890), Saskatchewan and Alberta (1905),
and Ontario (1912), as well as the execution of Métis leader Louis Riel
in 1885 and the start of the Boer War in 1899, drove many intellectuals, both lay and clerical, to exploit the old theme of providentialism
in order to legitimize the right of French Canadians to exist, not only
in Quebec, but across the country and even across North America. If
Providence itself had chosen French Canada to bear witness to Catholicism and to work towards its expansion, any attempt at assimilation,
be it linguistic, cultural, or religious, would itself be seen as bereft of
legitimacy. It is in this context that the Compact theory of Confederation would emerge, as Arthur Silver demonstrated in his classic 1982
study, *The French-Canadian Idea of Confederation*.[23] In the minds of the
new generation of nationalist thinkers, French Canada could consider
itself fully one of the two founding peoples of Canada, though not primarily because of the existence of any constitutional or legislative text,
but essentially as a result of its missionary past, present, and future.
Providentialism was no longer strictly a loyalist concept: the rising nationalist movement could claim it as well.

Though politician and journalist Henri Bourassa might have been
the first to define explicitly both the Compact theory and the alliance

of nationalism and providentialism,[24] no one devoted himself to the development of these ideas with as much zeal and conviction as Lionel Groulx. French Canada's providential mission, he explained, was the one thing that justified, above all others, its right to exist across the country and the continent.[25] Groulx's particular brand of nationalism led him to reject Chapais' loyalist interpretation of French-Canadian history and, above all, the Providential Conquest theory. In 1944, he published an article entitled 'La Providence et la Conquête anglaise de la Nouvelle-France,' an article meant to put the issue to rest once and for all. The Providential Conquest theory, he wrote, had nothing to do with the philosophy of history and much less to do with history itself at its most basic and empirical level. It was nothing more than misguided theology and, as such, entirely ahistorical. The question, he said, did not consist in determining whether or not the British Conquest was a providential act. Everything in history was providential, he explained, the good along with the bad. Groulx's profound voluntarism led him to believe in the absolute liberty of Man and Nation, both of whom possessed the freedom to either follow the path laid out for them by Providence or choose a different one. Nothing in history, including the Conquest, had therefore been preordained: 'The absolute universality of Providence is deduced from the absolute universality of supreme causality. History is the work of men, of free men, though they bustle under the watchful eye of God. Divine action, though sovereign, does not limit or set any constraints upon the prerogatives of human freedom. In rigorous truth, it can be said of men that they build their own lives, and of nations that they build their own histories. In the infinite passing of human events, God never loses sight of his own ultimate ends, the ends of creation and redemption to which all things are subordinated.'[26] In other words, Providence had more important things to do than look after such minutiae as the outcome of the Seven Years' War – which was not to say that it wasn't paying attention, but that its viewpoint was much more farsighted. Ultimately, if men possessed, for better or worse, the freedom to choose their own destiny and to conduct their lives as they saw fit, so too did nations, which were collective beings, possess the capacity to write their own histories, for history was nothing if not the life of a nation. Whether or not men and nations made their choices in accordance with the great design Providence had elaborated for mankind was, in the end, entirely up to them.

Groulx also used less theological and more prosaic arguments to deconstruct the Providential Conquest theory. He would go on to explain that the loss of Canada to the British had been provoked not by Providence, but rather by France itself, which had, under Louis XV (and even in the later years of Louis XIV's reign), essentially left the colony to fend for itself both demographically and economically, as if the *Canadiens* had been alone on the North American continent and did not have to contend with a formidable adversary directly to the south of them. Moreover, was it not strange to insist on seeing the instrument of divine intervention in Protestant and anti-papist Britain, a nation which had spawned Locke and Bentham, as well as many other philosophers who were to sow the revolutionary seed throughout Europe over the course of the eighteenth century?[27] After all, Voltaire and Diderot had not fallen directly from the sky. Had the domination of Britain been any more benign than would have been the continued rule of France, even of a republican France?

Groulx's analysis of Canadian history after 1760 would provide a resounding 'no' to this question. His first substantial analysis of the early years of the British regime, entitled *Lendemains de Conquête*, was published in 1920, only a year after the first volume of rival Chapais' *Cours d'histoire du Canada*. After having studied the French regime the previous year in *La naissance d'une race*, a book that was meant to describe the early formation of the French-Canadian religious and national character,[28] Groulx now turned his attention to the many hardships faced by the young society in the aftermath of the Seven Years' War. The historian's position on the issue was for the most part devoid of ambiguity. The Conquest, far from being a providential blessing in disguise, represented an event of cataclysmic proportions and had threatened to compromise the *Canadien* nation's normal and organic development, even its very existence:[29] 'The British Conquest had suddenly halted the growth of the French-Canadian nationality. A violent jolt shook the organism of the young race. Some of its life sources would be significantly impoverished, others would run entirely dry. In the destiny of our people, it was … a trial that would take on the proportions of a catastrophe.'[30]

In the short term, the *Canadiens* had to rebuild the economic infrastructure the war had destroyed and could not count on anyone but themselves. They had also been deprived of the progressive agricultural techniques soon to be developed in France, as the new British elite cared little for agricultural development, over which it had clearly preferred more profitable mercantile ventures. Moreover, the British had rendered nearly impossible any form of contact with France, whether commercial, intellectual, or religious. This had singularly impoverished French-Canadian society from the standpoint of both culture and education. True, French Canadians had been shielded from the horrors of the French Revolution, but they had also been cut off from 'la saine pensée française'[31] – that of Catholic and traditionalist France, which had not accompanied the *ancien régime* into oblivion. More important, the 'Conqueror,' as he continued to call the British, had suspended clerical recruitment among the Catholic religious orders of France. The Canadian clergy were the only natural leaders the fledgling society had left after the departure of its political and economic elite, but the Church had to rely solely on its own vastly insufficient internal growth to keep its own head above water. Barely an adolescent society, French Canada had hardly been ready to fend for itself.

Groulx underscored what he considered the willingness of the Conqueror to take advantage of the colony's weakened state. The Royal Proclamation of 1763 had amputated from Quebec a large part of its former territory in order to stifle the *Canadiens* and park them in the St Lawrence Valley.[32] More important, Groulx argued, the Proclamation had established that the infamous Test Oath had to be taken by all administrative officers, requiring them to renounce their Catholicism, a sure way to rid the colony of any 'papist' influence. Even after the passing of the Quebec Act in 1774, which had restored some measure of religious freedom in the colony, the *Canadiens* still had new obstacles to overcome. Groulx explained that, in 1791, the intention of the British, while instituting the parliamentary system in the new province of Lower Canada, had been to marginalize the use of the French language to further anglicize the national character of the *Canadiens*. In a series of studies entitled *Nos luttes constitutionnelles*, he rejoiced in the ability of the early French-Canadian parliamentarians to thwart, time and time again, the assimilation tactics of the Conqueror, including the projected unification of Upper and Lower Canada in the early 1820s.[33] Even after the defeat of the rebellions – which Groulx refused to condemn as straightforwardly as had Chapais – and despite the hated Act of Union of 1841, the French-Canadian political class had succeeded once again in restoring the language rights of their compatriots and, with the assistance of progressive-minded Upper Canadians, finally obtained responsible government, greatly advancing the cause of French-Canadian political autonomy. The principal artisan of these victories had been, of course, Louis-Hippolyte La Fontaine, who had even convinced a majority of his colleagues to extend religious schooling rights to Upper-Canadian Catholics, despite vociferous opposition from Grits and Orangeists alike.

The historical picture Groulx was in the process of painting was that of an 'upward curve': the political and religious situation of French Canadians had indeed steadily and substantially improved after the Conquest. On this basic level, he was in agreement with his rival, Thomas Chapais. But the two historians fundamentally disagreed on the cause of such a strengthening of the French-Canadian nation. For Groulx, if French Canadians had been able to overcome the cataclysmic effects of the Conquest, there were no thanks to be given to the British, only to themselves. More specifically, he attributed such progress to the fact that the French-Canadian people had been governed by true leaders in both the political and religious spheres, leaders who had remained faithful to the providential mission that had been bestowed upon their nation at the moment of its birth.

Lionel Groulx's ideology, and even his historical interpretations, were clearly not devoid of theological and even messianic considerations – that much is an understatement. Though Providence, contrary to what Chapais and some of his predecessors appeared to believe, did not operate on a microscopic scale, it nonetheless did have some great design for humanity, and called upon the nations it had created to do their part in its accomplishment. French Canada's mission was to spread Catholicism across the North American continent, a mission it had readily carried out since the early days of New France – the French-Canadian minority groups dispersed across Canada and the United States were indeed witnesses to this fact, as Groulx repeatedly pointed out. As long as French Canadians kept the faith and continued to stay the course, Providence, in its infinite wisdom, would not fail them but would guarantee their continued survival as a nation, regardless of the Conqueror's efforts to repress them.[34]

The 'upward curve' of French-Canadian history would reach its zenith in 1867. Much has been said and written about Lionel Groulx's so-called separatism and his critique of Confederation, and though it is true that he found much to deplore, his criticisms were rarely aimed at the institutions of 1867 themselves, but rather at the men who ran them. In fact, Groulx lauded the passing of the British North America Act as nothing less than the 'political resurrection of French Canada.'[35] Confederation was the embodiment of the political victories French Canadians had accumulated since the Conquest. Not only had it granted them a state, federated as it was to a larger whole, it had also freed them from the tutelage of Upper Canada. In short, it represented the constitutional recognition of the Compact theory. Groulx was steadfast in his belief that the new Dominion of Canada had been freely founded by two autonomous peoples, two nations, equal in rights and free to remain true to their religious ideals and national character anywhere in the country. Canada was more than merely bilingual; it was binational. Again, the victory of Confederation had been made possible by the earnestness, integrity, and unwavering faith of the French-Canadian clerical elite, but also, in this case, its political elite. Groulx, of course, found the subsequent chapters of Canadian history to be less inspiring, as was evidenced by English Canada's attempt to limit French-Canadian influence to what he ironically called the 'Quebec reservation.' He also deplored the crushing of the Western Métis, the 'persecution' of French-Canadian and Catholic minorities in most provinces, and, after the Great War, the massive Americanization of Quebec's economy, as well as its way of life – a phenomenon Groulx even likened to a 'Second Conquest.'[36] What was at fault, however, was not the 'pact' of 1867 as such, but rather English Canada's refusal to abide by both its terms and its spirit and, even more important, the inability of French-Canadian political leaders to demonstrate the same nationalist and religious conviction as their pre-1867 counterparts. Once again, French Canada, like all nations, possessed the freedom not to follow the path laid out for it by Providence. Groulx began to question seriously his contemporaries' willingness to ensure their own survival as a nation, a fear that would only grow as he witnessed Quebec's economic and social transformation over the course of the twentieth century. The root of the problem was, in a sense, fundamentally spiritual. Unless they recovered their senses, French Canadians would have only themselves, and not the Conquest or the British, to blame for their own gradual demise.

Groulx's interpretation of French-Canadian history since 1760 would not find unanimity among all of his colleagues in the historical profession. Thomas Chapais' successor at the Université Laval, Abbé Arthur Maheux, would oppose a more *bonne ententiste* view of history to Groulx's nationalist ideas. In *Ton histoire est une épopée*, published at the outset of the Second World War, Maheux attempted to demonstrate that the Conquest, far from having been a catastrophe for French Canadians – especially in light of the atrocities being committed in Europe at the same time – had in actuality rendered possible the alliance of the two great peoples who would go on to found Canada in 1867.[37] A year following the 1942 conscription crisis, Maheux, apparently deeply upset over the results of the plebiscite, which had pitted French and English Canadians against each other, suggested that, to solve the country's ills, a single interpretation of Canada's national history should be taught in all schools from coast to coast, regardless of linguistic or religious identity. He phrased the title of his piece in the form of a question: *Pourquoi sommes-nous divisés?* (Why are we divided?), leaving the door wide open for Groulx, who would take on the challenge of answering Maheux's question in a counterattack he affirmatively titled *Pourquoi nous sommes divisés* (Why we are divided).[38] By deconstructing Maheux's *bonne ententiste* and loyalist plea for national unity, Groulx sought to prove the folly of a single interpretation of history in a country that housed two distinct and separate nations. Collaboration and harmony between the two founding peoples were indeed possible, in Groulx's mind, but only insofar as each could retain its own clearly defined national identity. As Bourassa had done before him, Groulx firmly rejected the idea that 'la fusion des races' represented the only path to Canadian unity.

Maheux, however, did not pose a significant threat to Groulx's status as French Canada's leading historian. Only after the Second World War would his historical legacy be more seriously challenged by a new generation of historians eager to rest their discipline on entirely 'scientific' grounds and to develop a more materialistic interpretation of Quebec's past. These young scholars were divided into two opposing factions: the neo-nationalist Montreal school and the less-than-nationalist Laval school. In the context of the post-war economic boom, itself fuelled by American investments and the expansion of the Canadian welfare state, a growing number of intellectuals and scholars sought a better understanding of the historical origins of what they considered to be French Canada's economic inferiority.[39] On either side of the nationalist divide, all things traditionalist and clerical were criticized for having shielded Quebec from modernity and economic progress. There was considerable disagreement, however, between the two schools of thought over the role played by the British Conquest of New France in the economic marginalization of French Canada.

The Laval school consisted of historians who, in a sense, might be considered heirs to Chapais and Maheux, inasmuch as their viewpoint proved to be severely critical, for the most part, of any and all nationalist interpretations of French-Canadian history.[40] The three main figureheads of the Laval school were Marcel Trudel and his pupils, Jean Hamelin and Fernand Ouellet. As Charles-Philippe Courtois points out in a recently published anthology of the major historiographical texts relating to the Conquest, Trudel, a specialist on the French regime, revisited the Providential Conquest theory not by positing that it had saved

French Canada from the horrors of the French Revolution, but instead by underscoring that it had delivered the colony from French absolutism.[41] The conservatism and clericalism of Chapais and Maheux might be things of the past, but their loyalism, apparently, was not entirely. Hamelin, for his part, in his work on the economic and social history of New France, attempted to demonstrate that French-Canadian culture had been incompatible with capitalism and had deprived the colony of a true bourgeoisie before the advent of the British.[42] Ouellet would pursue and develop this line of reasoning in his groundbreaking work on the economic and social history of the British regime and Lower Canada. French Canadians, in his view, had been plagued by an *ancien régime* mentality that had kept them from actively pursuing their own economic development and modernization.[43] In both Hamelin's and Ouellet's accounts, the Conquest was purged of its catastrophic and dramatic characteristics and presented as a relatively negligible event, a simple change of metropolis for a colony that had never showed much interest, in any case, in its own economic progress. In short, the economic inferiority of French Canada was no fault of the British. French Canadians had only themselves to blame.[44]

The Laval school's interpretation of Canadian history after 1760 would be challenged by its nationalist competitors of the Montreal school. The figureheads of this movement, Maurice Séguin, Guy Frégault, and Michel Brunet, were former disciples of Lionel Groulx, and the point of view they succeeded in developing on the Conquest was not entirely dissimilar to that of the patriarch of French-Canadian historians. Like Groulx, they were firm believers in the idea that the Conquest had been a catastrophe, but one that had plunged the *Canadiens* into a state of mediocrity and economic inferiority from which there had been no escape. Gone was Groulx's 'Upward Curve' theory, along with his messianism. Indeed, these young historians made every effort to purge their profession of what they considered to be the 'compensatory' myths scattered throughout their predecessors' work. By focusing primarily on the religious and political aspects of French Canada's past and by ultimately subordinating their understanding of history to such an intangible and evasive concept as Providence, the historians of previous generations had not recognized the true economic degradation that had plagued French Canada's national existence since 1760.

Frégault, for his part, devoted a masterful study to the causes and consequences of the Seven Years' War, a study that remains a classic today, more than half a century after its publication. The future undersecretary of cultural affairs in the Lesage government of the 1960s concluded that the Conquest had put an end to the *Canadiens'* 'normal' development: initially a commercial people, they had been forced after 1760 to rely on the meagre offerings of the land in order to survive, the reins of the colony's commercial activities having been handed over to the Conqueror.[45] Two centuries later, little had changed: French Canadians were still not *'maîtres chez eux.'* The only difference was that, instead of farming the land, they had become labourers in Quebec's new industrial economy.

No one, however, was more vocal than Brunet in his critique of traditional historiography. In the late 1950s, he published a scathing article that deplored what he viewed as the three 'constants' in French-Canadian intellectual life since 1760: agriculturalism, antistatism, and messianism.[46] Before the Conquest, New France had been a 'normal' society and had developed similarly to other colonial societies during the same period. The *Canadiens* had not been less commercially active than people in other colonies; they had not been wary of using government to favour economic growth; and they had certainly not adhered to the idea that their destiny, as dictated by Providence, had been limited to spiritual and agricultural endeavours. To the contrary, each and every one of those ills had been a direct consequence of the Conquest. In *Les Canadiens après la Conquête* (1969), Brunet would develop his ideas more explicitly on the 'social decapitation' of *Canadien* society after 1760.[47] New France's economic and political elite had been forced either to leave the colony after the Seven Years' War or run the risk of being marginalized. The British elite, who benefited from Britain's mercantilist policies, had taken over the former *Canadien* commercial network, which had granted them control over the St Lawrence hydrographical system and, as a result, the lucrative fur trade. The *Canadiens*, for their part, had been reduced to toiling on the land. The clerical elite, who had stepped in to replace the former political and economic leaders of New France, compensated for this marginalization by diffusing 'compensatory myths' that represented French Canadians as more spiritually pure than their materialistic Anglo-Protestant counterparts and the recipients of an absurd providential and agricultural mission. In Brunet's mind, French Canada's *déchéance* had lasted for two centuries. It was high time to envision a change: 'The French-Canadian nation of Quebec faces a crossroads it does not have the liberty to avoid. Will it continue, without reacting, to endure the tragic determinisms of its history since the Conquest? Or will it efficiently exploit the means it has at its disposal [the development of Quebec's state apparatus] in order to rise above these determinisms while it still has the capacity to do so?'[48]

Of the three neo-nationalist historians, Séguin was the one who gave these ideas the better part of their theoretical substance. In fact, both Brunet and Frégault would be influenced heavily by his ideas. Séguin, who had written his PhD thesis on French-Canadian agriculture between 1760 and 1850 under the supervision of Groulx himself, endeavoured in *Les normes* to demonstrate that a people who lost the control of its economic structures had essentially lost the capacity to choose its own destiny and was condemned to a mediocre existence at best. Such had been the case when New France was lost to the British, who, through the control they then exerted over the colony's commercial and, later, industrial development, confined the *Canadiens* to the countryside, where they were compelled to practise subsistence agriculture and to take refuge under the clergy's iron rule.[49] Unable to amass capital in any significant way, their transition to the industrial era once again would reduce them to a subordinate position in the global North American economy, this time as mere labourers in a system ruled by Anglo-Saxon capital (British, Canadian, and American). Lord Durham's predictions about the unavoidable economic marginalization of French Canada had proven correct: 'The Durham Report even foresaw the future: the *Canadiens* would abandon their quiet country lifestyle; the mass of the *Canadien* population was destined, to a certain degree, to hold an inferior position in Lower Canada's economy; the national distinction between the *Canadiens* and the British would coincide with the socio-economic distinction between classes, between workers and capitalists.'[50] For Séguin, the root of French Canada's economic inferiority was structural, not political, much less spiritual. It could be traced back to the Conquest, no amount of constitutional change ever having made even the slightest dent in the problem. What was needed, therefore, was a complete and radical reappropriation of French Canada's economic structures, a prospect about which Séguin himself was in fact quite pessimistic.

The constitutional and political victories Groulx had celebrated over the years appeared rather pathetic, in retrospect. But the elder scholar was not one to take this sort of criticism lying down. In Groulx's mind, historical pedagogy and the ability to make sense of a people's collective existence in order to better enlighten its path were central aspects of the historian's function. By depicting French Canadians' past in such a negative and uninspiring light, he feared his compatriots might succumb to discouragement and lose their willingness to roll up their sleeves and continue the struggle for autonomy. If French Canada had accomplished nothing of value over the past two hundred years, what was the point, then, of carrying on? By evacuating the metaphysical from their conceptual edifice, the young neo-nationalists, Groulx feared, also ran the risk of eliminating every good reason French Canadians had to place their hope in the future, for no obstacle, no matter how great, was impossible to overcome for a people who remained true to its providential calling.[51]

Groulx questioned his young disciples' ability to appreciate fully the 'ultimate consequences of their historical philosophy.'[52] He discussed the issue repeatedly with Michel Brunet, the historian among the three members of the Montreal school with whom he entertained the closest and most paternal relationship. In the late 1950s, Groulx worried that Brunet and Frégault had been too long under the harmful influence of Séguin, whom he described as 'pitifully repressed' and incapable of 'secreting anything but a fundamental and total pessimism.'[53] The Montreal school's interpretation of French-Canadian history was, in his view, severely limited by its unbending 'economic determinism.' By relying exclusively on an ostensibly 'scientific' and materialistic approach to the study of history, by eliminating from its conceptual edifice the very principles of providentialism and human voluntarism, it had done nothing more than replace the old traditionalist myths with new, far less inspiring ones.[54] Brunet, on the other hand, sought to defend his colleagues' ideas from his mentor's criticisms. History, as a discipline, needed to be purged of all 'romanticism' and 'messianism,' he wrote Groulx. Only then could it achieve an 'objective' and 'scientific' understanding of the French-Canadian situation as it truly was.[55] In the end, the (scientific) truth would set French Canada free. It seemed clear that there would be no bridging of the gap between Groulx and the new generation of nationalist historians.

The Montreal school's interpretation of French-Canadian history would have a tremendous impact not only in academic circles, but within the greater nationalist movement as well. If the source of the economic inferiority of French Canadians was essentially structural, if the Conquest had robbed them of the ability to control their own economic and political structures and, in the end, their own destiny, it is not difficult to understand how many, in a context dominated by Keynesian economics, might conclude that the only viable solution to the problem was to regain control through the formation of a strong – and independent – nation-state. The Quiet Revolution of the 1960s would see these ideas relayed by a large number of publications, intellectuals, and political parties – some much more radical than the Montreal school – who would give birth, collectively, to the modern sovereigntist movement, often by borrowing heavily from the anticolonial ideologies in wide circulation during the 1960s throughout the world. The marginalization of the Catholic Church as a structuring force for French-Canadian society, the rapid growth of the Quebec state and its substantial interventions in matters of economy, social welfare, culture, and language – all of these factors ultimately would transform French Canada's national identity, now defined as *Québécois*, even to the exclusion of French-Canadian minorities dispersed across the country.[56]

Groulx, for his part, rejoiced at the sudden surge of political and economic nationalism during the 1960s, though he was greatly disheartened by the relatively swift secularization of French-Canadian society that accompanied it.[57] His views on the Quiet Revolution were consistent with his judgment on the Montreal school's 'historical philosophy,' as he once put it. Was there nothing of value in all that had been accomplished by French Canadians since the Conquest? Was it wise for them to attempt to erase two full centuries of history from their collective memory simply because the dominant ideology had become hypercritical of Catholicism and traditionalism in all its forms? Did the younger generation of nationalist historians and intellectuals not see the danger of espousing a purely materialistic view of the past, devoid of the hope that faith in Providence could alone provide? By defining progress simply as the process of 'catching up,' economically, with Anglo-Saxon society and by forgoing the deeper spiritual realities that had given meaning to its existence and history, did the French-Canadian nation not ultimately run the risk of losing its soul, the one thing that made it unique and original in North America and even the world? Groulx was plagued by such questions in the final years of his life.

The conflict between Groulx and the Montreal school was deeply epistemological. The function of the historian, in the elder scholar's opinion, was not to denigrate his society's collective historical experience, as he believed the neo-nationalists were doing, but to uncover the true 'substance' of his nation's identity, a substance that could evolve and enrich itself over time, but whose defining characteristics would remain consistent.[58] Only then could a society achieve true progress – and true nationhood. So, with the same tenacity he had fought the Providential Conquest theory some forty years earlier, Groulx sought to repel his young disciples' materialistic and 'depressing' approach to French-Canadian history since 1760. He did so until the bitter end, which for him would come in 1967. This time, however, it was he who would suffer defeat: the materialistic paradigm would prove to be far too powerful to suppress, as the future of Quebec historiography – and, as he feared, Quebec society generally – would quickly demonstrate. But Groulx's contribution to Quebec's and French Canada's intellectual and political effervescence far exceeded this single issue. Indeed, his views on the catastrophic consequences of the Conquest would continue to nourish the nationalist movement throughout the Quiet Revolution and beyond.[59] Few intellectuals in Quebec have had such an impact.

NOTES

1 Groulx's appointment was at the Université Laval de Montréal, founded in 1876 as a branch of Quebec City's Université Laval. In 1919, it obtained a rescript from Pope Benedict XV granting it full autonomy, thus becoming the Université de Montréal.

2 See, for instance, Pascale Ryan, *Penser la nation: la Ligue d'action nationale, 1917–1960* (Montréal: Leméac, 2006); Michel Bock, 'Apogée et déclin du projet national groulxiste: quelques réflexions autour de *Directives* (1937),' in *1937: Un tournant culturel*, ed. Yvan Lamonde and Denis Saint-Jacques (Québec: Presses de l'Université Laval, 2009); Denis Chouinard, 'Des contestataires pragmatiques: les Jeune-Canada, 1932–1938,' *Revue d'histoire de l'Amérique française* 40, no. 1 (1986): 5–28; and Robert Comeau, 'Lionel Groulx, les indépendantistes de *La Nation* et le séparatisme (1936–1938),' *Revue d'histoire de l'Amérique française* 26, no. 1 (1972): 83–102.

3 Hubert, cited in Yvan Lamonde, *Histoire sociale des idées au Québec,* vol. 1, *1760–1896* (Montréal: Fides, 2000), 45.

4 'Quel bonheur pour nous que la Providence nous … ait détachés [de la France] avant qu'elle s'abandonnât à ce déplorable aveuglement [la Révolution], et nous ait soumis, par une bonté que nous ne méritions pas et que nous ne pouvons assez reconnaître, au Gouvernement libéral et bienfaisant, de Sa Tr. Gr. M. le Roi de la Grande-Bretagne … Ce généreux Empire a senti dès le commencement de la Révolution Française les suites funestes que pouvoient avoir les principes d'anarchie et de liberté mal entendue qui en faisoient la base'; Plessis, cited in Lionel Groulx, 'La Providence et la Conquête anglaise de la Nouvelle-France,' in *Notre maître, le passé*, vol. 3 (Montréal: Granger Frères, 1944), 139.

5 François-Xavier Garneau, *Histoire du Canada depuis sa découverte jusqu'à nos jours* (Québec: Imprimerie N. Aubin, 1845–52).

6 Ronald Rudin, *Making History in Twentieth Century Quebec* (Toronto: University of Toronto Press, 1997), 25–6. See also Serge Gagnon, *Le Québec et ses historiens de 1840 à 1920* (Québec: Presses de l'Université Laval, 1978).

7 Jean-Baptiste-Antoine Ferland, *Cours d'histoire du Canada* (Québec: A. Côté, 1861–5). For an excellent analysis of the diverging interpretations on the British Conquest in nineteenth-century French-Canadian intellectual circles, see Michel Ducharme, in this volume, as well as David Hayne, 'Conquête providentielle et révolution diabolique: une constante de la littérature québécoise du XIXe siècle,' in *La Révolution française au Canada français*, ed. Sylvain Simard (Ottawa: Presses de l'Université d'Ottawa, 1991).

8 'Les hautes sphères de notre société canadienne avaient besoin d'être purifiées par l'épreuve. Elles le furent. Le cataclysme qui coupa en deux notre histoire, s'il parut désastreux à nos pères, nous sauva de bien des déchéances. Et, par un dessein de miséricorde, le Dieu qui avait veillé sur notre berceau voulut que, même à l'heure où il nous envoyait la guerre, l'invasion et tout leur sinistre cortège, notre défaite et notre chute fussent illuminées d'un reflet de gloire qui rayonnât sur notre avenir. Montcalm fut le soldat qu'il suscita pour cette fin, et ses exploits, ses triomphes, aussi bien que sa mort au champ d'honneur, couronnèrent le trépas de la Nouvelle-France d'une auréole, qui continua de briller sur le Canada français orienté vers des destins nouveaux'; Thomas Chapais, *Le marquis de Montcalm, 1712–1759* (Québec: J.-P. Garneau, 1911), xi–xii.

9 'Une chose était frappée de mort: la domination française; une chose était menacée de mort: la nationalité française. La domination française avait vécu. Dans les conditions où se trouvait l'Europe à l'issue de la guerre de Sept [A]ns, rien ne pouvait faire concevoir la possibilité de sa résurrection. Nos destinées avaient fait un pas irrévocable. La Providence, qui gouverne les événements suivant de mystérieux desseins, avait décrété ce changement de souveraineté contre lequel nous ne pouvions nous insurger. Force nous était de nous adapter au régime nouveau. Cette adaptation constituait-elle vraiment pour nous une obligation très difficile? Non, Messieurs, nous devons le reconnaître si nous scrutons les réalités de la situation'; Thomas Chapais, *Cours d'histoire du Canada*, vol. 1 (1919; Trois-Rivières, QC: Boréal Express, 1972), 21.

10 'Non, de quelque côté que l'historien canadien-français et catholique envisage la question, il ne saurait amnistier les mouvements insurrectionnels de 1837 et de 1838'; Chapais, *Cours d'histoire du Canada*, vol. 4 (1923; Trois-Rivières, QC: Boréal Express, 1972), 229.

11 Chapais, *Cours d'histoire du Canada*, vol. 6 (1933; Trois-Rivières, QC: Boréal Express, 1972), 201–7.

12 '[L]e spectacle de l'inauguration, en 1867, d'une législature française, créée par un acte du parlement d'Angleterre, pour administrer librement une province française, formée de tout le territoire qui constituait jadis la partie principale de l'ancienne Nouvelle-France'; Chapais, *Cours d'histoire du Canada*, vol. 8 (1934; Trois-Rivières, QC: Boréal Express, 1972), 215.

13 Rudin, *Making History in Twentieth Century Quebec*, 39–40.

14 Lionel Groulx, *Mes mémoires*, vol. 3, *1926–1939* (Montréal: Fides, 1972), 175. For Groulx's 1937 speech, see idem, 'L'Histoire, gardienne des traditions vivantes,' in Groulx, *Directives* (Montréal: Zodiaque, 1937), 205–42. For an analysis of the 1937 controversy, see Bock, 'Apogée et déclin du projet national groulxiste,' 27–38.

15 Groulx, *Mes mémoires*, vol. 3, 175. Groulx's candidacy would also be supported by the Archivist of Canada, Arthur Doughty, but would ultimately be unsuccessful.

16 Lionel Groulx, 'M. Thomas Chapais,' *Liaison* 1, no. 1 (1947): 14.

17 'En ce domaine où le dogmatisme n'appartient qu'aux suffisants, il n'était pas si sûr de ses opinions qu'il ne les crût faillibles'; ibid., 12.

18 'La dirons-nous malheureusement chargée de toutes les déformations que les milieux politiques ont fait subir à l'auteur? Répétons-le: [Chapais] est de l'époque d'après la Confédération, époque où les politiciens tournent le dos au vieil idéal d'indépendance canadienne, pour céder au retour offensif de l'impérialisme anglais. Nulle part, plus que dans le Québec, pour se faire pardonner ses origines françaises, l'on ne se plaît aux professions de loyalisme. M. Thomas Chapais, homme politique, ne pouvait écrire qu'une histoire loyaliste'; ibid., 16.

19 'Pour tout dire, leur idéologie de clan nous a ramenés à l'enfance politique'; ibid., 15.

20 Lionel Groulx, *Mes mémoires*, vol. 4, *1940–1967* (Montréal: Fides, 1974), 162.

21 Ibid.

22 See Michel Bock, 'Se souvenir et oublier: la mémoire du Canada français, hier et aujourd'hui,' in *L'espace francophone en milieu minoritaire au Canada: nouveaux enjeux, nouvelles mobilisations*, ed. Joseph Yvon Thériault, Anne Gilbert, and Linda Cardinal (Montréal: Fides, 2008).

23 Arthur I. Silver, *The French Canadian Idea of Confederation, 1864–1900* (Toronto: University of Toronto Press, 1982).

24 See, for instance, Henri Bourassa, *Religion, langue, nationalité: discours prononcé à la séance de clôture du XXIe Congrès eucharistique à Montréal, le 10*

septembre 1910 (Montréal: Le Devoir, 1910); and idem, *Le Canada apostolique* (Montréal: Bibliothèque de l'Action française, 1919).

25 Lionel Groulx, *Dix ans d'Action française* (Montréal: Bibliothèque d'Action française, 1926), 201.

26 'L'universalité absolue de la Providence se déduit de l'universalité absolue de la causalité suprême. L'histoire est œuvre d'homme, d'homme libre, mais s'agitant sous la main de Dieu. La souveraineté de l'action divine n'enchaîne ni n'entame aucunement néanmoins les prérogatives de la liberté humaine. En rigoureuse vérité l'on peut dire d'un homme qu'il fait sa vie, et d'un peuple, qu'il fait son histoire. De même, dans le déroulement indéfini des événements humains, Dieu ne se relâche point des fins qui sont les siennes: fins de l'œuvre créatrice et rédemptrice. Fins ou exigences auxquelles tout se subordonne et qui peuvent porter loin l'intervention d'en haut'; Groulx, 'La Providence et la Conquête anglaise de la Nouvelle-France,' 125–6.

27 Ibid., 154–5.

28 Lionel Groulx, *La naissance d'une race* (Montréal: Bibliothèque de l'Action française, 1919).

29 Lionel Groulx, *Lendemains de conquête* (Montréal: Bibliothèque de l'Action française, 1920), 182–3.

30 'La conquête anglaise survint qui arrêta brusquement [la] croissance [de la nationalité canadienne-française]. Une secousse violente agita l'organisme de la jeune race. Quelques sources de sa vie s'en trouvèrent appauvries, d'autres entièrement taries. Dans la destinée de notre peuple, ce fut une courbe soudaine, une épreuve qui prit les proportions d'une catastrophe'; ibid., 13.

31 Ibid., 199.

32 Lionel Groulx, *Nos luttes constitutionnelles*, vol. 5, *Les Droits du français* (Montréal: Le Devoir, 1916), 5.

33 Lionel Groulx, *Nos luttes constitutionnelles*, 4 vols. (Montréal: Le Devoir, 1915–16); see also idem, *Histoire du Canada français depuis la découverte*, 4 vols. (Montréal: L'Action nationale, 1950–2).

34 Michel Bock, *Quand la nation débordait les frontiers: les minorités françaises dans la pensée de Lionel Groulx* (Montréal: Hurtubise HMH, 2004).

35 '[N]ous avons fait triompher le principe fédératif, nous avons obtenu la résurrection politique du Canada français'; Lionel Groulx, 'L'histoire gardienne des traditions vivantes,' in Groulx, *Directives*, 205–42. For an analysis of Groulx's involvement with the separatist movement during the inter-war years, see Bock, *Quand la nation débordait les frontières*, 297–343.

36 Frédéric Boily, *La pensée nationaliste de Lionel Groulx* (Sillery, QC: Septentrion, 2003), 90–8.

37 Arthur Maheux, *Ton histoire est une épopée* (Québec: Cherrier & Dugal, 1941).

38 Arthur Maheux, *Pourquoi sommes-nous divisés?* (Montréal: Radio-Canada, 1943); and Lionel Groulx, *Pourquoi nous sommes divisés* (Montréal: L'Action nationale, 1943).

39 Bock, *Quand la nation débordait les frontières*, 345–412. See also Michael D. Behiels, *Prelude to Quebec's Quiet Revolution: Liberalism versus Neo-Nationalism, 1945–1960* (Montreal; Kingston, ON: McGill-Queen's University Press, 1985).

40 Rudin, *Making History in Twentieth Century Quebec*, 129–70.

41 Charles-Philippe Courtois, *La Conquête: une anthologie* (Montréal: Typo, 2009), 378. See also Marcel Trudel, *Mythes et réalités dans l'histoire du Québec*, 4 vols. (Montréal: Hurtubise HMH, 2001–9).

42 Courtois, *Conquête*, 365–7. See also Jean Hamelin, *Économie et société en Nouvelle-France* (Ste-Foy, QC: Presses de l'Université Laval, 1960).

43 See Fernand Ouellet, *Histoire économique et sociale du Québec, 1760–1850* (Montréal: Fides, 1966).

44 Rudin, *Making History in Twentieth Century Quebec*, 129–70.

45 Guy Frégault, *La Guerre de la Conquête* (Montréal: Fides, 1955).

46 Michel Brunet, 'Trois dominantes de la pensée canadienne-française: l'agriculturisme, l'anti-étatisme et le messianisme,' in Brunet, *La Présence anglaise et les Canadiens* (Montréal: Beauchemin, 1958).

47 Michel Brunet, *Les Canadiens après la Conquête, 1759 à 1775: de la révolution canadienne à la révolution américaine* (Montréal: Fides, [1969]).

48 'La nation canadienne-française du Québec fait face à une échéance qu'elle n'a pas la liberté de reculer. Continuera-t-elle à subir presque sans réagir les tragiques déterminismes de son histoire depuis la Conquête? Ou saura-t-elle utiliser efficacement tous les moyens d'action dont elle dispose pour les dominer dans la mesure où elle en a encore la liberté?'; Brunet, 'Trois dominantes de la pensée canadienne-française,' 166.

49 *Les normes* would only be published in 1999, some fifteen years after Séguin's death; see Maurice Séguin, *Les normes de Maurice Séguin, le théoricien du néo-nationalisme* (Montréal: Guérin, 1999).

50 'Le *Rapport* [*Durham*] prévoit même l'avenir, les Canadiens devront abandonner leur quiétude paysanne; la masse de la population canadienne est vouée, dans une certaine mesure, à tenir une position inférieure dans l'économique du Bas-Canada; la distinction nationale entre Canadiens et Britanniques se confondra de plus en plus avec la distinction économico-

sociale entre classes, entre prolétaires et capitalistes'; Maurice Séguin, 'La Conquête et la vie économique des Canadiens,' *L'Action nationale* (1946), cited in Courtois, *La Conquête*, 402.

51 Bock, *Quand la nation débordait les frontières*, 345–412. See also Jean Lamarre, *Le devenir de la nation québécoise selon Maurice Séguin, Guy Frégault et Michel Brunet, 1944–1969* (Sillery, QC: Septentrion, 1993).

52 '[L]es ultimes conséquences de [leur] philosophie d'histoire'; Lionel Groulx, letter to François-Albert Angers, 8 December 1958, cited in Bock, *Quand la nation débordait les frontières*, 363.

53 '[P]auvre refoulé qui ne pourra jamais secréter qu'un pessimisme foncier et total'; Lionel Groulx, letter to Michel Brunet, 2 August 1957, cited in ibid., 366.

54 Lionel Groulx, letter to Michel Brunet, 23 December 1958, cited in ibid., 366–7.

55 Michel Brunet, letters to Lionel Groulx, 18 May 1955 and 3 August 1957, cited in ibid., 365–6.

56 Ibid., 345–412.

57 See Lionel Groulx, *Chemins de l'avenir* (Montréal: Fides, 1964).

58 Lionel Groulx, 'L'Histoire, gardienne des traditions vivantes,' in Groulx, *Directives*, 208–9.

59 It must be noted, however, that, as of the 1960s, support for the Conquest-as-catastrophe theory would come not from academic circles, but from polemical ones, as Brian Young and Alexis Lachaine demonstrate in their respective contributions to this volume. Ronald Rudin has argued that many of the professional (or 'revisionist') historians of the following decades tended to relinquish the field of 'national history' to historical popularizers, of which Denis Vaugeois might be considered a fine example. The 'revisionists' consequently would focus their efforts on proving that Quebec, from a social and economic perspective, had always been a 'normal' society, as modern as any other in North America. In this new narrative, the Conquest was no longer seen as the pivotal event in Quebec history that crippled its subsequent development. The memory of 1759 thus would be kept alive elsewhere than within the walls of the academy. See Rudin, *Making History in Twentieth Century Quebec*, 171–218; and idem, 'L'historien professionnel et le grand public: réflexions québécoises alimentées par l'expérience irlandaise,' in *Les idées mènent le Québec*, ed. Stéphane Kelly (Québec: Presses de l'Université Laval, 2003).

8

Intervening with *abandon*: The Conquest's Legacy in the Canada-Quebec-France Triangle of the 1960s

DAVID MEREN

As Nicole Neatby explores in her contribution to this volume, the controversy surrounding the two hundred and fiftieth anniversary of the Battle of the Plains of Abraham was a dramatic reminder of how the Conquest – or, more accurately, the historical memory of the Conquest – continues to resonate in Quebec and the rest of Canada, and the ease with which this memory can lend itself to dissension. The media storm that arose when the militant pro-independence group the Réseau de Résistance du Québécois threatened to disrupt a re-enactment of the battle led the National Battlefields Commission to cancel the event. The winds of disagreement blew just as fiercely over the *Moulin à paroles* that was organized in place of the re-enactment, stemming in part from the fact that sovereigntist elements were linked closely to the event, and more immediately because of the recitation of the manifesto of the Front de libération du Québec (FLQ).[1]

These linked disputes demonstrated how the Conquest serves as a foundational myth, the pivot around which revolves a specific narrative of Quebec history, and one occupying a central place in the public mind, as is revealed in Brian Young's discussion of the work of Jacques Lacoursière and Denis Vaugeois. In this narrative, North America's francophone population, notably that of Quebec, is depicted as a tragic hero, one boasting the bittersweet virtue of having been conquered. Fate has accorded this population the historical mission of transcending this defeat through the achievement of independence; until this objective is realized, it is the population's duty to recall earlier failed attempts to do so – including remembering those forces and figures alleged to have contributed to these replicated defeats and reinforced conquest. By staging a performance of the key texts in Quebec history from the two and a half centuries preceding and following the battle of the Plains of Abraham, the *Moulin à paroles* was designed to highlight the intellectual and political sedimentation that has accumulated on the historical bedrock that is the Conquest.

While it was the reading of the FLQ manifesto that grabbed the lion's share of headlines in both the anglophone and francophone press, the *Globe and Mail* also noted reprovingly the recitation of the remarks – especially 'Vive le Québec libre' – that Charles de Gaulle delivered from the balcony of Montreal's city hall in July 1967.[2] It was fitting that the events of 1967 should have been included in the commemoration, in 2009, of events that took place in 1759. The linking of these three moments in time is consistent with Jocelyn Létourneau's observation that 'narrative is not only a consubstantial element of the factuality of action, but also its effective fulfillment,' so that '1759 is the inseparable sum of what has been and what has been said of it in the past and present.'[3] The French president's visit and the developments preceding it in the Canada-Quebec-France triangle had been informed by the narrative of the Conquest and its consequences. And, through his actions, de Gaulle added another layer to this narrative. This becomes apparent when the events of the 1960s are examined through the prism of the Conquest and the idea of *abandon*: the notion that France abandoned its New World outpost and its population. The long-term geopolitical and cultural consequences arising from this abandonment figured prominently in the emergence of the special relationship between Paris and Quebec City.

In the little over two decades between the end of the Second World War and de Gaulle's visit, a complex triangular dynamic had emerged between France, Quebec, and Canada. The acceleration of interdependence and transnational exchanges under the auspices of preponderant American power in the West, and the intersection of this global trend with domestic circumstances on both sides of the Atlantic, contributed to the rise to power of Quebec neo-nationalism and the Gaullist variant of French nationalism. This development was paralleled by a growing rapprochement between France and Quebec. Anticipated by the proliferation of cultural and economic exchanges in the private sphere, links of an increasingly official nature multiplied between Paris and Quebec City following the establishment of the Fifth Republic and the election of the Lesage government in Quebec. Gaullism and Quebec neo-nationalism aligned to challenge fundamental assumptions and objectives of pan-Canadian nationalism. The dynamic was equally true in reverse, so that the growth of relations in the triangle was accompanied by that

of suspicion, tension, and confrontation. The burgeoning special relationship between Paris and Quebec City presented a dilemma for Ottawa, one that became more and more complicated as Paris adopted an
increasingly overt two-nation stance that favoured Quebec and marginalized federal authority. In an immediate sense, the shift in Paris's
approach stemmed from a growing French consensus that the Quiet
Revolution necessitated fundamental changes to the Canadian political
order, ranging from a reformed federalism to independence for Quebec. Gaullist France's 'Quebec policy' and the triangular tensions that
flowed from it were equally attributable, however, to geopolitical and
ethnocultural motivations that could be traced to the Conquest and its
consequences.[4]

   To a significant extent, Paris's actions were a bid to contest the geopolitical legacy of the events of 1759 – namely, the rise to global predominance, in their turn, of Britain and the United States. To be sure,
there had existed a great deal of ambivalence in France about its North
American outpost. The colony faced the antipathy that some people
in France reserved for the Americas and colonialism.[5] Voltaire would
most famously express such sentiment at the height of the Seven Years'
War when he dismissed New France as a few acres of snow.[6] A greater
French appreciation of North America's geopolitical significance was
apparent in the century that followed the Treaty of Paris (1763), which
saw France cede virtually all of its North American possessions to Britain, opting to retain what at the time were the more valuable possessions of Guadeloupe and Martinique. As the treaty was being drafted,
Louis XV's chief minister, Étienne François, duc de Choiseul, had con-
soled himself and his compatriots over the cession of New France with
the prediction that Britain's acquisition of the colony ultimately would
serve French interests in the longer term by sowing the seeds of revolt
in the thirteen colonies. When this occurred, Louis XVI came to the material and moral aid of the American revolutionaries in a bid to thwart
a British rival that had seen its international position enhanced by the
Conquest. Decades later, Napoleon III, profiting from the United States'
Civil War, launched his ill-fated intervention in Mexico, hoping to hem
in the rising American power by extending the Second Empire's global
reach to Latin America. By the mid-twentieth century, the Conquest's
geopolitical legacy was all too apparent: in the wake of the Second
World War, France was forced to grapple with its diminished international standing and manage what would prove to be a tempestuous
relationship with the new American superpower.

France's geopolitical dilemma was not wholly dissimilar from that of its former North American outpost – Canada also had to come to terms with the United States' enhanced geopolitical weight. Ottawa's and Paris's responses to Cold War realities, not least preponderant American power, shaped their post-war relationship. For a time, the fact that the two capitals shared an Atlanticist foreign policy response to the global situation, reflected in their common membership in the North Atlantic Treaty Organization (NATO), facilitated more substantive relations. However, the two capitals viewed the Cold War through different prisms, conditioned by diverging interpretations of the nature and organization of the international system, different histories, and the respective places Canada and France occupied on the world stage. Ottawa and Paris thus embraced Atlanticism with different expectations, and by the mid-1950s the discrepancy between the Canadian and French understandings of this foreign policy response made it a growing source of bilateral discord. Paris, wrestling with the twin challenges of a reduced international stature and decolonization, chafed under Atlanticism's constraints. It resented the realities of a NATO alliance perceived increasingly as a thorn in the side of French interests. Such frustration fuelled an increasingly nationalist foreign policy and, exacerbated by the quagmire of the Algerian Revolution, culminated in the collapse of the Fourth Republic and de Gaulle's return to power.

The general had observed ruefully in 1944 that the United States was 'already trying to rule the world.'[7] Nothing had occurred in the intervening years to disabuse him of that notion. Despite repeated French efforts since its inception, NATO had not assured Paris the equal strategic partnership with Washington and London that it desired. Strikingly evident in the dying days of the Fourth Republic, French dissatisfaction with the transatlantic alliance and the preponderant Anglo-American influence in it only increased following the birth of the Fifth. De Gaulle scorned the Fourth Republic's Atlanticism as having subjected France 'to the hegemony of the Anglo-Saxons.'[8] Returned to office, he strove to end France's second-tier status in the strategic direction of the West; although France would continue to confront the Soviet threat alongside the United States and the NATO allies, the foremost Gaullist aim was to ensure that France recovered its rightful geopolitical rank while increasing its autonomy from and influence with Washington.[9] The Franco-American differences that arose from these efforts were reflected in the rival 'Grand Designs' that Paris and Washington proposed for the transatlantic relationship.[10]

The shifting French position presented Ottawa with a dilemma. Nationalist concern in Canada over the country's thickening web of links with the United States had grown parallel to the declining importance of relations with Britain and the Commonwealth after 1945. Ottawa continued to consider Atlanticism the most effective response to the country's asymmetrical relationship with Washington and the best means to maximize Canada's ebbing international influence. As the Gaullist storm broke, Ottawa tied itself to the mast of Atlanticism, striving to reconcile France and NATO in an attempt to preserve the transatlantic framework that provided Canada with a crucial counterweight to American power. Added to this was a domestic motivation that would grow in prominence throughout the 1960s: it was believed that strengthening relations with France for Atlanticist ends would also have the salutary benefit of responding to Quebec nationalist charges that Canadian foreign policy inadequately addressed French Canada's need for relations with the francophone world.[11]

The Pearson government was thus strongly compelled to respond to the Gaullist challenge to Atlanticism. Aware of Franco-American differences, the secretary of state for external affairs, Paul Martin, told France's ambassador in mid-1963 that Ottawa was examining how it could help reactivate the dialogue between Paris and Washington.[12] Martin claimed repeatedly in conversations with his international counterparts that Canada, by virtue of its bicultural heritage and historic links to France, was well positioned to improve the climate between Paris and Washington, as well as the rest of NATO.[13] When Lester Pearson visited France in 1964, he emphasized the importance of the Atlanticist framework to Canada and urged French understanding of American global responsibilities. In talks with de Gaulle, he acknowledged the closeness of Canada's relations with Washington, and cited this as the reason for the high priority that Ottawa assigned to strong transatlantic links.[14]

The Canadian assessment of Pearson's visit was positive, feeding a hope that it was the beginning of more substantive Franco-Canadian relations.[15] This was wishful thinking. If a common NATO membership had previously provided opportunities for bilateral contact and cooperation, the differing post-war experiences of Canada and France meant that by the 1960s Atlanticism had evolved into a source of divergence, hollowing out the bilateral relationship. Canadian efforts to develop relations with France and to act as a transatlantic linchpin were suspect in Gaullist eyes, which had turned to Canada (and elsewhere) as Washington thwarted Paris's bid for a French-led Western Europe in strategic partnership with the United States. Ottawa's efforts on behalf of Atlanticism only confirmed a French conviction that Canada had become the servant of American geopolitical interests. Indeed, tellingly for French perceptions, the 1963 federal election that had brought the Pearson government to power was the first vote in Canadian history in which the side championing the anti-American position had failed to carry the day.[16] Notwithstanding the fact that domestic considerations loomed increasingly large in Ottawa's quest for strong links with France, within months of the Pearson government's election, French officials were interpreting its overtures as inspired primarily by Atlanticist considerations, and thus proof of Canada's satellization.[17]

The French assessment of Canada's geopolitical situation surfaced when Pearson went to Paris. The Canadian embassy sensed a French 'assumption' during the visit that Ottawa's policies were shaped primarily by its relations with Washington.[18] In referring to the Quiet Revolution, France's prime minister, Georges Pompidou, told his Canadian counterpart that rather than any question of unity, the real challenge that Canada faced was maintaining its independence and distinctiveness from the United States.[19] Pierre Trottier, the embassy's cultural counsellor, claimed subsequently that de Gaulle had tested Pearson during his stay in the French capital, dangling the prospect of Paris's cooperation in exchange for undertaking to move Canada out of the American geopolitical orbit. Pearson did not rise to the bait, however, and thereby reinforced the Gaullist analysis.[20]

The Franco-Canadian divergence was fundamental. The more Paris challenged the Atlanticist framework and the more Franco-Canadian relations deteriorated, the more Ottawa strove to forge links with Paris. Ultimately, however, the circle could not be squared between the Canadian aim to help resolve the divisions plaguing the transatlantic alliance, and Paris's determination to provoke fundamental change. The dynamic was all too apparent to Canada's ambassador, Jules Léger, who questioned the wisdom of Ottawa's dogged attempts to reconcile Paris to NATO.[21] He emphasized that de Gaulle dismissed the notion that Ottawa was well placed to act as a linchpin; rather, the general was attracted to Canada to the extent that its foreign policy asserted independence from Washington.[22]

Ottawa's exertions on behalf of reconciling Paris to Atlanticism came to naught in March 1966 when de Gaulle announced that France was withdrawing from NATO's integrated military command and that allied forces would be asked to leave French territory. For want of any viable alternative and mindful of the need for Paris's benevolence amid Canada's deepening unity crisis, Ottawa's impulse for conciliation endured. Paul Martin argued well into 1967 that Ottawa should act as a 'helpful fixer' in the multilateral sphere in order to convince Paris of the benefits that flowed from good relations with Canada.[23] The minister, however, had matters upside-down; instead of strengthening the Canadian position, Ottawa's conciliatory approach reinforced the Gaullist conviction regarding Canada's satellization and thus exacerbated the Franco-Canadian divergence.

Differences in the multilateral sphere spilled into the bilateral domain. Confronted with a Canada it viewed as firmly ensconced in the Anglo-Saxon world and an American satellite, Gaullist France was encouraged to establish direct, privileged relations with Quebec. Attributing Canada's geopolitical situation to its anglophone-dominated federal state, de Gaulle sought to provoke a fundamental change to the Canadian political order. Brought about with French assistance, a sovereign Quebec partnered with the rest of Canada would ensure the independence of the 'Canadas' in a new entity better able to resist American pressures and serve as a useful French ally by counterbalancing the United States on the North American continent.[24] While one could argue (and it certainly was on both sides of the Atlantic) that the Gaullist approach failed to recognize that a collapse of the Canadian federation would enhance American geopolitical strength, to de Gaulle's eyes the status quo was already producing this result, and therefore intervention was justified.[25]

The general's analysis was by no means idiosyncratic: throughout the post-war period French observers had recognized Quebec's significance to Canada's independence, and the geopolitical dimension of Gaullist France's Quebec policy was anticipated in a report prepared by members of the French National Assembly who visited Canada in 1963. The deputies concluded that a renewed French Canada was the surest safeguard of Canadian autonomy, one that would permit Canada to realize its mission as a linchpin between North America and Europe.[26] Even such a prominent critic of de Gaulle as Claude Julien recognized Canada's geopolitical significance. Decrying Europe's lack of appreciation of the country's importance, the Le Monde journalist argued that European independence was at stake in Canadian efforts to resist the American geopolitical pull. Invoking the memory of the Conquest, Julien warned that the loss of Canada's economic potential to the United

States would be a defeat with ramifications far in excess of that which France had experienced on the Plains of Abraham.[27]

Geopolitical calculations stemming from the legacy of the Conquest thus figured prominently in de Gaulle's visit in July 1967. One of his biographers, Jean Lacouture, argues that the French leader's speech at the banquet hosted by Premier Daniel Johnson in Quebec City was in a sense more provocative than his Montreal remarks in that he called not only for Quebec self-determination, but for Canada as a whole to free itself from American tutelage. Not only was Quebec to be sovereign, but in saving itself (with French assistance), it would save the rest of Canada from the American embrace.[28] Indeed, the official account of the visit that the Quai d'Orsay sent to French diplomatic posts around the world explained that the actions of France's president had been intended to underline that Quebec's ferment would result in a new political order that would ensure a better 'general equilibrium' on the North American continent.[29] One Gaullist baron, Michel Debré, echoed this idea in describing the *cri du balcon* as 'a warning against U.S. hegemony over Quebec, the rest of Canada, and indeed much of the rest of the globe.'[30] De Gaulle subsequently told one of his closest advisors that Quebec would one day become a 'great power,' making it crucial that France have 'a foothold over there.'[31] If de Gaulle did not expect to reverse Montcalm's defeat, he did hope to mitigate its geopolitical legacy as much as possible for the francophone populations on both sides of the Atlantic.

Quebec's prominence in Gaullist geopolitical manoeuvrings draws attention to the ethnocultural dimension of the special relationship between France and Quebec. Cultural exchanges between France and French Canada were never completely severed after the Conquest, and these reflected an array of political and ideological positions. Quebec's traditional nationalist elites, for example, distinguished between *France éternelle* and *France moderne*, favouring the former pre-1789 incarnation as an ally in maintaining French Canada's religious and linguistic specificity, and condemning the latter as a Trojan horse for liberal secularism.[32] Regardless of whether contacts boasted a more traditional or liberal hue, however, they were infused with a French-Canadian ambivalence that arose in large measure from the notion of the *abandon* of 1763 and, more broadly, the Conquest's cultural and political ramifications.[33]

The dynamic was apparent, for example, in the traditional nationalist antipathy for *France moderne* that informed a view of the Conquest as a providential blessing. As Michel Ducharme and Michel Bock set out in their respective chapters in this volume, the loss on the Plains of Abraham in this telling had meant that Quebec was sheltered from the French Revolution's secularizing upheaval.[34] Similarly indicative of the complex Quebec attitudes regarding France was the intellectual evolution of the neo-nationalist historian Guy Frégault. Writing in the 1930s, Frégault expressed the desire to see French Canada be active in the 'vital structures of the French nation,' and to see restored 'the sense of close contact and fraternal harmony with the rest of the French nation that it had lost.' Frégault claimed French Canada had suffered horribly as a result of the 'brutal separation' of the Conquest.[35] Notwithstanding his claims to francophilia, however, Frégault became increasingly harsh in his criticism of France's management of its North American territories, taking it to task for abandoning the *Canadiens*.[36] Frégault's colleague at the Université de Montréal, Michel Brunet, was similarly hostile, once making public remarks about France that were considered so antagonistic that the university's rector felt obliged to invite Paris's ambassador to deliver a speech as a compensation.[37] The resentment linked to the notion of *abandon* that some French Canadians harboured for France was perhaps most colourfully revealed when de Gaulle visited Canada in 1960: at a wreath-laying ceremony in Quebec City, the band had scarcely finished performing the national anthems when the Quebec lieutenant-governor's aide-de-camp turned to de Gaulle's and, through clenched teeth, declared 'and thus, you damned French abandoned us.'[38]

Notwithstanding the complex Quebec attitudes about France, there was a growth and evolution of cultural relations between France and francophone Quebec in the fifteen years after the Second World War. Consistent with broader developments in the province, links of a more traditional and conservative nature declined in importance relative to those of a more secular and liberal orientation. Moreover, the global trend towards increased transnational exchanges, of which the expanded Franco-Canadian cultural contact was but one example, also carried with it a more defensive impetus that reinforced the desire to develop links. Amid the eclipse of traditional French-Canadian nationalism, concerns grew that the socio-economic changes in Quebec were promoting anglophone cultural influences, notably those of the United States. Concerns about French Canada's cultural survival provoked calls from the rising generation of Quebec neo-nationalists for a more activist Quebec state that would forge links with France.[39]

Indeed, the acceleration, under the aegis of American predominance, of what is referred to today as globalization, contributed to crises of national identities on both sides of the Atlantic. The evolving Quebec interest in France coincided with a reinforced French cultural diplomacy. A French anti-Americanism that had been evident well before the Second World War and crossed the country's deep political divides underpinned the determination of the political class and intelligentsia after 1945 to ensure France's cultural *rayonnement* – its radiance – at home and abroad in the face of the United States' cultural power.[40] Such American influences appeared all the more problematic to a France still nursing the deep wounds that the war years had inflicted on the body politic and that sought a restored sense of identity and renewed sense of purpose through its cultural life.[41] French preoccupations extended to Canada and, specifically, to Quebec's *francité* – its 'Frenchness.' Paris's concerns about French Canada's survival might not have been new, but the manner in which these were manifested was transformed after Gaullist nationalism arrived in office. Quebec neo-nationalism, and efforts to equip the Quebec government to serve as the political expression of the French-Canadian nation and as protector and promoter of North America's *fait français* – its French fact – found an enthusiastic partner across the Atlantic. Paris increasingly favoured Quebec City, viewing it as the seat of the only viable national entity that, with French help, could resist American cultural power.

If French notions of nationhood historically have been predominantly *political* in orientation, they also have been marked by efforts to achieve *cultural* unity; moreover, the ethnocultural dimension has at times overshadowed civic and political attributes.[42] Gary Wilder argues in his exploration of French imperialism and its relationship to questions of national identity that one can view the post-1789 history of the French nation-state as a series of crises linked to questions of membership in a claimed universalism.[43] Wilder's analysis highlights how, notwithstanding claims to civic-political notions of nationalism and identity, the very efforts to achieve these carry in them an ethnocultural content. Hence, the value placed on any *a priori* understanding of national identity has the potential to lend itself to a chauvinistic and more ethnocultural strain of nationalism. It is thus not surprising that, as France's multi-ethnic empire dissolved and amid heightened French sensitivities regarding Americanization, the ethnocultural dimension of French identity took on greater salience, and that there should have been an increased appreciation of *French* Canada.

Indeed, despite the assertions of Quebec figures regarding French Canada's distinctiveness from France, de Gaulle tended to view French

Canadians as a branch of the French nation.[44] When Jules Léger presented his credentials as Canada's ambassador in 1964, the general declared provocatively that France was present in Canada by virtue of the
fact that numerous Canadians were of French blood, language, culture,
and thought, and were essentially French in all areas except their sovereignty.[45] De Gaulle also interrupted a French cabinet discussion of
Quebec to insist that, rather than 'francophone' and 'anglophone,' the
terms 'French' and 'English' be used to refer to Canada's two principal
linguistic communities.[46] In the months preceding the 1967 visit, the
Elysée's diplomatic counsellor explained to a senior Canadian diplo-
mat that French Canadians were 'of course' Canadians, but they were
also 'former Frenchmen,' thus making them for France's president a
'very special case' to which 'normal rules [did] not apply.'[47]

There were, however, French acknowledgments of Quebec's 'American' dimension. A French foreign ministry report explained that, amid
the budding special relationship, Paris had to remain mindful of Quebec's Canadian and North American character, and recognize that
France and Quebec had followed separate historical paths since the
Conquest.[48] André Malraux, France's minister of culture, came away
from a visit to Canada in 1963 with the view that neither Quebec *indépendantistes* nor the general population were anti-American; rather,
they were anti-English-Canadian, wanting to see francophones own
Montreal's skyscrapers.[49]

Yet such awareness of the North American aspect of Quebec realities fuelled French fears that the United States' growing influence in
the province constituted a threat to the 'French' component of its identity.[50] Such fears had been growing throughout the post-war period;
by the close of the 1940s, France's consulate general in Quebec City
was linking the rapid changes in French-Canadian life to the expanding American presence, observing ruefully that, after two centuries of
resisting the Anglo-Saxon influence represented by Britain, Quebec appeared to be rapidly embracing that of the United States.[51] Members of
the French National Assembly's foreign affairs committee who visited
in the early 1960s pronounced it France's national interest and duty as
a 'sister nation' to intensify economic and cultural links with Canada
– specifically Quebec – to protect it from falling irretrievably into the
American orbit.[52] Georges Pompidou told Jean Chapdelaine, the Quebec government's representative in Paris, that he was concerned about
Quebec's ability to maintain its identity in the face of 'the American
colossus.'[53]

Developments in Quebec were regarded in French intellectual circles as having a special relevance for France. Jean-Marie Domenach, editor of the review *Esprit*, argued that Quebec was a testament to American civilization's assimilatory capacity and, as a consequence, to the tremendous challenge of maintaining a distinct political and socio-economic system while embracing the American way of life.[54] Joffre Dumazedier declared that the very future of France's culture, society, and economy was at play in Quebec's 'feverish revolt' against the Anglo-Americans. The French sociologist, who had spent time at the Université de Montréal, expressed the hope that Quebec could invent 'a second America, an America of French culture where the values of justice, liberty, truth, and beauty would be better incarnated in communal and individual daily life.'[55]

Most significant to the triangular tensions were the efforts of the 'Quebec lobby,' a group of French politicians, civil servants, and other personalities. If members of this informal group differed in terms of ideological and political affiliations, and were not even entirely agreed over the ideal political status for Quebec, they did share a nationalist-inspired concern for the international *rayonnement* of French culture, and were thus predisposed to sympathize with Quebec neo-nationalism. Lobby members conflated the promotion of North America's *fait français* with French national interests – cultural and otherwise.[56] Encouraged by a *'francolâtre'* (an excessive love of France) and motivated by a nationalism influenced by an anti-American discourse that dated to the nineteenth century and posited a global struggle between the Anglo-Saxon and Latin races, Quebec lobby members displayed a predilection to imagine Quebec as part of a transatlantic French community. At the same time, they were less inclined to acknowledge its Canadian and North American components.[57]

André Malraux's visit in 1963 reflected the official significance Paris attached to relations with Quebec and the *épanouissement* – the flowering – of North America's francophone population. In improvised remarks in Montreal, he claimed that nowhere else in the world was French energy on display as much as it was in Quebec, and declared triumphantly that 'we will build the next civilization together!'[58] Malraux's call to arms was one example of the multiplying references to a cultural solidarity between the francophone populations on either side of the Atlantic in the face of American cultural power.

The most dramatic manifestation of this notion of cultural solidarity was, of course, de Gaulle's 1967 visit. On the eve of the general's arrival, Daniel Johnson predicted it would signal to the world that 'we exist, and we are no longer alone.'[59] Here was to be the acknowledgment, from one of the most prominent figures in French history, of the cultural resistance that the descendants of New France's *habitants* had waged for two centuries, a declaration of fraternal support to compensate for what was condemned in certain French-Canadian quarters as decade after decade of official indifference and neglect. Indeed, France's leader was determined to use the occasion not only to recognize and laud French Canadians, but also to highlight the links uniting his country and Quebec. De Gaulle's remarks during his stay, not least his speech from the city hall of 'the *French* city of Montreal' were replete with references to cultural solidarity, going so far as to intimate French-Canadian membership in a transatlantic French collectivity that was acting to counter American cultural power around the globe.[60] On the last day of his visit, after acknowledging their differing circumstances, de Gaulle affirmed that the tasks before the 'Français de Canada' and the 'Français de France' were bound inextricably together and derived from a common inspiration.[61] The Quai d'Orsay's account of the visit cited the rapturous welcome that the population had accorded the French leader, not least the crowds' enthusiastic renditions of *La Marseillaise*. The negative federal reaction, meanwhile, was ascribed to Ottawa's acting under pressure from 'British Canadians.' The account concluded by emphasizing the importance of assisting the Johnson government in its efforts to ensure the progress of North America's 'French nation.'[62]

Relations in the Canada-Quebec-France triangle had evolved significantly from the early 1950s, when one of de Gaulle's predecessors, Vincent Auriol, had enquired of Canada's ambassador whether it would offend Ottawa if, during his upcoming visit, he were to give Prime Minister Louis St Laurent a book on the coronation of Louis XV, as it had been published when Quebec was still a French colony.[63] Indeed, the ethnocultural dimension of de Gaulle's 1967 visit underscored how events were being influenced by the historical memory of the Conquest and its legacy. The French anti-Americanism encouraging the Gaullist intervention had been informed in part by a romanticized view of pre-Conquest North America, one consistent with a worldview emphasizing the historical struggle between France and the 'Anglo-Saxons.' Writing in the 1880s about the United States, for example, Frédéric Gaillardet alluded to an era of pastoral harmony between the colonists of New France and North America's aboriginal population. In *L'Aristocratie en Amérique*, he grouped together Acadians and aboriginal peoples as victims, each in their turn, of the rapacious Britain and United States. Anticipating the words of Dumazedier by eight decades, Gaillardet portrayed New France and Acadia as an alternate America, a better America, one that had been brought to a tragic end by the outcome of the Seven Years' War.[64]

A number of anniversaries took place in the lead-up to the *cri du balcon*. In addition to the bicentenaries of the Acadian deportation, the Conquest, and the Treaty of Paris, there was the centennial of Confederation. When Ottawa requested a congratulatory message from de Gaulle that could be broadcast at the outset of Canada's centennial year, the *Amérique* division of France's foreign ministry recommended that the content be carefully weighted to ensure that it maintained a strict neutrality regarding the British North America Act.[65] De Gaulle rejected even this, however, declaring that France had no reason to celebrate the incorporation of 'a part of the French people' into a British entity that was the product of a French defeat.[66] Indeed, consistent with de Gaulle's antipathy for the political consequences that had flowed from the Conquest and his determination to give a boost to the cause of Quebec nationalism, drafts of the speeches prepared for the French leader to deliver in Ottawa reveal that, had this portion of his visit been realized, he would have made no mention of Confederation's anniversary.[67]

The general's attitude regarding the centennial pointed to his keen sense of history. This had been inculcated by his grandfather, a historian, and his father, who was a professor. During his schooling, de Gaulle demonstrated a particular interest in the eighteenth century; writing a paper in 1913 on the theme of 'patriotism,' he ranked Louis-Joseph de Montcalm alongside the heroes of the Hundred Years' War, Jeanne d'Arc and Bertrand du Guesclin.[68] De Gaulle's decision was consistent with the rehabilitation Montcalm's reputation had undergone in France in the late nineteenth century, as Michel Ducharme discusses in his contribution to this volume. As Jean Lacouture argues, de Gaulle, by virtue of his worldview and sense of history, was compelled to take action on behalf of a 'fragment of the French people ... that had survived in a pure state from the centuries of the Valois and Bourbons.'[69]

Adding to this burden of the past was, of course, de Gaulle's sense of his own place in it. The general conceived of himself as one of the mythical actors of French history – Stéphane Monclaire has emphasized how Charles the man acted in accordance with the dictates of de Gaulle the historical figure.[70] At the time of the Liberation, de Gaulle had felt himself 'an instrument of fate'; as he prepared for his 1967 visit, so, too, did he see himself as history's agent, repaying the debt of Louis XV and atoning for France's having abandoned the colonists of New France to their fate. Such a legacy surely had to take on greater resonance in the mind of someone who, notwithstanding his disdain for the advocates of *Algérie française*, had just overseen France's withdrawal from Algeria. Before leaving for Quebec, de Gaulle confided to his son-in-law that it was the 'last chance to rectify the cowardice of France.'[71] It was similarly telling of the French leader's state of mind that, in the wake of the dramatic events that followed, he asserted to one of his advisors that had he not acted he 'no longer would have been de Gaulle.'[72]

Gaullism has been described as being at least as much an emotion as an ideology,[73] and so it was fitting that the general's triumphal tour up Quebec's North Shore was bathed in historical and cultural symbolism. De Gaulle had played a significant personal role in its planning. It originally had been suggested that, instead of travelling the chemin du Roy, the highway linking Quebec City and Montreal that dated to the 1730s, he would sail up the St Lawrence at night, past bonfires of greeting on the riverside. But such an arrangement was impractical given the width of the river; moreover, it meant he would be denied the direct contact he desired with the population. Matters were quickly put right. The arrival of France's head of state recalled the route that French explorers and colonists had taken in past centuries; after stopping at St-Pierre-et-Miquelon, the last vestiges of France's North American territory, de Gaulle arrived in Quebec City on the naval cruiser *Colbert*, named for the French minister who had played a pivotal role in New France's development. His point of disembarkation was wholly appropriate to the task he had set himself: L'Anse au Foulon, the cove where British forces had landed before scaling the cliffs to reach the Plains of Abraham. Triumphal arches and flags abounded along the route that took de Gaulle to Montreal, *fleurs-de-lys* were painted on the pavement at two-metre intervals, and villages were designated to represent various regions of France. The Johnson government declared a public holiday, and buses were arranged to bring the population into communion with France's leader.[74] Michel Hébert and Lyse Roy have gone so far as to compare the ceremonial aspects of the visit to those of receptions granted *ancien régime* monarchs.[75]

De Gaulle's visit was an occasion for the vaunting and celebration of links between France and Quebec. It was indicative of the significance of de Gaulle's visit, as well as the resonance of the Conquest in Quebec historical memory, that prominent conservative nationalist François-

Albert Angers was moved at the time to rank the general's 'Vive le Québec libre!' alongside Quebec's founding and the Conquest as one of the three most important dates in French-Canadian history.[76] At the opposite end of Quebec nationalism's ideological spectrum, *indépendantiste* Pierre Bourgault was pleasantly astonished at what he described as Quebecers' enthusiastic demonstration of their *francité* during the visit, claiming that 'despite their history, despite the English, despite the notables, and alas, despite us, the Québécois had stayed French. I could not get over it. This people had no need to be told to assert their French pride to the entire world. They had an overwhelming desire to demonstrate this, and they did so.'[77] His fellow *indépendantiste*, Reggie Chartrand, claimed that de Gaulle had filled with joy the heart of 'a French nation in North America' that too often had been humiliated and hidden from view. Chartrand's Chevaliers de l'indépendance subsequently released a communiqué in support of de Gaulle, declaring that French Canadians were thankful for the generous support of 'this fearless champion ... not just of France but of New France.'[78]

It did not take long for the effects of de Gaulle's visit to spill into Quebec cultural life. Claude Jasmin was moved after the visit to lay claim to his French heritage. The Quebec writer observed that 'we had forgotten that we were sons of France, and grandsons of Navarre, Normandy, Britanny or Berri,' asserting that 'I have a right to Corneille and Lafontaine, Renan is a relative of mine, Pasteur is part of my family, Lumière is French and I am French too.' Jasmin reminded his readers that, rather than being born spontaneously after Jacques Cartier's arrival, Quebecers were colonists and sons of colonists whose roots lay in France. With this in mind he emphasized the need of the youth of France and Quebec to meet one another, so that the 'French spirit [would be] able to make its presence felt once again on this side of the Atlantic,' before commanding: 'stand up Frenchmen of the New World!'[79]

Yet 1967 was not 1759. Notwithstanding the thunderous cheer that greeted 'Vive le Québec libre!' the reaction in Quebec to the French leader's actions was complicated. In his enthusiastic support of Quebec nationalism, his tendency to see French Canada as a branch of the French nation, and his preoccupation with countering American global power, de Gaulle tended to ignore those aspects of the Quebec identity – not least its Canadian component – that distinguished it from France. When Jean Chapdelaine gently hinted to his high-ranking interlocutors in Paris that Quebec City preferred the term *Canadiens français* to the *Français du Canada* that de Gaulle had a penchant to employ, he was rewarded only with a polite smile and a warning that there was little hope of changing the language that the general used.[80]

If there existed a complementarity between Gaullism and Quebec nationalism, there were also differences. Indeed, Daniel Johnson made a point during de Gaulle's visit of referring to the distinct North American identity that New France's *Canadiens* were displaying before the Conquest.[81] Similarly, even while François-Albert Angers was adamant that Quebec needed to be united in its support of de Gaulle's intervention, and that it should seize the opportunities this afforded to advance the cause of independence, he was also sure to warn against too heavy a reliance upon France and its leader. He argued that 'we should not necessarily lend ourselves, in servile fashion, to all of the plans for which [de Gaulle] may be thinking he wants to use us – all human activities, even the highest and most noble are never devoid of ulterior motives ... We must stay Québécois vis-à-vis France, just as we asked Canadians to vis-à-vis England.'[82] A report in the radical-left publication *Parti pris* took a similar stance, playfully noting that those who suggested Quebec was attempting to re-establish the old colonial link with France needed to be reminded that the chemin du Roy remained a secondary route for the overwhelming majority of Quebecers. At the same time, however, Thérèse Dumouchel could not completely dismiss the ethnocultural dimension of events, declaring it only logical that a people increasingly aware of its collective existence and struggling to see this acknowledged would seek recognition first of all from its more powerful closest relation. Dumouchel claimed this was all the more natural because de Gaulle was doing his utmost to rally the international French-speaking community and neutralize the 'Anglo-Saxon cultural bloc,' and that the Gaullist preoccupation with *francité* on a global scale was consistent with Quebec's local situation and concerns. Dumouchel made sure to add, however, that the French had to renounce their cultural monopoly as francophone populations around the world – including Quebec's – were undergoing a cultural *épanouissement* that coincided with their accession to independence.[83] For his part, Quebec writer Hubert Aquin was subsequently scathing and sarcastic in dismissing the notion that Quebec francophones were part of a transatlantic French nation.[84]

It was perhaps Montreal's francophile mayor, Jean Drapeau, who at the time best captured the complexities of francophone Quebec's evolving identity. Speaking at a luncheon amid the controversy that de Gaulle's speech had provoked, Drapeau acknowledged the ties of culture and history linking France and Quebec. He explained that French Canadians were grateful for de Gaulle's interest in their fate, but he also used the occasion to tell the French president that they harboured a degree of ambivalence for the country he led, arising from the struggle for survival they had had to wage alone for two centuries. Drapeau concluded by declaring that the roots of French Canadians were planted firmly in Canadian soil. In the weeks that followed, a poll showed that it was the mayor's response to de Gaulle's actions that received the greatest level of support from Quebecers.[85]

This same poll, however, showed that a majority of respondents had come to approve of de Gaulle's visit and his remarks at Montreal's city hall.[86] To be sure, a degree of cultural essentialism had characterized the Canada-Quebec-France triangular dynamic of the 1960s. It had been presumed (and feared) that ethnocultural affinities between France and Quebec made them natural allies. Yet such affinities by no means dictated a perfect harmony, especially given the lengthy history of ambivalence between French Canada and France. Even amid the multiplying references to a cultural solidarity, there was a certain disconnect between two nationalist reactions that, ultimately, were using one another to advance their respective political agendas. Nevertheless, the roar of approval that greeted de Gaulle's *cri du balcon* in Place Jacques-Cartier revealed that he had tapped into something profound. His words resonated in 1967 – and do so today – because they went to the core of what Jocelyn Létourneau describes as a narrative of a 'past seen as one of ordeals and sacrifices requiring an undying memory and necessitating reparation or redemption.'[87] The general's visit was not simply a celebration of the existence of the *fait français* in North America more than two centuries after the Conquest, but a bid for redemption – as much for France as for New France – for the events that unfolded on the Plains of Abraham in 1759.

NOTES

1 Isabelle Porter, 'Trop bavard au goût de certains,' *Le Devoir*, 5 September 2009, A2.

2 '"Sovereigntist show" spurs boycott,' *Globe and Mail*, 5 September 2009, A2.

3 Jocelyn Létourneau, *A History for the Future: Rewriting Memory and Identity in Quebec*, trans. Phyllis Aronoff and Howard Scott (Montreal; Kingston, ON: McGill-Queen's University Press, 2004), 99.

4 David Meren, *With Friends Like These: Entangled Nationalisms in the Canada-Quebec-France Triangle, 1944–1970* (Vancouver: UBC Press, 2012).

5 Philippe Roger, *The American Enemy: A Story of French Anti-Americanism*, trans. Sharon Bowman (Chicago: University of Chicago Press, 2005), 2–4.

6 This is by no means to suggest that French opinion regarding the cession of Canada was monolithic. In this regard, see William James Newbigging, 'The Cession of Canada and French Public Opinion in France in the New World,' in *Proceedings of the 22nd Annual Meeting of the French Colonial Historical Society*, ed. David Buisseret (East Lansing: Michigan State University Press, 1998).

7 Quoted in Raoul Aglion, *Roosevelt and De Gaulle, Allies in Conflict: A Personal Memoir* (New York: Free Press, 1988), 180–1.

8 Charles de Gaulle, *Memoirs of Hope, Renewal*, trans. Terence Kilmartin (London: George Weidenfeld and Nicholson, 1971), 9–10.

9 Serge Berstein, *Histoire du Gaullisme* (Paris: Perrin, 2001), 294; Maurice Vaïsse, *La grandeur: politique étrangère du général de Gaulle, 1958–1969* (Paris: Fayard, 1998), 117–23; Alfred Grosser, *The Western Alliance: European-American Relations since 1945*, trans. Michael Shaw (New York: Continuum, 1980), 183–5; and Edward L. Morse, *Foreign Policy and Interdependence in Gaullist France* (Princeton, NJ: Princeton University Press, 1973), 117.

10 Jeffrey G. Giauque, *Grand Designs and Visions of Unity: The Atlantic Powers and the Reorganization of Western Europe, 1955-1963* (Chapel Hill: University of North Carolina Press, 2002), 98–125.

11 Meren, *With Friends Like These*, 30–3.

12 European Division to Under-Secretary, 10 September 1963, Library and Archives Canada (hereafter cited as LAC), RG 25, G-2, vol. 5289, 9245-40/6.1.

13 Canadian Embassy, Washington to Department of External Affairs (hereafter cited as DEA), 9 and 25 September 1963, LAC, RG 25, A-3-c, vol. 10097, 20-1-2-FR/1.1; Canadian Mission, United Nations to DEA, 3 October 1963, LAC, RG 25, A-3-c, vol. 10097, 20-1-2-FR/1.1.

14 Document 29, Compte-Rendu de l'Entretien entre le Général de Gaulle et M. Lester Pearson, Premier Ministre du Canada à Paris, le 15 janvier 1964,' in *Documents diplomatiques français*, 1964, vol. 1, 1er janvier-30 juin, ed. Colette Barbier, Nathalie Buffet, Antoine Daveau, et al., sous la dir. de Maurice Vaïsse (Paris: Ministère des affaires étrangères, 2002).

15 Halstead, Canadian Embassy, Paris to DEA, 21 February 1964, LAC, RG 25, A-4, vol. 3497, 19-1-BA-FR-1964(3).

16 J.L. Granatstein, *Yankee Go Home? Canadians and Anti-Americanism* (Toronto: Harper Collins, 1996), 143.

17 Bousquet to Couve de Murville, Ministère des Affaires Étrangères

(France), Amérique, 31 December 1963, Archives du Ministère des Affaires Étrangères (hereafter cited as MAE), Série B, Amérique, Sous-Série Canada, vol. 137.

18 Halstead, Canadian Embassy, Paris to DEA, 21 February 1964, LAC, RG 25, A-4, vol. 3497, 19-1-BA-FR-1964(3).

19 'Document 31, Compte Rendu de l'Entretien entre M. Georges Pompidou et M. Lester Pearson, Première Ministre du Canada, à l'Hôtel Matignon, le 16 janvier 1964,' in *Documents diplomatiques français* (see note 14).

20 Dale Thomson, *Vive le Québec libre!* (Toronto: Deneau 1988), 124–5.

21 Canadian Embassy, Paris to USSEA, 8 October 1965, LAC, RG 25, A-3-c, vol. 10295, 27-4-NATO-3-1-FR/1.

22 Léger to DEA, 8 September 1965, LAC, RG 25, A-3-c, vol. 10098, 20-1-2-FR/3.1.

23 Martin to Pearson, 24 June 1966, Lester B. Pearson Papers, LAC, MG 26, N6, vol. 9, Memoranda, Pearson and Paul Martin, Private Statements, Pearson, 1959–1967; Martin to Pearson, 24 January 1967, LAC, RG 25, A-3-c, vol. 10045, 20-1-2-FR/5; Personal Journal, 14 July 1967, Marcel Cadieux Papers, LAC, MG31-E1, vol. 8, 15.

24 Jacques Filion, 'De Gaulle, la France et le Québec,' *Revue de l'Université d'Ottawa* 45, no. 3 (1975): 298–306, 317.

25 Leduc to Couve de Murville, MAE, Amérique, 11 May 1967, MAE, vol. 278; Léger to Cadieux, 20 September 1967, LAC, RG 25, A-3-c, vol. 10045, 20-1-2-FR/9; Leduc to Debré, MAE, Amérique, 26 June 1968, MAE, vol. 189.

26 Basdevant, Charge d'Affaires a.i., to Schuman, MAE, Amérique, 22 June 1950, MAE, vol. 41; Letter from Duranthon, Consul Général de France à Québec et Halifax, to Schuman, MAE, Amérique, 4 July 1950, MAE, vol. 42; Triat, Ministre Plenipotentiaire, Charge du Consulat Général de France à Montréal, to Guérin, 17 March 1955, MAE, vol. 114; Rapport d'Information, MM. Bosson et Thorailler, Députés, Assemblée Nationale, 18 March 1963, MAE, vol. 101.

27 Claude Julien, *Canada: dernière chance de l'Europe* (Paris: Grasset, 1965), 6.

28 Jean Lacouture, *De Gaulle: The Ruler, 1945-1970*, trans. Alan Sheridan (New York: W.W. Norton, 1992), 452–3.

29 Translation of 'équilibre générale' in de Leusse, Affaires Politiques, Télégramme Circulaire à Tous Postes Diplomatiques, 28 July 1967, MAE, vol. 210, Réactions.

30 Foreign Broadcast Information Service, French Minister's Article, Paris, Agence France-Presse, 4 August 1967, LAC, RG 25, A-3-c, vol. 10045, 20-1-2-FR/7.

31 Translation of 'une grande puissance' and 'un pied là-bas' in Jacques Foccart, *Tous les soirs avec De Gaulle, Journal de l'Élysée*, vol. 1 (Paris: Fayard/Jeune Afrique, 1997), 684–6.

32 For discussions of links between France and Quebec prior to 1945, see Centre culturel canadien, *Les Relations entre la France et le Canada aux XIXe siècle*, Colloque, 26 April 1974, organisé par le Centre culturel canadien (Paris, 1974); Pierre Savard, 'Les Canadiens français et la France de la "cession" à la "révolution tranquille,"' in *Le Canada et le Québec sur la scène internationale*, ed. Paul Painchaud (Montréal: Centre québécois de relations internationales, 1977); Luc Roussel, 'Les relations culturelles du Québec avec la France, 1920–1965' (PhD thesis, Université Laval, 1983); Katherine Pomeyrols, *Les intellectuels québécois: formation et engagements, 1919–1939* (Paris: L'Harmattan, 1996); and Yvan Lamonde, *Allégeances et dépendances: l'histoire d'une ambivalence identitaire* (Québec: Éditions Nota bene, 2001), 137–66.

33 Xavier Gélinas, *La droite intellectuelle québécoise et la Révolution tranquille* (Québec: Les Presses de l'Université Laval, 2007), 45. For discussions of the complex French-Canadian attitudes about France, see Gérard Bouchard, *Entre l'Ancien et le Nouveau Monde: le Québec comme population neuve et culture fondatrice* (Ottawa: University of Ottawa Press, 1996); and Lamonde, *Allégeances et dépendances*, 137–59.

34 Jean-Pierre Wallot, 'La Révolution française au Canada, 1789–1838,' and Pierre Savard, 'Autour d'un centenaire qui n'eût pas lieu,' both in *L'image de la révolution française au Québec 1789–1989*, ed. Michel Grenon (Lasalle, QC: Hurtubise HMH, 1989).

35 Translation of 'cadres vitaux de la nation française,' 'le sentiment de contact intime, de vibration fraternelle avec le reste de la nation française, qui s'est perdu,' and 'arrachement brutale' in Christian Roy, 'Le personnalisme de L'Ordre Nouveau et le Québec, 1930–1947, son rôle dans la formation de Guy Frégault,' *Revue d'Histoire de l'Amérique française* 46, no. 3 (1993): 469–70.

36 Ronald Rudin, *Making History in Twentieth-Century Quebec* (Toronto: University of Toronto Press, 1997), 143. Frégault went on to play a central role in the official rapprochement between France and Quebec as deputy minister of cultural affairs.

37 Lacoste to Couve de Murville, MAE, Affaires Culturelles, 8 August 1958, MAE, vol. 172.

38 'C'est alors que vous autres, maudits Français, vous nous avez abandonnés'; François Flohic, *Souvenirs d'Outre-Gaulle* (Paris: Librairie Plon, 1979), 84.

39 Meren, *With Friends Like These*, chaps. 2–3.

40 Roger, *American Enemy*, 122, 275–6.

41 Herman Lebovics, *Mona Lisa's Escort: André Malraux and the Reinvention of French Culture* (Ithaca, NY: Cornell University Press, 1999), 4.

42 Rogers Brubaker, *Citizenship and Nationhood in France and Germany* (Cambridge, MA: Harvard University Press, 1992), 1–13; and Eugèn Weber, *Peasants into Frenchmen: The Modernization of Rural France, 1870–1914* (Stanford, CA: Stanford University Press, 1976).

43 Gary Wilder, *The French Imperial Nation-State, Negritude & Colonial Humanism between the Two World Wars* (Chicago: University of Chicago Press, 2005), 15–18.

44 Filion, 'De Gaulle, la France et le Québec,' 317.

45 Cl. Lebel, MAE, Services de Presse et d'Information to French Embassy, Ottawa, 2 June 1964, MAE, vol. 195; Canadian Embassy, Paris to DEA, 4 June 1964, LAC, RG 25, vol. 10098, A-3-c, 20-1-2-FR/2.1.

46 Alain Peyrefitte, *De Gaulle et le Québec* (Montréal: Stanké, 2000), 37.

47 Le Général de Gaulle en Visite au Canada (undated), p. 12, LAC, RG 25, A-4, vol. 9568, MF241.

48 Note sur la Province de Québec, MAE, Amérique, 9 October 1961, MAE, vol. 135.

49 Peyrefitte, *De Gaulle et le Québec*, 30.

50 Boyer Ste-Suzanne, Consul Général de France à Montréal, to Roux, Directeur Général adjoint des Affaires Politiques au Département, 23 August 1961, MAE, vol. 146.

51 Del Perugia, Gérant le Consulat Général de France à Québec, to MAE, Amérique, 21 May 1949, MAE, vol. 41.

52 Translation of 'nation-sœur' in Rapport d'Information, MM. Bosson et Thorailler, Députés, Assemblée Nationale, 18 March 1963, MAE, vol. 101.

53 Thomson, *Vive le Québec libre!*, 158.

54 Jean-Marie Domenach, 'Le Canada Français: controverse sur un nationalisme,' *Esprit* 33, no. 335 (1965): 321–2.

55 Translation of 'fièvre révolte' and 'une seconde Amérique, une Amérique de culture française où les valeurs de justice, de liberté, de vérité, et de beauté seraient mieux incarnés dans la vie quotidienne des collectivités et personnes' in Pierre Godin, 'L'indépendance économique de la France se joue dans la lutte du Québec pour la libération,' *La Presse*, 5 September 1967.

56 The most comprehensive discussion of the Quebec lobby may be found in Paul-André Comeau and Jean-Pierre Fournier, *Le Lobby du Québec à Paris: les précurseurs du Général de Gaulle* (Montréal: Éditions Québec-Amérique,

2002). See also J.F. Bosher, *The Gaullist Attack on Canada, 1967–1997* (Montreal; Kingston, ON: McGill-Queen's University Press, 1999), 63–83, detailing what he terms the 'Quebec mafia.'

57 Comeau and Fournier, *Lobby du Québec*, 28–9; and Roger, *American Enemy*, 86–7, 202.

58 'La prochaine civilisation, nous la ferons ensemble!'; Bousquet to Couve de Murville, MAE, Amérique, 21 October 1963, MAE, vol. 101.

59 '[N]ous existons, et nous ne sommes plus seuls'; François-Albert Angers, 'Éditorial – I, "Le monde saura que nous existons, et nous ne sommes plus seuls,"' *L'Action Nationale* 57, no. 1 (1967): 8.

60 Translation of 'la ville Montréal française,' with de Gaulle's emphasis on 'française,' in Renée Lescop, *Le pari québécois du général de Gaulle* (Montréal: Boréal Express, 1981), 154–73.

61 Ibid., 170–3.

62 Translations of 'canadiens britanniques' and 'nation française' in de Leusse, Affaires Politiques, Télégramme Circulaire à Tous Postes Diplomatiques, 28 July 1967, MAE, vol. 210, Réactions. See also Benedict Anderson, *Imagined Communities, Reflections on the Origin and Spread of Nationalism* (New York: Verso, 1991), 145. Anderson cites the singing of national anthems as an example of *unisonance* that contributes to a sense of nation. As such, the singing of *La Marseillaise* during de Gaulle's visit might be construed as a manifestation of and appeal to an 'imagined community.' This certainly appears to have been the subtext of the Quai d'Orsay's reference to it.

63 Vanier to Heeney, USSEA, 26 February 1951, LAC, RG 25, G-2, vol. 8300, 9908-AD-2-40/2.1.

64 Roger, *American Enemy*, 115, 121.

65 Jurgensen to Secrétaire-Général, MAE, 9 December 1966, MAE, vol. 199.

66 Translation of 'une partie du peuple français' in Note du Secrétaire Général de la Présidence de la République, à M. le Ministre des Affaires Étrangères, 9 December 1966, Maurice Couve de Murville Papers, Archives d'histoire contemporaine, vol. 8, 1966.

67 Ch. de Bartillat, Affaires Politiques, Amérique, 23 June 1967, MAE, vol. 208, Dossier Général, Antérieur au Voyage, au 23 juillet 1967; Allocution du Président de la République à son arrivée à Ottawa, le 26 juillet, MAE, vol. 209, Discours; Draft of speech to have been delivered in Ottawa on Parliament Hill, MAE, vol. 209.

68 Marine Lefèvre, *Charles de Gaulle, du Canada français au Québec* (Montréal: Leméac, 2007), 8–9.

69 Lacouture, *De Gaulle*, 450.

70 Stéphane Monclaire, 'Histoire et référents historiques dans le discours du président de Gaulle,' in Institut Charles de Gaulle, *De Gaulle en son siècle, Actes des Journées internationales tenues à l'Unesco, Paris, 19–24 novembre 1990*, vol. 7, *De Gaulle et la culture* (Paris: Plon/La Documentation Française, 1992), 193–4.

71 Thomson, *Vive le Québec libre!*, 101, 199.

72 'Je n'aurais plus été de Gaulle si je ne l'avais pas fait'; Anne Rouanet and Pierre Rouanet, *Les trois derniers chagrins du Général de Gaulle* (Paris: Bernard Grasset, 1980), 27.

73 Andrew Knapp, *Le Gaullisme après de Gaulle* (Paris: Éditions de Seuil, 1996), 15.

74 Dorin to Masse, 25 March 1996, Jean Chapdelaine Papers, Bibliothèque et archives nationales du Québec (hereafter cited as ANQ), P776, 2001-01-006, vol. 4, Ministère des Affaires Intergouvernementales, 1969-1996; Comeau and Fournier, *Le Lobby du Québec à Paris*, 51; Thomson, *Vive le Québec libre!*, 197; and Rouanet and Rouanet, *Les trois derniers chagrins*, 103–33.

75 Michel Hébert and Lyse Roy, 'Amour sénarisé, amour vécu: l'entrée solennelle de Charles de Gaulle au Québec en juillet 1967,' *Bulletin d'histoire politique* 14, no. 1 (2005): 147–59.

76 Angers, 'Éditorial,' 5.

77 '[M]algré l'histoire, malgré les Anglais, malgré les notables et un peu aussi malgré nous hélas! Le peuple québécois était resté français. J'en fus violemment retourné. Ce peuple n'avait pas eu besoin de directives pour affirmer sa fierté française à la face du monde entier. Il avait une envie folle de se manifester et il le fit'; Pierre Bourgault, *Écrits polémiques 1960–1981*, vol. 1, *Le politique* (Montréal: vlb éditeur, 1983), 133–5. Indicative of the complexity of the francophone Quebec identity was the fact that, in this remembrance of the events of July 1967, Bourgault rejects categorically the accusation that his Rassemblement pour l'indépendance nationale (RIN) harboured an exaggerated francophilia and wished to renew colonial links with France. To the contrary, Bourgault claims that the RIN was the first political initiative in two hundred years to owe nothing to anyone and to assert itself proudly as 'made in Québec.'

78 Translation of 'une nation française en Amérique du Nord' and 'ce champion sans peur … non seulement de la France mais aussi de la Nouvelle-France' in Reggie Chartrand, *La dernière bataille* (Montréal; Québec: Éditions Parti pris, 1972), 8, 88, 203. Indicative of Chartrand's worldview was that he dedicated this book to England, which he alleged had kept the *Québécois* people colonized for 226 years, and to all those in and outside of the province who had kept Quebec in this colonized state.

79 '[N]ous avions fini par oublier que nous étions fils de France, petit-fils de Navarre et de Normandie de Bretagne ou de Berri … j'ai droit à Corneille et à Lafontaine, Renan est mon parent, Pasteur est de ma famille, Lumière est français et je suis français aussi … que l'esprit francais puisse s'essayer encore une fois de ce côté-ci de l'Atlantique … [d]ebout, Français d'ici!'; Claude Jasmin, *Rimbaud, mon beau salaud!* (Montréal: Éditions du Jour, 1969), 41–3.

80 Chapdelaine to Morin, 5 December 1967, Jean Chapdelaine Papers, ANQ, P776, 2001-01-006, vol. 1, Reportage Politique, 1967–1974.

81 Allocution de M. Daniel Johnson, Premier Ministre du Québec, Dîner Offert par le Général De Gaulle, Président de la République Française, Pavillon de la France, 25 July 1967, MAE, vol. 209, Discours prononcés.

82 Angers, 'Éditorial,' 8. 'Nous n'avons pas nécessairement à servir "servilement" toutes les combinaisons auxquelles peut-être il pourrait songer à vouloir nous utiliser – toutes les entreprises humaines mêmes les plus hautes et les plus nobles ne sont jamais sans cette part de faiblesse … Nous devons rester des Québécois, vis-à-vis de la France, comme nous leur avons demandé de rester des Canadiens vis-à-vis de l'Angleterre'; idem, 'L'épilogue de la visite du Général de Gaulle,' *L'Action nationale* 57, no. 2 (1967): 180.

83 Translation of 'bloc culturel anglo-saxon' in Thérèse Dumouchel, 'De Gaulle, un point tournant,' *Parti pris* 5, no. 1 (1967): 27.

84 Hubert Aquin, 'Nos cousins de France,' in *Point de Fuite* (Montréal: Cercle du Livre de France, 1971), 67–70.

85 Le Général de Gaulle en Visite au Canada (undated), 93–5, LAC, RG 25, A-4, vol. 9568, MF241; Thomson, *Vive le Québec libre!*, 212–14, 234–36.

86 Thomson, *Vive le Québec libre!*, 236.

87 Létourneau, *History for the Future*, 4.

9

A Nightmare to Awaken from: The Conquest in the Thinking of *Québécois* Nationalists of the 1960s and After

> History (...) is a nightmare from which I am trying to awake.
>
> – James Joyce, *Ulysses* (1922)

On the night of 25 September 1962, mere weeks before the Cuban Missile Crisis grabbed hold of newspaper headlines around the world, Hubert Aquin, a thirty-three-year-old French-Canadian writer and nationalist militant, wrote the following words in his diary: 'The novel? But my mind is devoid of everything that does not speak to me of this crazy and degrading connection between myself and my real country. Maybe, out of this obsessive line of thinking, I could write a novel: something which would be the insurrectional brothel (Behan: *The Hostage*) which endlessly fills me with what nourishes all my thoughts, and all my conversations.'[1] The reference to Irish nationalist playwright Brendan Behan's 1958 play *The Hostage* is an interesting one,[2] but even more revealing is his mention of Irish novelist James Joyce a few sentences later in his journal entry: 'And so – the only possible level is that of language, of speech. It's in language that I can fornicate this damn country, unreal in every way except in the language with which we describe it! Second-rate Ireland. French Canada has a revolutionary problem of which we will find linguistic and symbolic solutions! The detective novel: yes, on the structure of the detective novel build, like Joyce did with the Odyssey, my novel which can only be inspired by an English detective novel, by the way.'[3] A few months earlier, in his celebrated essay 'La fatigue culturelle du Canada français,' Aquin had evoked Joyce in his analysis of the colonized state of the French Canadian; he emphasized how Joyce had subverted the English language in his novels, turning a colonial relationship to language and the 'canon' on its head. 'Condemned to speak a foreign language,' Aquin pointed out with reference to the exiled Irish modernist, 'he took his mysterious revenge by making it foreign unto itself.'[4] Now, seeking to write a novel whose content and form could adequately capture the chaotic and fragmented condition of French Canada in the early 1960s, and musing upon the revolutionary potential of Quebec at that tumultuous moment in its history, Aquin, ever looking for outside examples to better understand the condition of his own people at home, turned once again to Ireland, and more particularly Joyce, as he embarked upon his enterprise.

That enterprise, Aquin's first novel, published three years later under the somewhat vacillating title of *Prochain épisode*, would shatter the conformity of French-Canadian literature, and of politics and culture, like a bomb. Critics hailed it as a masterpiece, the long-awaited novel of a new Quebec – revolutionary, modern, a stunning feat of innovative form and searing style. 'We now have him, our great writer,' Jean-Ethier Blais affirmed emphatically in *Le Devoir*. 'The first novel of the literary season is a bomb,' the esteemed literary critic Gilles Marcotte wrote in Montreal's *La Presse*. Even Lionel Groulx, that aging dean of French-Canadian nationalism, in a private letter to the first-time novelist, had hopeful things to say.[5] Narrated by a French-Canadian nationalist who, while incarcerated for his revolutionary activities and awaiting trial, embarks upon the writing of an espionage novel, all the while reminiscing in a highly lyrical and elliptical manner about his past, his loves, and his revolutionary failures, Aquin's novel sought to capture, both in content and in form, the fractured and fragmented nature of the Quebec revolution – violent, disordered, hesitant, and suicidal.

What is striking about Aquin's novel is that history, it seems, is something looming in the future, not the past. For Aquin, and for his narrator, history does not – *cannot* – exist under the present colonized condition of the French Canadian; it will commence only once the violent revolutionary struggle for national liberation has begun. 'It's true that we have no history,' Aquin's narrator declares in an allusion to Lord Durham's oft-quoted statement about French Canadians, adding: 'Our history will begin at the unknown moment when the revolutionary war begins.'[6] This passage from *Prochain épisode* is crucial to our understanding of Aquin and a number of French-Canadian nationalists of the 1960s, who were looking forward, rather than to the past. The burden of the past weighed heavily upon them. Faced with a past replete with failure and non-entity, a laundry list of waverings and indecisions, they sought to free themselves from its clutches, to look with eyes wide open at the avenues that pointed to a liberated future. 'History is a nightmare from which I am trying to awake,' Joyce had Stephen Dedalus declare in that now-famous passage from *Ulysses*; and in the riotously shifting society that was Quebec in the 1960s, Hubert Aquin, and other French-Canadian nationalists, no doubt would have agreed. As Aquin's melancholic narrator stridently proclaimed: 'History will begin to write itself when we give to our pain the rhythm and the blinding power of war. Everything will take on the flamboyant colours of history when we march into battle, machine-guns at the ready.'[7]

If the burden of the past weighed heavy on their shoulders, no event, perhaps, weighed heavier than that of the British Conquest of 1759. Indeed, for well over a century, generation upon generation of French-Canadian nationalists had debated and argued the effects of the Conquest, seeking in its calamitous consequences the roots of their own inferiority in the country that emerged from its ashes. 'Each generation of French Canadians appears to fight, intellectually, the Battle of the Plains of Abraham again,' historian Ramsay Cook declared in his 1966 essay, 'Conquêtisme.'[8] From François-Xavier Garneau to Lionel Groulx, from Benjamin Sulte to Michel Brunet, French-Canadian nationalist historians had regarded the Conquest as *the* seminal event of the French-Canadian existence – the event they kept going back to, ruminating over its meaning, rummaging through its detritus to make some sort of sense of French Canada, as it stood in their time. Whatever the Conquest meant, it was *there*. This was the burden *Québécois* nationalists of the 1960s tried to relieve themselves of – the nightmare, to paraphrase Joyce, from which they were trying to awake.

This chapter seeks to explore the place of the Conquest in the thinking of *Québécois* nationalists of the past few decades.[9] Its focus, however, is on the 1960s, a period of tumultuous change in Quebec widely referred to as the 'Quiet Revolution,' though for nationalists in this decisive time the revolutionary potential of the events taking place in the province was far greater than that name implies. As Jean-Christian Pleau explains, the term 'Quiet Revolution' fails to capture the truly revolutionary spirit that hovered in the air: 'at the beginning of the 1960s, we were all the same a little more demanding, we waited and hoped for a spectacular break with the past: independence, preferably accompanied by a widespread proletarian uprising and followed by the advent of a socialist Quebec.'[10] As decolonization struggles raged around the globe and more and more formerly colonized peoples took their place at the concert of nations as newly independent states, *Québécois* nationalists borrowed from, adapted, and refashioned their discourses, symbols, and ideas to proclaim their own right to overthrow what they saw as the shackles of their own colonialism and assume their full *globalité*, or totality, as a people and a nation in the world.[11] In order to do this, they hoped to move beyond the Conquest, and look not so much towards the past as to the future, one replete with all the trappings of a total liberation from a French-Canadian past of colonialism, apathy, and fatigue. Liberation and revolution were the catchwords of the day; the Conquest had little place in the revolutionary discourse of emancipation.

In a crucial chapter of *Prochain épisode*, towards the end of the novel, Aquin's narrator finds himself waiting, gun at the ready, in the vast rooms of his mysterious and elusive enemy H. de Heutz's opulent abode, hoping to kill the very man who represents all those nefarious forces keeping French Canadians in a permanent state of bondage. 'It's strange, being all alone in this grand residence,' the musing narrator declares. 'In every room I race through, I keep discovering *objets d'art*, displayed more or less conspicuously.'[12] Among the *objets d'art* the would-be assassin discovers in H. de Heutz's possession is an engraved reproduction of Benjamin West's famous eighteenth-century painting 'The Death of General Wolfe.' What is curious about the painting, that potent symbol of the Battle of the Plains of Abraham, and its place in the novel, is that it seems more a museum piece than anything else – an object to collect and admire but with little relevance to the broader concerns of the modern-day world. Indeed, for Aquin's narrator, the painting elicits not some grave and tragic memory (the Conquest), but rather the epitome of fine taste and lavish living. 'This brilliant copy of "The Death of General Wolfe," which was purchased by George III some centuries before H. de Heutz bought his, thrills me!' he exclaims. 'For that matter the remarkable luxury and good taste throughout this chateau fill me with a kind of haunting memory I've never known before: the pleasure of living in a house can then resemble the bewildered complacency I experience in this sweeping, majestic salon.'[13]

Of course, there are other references to the Conquest in Aquin's novel, but they are never as explicit and never seem to take on the same importance as that of another seminal event in French-Canadian history – the rebellion of 1837–8. *Prochain épisode* is replete with allusions to the *Patriotes* and the Lower-Canadian rebellion; indeed, along with the Cuban and French revolutions, one could argue that the rebellion of

1837–8 constitutes an important historical signpost to the revolutionary struggle taking place in the narrative. For example, at numerous points in the novel, Aquin's narrator lyrically evokes driving through the Quebec countryside with his lover, K, past the sights of the *Patriotes'* more famous battles – such as St-Denis and St-Eustache. And the failure of the rebellion serves as a powerful reminder to the narrator of his own failed revolutionary action, in the end. Indeed, a number of critical passages clearly anchor the present-day struggle of Quebec revolutionaries (the members of the Front de libération du Québec, FLQ) with that of the *Patriote* rebels of a century before: 'I'll have to answer for my brothers who took their own lives after the defeat at Saint-Eustache,'[14] the narrator declares in a particularly moving passage.

In many ways, Hubert Aquin was obsessed with the *Patriotes'* uprising. As early as 1962, he had recorded in his journal that he planned to write a historical novel about Louis-Joseph Papineau and the Lower-Canadian rebellion,[15] and his interest in the subject neither abated nor waned over the years; in 1968 he even wrote the introduction and commentary to a published edition of Papineau's account of the rebellion, *Histoire de l'insurrection au Canada*.[16] Perhaps it was in his 1965 essay, 'L'Art de la défaite,' however, that Aquin's analysis of the rebellion was most explicitly made.[17] But 'L'Art de la défaite' was no dry historical analysis; in it Aquin offered a scorching critique of the *Patriotes'* role in their own defeat and an examination of the rebellion through the lens of decolonization and the wars for national liberation taking place in the Third World at the time. Armed with the analytical tools of such decolonization theoreticians as Frantz Fanon and Aimé Césaire, Mao Tse-tung and Ernesto Che Guevara, Aquin argued that had the *Patriotes* fought a war of national liberation – that is, a guerrilla war – through to the end, and neither wavered nor shown any hint of indecisiveness in their desire to pursue it to the end, they would have been successful. Wars of national liberation must be fought unflinchingly – this was the logic Aquin drew from his analysis of the rebellion; and the parallels to the FLQ bombing campaign that had begun in Quebec in 1963 would have been evident to many readers at the time. With the emphasis on revolution and anticolonial struggles in the 1960s, in both Quebec and the Third World, it comes as little surprise that Aquin chose to explore the one moment in French-Canadian history when revolution seemed a possibility.

Aquin was far from alone in this view. 'We must attribute our precarious situation to the Conquest,' Pierre Vadeboncoeur wrote in his

influential 1962 essay, 'La Ligne du Risque,' 'but we must go back to
the failure of the Rebellion in order to understand our strange career
of accepted political impotence and our abdication of the spirit of freedom.'[18] Vadeboncoeur, Aquin's contemporary and a notable intellectual in his own right, echoed Aquin's sentiments that the rebellion of
1837–8, rather than the Conquest, constituted the crucial event of the
French-Canadian past, although he put less importance on the armed
component of the struggle, and more on the intellectual impact of the
rebellion's failure on the development of French-Canadian society. As
Vadeboncoeur succinctly put it, '[i]t was in 1837 that we were broken,
more in our own mind than by any military victory. The legacy of the
red-coats was taken over by our reactionaries. Vanquished militarily
for the second time in less than a century, we would be vanquished for
the first time in our own mind and by our own hand.'[19]

The year *Prochain épisode* was published, Pierre Vadeboncoeur released a second book of essays, entitled *L'autorité du peuple.* In the book's
closing essay, 'Les solutions et leurs problèmes,' Vadeboncoeur once
again tackled the idea of freedom, or 'liberté,' in the province, but this
time as it stood after five years of rapid social change. Some progress
had been made since the advent of the Quiet Revolution in the 1960s,
he argued; freedom was finally, now, 'exerting' itself – 'elle s'exerce.'[20]
Moreover, in Quebec, '[w]e can now finally see that freedom, while exerting itself among us, has taken on a revolutionary style.'[21] And here,
in Vadeboncoeur's essay, we hear more echoes of Aquin: 'In a sense,
the Québécois do not have a history. History, for us, is simply what is
passed. Few western peoples, perhaps, have been as little penetrated
with history as ours has; whose past, that is, is so effectively over ... We
do not have a history.'[22]

A people without a history: although Vadeboncoeur did not read
Aquin's novel until after he wrote this essay – he reviewed *Prochain
épisode* in 1966 in *Le Devoir*, and sent a private letter to Aquin telling
him that the novel had left him 'favourably impressed'[23] – these words
could have been written by Aquin himself. And this is where Vadeboncoeur's essay gets interesting. France has a history, he wrote, because,
projected by forces of its own, it passed through successive stages – in
other words, it underwent revolutions, and revolutionary changes, political, social, cultural, economic. 'The history of France is articulate and
alive,' Vadeboncoeur declared, 'and the present still resonates with its
last two centuries of struggles. This is because the people still live these
struggles, or at least remember them for having triumphed over them

with great difficulty. And this is what having a history means: to still combat side by side with those who are gone, or else triumph along with them even today.'[24] French Canada, however, lacks such a history – or a history at all – because French Canadians were – and had always been – passive.

The only exception to this, and only up to a certain point, Vadeboncoeur pointed out, was the period leading up to the rebellion of 1837–8 ('the period from the Conquest to the Rebellion'), which still resonated somewhat in the present day. He made it quite clear that this exception did not include the Conquest itself, as 'When we talk about *la Défaite*, we do not even know what we are talking about: we have to unearth it. It almost makes you believe there had not been a Conquest. In fact, the Conquest has so little importance that, just a few years ago, we sought to celebrate 1760 as a historical event, and the very idea of opposing this seemed incongruous!'[25] The Conquest as a museum piece, to borrow the metaphor from Aquin's novel; indeed, the problem with the Conquest, Vadeboncoeur argued, was that French Canadians, in a certain sense, did not even participate in it and thus were never truly vanquished – France was. French Canadians were merely engulfed, or devoured. And this passivity at the hands of broader historical forces had defined the French-Canadian existence until very recently, he revealingly declares: 'Until very recently we were drifting aimlessly on a history which we would say had been written in advance in 1867, or even earlier, in order to avoid having to live it.'[26] French Canadians are without a history because it was written in advance for them, and they never actively participated in it; only the rebellion of 1837–8 formed an exception, Vadeboncoeur said, as did the present day (the 1960s), when socialism and independence were on the agenda: 'Ever since we [began to] speak of socialism and independence it's truly the first time since 1837 that we seem to actually want something.'[27] Aquin could not have said it better.

The examples of *Québécois* nationalist writers and intellectuals of the 1960s who saw the rebellion, rather than the Conquest, as the seminal event of the French-Canadian past are many indeed. Here is another example – a play, this time. *Les Grands Soleils*, by the doctor-writer Jacques Ferron, an early proponent of decolonization and left-wing French-Canadian nationalism, first appeared in 1958, but was revived in 1968 in a popular production performed in forty-four cities across Quebec, New Brunswick, and Ontario.[28] The production, put on by the Théatre du Nouveau-Monde, was widely covered in Quebec's newspapers, garnering Ferron a great deal of attention for his original treatment of a well-known historical event and for making explicit links between French Canada and the broader decolonization struggles taking place at the time. As Ferron explained in an interview with André Major in *Le Devoir* the year the play was revived, 'I wanted to link our liberation struggle to all the other liberation struggles in the world.'[29]

The play dramatized Jean-Olivier Chénier, the *Patriote* hero-martyr of the Lower-Canadian rebellion in an explicitly political manner, eschewing traditional contextual analysis of French-Canadian history and, in what today would seem as an early post-modernist stroke, linked his struggle and fate to that of Third World movements of national liberation, particularly those in Asia in the period following the Second World War. Indeed, in *Les Grands Soleils*, Chénier, who perished at the hands of British troops at the Battle of Ste-Eustache in 1837, served as both symbol and martyr for the French-Canadian national liberation struggle. Burned to death in a church where he and other *Patriote* rebels had hoped to make a last stand against British troops during the battle, Chénier's death was symbolically linked, through Ferron's innovative dramatic re-enactment and retelling of the story on the stage, with that of Chinese communists torched by napalm in their floating pagodas during the Korean War. A direct link was thus made between the rebellion – French Canada's struggle for 'national liberation' – and Third World national liberation movements of the post–Second World War era. Again it was the rebellion, and not the Conquest, that was used.

Turning to perhaps the most famous autobiography and political tract of the period, Pierre Vallières' *Nègres blancs d'Amérique*, we see a similar view of the Conquest as an event of only minor importance. Written in an intense creative burst from late October 1966 to early January 1967, while Vallières, the FLQ's foremost intellectual, was imprisoned in the Manhattan Detention House for Men for having protested at the United Nations in New York with fellow *felquiste* Charles Gagnon, and just before he was extradited back to Canada to face trial for his role in a 5 May 1966 bomb blast that had taken a life at the Montreal La Grenade shoe factory and a botched attempt to dynamite a Montreal Dominion Textile Plant a few months later, the book's manuscript pages were smuggled to the editors of the left-wing nationalist magazine *Parti pris*, where it was published shortly thereafter. Its success was immediate, and notorious. Aided by the publicity of Vallières' trial, it went on to become a bestseller, and was published in a number of countries, including France, the United States, Germany, and Mexico.[30]

In an early chapter of *Nègres blancs d'Amérique*, Vallières offered a highly personal analysis of French-Canadian history, heavily tinted with decolonization theory, French-Canadian revolutionary nationalism, and New Left Marxist politics. In light of this, it is perhaps unsurprising that Vallières placed little emphasis on the Conquest in his analysis of the French-Canadian past and in his understanding of its road to national liberation. Indeed, like other 1960s nationalist intellectuals, Vallières placed revolutionary action above all else, and found little relevance in stale debates over the Conquest and whatever significance it may have held. He offered instead an alternate reading of French-Canadian history that concentrated on the condition of the French Canadian as *nègre*, or exploited cheap labour, to imperial and colonial economic interests. In doing so, he eliminated any distinctive peculiarities from the French Canadian's past, thus making it easier to understand them as *nègres blancs*, or 'white niggers' – a people on a par with American blacks and other exploited, colonized peoples of the world. Through his Marxist economic interpretation of French-Canadian history, he thus made it easier to depict French Canadians as faceless, cut-out characters on which the features of the world's oppressed could then be superimposed; what resulted was an image of French Canadians as exploited workers whose fate was controlled by the whims of broader economic forces beyond their control. The Conquest, then, had little relevance to his interpretation. Writing about the effect of the Conquest on the average French Canadian, Vallières was succinct and to the point: 'Nothing changed in the frugal and monotonous life of the Habitants. They were still beasts of burden, despised in a hostile country.'[31]

This is not to say that the Conquest had no role, symbolic or otherwise, in *Québécois* nationalist politics of the 1960s. Rather, it is that the Conquest – for many nationalists the root, or genesis, of French-Canadian inferiority at the hands of their English-speaking colonial masters – had to be surpassed. It had to be acted upon. Of course, the symbolism of the Conquest did appear at times in Quebec nationalist politics during this period, and perhaps never so vividly as during the queen's visit to Quebec City in October 1964, and the demonstrations by the Rassemblement pour l'indépendance nationale against the visit, which resulted in a stunning episode of police repression against the demonstrators – the *samedi de la matraque*. Indeed, the symbolism of the queen's arrival by boat at L'Anse au Foulon, the famed spot that General Wolfe, two centuries before, had scaled with his troops under cover of darkness to surprise the French the following morning on the Plains of Abraham, would not have been lost on anyone. As the lead of the front page article in *Le Devoir* on 10 October 1964 put it to its readers, '[t]wo hundred five years and one month after General James Wolfe, the Queen will disembark this morning at 10.02 at l'Anse au Foulon.'[32] But such examples do not take away from the fact that the Conquest, for a great number of *Québécois* nationalists of the 1960s, ultimately had to be surpassed, and could only be surpassed, through action – revolutionary or otherwise. Even the FLQ, through its publication *La Cognée*, condemned any possible assassination attempt on the person of the queen during her visit to Quebec, arguing that she was nothing but a 'symbol of colonialism.'[33]

More important, for a large component of nationalist intellectuals of the 1960s in Quebec, was the revolutionary action of the present and the future, for only through national revolution and independence, it was argued, could French Canadians – or *Québécois*, rather – enter into the field of history. As Gaston Miron, perhaps the most important *Québécois* nationalist poet of the period, put it in his poem 'Octobre':

we will make you, Land of Quebec
a bed of resurrections
and a thousand lightning metamorphoses
of our leavens from which the future shall rise
and of our wills which will concede nothing
men shall hear your pulse beating through history
this is us winding through the October autumn
the russet sound of roe-deer in the sunlight
this is our future, clear
                              and committed[34]

In October 1970, as the War Measures Act was declared and soldiers took over the streets of Montreal, Miron was imprisoned along with some five hundred other FLQ sympathizers, nationalist intellectuals, and political activists. At a conference held at the Université de Montréal to protest Miron's incarceration, the poet Yves Préfontaine declared, 'Miron in prison – it's our very speech that's being locked up.'[35] The October Crisis, as it became known, was in full swing, though it was short lived; the 1960s, in Quebec at least, came to a close in violence, fear, and in repression.

If the October Crisis served to delegitimize the use of violent revolutionary action in the eyes of the vast majority of *Québécois*[36] – even

Pierre Vallières abandoned his support for violent revolutionary action shortly after his release from prison[37] – it did not change much in the way *Québécois* nationalist intellectuals perceived the Conquest. With the growing popularity, under René Lévesque, of the social-democratic sovereigntist Parti Québécois (PQ), the eyes of nationalist intellectuals were still very much turned towards the future, as the dream of Quebec independence – albeit different, and much more compromise ridden, from that of the revolutionary politics of the 1960s – began to take shape. And with the stunning PQ victory in the 1976 provincial election, the possibility of achieving this dream seemed clearly within reach. Independence, the idea went, would usher in the history that, for French-Canadian nationalist intellectuals, had been so sorely lacking.

In his 1968 book *Option Québec*, Lévesque had said this about the Conquest: 'Then came the conquest. We were a conquered people, our hearts set on surviving in some small way on a continent that had become Anglo-Saxon.'[38] And then, a few chapters later, under the subheading 'Making History Instead of Submitting To It,' he brought out, in somewhat different form, the argument for independence that nationalist intellectuals and writers of the 1960s had been making since the early part of the decade: 'The future of a people is never born without effort. It requires that a rather large number of "midwives" knowingly make the grave decision to work at it. For apart from other blind forces, and apart from all the imponderables, we must believe that basically it is still men who make man's history.'[39] History, again, was something to be *made*. And 'making history,' for the *Québécois* people, so the argument went, meant achieving independence. So long as the dream of 'making history' remained – and it remained until the sovereigntist defeat in the 1980 referendum and again for a brief period from the failure of Meech Lake to the much narrower sovereigntist defeat in the 1995 referendum – nationalist intellectuals in Quebec could forget the Conquest and focus on the future, on the 'history' that would begin with the advent of an independent state. When that dream waned, the Conquest, or the significance of the Conquest, quite naturally, grew. Is it a surprise then that, today – when the sovereigntist option seems, to many, less urgent in the minds of the majority of *Québécois* and *Québécoises*, and something that perhaps will not be realized in the immediate future – the significance of the Conquest and the Battle of the Plains of Abraham has taken on, at least among a certain segment of *Québécois* nationalists, a new urgency once again?[40] For these nationalists, history is still a nightmare: they have not awoken from it yet.

NOTES

1 'Le roman? Mais j'ai l'esprit vide de tout ce qui ne me parle pas de cette liaison folle et dégradante entre mon pays réel et moi. Peut-être pourrais-je faire un roman dans cet axe d'obsession: quelque chose qui serait le bordel insurrectionel (Behan: *The Hostage*) qui me gave à jamais de ce qui nourrit toutes mes pensées, toutes mes conversations'; Hubert Aquin, *Journal, 1948–1971*, ed. Bernard Beugnot (Montréal: Bibliothèque Québécoise, 1999), 247.

2 In an interview three years later, Aquin declared, in reference to a statement about the drama of the *Québécois* as one who is an exile in his own country, 'Je pense à Brendan Behan qui est mort saoul, ou saoul mort, dans un ruisseau. C'est une belle mort. La situation peut m'amener au suicide, je le pressens. Mais ce qui compte c'est de mourir en beauté'; 'Entrevue avec Hubert Aquin: "Prochain épisode"... Est-ce le roman d'un grand rêve?' *Le Petit Journal*, 7 November, 1965, in *Hubert Aquin: dossier de presse 1965–1980* (Sherbrooke, QC: Bibliothèque du Séminaire de Sherbrooke, 1981), 3.

3 'Alors – le seul niveau possible est celui du langage, du parler. C'est dans la langue que je peux forniquer ce pays maudit, irréel en tout sauf dans la langue par laquelle on le décrit! Irlande au second degré. Le Canada français a un problème révolutionnaire dont on trouvera des solutions linguistiques ou symboliques! Roman policier: oui, sur une structure de policier construire, comme Joyce avec l'Odyssée, mon roman qui ne peut être inspiré que par un roman policier anglais, d'ailleurs'; Aquin, *Journal, 1948–1971*, 247.

4 Hubert Aquin, 'The Cultural Fatigue of French Canada,' in *Writing Quebec: Selected Essays By Hubert Aquin*, ed. Anthony Purdy, trans. Paul Gibson, Reva Joshee, Anthony Purdy, and Larry Shouldice (Edmonton: University of Alberta Press, 1988), 40.

5 'Nous le tenons, notre grand écrivain'; Jean-Ethier Blais, 'Un roman d'Hubert Aquin: "Prochain épisode,"' *Le Devoir*, 13 November 1965; '*Le premier roman de la saison littéraire est une bombe*'; Gilles Marcotte, 'Une bombe: "Prochain épisode,"' *La Presse*, 13 November 1965; Lettre de Lionel Groulx à Hubert Aquin, 30 December 1965, Fonds Hubert Aquin, Archives de l'Université du Québec à Montréal, 44P-030/3.

6 Hubert Aquin, *Next Episode*, trans. Sheila Fischman (Toronto: McClelland and Stewart, 2001), 65.

7 Ibid.

8 Ramsay Cook, *The Maple Leaf Forever: Essays on Nationalism and Politics in Canada* (1977; Toronto: Copp Clark Pitman, 1986), 82.

9 In this collection, the contributions by Michel Bock and Brian Young focus specifically on the role of historians, both popular and professional, in the creation of the historical memory of the Conquest in Quebec. This chapter, in contrast, explores a different set of intellectuals in the province – writers, poets, essayists, and other types of nationalist militants active in the often heated politics and discourse of the 1960s and after. In doing so, it tells a different, yet complementary, story.

10 Pleau's full quote is: 'La Révolution Tranquille, c'est en somme ce qui frappe de non-lieu la Révolution tout court. Or, au début des années soixante, on était tout de même un peu plus exigeant, on attendait, on espérait une rupture spectaculaire avec le passé: l'indépendance, de préférence accompagnée d'un soulèvement général du prolétariat et suivie de l'avènement d'un Québec socialiste'; Jean-Christian Pleau, *La Révolution québécoise: Hubert Aquin et Gaston Miron au tournant des années soixante* (Montréal: Fides, 2002), 8.

11 For a history of decolonization in Quebec during the 1960s, see, for example, Magali Deleuze, *L'une et l'autre indépendance 1954–1964: les médias au Québec et la guerre d'Algérie* (Montréal: vlb éditeur, 2001); Alexis Lachaine, 'Black and Blue: French Canadian Writers, Decolonization and Revolutionary Nationalism in Quebec, 1960–1969' (PhD thesis, York University, 2007); and Sean Mills, 'The Empire Within: Montreal, the Sixties, and the Forging of a Radical Imagination' (PhD thesis, Queen's University, 2007). For a colourful and still relevant account, see also Malcolm Reid, *The Shouting Signpainters: A Literary and Political Account of Quebec Revolutionary Nationalism* (Toronto: McClelland and Stewart, 1972). For an excellent and lively overview of the broader decolonization and Third World national liberation project in this period, see, for example, Vijay Prashad, *The Darker Nations: A People's History of the Third World* (New York; London: New Press, 2007).

12 Aquin, *Next Episode*, 86.

13 Ibid., 90.

14 Ibid., 53.

15 See Hubert Aquin, *Journal*, 243. This historical novel would never be written, although, as we have seen, the rebellion had an important symbolic place in *Prochain épisode*. Interestingly, it seems Aquin had been planning to return to the period of the Lower-Canadian rebellion in his last novel, *Obombre*, which was left unfinished by his shocking death in 1977.

16 Louis-Joseph Papineau, *Histoire de l'insurrection au Canada*, with an introduction and commentary by Hubert Aquin (Ottawa: Leméac, 1968).

17 Hubert Aquin, *Blocs Erratiques* (Montréal: Les Editions Quinze, 1977), 113–22.

18 'C'est à la Conquête qu'il faut attribuer notre situation précaire, mais c'est à l'échec de la Rébellion qu'il faut faire remonter notre étrange carrière d'impuissance politique acceptée et de démission de l'esprit de liberté'; Pierre Vadeboncoeur, *La ligne du risque* (1963; Montréal: Éditions Hurtubise, 1977), 197.

19 'C'est en 1837 qu'on nous a rompus, non pas tant par une victoire militaire que dans notre pensée. La succession des Habits rouge fut prise par nos réactionnaires. Vaincus militairement pour la deuxième fois en moins d'un siècle, nous allions l'être pour la première fois dans notre esprit et par nos propres soins'; ibid.

20 Pierre Vadeboncoeur, *L'autorité du peuple* (Bourgainville, QC: Éditions de l'Arc, 1965), 119.

21 'On voit bien que finalement la liberté en s'exerçant a pris chez-nous un style révolutionnaire'; ibid., 126.

22 'En un sens, les Québécois n'ont pas d'histoire. L'histoire, pour nous, est simplement du passé. Il y a peut-être peu de peuples occidentaux si peu pénétrés d'histoire que le nôtre, c'est-à-dire dont le passé soit effectivement si révolu ... Nous n'avons pas d'histoire'; ibid.

23 '[F]avorablement impressionné'; lettre de Pierre Vadeboncoeur à Hubert Aquin, 1966 (no precise date is given), Fonds Hubert Aquin, Archives de l'Université du Québec à Montréal, 44P-030/4.

24 'L'histoire de France depuis 1789 est articulée et vivante, et le présent résonne encore des deux derniers siècles de luttes, parce que le peuple vit encore ces luttes ou bien s'en souvient pour y avoir durement triomphé. Voilà ce que c'est que d'avoir une histoire: c'est de combattre encore côte à côte avec des disparus ou bien triompher encore aujourd'hui avec eux'; Vadeboncoeur, *Autorité du peuple*, 126.

25 'Quand on parle de la Défaite, on ne sait pas de quoi l'on parle: il faut la déterrer. C'est à croire qu'il n'y aurait pas eu de Conquête; il y en aurait tellement peu eu que, voici à peine quelques années, on songeait à célébrer 1760 en tant qu'événement historique, et l'idée de s'y opposer paraissait incongrue!'; ibid., 127.

26 'Jusqu'à tout récemment, nous flottions à la dérive sur une histoire dont on dirait qu'on l'a écrite d'avance en 1867 ou plus tôt pour nous éviter d'avoir à la vivre'; ibid.

27 'Depuis que nous parlons de socialisme et d'indépendance, c'est vraiment la première fois depuis 1837 que nous semblons vouloir quelque chose'; ibid.

28 Jacques Ferron, *Théâtre 1: Les Grands Soleils, Tante Élise, Le Don Juan chrétien* (Montréal: Librairie Déom, 1969). For a discussion of Ferron and decoloni-

zation, see Alexis Lachaine, 'Jacques Ferron, the Third World, and Decolonization in 1960s Quebec,' in *Jacques Ferron Hors Québec – Jacques Ferron Outside Québec*, ed. Ray Ellenwood and Betty Bednarski (Toronto: Éditions du GREF, 2010), 211–46. For an insightful overview of the relationship between politics and the theatre in Quebec, see, for example, Elaine F. Nardocchio, *Theatre and Politics in Modern Québec* (Edmonton: University of Alberta Press, 1986). The late 1960s saw the rise of an important radical theatre in English Canada as well. For an excellent study of radical theatre in Toronto in this period, see Denis W. Johnston, *Up the Mainstream: The Rise of Toronto's Alternative Theatres, 1968–1975* (Toronto: University of Toronto Press, 1991).

29 'J'ai voulu rattacher notre lutte de libération à toutes les luttes de libération dans le monde'; André Major, 'Un rôle de révélateur,' *Le Devoir*, 27 April 1968, 13.

30 Luc Fournier, *FLQ: histoire d'un mouvement clandestin* (Montréal: Québec-Amérique, 1982), 163.

31 Pierre Vallières, *White Niggers of America*, trans. Joan Pinkham (Toronto: McClelland and Stewart, 1971), 25.

32 'Deux cents cinq ans et un mois après le général James Wolfe, la reine débarquera ce matin à 10.02 à l'Anse au Foulon'; *Le Devoir*, 10 October 1964, 1.

33 Fournier, *FLQ*, 95.

34 Gaston Miron, *The Agonized Life*, trans. Marc Plourde (Montreal: Torchy Wharf Press, 1980), 39.

35 'Miron en prison, c'est notre parole même qu'on enferme,' *La Barre du jour* 26 (October 1970), 9.

36 Éric Bédard, *Chronique d'un insurrection appréhendée: la Crise d'Octobre et le milieu universitaire* (Sillery, QC: Septentrion, 1998).

37 See Pierre Vallières, *L'urgence de choisir* (Montréal: Parti pris, 1971).

38 René Lévesque, *An Option for Quebec* (Toronto: McClelland & Stewart, 1968), 14.

39 Ibid., 30.

40 I am referring, of course, to the recent controversy over the re-enactment of the Battle of the Plains of Abraham in Quebec City to celebrate the two hundred and fiftieth anniversary of that battle; see also the chapter by Nicole Neatby, in this volume.

10

Below the Academic Radar: Denis Vaugeois and Constructing the Conquest in the Quebec Popular Imagination[1]

BRIAN YOUNG

Although generally below the academic radar, Jacques Lacoursière and Denis Vaugeois, two historians from Trois-Rivières with neither PhDs nor tenured academic posts, have had an underestimated place in the internalization of the Conquest in the popular *Québécois* mindset.[2] In this chapter, I suggest how their choice of the Conquest as a pivotal event has been used to organize the historical dominos of ethnicity, identity, and national psyche. In that sense, the chapter fits directly into international debates over the construction and purveying of national histories in democratic societies.[3] I show how two history entrepreneurs embraced modernity. Using technologies, art forms, distribution techniques, and media savvy drawn from the pre–Quiet Revolution conservative and Catholic milieu of their youth, they easily eclipsed university historians in purveying their interpretation of Quebec history.

My interest in Vaugeois' half-century of entrepreneurship in popular history was prompted by curiosity as to where *Québécois* concepts of history *actually* originate. In my university career, teaching the Canadian survey course, sitting on history teaching commissions, writing history texts, and interacting with professional *Québécois* historians, I was struck by the contrast between academic discourses and popular expressions of the Quebec historical narrative. With an office just two doors down from Louise Dechêne, the distinguished historian of New France, I was puzzled by the tidal differences between the history she and other social scientists wrote and the perception of arriving francophone students as to the place of the Conquest, race, and minority status.[4] Interested in structures, demography, and the economy, Dechêne emphasized the persistence of French institutions in New France and similarities between peasant and merchant experiences on both sides of the French Atlantic. With an interest in regional studies, in prices, and in urban conditions, she did not give great significance to the Conquest, remarking to a Radio-Canada interviewer that there was little reason to view 1760 'as a watershed.'[5] This interpretation, however, was foreign to arriving students, as were the interpretations of other contemporary historians such as Gérard Bouchard or Jean-Marie Fecteau. I watched Jocelyn Létourneau test McGill students as part of a Quebec-wide inquiry into student attitudes to Quebec history. His chapter in this collection confirms the centrality of the Conquest, of the *nous* and *l'autre*, and of a sense that the history of Quebec coincides with the physical territory of Quebec.[6] These conceptions stretched back at least to 1970, when, in their report prepared for the Royal Commission on Bilingualism and Biculturalism, Marcel Trudel and Geneviève Jain identified what they called a 'history of grievances, revenge, and survival' from exposure to a 'superheated provincial nationalism' and the conviction that 'history should serve "la cause nationale."' Textbooks, they concluded, had become 'vehicles of a French and Catholic apologia. When we consider that today's French-speaking youth has received its historical education from these books, we can hardly wonder at the great vogue for the separatist movement among young people.'[7]

We need to move beyond academic examinations of the Conquest to understand its assimilation into popular culture: how does it fit with post 1960, with teaching, television, and Culture with a capital 'C'?[8] How do the Conquest and narratives of Quebec history relate to larger aspects of public culture, elements that include language, music, urban landscapes, or political discourses? From this perspective, Lacoursière and Vaugeois are far from being bottom feeders in the hierarchy of purveyors of national history. Rather, they have been highly effective communicators and writers of popular history and, while it is an unfair simplification to reduce their lifeworks to a focus on one event, they have been major players in weaving, repeating, and embedding the Conquest as the central trope in the Quebec national narrative. Borrowing from Tony Bennett, who, in turn, reaches to Robert Young's work, they can be described as 'crucial conceptual operator[s] in the history of difference.'[9]

Born in the mid-1930s and trained in mid-century Trois-Rivières in a milieu of vigorous Catholic popular education and first specializing in pedagogy, Lacoursière and Vaugeois understood quickly that the visual, the presentation, and the form of the message, along with the public personality of the messenger, matter. As the history of Quebec, nourished by the national movement of the 1960s, became an increasingly popular and politically sensitive subject, they cut a broad swath in both public and official domains. Quick learners, they linked their 1950s seminarian and community instincts with mastery of the technologies, new communications forms, and nationalist discourses of the new Quebec. Populists, they respected their public's preference for historical narratives, great events, heroes, humour, and fun. Experienced communicators and entrepreneurs, they caught the wave of expanding state investment in education and culture catering to secondary school and CEGEP (Quebec's junior college system) markets for textbooks, teachers' manuals, reading and documentary materials, and Quebec history productions for the mass media. These initiatives were particularly apt as rapid secularization reduced, practically overnight, traditional Catholic texts and history narratives to the category of anachronisms. Their peers moved in the 1960s and 1970s to positions of academic authority in CEGEPs, universities, academic presses, and archives in Ottawa and Quebec. For their part, they did not dabble with Marx, interdisciplinary junctures between history and anthropology, or emerging social science morasses of class, demography, or gender as debated in the learned journals. Instead, and always moving fast with a necessary eye on the cash register, they used their publishing success with a tabloid history journal, Le Boréal Express, to propel careers in the writing of popular history and in the media, politics, and publishing.[10] Their advance was aided by their attractive public personalities: engaging, congenial, and reassuring in their traditional masculinity and down-home québécité. Their Yin and Yang partnership as complementary, interacting opposites has served them well over five decades: Vaugeois bringing efficiency, technocracy, entrepreneurship, and ideological certainty, Lacoursière offering humanism, encyclopedic memory, the geniality of the raconteur, and marketability as a major media personality.

This effective communications twosome, particularly with Vaugeois' leadership, made the Conquest one of their principal mantras, and this forms the theme of the second part of the chapter. Seizing upon Université de Montréal professor Maurice Séguin's vision of Canadian history, they confirmed 1760 as the tipping point for French-Canadian identity and nationhood. Séguin's influence, and a similar point is made in this volume in Jocelyn Létourneau's contribution, is particularly evident in Vaugeois' writing of history, in his publishing, and in his politics and public career. In 1962, even before Le Boréal Express began, Vaugeois published his first monograph: the word *Conquête* appears as part of his title. Now in their seventies, the team persists with both medium and message. As part of the commemoration of the two hundred and fiftieth anniversary of the Battle of the Plains of Abraham (see Nicole Neatby's treatment of the event in this volume), they brought out *Québec ville assiégée, 1759–60: d'après les acteurs et les témoins*, with Lacoursière as co-author and Vaugeois as publisher through his publishing house, Les Éditions du Septentrion. A 259-page document collection, based on some two thousand five hundred research filing cards prepared by Lacoursière in 1961 for their tabloid, the book is a straightforward apolitical chronology of the political and military events of 1759–60. The presentation, format, style, and backers bear witness to their ongoing ability to repackage, repeat, and massage familiar messages and their capacity to attract deep-pocketed corporate and state sponsors.[11]

The cover is a reproduction of J. Walker's engraving of the Battle of Ste-Foy, a map of the Plains serves as frontispiece and is followed by a period view of Quebec. Careful attention is given to the cult of Lacoursière as one of the best *vulgarisateurs* of Quebec history and as author of the *Histoire populaire du Québec*, a five-volume steamroller that the publisher's website tells us has sold three hundred thousand copies. The text itself – and it is not easy to market a document collection – is skilfully presented. As is common in Lacoursière's works published by Septentrion, Vaugeois intervenes directly in the text, in this case writing the preface. Here, he emphasizes that the *Canadien* people, in place by 1760, were no longer French – abandoned, in fact, by a France that 'had not made the necessary effort' and creolized through contact with natives.[12] These are themes, as we will see, that he has emphasized throughout his lifetime.

The components of the standard historical work – index, bibliography, sources for illustrations – are all imaginatively presented with a view to attracting the popular reader of history. Instead of footnotes, sidebars are used to identify the documents. Reaching back again to techniques first employed in the 1960s, they use the *fleur-de-lys* and English lion as symbols to give each event its national French-British context, visual confirmation from the battlefield itself of the inexorable reality of *deux nations*. Illustrations – guns, victorious generals, scenes of urban ruin – fill dead spaces or form background to the text. From the monograph, the reader is invited to search for keywords on Septentrion's web page; Vaugeois' blog and access to the publisher's photo archives also encourage reader interactivity.

The influence of these two Trifluvians suggests that we may have underestimated the contribution of regions outside the two metropolises to the construction of the post-1960 Quebec identity. More than a dull industrial cityscape between Montreal and Quebec City and the legendary home of a reactionary *Duplessisme*, Trois-Rivières and its region is home to a vibrant and influential cultural tradition in music, poetry, art, archaeology, and popular history: Félix Leclerc, Gérald Godin, and, from the South Shore, artist Rodolphe Duguay come immediately to mind. As the third administrative centre of New France, it is an area rich in the vestiges of its native, colonial, and economic history. Its local history has been encouraged by intellectuals such as Benjamin Sulte and sustained by active historical and national societies, by an excellent newspaper, *Le Nouvelliste*, by federal and provincial investments in prominent historical sites and memorials, and by the archival and historical consciousness of Catholic institutions such as the Ursulines and the seminaries in Trois-Rivières and Nicolet. The region also had a strong male mentoring tradition through a clerical network based at the Séminaire de Trois-Rivières, centring on the hugely influential Monsignor Albert Tessier (1895–1976). Far from 'l'immobilisme social et intellectuel' suggested in Denis Monière's analysis, this network, albeit dead weight on questions of family, gender, or social reform, had an enduring interest in popular education, in new technologies, in art, theatre, poetry and literature, in regional history and community associations, and in international youth and intellectual currents useful in communicating with the popular classes in the forest and industrial towns they served as teachers, journalists, booksellers, or clergymen.[13]

A tireless organizer, documentary film-maker, archives aficionado, administrator, and university and popular educator, Albert Tessier was the region's intellectual and cultural tower. A native of the region and a graduate of the Séminaire de Trois-Rivières' classical and theological colleges, Tessier studied in Rome and Paris, returning to teach at his alma mater. From this seminary base, his intellectual influence spread across the region through community groups, adult education, and local publications and associations. Tessier had been a graduate theological student in Rome when Mussolini came to power and, back in Trois-Rivières, he frequently and approvingly drew the attention of colleagues to the model of Mussolini, himself an elementary school teacher, and his use of new school texts to recall the glory of Rome. Tessier took up writing, teaching, researching, and what he called the 'vulgarization' of history as a personal mission.[14] He was secretary of the local history society (1926), founded a publishing house, les Éditions du Bien public (1932), and often contributed to local newspapers, particularly in the form of a popular history column, 'la Grande et la Petite histoire.'[15] In 1927, with the collaboration of the journal *L'Action française* and the local history society, he organized a pilgrimage to Les Vieilles Forges, the historic iron works on the St-Maurice. After a speech by Lionel Groulx, a cross was erected near the ruins, an act that seamlessly merged Catholicism with a historic landscape and a nostalgic French past.[16] In celebration of the tercentenary of Trois-Rivières in 1934, the courtyard of the seminary was used to depict twenty living scenes from the history of the city, with three hundred vocalists and a thousand female figurants in period costume: for the occasion, Tessier produced a film, 'Trois-Rivières.'

Just below the rank of Groulx and Thomas Chapais, Tessier emerged as one of Quebec's most prominent historians in the 1930s and 1940s, publishing multiple works on the history of Canada and the St-Maurice region. He taught literature and Canadian history at the seminary, served as the seminary archivist, and, for a period in the 1930s, replaced Chapais in the Chair of Canadian History at l'Université Laval. A member of the Société des Dix and the Royal Society of Canada, Tessier hosted a weekly fifteen-minute show on Radio-Canada from 1941 to 1947. He was a strong promoter of St-Maurice native Félix Leclerc, editing and publishing the musician's works. A tireless public speaker, he presented some three thousand addresses on the history of the *Mauricie*, illustrating his talks with photos and films drawn from his own collection.[17] Beginning in 1925, he produced seventy documentary films unabashedly describing them as 'propagande par le film.'[18]

At the same time Tessier had expanding social influence across French Canada. In 1937, Premier Maurice Duplessis named him inspector of the province's sixteen schools of household education. This gave him a public platform to emphasize female education as separate from that of males, part of a girl's technical and moral training for her 'destiny' as the soul of the Quebec family.[19] In 1942, he became principal of the Institut de pédagogie familiale, a normal school for girls established in Montreal to train teachers of household education. Even in the late 1960s, amid the collapse of these institutions and their ideologies, Tessier would remain a strong pedagogical defender of the traditional Church/family/nationalist discourse.

Tessier developed strong social bonds with younger clerics and promising seminarians; to this day, Lacoursière and Vaugeois attribute their passion for history and archival research to this encouragement. In 1951, Tessier organized a country retreat, Tavibois, north of Trois-Rivières and not far from the St-Maurice home towns of Lacoursière and Vaugeois. Tavibois emphasized sociability and intellectualism around a model of clerical masculinity. Tessier lived at his Tavibois cottage, opening the site as a retreat and worksite for fellow clerics, student protégés, and local artists, as well as visiting Catholic intellectuals from France.[20] Le Cercle littéraire, based at the seminary and to which Vaugeois belonged for years, met there on Sundays. Lacoursière and Abbé Gilles Boulet, a member of the board of Le Boréal Express, shared a chalet on the Tavibois domain. Another Boréal editor, Abbé Lévis Martin, then an art teacher at the seminary, also built a chalet. This clerical milieu gave Lacoursière and Vaugeois a sense of balance, male space, intellectual richness, and a conservative rudder until 1968 – and thus deep into the era not only of the Quiet Revolution but also of Herbert Marcuse, women's liberation, and the Vietnam War.

In 1961, Lacoursière and Vaugeois, working out of the seminary archives, began planning what would become Le Boréal Express – their mock-ups were designed in tabloid form, the preferred format of the popular reader – and sought support from Tessier and senior clerics in the seminary/Tavibois network. Tessier agreed to serve on their board, and publication of the journal began in 1962. Besides Lacoursière, Vaugeois, and Tessier, the original editors included Abbés Gilles Boulet and Lévis Martin, and bookshop owner and journalist Pierre Gravel. Since Gravel had studied to be a Franciscan and Lacoursière had begun theological studies, five of the six editors, as Vaugeois remarked, had taken the soutane: none was a professional historian. If Tessier was the éminence grise, he was often absent from the editorial meetings held variously in their offices, at Lacoursière's home, and occasionally at Tavibois. Rather than meetings of a fledgling business enterprise, editors recall evenings of social and intellectual bonding, with elaborate dinners prepared by gourmet cook Lacoursière and the reading aloud of draft articles.[21] Lévis Martin (b. 1929) and Gilles Boulet (1926–97) were critical members of this editorial circle. Martin knew Lacoursière (b. 1932) and Vaugeois (b. 1935) through the seminary, where he taught art and literature from 1954 to 1972. As Tessier's presumed successor as cultural mentor, Martin liaised with Tessier, dealt with deadlines, and was known for quick articles on art and music. Responsible for art layout, he gave substance to Tessier's emphasis on the visual. Trained in Europe and Washington, he ensured the tabloid's youthful look by spreading stories and art across two-page spreads and imitating the modernistic, bloc style of Piet Mondrian. It was Martin who drew 'Pee Wee,' a popular cartoon presented without text and featuring a native boy.[22] Gilles Boulet, from an elite family in Vaugeois' home town of St-Tite, took an MA at the Catholic University of Paris after theological studies at the seminary. A literature teacher in Shawinigan by day, Boulet was known across the region for his leadership in popular education, for his interest in local history and archaeology, and, thanks to family wealth, for clerical dash through his Jaguar and yacht. He was also the author of French-language textbooks and director of both the Musée d'Archéologie et de Préhistoire de Trois-Rivières and the *Cahiers d'archéologie québécoise*. In 1960, he was named by the bishop to head a new Centre d'études universitaires that would coordinate diverse university courses being offered in the diocese by the seminary, Jesuits, nuns, and normal school.[23] Alongside his elevation of local university programs to Quiet Revolution respectability – and, in 1969, the Centre evolved into the Université du Québec à Trois-Rivières – Boulet encouraged extension and adult courses through the Centre. Boulet used the Centre to provide *Le Boréal Express* with office space as well as a start-up loan of $2,000, and he wrote articles for the tabloid on science and technology.[24]

Presented as a newspaper of the period, each twelve-page edition of *Le Boréal Express* focused on the events, personalities, and anecdotes of a single year. Publicity pamphlets spoke to its 'revolutionary' presentation of Canadian history, its 'authenticity,' its 'modern allure,' its 'sensational headlines,' its women's and sports columns, and its placing of Canadian history in a global context.[25] The first issue treated 1524 and the sixteenth, published in June 1964, ended the history of New France. A later series took the tabloid to 1841. Three of these – 1756, 1760, and 1763 – were devoted to the seven-year Conquest period. Priced at 35 cents a copy or $3.00 a year, each issue used headlines, illustrations, photos, drawings, cartoons, and crossword puzzles to underline a visual, journalistic presentation. A sense of moment and mood was captured: for the issue dealing with the Conquest, for example, the editors announced that, given the urgency of the time, they were suspending the women's column. Readers' comments were invited, and the editors reached out to the public through presentations to book fairs, teachers' meetings, and rotary luncheons. Behind the chat and interactivity, each issue had serious intellectual content through texts and strategic use of original documents, usually constitutional and often drawn from

Adam Shortt and Arthur G. Doughty's *Documents Relating to the Constitutional History of Canada, 1759–1791* (1911). Reviews, such as popular journalist and nationalist activist Pierre Bourgault's description of the tabloid as a 'tour de force,' were cited along with clerical recommendations from Chanoine Lionel Groulx and Sister Suzanne Pouliot of the Centre Marie de l'Incarnation and historians Michel Brunet, Pierre Savard, and Marcel Trudel.[26]

A teachers' guide to each issue was published and sold separately. These included films and other audiovisual didactic materials, course outlines, bibliographies, supplementary documents and maps, and an index to the issue. Teachers were encouraged to present the opposing views of historians such as facing-page quotations from Donald Creighton (in English) and Guy Frégault as to the significance of the Treaty of Utrecht: this was accompanied by a series of questions to animate class discussion.[27] The teachers' guides were used for announcements –history association meetings and local book fairs – and for promotions such as Christmas subscriptions. In October 1963, for example, the editors announced to teachers that *Le Boréal Express* had received official approval as classroom material from the Catholic Committee of the Council of Public Instruction.[28] In 1964, the editors began to repackage their product, offering the tabloid and teachers' guides in separate bound volumes. The three large book-form volumes of *Le Boréal Express*, covering the years 1524–1760, 1760–1810, and 1810–41, were given added academic credibility through prefaces written by historians from both of Quebec's French-language universities: Michel Brunet of the Université de Montréal and Marcel Trudel and Jean Hamelin of Laval.

Encouraged by their tabloid breakthrough into the popular history market and with Vaugeois well placed – first in the history section of the Ministry of Education and then in the Centre franco-québécois de développement pédagogique – to gauge the growing textbook market, he and Lacoursière undertook in 1968 to write a survey text. Part of their motivation was frustration with the publication in 1967 of a Canadian history text, part of Canada's centenary celebrations. Published first in English in Toronto, authored primarily by an Ontario academic, and with a title they saw as a 'political slogan,' *Canada: Unity in Diversity* included sections on Quebec written by Marcel Trudel, Fernand Ouellet, and Jean Hamelin.[29] Totally opposed, as Vaugeois put it, 'to the use of history as propaganda' and to the introduction into Quebec schools of a translated text from Ontario, they first set out to revise the Clercs de St-Viateur text, *l'Histoire du Canada*, published in 1934 by

Fathers Paul-Émile Farley and Gustave Lamarche.[30] In writing what quickly evolved into a new synthesis, Lacoursière and Vaugeois were joined by Jean Provencher, another Trifluvian, with research assistance from a young Montreal graduate of the Université de Montréal, Paul-André Linteau: in 1968, they published *Histoire 1534–1968*, re-edited a year later as *Canada-Québec: synthèse historique*. Although it did not conform to the Ministry of Education program, their text was approved for use in Quebec Catholic schools in 1970 or 1971. Frequently republished over the years, the work had huge success, with teachers and school administrators buying hundreds of thousands of copies for classrooms across the province.[31] The graphics and maps, the placing of an illustration or document on virtually every facing page, and the historiography, comments, and definitions instantly available at the page bottom were techniques copied from *Le Boréal Express*. Although outdated by Ministry of Education history curricula introduced in the early 1980s, *Canada-Québec: synthèse historique* was still in use in Quebec high schools as late as 1989.

The publication of the tabloid, the writing of their survey text, and then, also in 1968, the establishment of their publishing house, Les Éditions du Boréal Express, represented only part of the almost frantic teaching, entrepreneurial, media, and public activities of Vaugeois and Lacoursière, as both used rising stardom in popular history to support young families. In 1965, Vaugeois attracted wide media attention with his three-week appearance on a popular television history quiz show, 'Tous pour un,' culminating in a $5,000 prize. This TV celebrity was instrumental in Vaugeois' nomination in September 1965 to direct the Ministry of Education's history division.[32] In three years at the ministry, he initiated reforms in the training of history teachers, and in 1966 published two important guides: *La civilisation française et catholique au Canada* and *Un projet de classe-laboratoire pour l'enseignement de l'histoire*. The emphasis in these reforms on student participation and the use of historical documents cloned pedagogical techniques mastered in *Le Boréal Express*.

In the late 1960s, the entrepreneurial Vaugeois caught other waves emanating from the expansion of the cultural state as Quebec and France increased their collaboration and investments in cultural and educational initiatives; David Meren examines this phenomenon elsewhere in this volume. From 1967 to 1969, Vaugeois served as co-director of the Centre franco-québécois de développement pédagogique; in 1969 and 1970 he directed the office of Marcel Masse, Minister of

Intergovernmental Affairs; from 1970 to 1974 he held the more senior position of director-general of international relations in the Ministry of Intergovernmental Affairs. Later in the 1970s, and as a part-time enterprise, he became co-owner of a trendy Quebec City record store, Mélomane. He had come a long way in the decade between leaving his normal school classroom in Trois-Rivières in 1965 and returning in 1976 as the city's member in the National Assembly. Travelling, collaborating at the highest levels with French cultural and educational officials, and directing the expansion of Quebec's overseas offices and then a major Canada-Quebec regional educational project in Morocco brought him an increased public profile. At the same time, his love of history and publishing remained strong. He and Lacoursière kept an old car in Paris and, whenever possible, indulged their passion for archives, researching from Paris to Rome. In 1973 he visited Chile, reporting on his visit in *Le Devoir*.

A contributor to the Parti Québécois since at least 1970, in 1976 Vaugeois ran successfully in Trois-Rivières, becoming a member of the first Lévesque government. There, he served as Minister of Culture (February 1978 to April 1981), Minister of Communications (September 1979 to November 1980), and Vice-President of the Treasury Board (November 1980 to April 1981). His instincts as minister, evident particularly in his museum and library policy, strongly reflected his belief in democratization, accessibility, and the freeing of institutions from old elites and self-interested professionals: 'My objective was to develop sites for popular and adult education. Libraries and museums were at the heart of my preoccupations and action.'[33] It was in fact his insistence on the renovation of popular urban neighbourhoods, as opposed to government subsidization of middle-class housing in the suburbs, that led to his dismissal from the Lévesque cabinet in April 1981.

For his part, Lacoursière flourished as a *raconteur* and writer of popular history. As early as 1968–9, he had a strong media presence through twenty-six half-hour radio programs. In 1979, *Nos racines, l'histoire vivante des Québécois*, co-authored with Hélène-Andrée Bizier, duplicated *Le Boréal Express*'s success in the Quebec popular market. Released in 144 weekly instalments, *Nos racines* served up Quebec history with an easy-to-follow chronological approach, superb illustrations, sidebars, bibliographies, and genealogies. In 1995, Lacoursière, this time with Vaugeois as his publisher, went back to the well of *Nos racines*, cutting and pasting parts of the original into another huge commercial success, the five-volume *Histoire populaire du Québec*. In 1995, his effective chairing of a commission on the teaching of history showed his persistent capacity to influence public policy and officials in the Ministry of Education. To this he added broad television exposure by participating in the founding and program development of Historia Television, Astral media's French-language history channel, as well as hosting and narrating a popular film history of Quebec. Directed by Gilles Carle and widely distributed as a four-disc DVD set, 'Épopée en Amérique: une histoire populaire du Québec' is still a regular repeat on late-night television. With Astral's anglophone ownership, the multiculturalism of the history commission, and his increasing Canada-wide recognition as a popular historian, Lacoursière, much more than Vaugeois, has tended to become ambiguous in applying the Conquest trope across Canadian history.[34]

In the early 1960s, however, with decolonization in the air and Quebec national feeling awaiting its tinderbox, confirmation of the Conquest as the Armageddon of a national narrative of popular history was a brilliant stroke. The Conquest is a deep line in the sand, an irretrievable moment of Before and After. Everyman understands its association with empires, war, violence, heroes, and glory and humiliation. The core identity, the culture, language, and religion of the defeated people are obvious: its destiny – and this three and a half centuries down the road – less so. From one perspective, undoing the Conquest leads inevitably to independence. From another – and this ambiguity is evident in Lacoursière and Vaugeois – the territorial magnitude of the pre-Conquest French Empire in North America facilitates nostalgia of an energetic and successful French Canada with explorers, traders, soldiers, and missionaries operating on a continental scale far beyond boundaries imaginable in modern Quebec. This construct of a positive and inextinguishable French contribution to North American civilization motors much of Vaugeois' recent work, particularly his descriptions of the Lewis and Clark expeditions and his historical atlas of North America.[35]

There was nothing inherently original about seeing the Conquest as the great divide in Quebec history. This had been one of the central themes of historians from Garneau to Groulx. But in the 1950s and 1960s the impact of the Conquest was forcefully reasserted by a group of historians at the Université de Montréal. Vaugeois, aided by his Tessier connections, went to study there in 1959, and he came away devoted to Maurice Séguin. If Tessier was his mentor in communications, popular education, and his sure sense of *patrie*, Vaugeois would give himself over ideologically to Séguin in adopting the master's conviction of the centrality of the Conquest. Writing more than four decades later, Vaugeois confirmed Séguin as 'my master, then my friend. I became his editor.'[36] Entitling one Séguin work as the 'Vision of a Prophet,' Vaugeois assessed Séguin as 'the intellectual who has perhaps had the most influence on the evolution of Quebec since 1960.'[37] Other observers give credence to this status. Jean Blain, himself a member of the Université de Montréal history department, noted that, although publishing relatively little, Séguin influenced his more prolific departmental colleagues Michel Brunet and Guy Frégault in their establishment of the neo-nationalist school and in their positioning of the Conquest as its centrepiece. Another historian and observer of the Université de Montréal school, Marcel Trudel, also pointed to Séguin's virtual obsession with the Conquest: 'Jovial, Maurice Séguin was not ... His courses and rare public lectures displayed a rigorous sense of logic. In fact his whole scheme of thought, constructed around a single event, the British Conquest of 1760 as the determining factor in French Canada's history, rested on the same rigorous logic. It was a tightly woven system, impregnable in its various parts. The basic premise was everything: either you accepted it or you didn't. Séguin wrote little, leaving it to his disciples (always a dangerous practice) to spread his ideas.'[38]

After graduating from the Université de Montréal with a *Licence ès lettres*, Vaugeois returned to Trois-Rivières and a teaching post at the École normale Duplessis: the Séguin shadow went with him. In his first book, *Union des deux Canadas: nouvelle Conquête?*, he placed Séguin alongside Lord Durham and Montesquieu in his frontispiece, quoting Séguin's dictum that, 'to be a minority people in a federation is to be an annexed people.'[39] Vaugeois went on to note that his book was a response to Séguin's appeal that 'THE GREATEST DUTY IN THE ORDER OF IDEAS IS TO DENOUNCE THE FUNDAMENTAL AND ESSENTIAL ALIENATION FROM WHICH FRENCH CANADA SUFFERS [his capitals] – to de-mask the imposture of the La Fontaine–Étienne Parent tradition, this good old myth that equality is possible between the two nationalities, or better yet of the possibility for French Canadians to be masters in a Quebec which remains within Confederation.'[40] With 'Union' and 'Conquest' both included in his title, Vaugeois emphasized Séguin's focus on the drama of 1760 and the critical importance of the period from the Conquest to 1840. His conclusion spoke to French Canada's 'collective mediocrity,' 'introduced by the Conquest,

renewed by the Union Act and given official status by Confederation,'
a situation that could be rectified only by regaining what Séguin had
called the capacity 'to think as a collective self.'[41]

While Vaugeois' own monograph attracted limited readership, the
Boréal Express and teachers' guides, his survey textbook of Canadian
history, his publishing house and its series '1760' opened mass readership to the Séguin interpretation throughout the 1960s and 1970s, re-
ceiving support from remaining Catholic institutions and publishers
and from the Quebec ministries of Education and Culture. It is hard to
imagine that any youth coming of age in the 1960s or 1970s in francophone Quebec missed exposure to Boréal Express publications. Le Boréal
Express for 1760 gave principal place to military heroes and the effects
of the Conquest, particularly on the Church. Illustrations showed, for
example, the ruined interiors of the Jesuit and Récollet churches. A column entitled 'Vie & Religion' appeared regularly with headlines that
spoke of the trial of the Jesuits and the 'immense sadness' of Rome.[42]
Séguin was reserved for the teachers' guide, which offered a six-page
presentation of what it called Séguin's 'norms,' by which nations were
established through colonization. The 'inevitable emancipation' of the
nation-fille might be found through outright independence, as in the
case of the United States, or within the cadre of the Commonwealth.[43]
In 1968, the Vaugeois/Lacoursière textbook Canada-Québec: synthèse historique gave full measure to the Conquest, portraying the collapse of
New France as the greatest defeat the French world had ever known.
Séguin was cited to the effect that the loss of Canada was more important than the defeat of Napoleon; it signalled the end of French hegemony and the triumph of the monde anglo-saxon. Students learned that
before 1760 a distinct Quebec nation was in place with a people who
had 'a spirit of independence and liberty.'[44]

Also in 1968, with the original Boréal team breaking up, with Tessier
embittered by Lacoursière's impending divorce, and with two of the
editorial board soon to be defrocked, Lacoursière and Vaugeois converted their tabloid operation into a publishing house, Les Éditions
du Boréal Express, with Vaugeois as principal shareholder. Its political
mission – 'development of the Québécois national consciousness' – was
worn up front.[45] Within the year, it had published a five-thousand-
copy run of Séguin's L'idée d'indépendance and, over the next decade
until Vaugeois' election in 1976, it published some fifty monographs.[46]
Séguin's book became the flagship of a new series entitled '1760' and
designed to 'suggest a major historical fact: the Conquest.'[47] A second

Séguin work, *La nation 'canadienne' et l'agriculture (1760–1840)*, rapidly sold three thousand copies.[48] The four remaining titles published in the series by 1974 included a collection of articles by Séguin's student, Jean-Pierre Wallot, as well as Vaugeois' own work on Jews in New France, Jean Provencher's study of Quebec under the War Measures Act of 1914, and Micheline Dumont-Johnson's study of missionaries in Acadia.[49]

In 1976, Vaugeois entered a new phase of his career as the member for Trois-Rivières in the National Assembly. In 1978, his role as Minister of Culture now putting him in a potential conflict of interest in that the ministry regularly subsidized his publications, he sold Les Éditions du Boréal Express. For Vaugeois, publishing might have been temporarily suspended: his attraction to a Séguin discourse from platforms as an MNA and then, as minister, as official spokesperson for Quebec culture, certainly was not. In 1978, for example, he explained the pre-Conquest origins of the nation in a guide written for Quebec women: 'New France generated a People, a *"Canadien"* People ... tenacious and light-hearted, fun-loving, keen on liberty – sometimes restless – and guardians of its French tradition ... From the eighteenth century to our own day, the "spirit of independence" of this people on the banks of the St Lawrence has been recognized.'[50] His explanation of 'the other,' of the Conquest 'traumatism,' and of his particular mission as a *Québécois* historian was presented in much blunter fashion to an English-Canadian audience in Sault Ste Marie, Ontario, in 1977. A *Canadien* nation existed before 1759, he told them, a society that 'had found its unity, its solidarity, its desire to last, even before your [nation] intervened in our national life.' The Conquest was 'the crucible event' that upset this 'equilibrium.' He reminded them of the Quebec historical tradition, applauding Lionel Groulx's scientific method, and concluding, '[as] a Québécois historian, I ask questions of a national past which is not yours. The space, time, and people of my inquiry are different than yours and I am researching elements of understanding that measure up to the preoccupations of the people of which I am a member, preoccupations different than those of the people to which you belong.'[51]

If almost every political moment could be given a 1760s connection, none was more pointed than language, particularly in the late 1970s and the period surrounding Bill 101. 'Since the reversal of power in 1760 by which we became a dominated national minority,' Vaugeois told a 1978 meeting of French-language teachers, 'our claims in favour of French-language rights for our society have never ceased.'[52]

His conception was profoundly ethnic, pointing out how the Conquest had marked French Canadians across the continent.[53] Commenting to a National Assembly committee on Acadian Antonine Maillet's winning of the French Prix Goncourt, Vaugeois noted that her achievement reminded him, as a historian, of Lieutenant-Colonel Winslow's reading of the 1755 orders of the seizing of the Acadians' goods and of their imminent exile. To the frustration of Liberal colleagues on the committee, he insisted that it was the Acadian tradition of keeping alive painful memories that was at the root of Maillet's achievement.[54] He had a similar discourse speaking to Louisianans in Quebec City to celebrate the old capital's three hundred and seventieth anniversary: the Conquest, they were reminded, could not 'annihilate the people already formed on its territories ... nothing ever will.' He continued, 'French America is all the charm of the American dream thought out and organized by the French spirit. It is the amalgam of the call of a fabulous territory, of the long-standing complicity between one of the great Western civilizations and the Amerindian peoples of this earth.'[55]

While Vaugeois has always accepted that the aboriginal peoples must be accorded status as charter members of pre-Conquest society, and while he is highly respectful of what he would call the nation of English Canada outside Quebec, his attitude towards the presence of the English in Quebec, and their language and institutions, has been less accommodating. His view of English-speaking minorities of European origin in Quebec is also problematic, since by reason of their arrival after 1760 and their language and culture, they are automatically consigned to the 'other' nation.[56] The Jews, however, form a minority that Vaugeois situates carefully in the Conquest narrative and are included, along with aboriginals, as charter minorities in the nation as it existed in 1760. He has regularly returned to their place in the Quebec historical experience, particularly to that of the small Jewish population in the Trois-Rivières of his youth, seeing their experience as raising issues of religious plurality and the dangers of xenophobia. Picking up on Tessier's emphasis on the role of the Jewish Hart family in Trois-Rivières and their family collection in the seminary archives, Vaugeois wrote the biographies of Aaron, Ezekiel, Moses, and Aaron Ezekiel Hart and of Samuel Jacobs for the *Dictionary of Canadian Biography*.[57] He has also used his Septentrion publishing house to publish a variety of books on the Jewish community. Although it was a stretch, since Jews were not permitted in New France, he entitled his second monograph, *Les Juifs de la Nouvelle-France* (1968) and included it in his series '1760.' Dedi-

cated to two Jewish friends, David Rome and Naïm Kattan, it spoke
to the dangers of anti-Semitism or of attributing the Seven Years' War
to an 'international Jewry or its subset the freemasons.' His conclusion
was that 'there is no cause and effect relationship between Jews and the
Conquest': while some Jews may have 'profited from the War of Conquest,' others were just suppliers and some even involuntarily aided
the French cause.[58] Vaugeois has also spoken regularly to Jewish audiences, inviting them to 'put their shoulder to the wheel,' integrating
into Quebec society and building a society à la Québécoise.[59]

Publication statistics give some measure of the Lacoursière/Vau-
geois impact in communicating their interpretation of Quebec history.
By 1963, just a year into publication, Le Boréal Express boasted some
nine thousand subscribers.[60] By 1974, the Boréal Express logo had appeared worldwide on over more than a million copies of the tabloid,
books, and other works.[61] Their textbook, Canada-Québec: synthèse historique, sold eighty thousand copies in the three years after its publication in 1968, and three hundred and fifty thousand by 2000.[62] Nor has
this communication energy diminished: Lacoursière's Histoire populaire
du Québec, published by Septentrion in the mid-1990s, has sold more
than three hundred thousand copies in the past decade. Many of these
works take the form of repackaged materials, the recycling of the same
primary documents, or repetition of a familiar message. Donald Fyson,
for example, points out that Histoire populaire reprints fifty-six chapters
from Nos racines, published in the early 1980s.[63] With fanfare at the 2009
Montreal Bookfair, Septentrion launched a reprint of the first volume
of Le Boréal Express (1524–1760), first printed as a history tabloid in the
1960s. If, as some cultural historians argue, all public culture can be
a form of propaganda, flagrant repetition, whatever the distaste for it
in academic corridors, can be a powerful commercial and communications tool.[64] And, if one comes back to one's initial theme of deep
student ruts in national history narratives constructed around the Conquest, this perspective is worthy of serious consideration. However
many the hoots from academicians, feminists, and federalists, Vau-
geois/Lacoursière have had a half-century of influence. Purveying and
sustaining a national history narrative is a complex function as societies, governments, and generations change. We must not underestimate
the long-term significance of a history tabloid and classroom texts, of
holding civil service positions in history teaching and international offices in the 1960s and 1970s, of elected office and cabinet posts in the
ministries of Culture and Communications at the end of the 1970s, of

intimate contact and lobbying with Ministry of Education officials into the 1990s, of publishing houses, and of ready and consistent presence in print, television, and film media.

Whatever the periodic bellicosity and ethnocentricity of the Séguin Conquest tropes, particularly in political crises like those of the patriation of the Constitution in 1982 and the referendum on sovereignty in 1995, Vaugeois' work ultimately reaches to a general overriding tolerance, an internationalism, and an essential religious plurality (best seen with respect to the Jews). At the same time, this has to be reconciled with the implicit contradiction that Quebec, like Trois-Rivières, must exist as a homogeneous society with a coherence built on its French-speaking, Catholic roots. These inclinations perhaps might be compared to Fernand Dumont's seeking a 'fraternal society,' or what Vaugeois – seeming constantly to struggle for solidarity and cohesion – at one point called a *sens commun*.[65] As Minister of Culture, Vaugeois insisted that culture be defined in its collective, rather than individual, context – a marker of both unity and difference. 'Culture,' he told a Montreal conference in 1978, 'is a powerful uniting force between men just as it is a clear demarcation line between societies.' Culture, he continued, is 'a limit, a frontier, and beyond its common sum, this society defines what is "the other," foreign. Culture then is a measure of difference ... A nation can integrate these groups without assimilating them on the express condition, nonetheless, that they share with the majority the essential of the national culture and contribute to it.'[66] And yet, even though he himself was an avid consumer of the Cannes Film Festival, the Smithsonian model of museums, and American music, history, and literature, he could not help noting that 'in a time of Chuck Mangione and Stevie Wonder ... at a time when the Ministry of Cultural Affairs subsidizes comic strips ... organized culture is the collective international subconscious to which we are all called ... on both sides of the Ottawa and on both sides of the Atlantic ... we are all brothers in a similar civilization.'[67]

Historical consciousness in Quebec undoubtedly has taken new dimensions from the Lacoursière/Vaugeois long march through Quebec popular culture. Grounded and coming of age in a coherent Catholic community just as the Quiet Revolution took form, they were advised, funded, introduced into schools, and published by Catholic authorities at every step of the way. At the same time, they had an easy touch for the modernity in French-Canadian culture, along with the energy, the didactic training, the love of history, and the business smarts to capital-

ize on the emergence of vigorous state cultural policies first introduced
by the establishment of the French Ministry of Culture under Malraux
in 1959 and in Quebec two years later. One might say that, in focusing
on the Conquest, Vaugeois was 'right on the money.' It was Fernand
Dumont, one of his principal advisers when he was Minister of Culture, who pointed out that one of the great challenges of modern society was determining how 'the individual can locate himself in a history,
construct a memory of his past, question his destiny.'[68] The Conquest
was perfect! It had a physical memorial site on the Plains of Abraham
and statues, fallen heroes, institutions, and commissions dedicated to
its safekeeping and memory, and ample art, maps, archival documents,
relics, memoirs, museums, and commemorations to keep an entrepreneurial publisher active over a lifetime. The Conquest, even in a modern and progressive society, was an irresistible marker readily inserted
in any *projet de société* that favoured patriotism and national autonomy.

NOTES

1 This chapter benefited from the thoughtful comments of Denyse Baillar-
   geon, Caroline-Isabelle Caron, John Dickinson, and Sean Mills.
2 Lacoursière and Vaugeois appear neither in Ronald Rudin, *Making History
   in Twentieth-Century Quebec* (Toronto: University of Toronto Press, 1997),
   which emphasizes the importance of historians such as Jean-Pierre Wallot
   and Louise Dechêne, nor in Denis Monière, *Le développement des idéologies
   au Québec des origines à nos jours* (Montréal: Québec/Amérique, 1977). For
   academic reviews of the *Histoire populaire du Québec* see Donald Fyson,
   Canadian Historical Review 78 (1997): 346–49; 79 (1998): 351–53, 791–93. Two
   long interviews with Vaugeois are available: 'Du Boréal au Septentrion:
   l'odyssée d'un historien' (Rencontre de Stéphane Stapinsky avec Denis
   Vaugeois), *Cahiers d'histoire du Québec au XXe siècle* 6 (automne 1996):
   83–109; and 'Rencontre avec Denis Vaugeois,' *Bulletin* (Association des
   professeures et des professeurs d'histoire des collèges du Québec) 8, no. 2
   (2002), http://vega.cvm.qc.ca/APHCQ/Bulletin/V08N2_APHCQ_
   Hiver2002-FWeb.pdf.
3 Controversy over versions of the American national past exploded over
   the issue of 'national history standards'; see Gary B. Nash, Charlotte
   Crabtree, and Ross E. Dunn, *History on Trial: Culture Wars and the Teaching
   of the Past* (New York: Knopf, 1998).
4 Having sat in the Ontario university classrooms of both Arthur Lower

and Donald Creighton, I more easily understood the ideology of English-speaking students summarized perhaps as a general disconnectedness with Quebec history, particularly pre-Conquest, an easy sense of the superiority of British institutions, and a still-existing vision of Canadian history (aside from angst over aboriginal issues and the environment), as José Igartua has put it, as a 'conflict-free progression from colony to nation within the comfortable orb of the British Empire'; see *The Other Quiet Revolution: National Identities in English Canada, 1945–71* (Vancouver: UBC Press, 2006), 72.

5 Cited in Rudin, *Making History in Twentieth-Century Quebec*, 181.

6 'L'histoire du Québec racontée par les élèves de 4e et 5e secondaire: l'impact apparent du cours d'histoire nationale dans la structuration d'une mémoire historique collective chez les jeunes Québécois,' *Revue d'histoire de l'Amérique française* 62 (Summer 2008): 69–94.

7 Both cited in Marcel Trudel, *Memoirs of a Less Travelled Road: A Historian's Life* (Montreal: Véhicule Press, 2001), 161.

8 This perspective in France is developed in Marc Fumaroli, *L'État culturel: essai sur une religion moderne* (Paris: Éditions de Fallois, 1992), 20.

9 Tony Bennett, *Culture: A Reformer's Science* (London: Sage, 1998), 78. For Robert Young, see his *Colonial Desire: Hybridity in Theory, Culture and Race* (London: Routledge, 1995).

10 One thinks, for example, of seminary classmates André Bureau in the media or Jean Chrétien in Ottawa politics.

11 The work was published in collaboration with the federal National Battlefields Commission with publishing subsidies from the Canada Council, SODEC, the Quebec government's Programme de crédit d'impôt pour l'édition de livres, and the federal government's Programme d'aide au développement de l'industrie de l'édition.

12 Denis Vaugeois, introduction to Jacques Lacoursière and Hélène Quimper, *Québec ville assiégée, 1759–60: d'après les acteurs et les témoins* (Sillery, QC: Septentrion, 2009), 16.

13 Monière, *Développement des idéologies*, 320; for internationalism, see Michael Gauvreau, *The Catholic Origins of Quebec's Quiet Revolution, 1931–1970* (Montreal; Kingston, ON: McGill-Queen's University Press, 2005), chap. 3.

14 Tessier stated his interest in vulgarizing history as editor of the thirty-nine-volume series, 'Pages Trifluviennes,' launched in 1932 as a prelude to Trois-Rivières' tercentenary. See Maude Roux-Pratte, 'Albert Tessier et les "Pages Trifluviennes" (1832–1939),' in *Nouvelle Pages Trifluviennes*, ed. Jean Roy et Lucia Ferretti (Sillery, QC: Septentrion, 2009), 167. His admira-

tion for Mussolini is outlined in Paul-Henri Carignan, *Mgr Albert Tessier, éducateur* (Trois-Rivières, QC: Éditions du Bien Public, 1977), 6.

15 See Roux-Pratte, 'Albert Tessier,' 167–98. The archives of Albert Tessier are held in the Archives du Séminaire de Trois-Rivières.

16 Albert Tessier, *Souvenirs en vrac* (Sillery, QC: Les Éditions du Boréal Express, 1975), 142.

17 Bibliothèque et archives nationales du Québec-Québec (hereafter cited as BANQ-Q), P655, Vaugeois Collection, box 218, Correspondance, Tessier file, newspaper clipping [n.d.].

18 Tessier, *Souvenirs en vrac*, 168.

19 Carignan, *Mgr Albert Tessier*, 19.

20 Interview with René Hardy, 9 July 2009.

21 Interviews with Denis Vaugeois, 5 August 2009 and Lévis Martin, 3 August 2009.

22 Interview with Lévis Martin, 3 August 2009. Martin left the clergy in 1972, teaching art history in Trois-Rivières until 1990.

23 Lucia Ferretti, *L'université en réseau: les 25 ans de l'Université du Québec* (Ste-Foy, QC: Presses de l'Université du Québec, 1994), 37. Boulet also left the clergy, becoming the first rector of the Université du Québec à Trois-Rivières and, later, president of the Université du Québec system. He also served on the board of Radio-Canada.

24 Interview with Denis Vaugeois, 5 August 2009. The final director on the first board was Pierre Gravel, director of the French review *Chantiers* as well of the Association catholique de la jeunesse canadienne française.

25 BANQ-Q, P655, Fonds Denis Vaugois, box 216, 'Brochure,' Salon du livre, Montréal, avril 1964, 'un genre révolutionnaire'; 'un journal d'allure moderne'; 'authentique'; 'titres à sensation.'

26 See *Bulletin pédagogique* 2, no. 1 (1963).

27 *Bulletin pédagogique* 2, no. 5 (1964).

28 *Bulletin pédagogique* 2, no. 2 (1963).

29 'Du Boréal au Septentrion' (see note 2); a French version, also published by Holt, Rinehart and Winston, appeared in 1968.

30 Ibid.

31 Jacques Lacoursière, Jean Provencher, and Denis Vaugeois, *Canada-Québec: synthèse historique 1534–2000* (Sillery, QC: Septentrion, 2000), 4.

32 Interview with Denis Vaugeois, 5 August 2009.

33 '[M]on objectif était de développer des lieux d'éducation populaire et permanente. Les bibliothèques et les musées ont été au coeur de mes préoccupations et de mes actions'; Denis Vaugeois blog, Septentrion website, 17 May 2009.

34 In 1996, for example, Lacoursière was awarded the Pierre Berton Award, Canada's top award for popularizing Canadian history.

35 Denis Vaugeois, *America 1803–1853: l'expédition de Lewis et Clark et la naissance d'une nouvelle puissance* (Sillery, QC: Septentrion, 2002); and Raymonde Litalien, Jean-François Palomino, and Denis Vaugeois, *La mesure d'un continent: atlas historique de l'Amérique du Nord 1492–1814* (Sillery, QC: Septentrion, 2008).

36 '[M]on maître, puis mon ami. Je deviendrai son éditeur'; Denis Vaugeois, *L'amour du livre: l'édition au Québec, ses petits secrets et ses mystères* (Sillery, QC: Septentrion, 2005), 22.

37 '[P]eut-être l'intellectuel qui a eu le plus d'influence sur l'évolution du Québec depuis 1960'; Denis Vaugeois, in Maurice Séguin, *Une histoire du Québec: vision d'un prophète* (Montréal: Guérin, 1995), v.

38 Trudel, *Memoirs of a Less Travelled Road*, 157; for Blain on Séguin, see the preface in Maurice Séguin, *La 'nation canadienne' et l'agriculture (1760–1850)* (Trois-Rivières, QC: Les Éditions du Boréal Express, 1970). Séguin is also treated in Rudin, *Making History in Twentieth-Century Quebec*; and in Jean Lamarre, *Le devenir de la nation québécoise: selon Maurice Séguin, Guy Frégault et Michel Brunet (1944–1969)* (Sillery, QC: Septentrion, 1993).

39 'Être un peuple minoritaire dans une fédération, c'est être un peuple annexé'; Denis Vaugeois, *Union des deux Canadas: nouvelle Conquête?* (Trois-Rivières, QC: Éditions du Bien Public. Éditions du Soc, 1962), viii.

40 'LE PLUS GRAND DEVOIR, DANS L'ORDRE DES IDÉES, EST DE DÉNONCER L'ALIÉNATION FONDAMENTALE ESSENTIELLE DONT SOUFFRE LE CANADA FRANÇAIS. De démasquer l'imposture de la tradition Lafontaine – Etienne Parent, ce bon vieux mythe d'une égalité possible entre les deux nationalités ou mieux de la possibilité pour les canadiens français d'être maîtres dans un Québec qui demeurait à l'intérieur de la Confédération' [capitalization in original]; ibid., xvi.

41 '[M]édiocrité collective,' 'introduite par la Conquête, reprise par l'Union et régularisée par la Confédération,' 'agir par soi collectif'; ibid., 223.

42 *Le Boréal Express an 1760* 2, no. 10 (1964).

43 *Bulletin pédagogique* 2, no. 4 (1963).

44 Denis Vaugeois, Jacques Lacoursière, and Jean Provencher, *Histoire 1534–1968* (Montréal: Éditions du Renouveau Pédagogique, 1968) 179, 187 ('l'esprit d'indépendance et de liberté').

45 '[L]a prise de conscience nationale des Québécois'; BANQ-Q, P655, Fonds Denis Vaugeois, box 216, Boréal Express, 'Catalogue 74,' n.p. (section 'L'équipe').

46 Vaugeois to Séguin, 28 October 1968, BANQ-Q, P655-26, Fonds Denis Vaugeois, box 218, Correspondance Séguin.

47 '[S]uggérer un fait historique majeur: la Conquête'; BANQ-Q, P655-26,
Fonds Denis Vaugeois, box 216, 'Catalogue 74.'

48 Vaugeois, *Amour du livre*, 158.

49 Maurice Séguin, *L'idée d'indépendance au Québec:* genèse et historique
(Trois-Rivières, QC: Les Éditions Boréal Express, 1968); idem, *La 'Nation
Canadienne' et l'agriculture* (Trois-Rivières, QC: Les Éditions Boréal Express,
1970); Denis Vaugeois, *Les Juifs de la Nouvelle-France* (Trois-Rivières, QC:
Les Éditions du Boréal Express, 1968); Jean-Pierre Wallot, *Un Québec qui
bougeait: trame socio-politique au tournant du XIXe* siècle (Trois-Rivières, QC:
Les Éditions Boréal Express, 1973); Jean Provencher, *Québec sous la loi des
mesures de guerre 1918* (Trois-Rivières, QC: Les Éditions Boréal Express,
1971); and Micheline Dumont-Johnson, *Apôtres ou agitateurs? La France missionnaire en Acadie* (Trois-Rivières, QC: Les Éditions Boréal Express, 1970).

50 'La Nouvelle France a généré un peuple, un peuple qu'on nomme canadien et qui se distingue rapidement de ces origines françaises. Les nécessités
physiques de l'adaptation au pays y ont contribué, plus encore l'apport
des cultures amérindiennes a-t-il été décisif. Ce peuple est tenace et
insouciant, avide de liberté – parfois indocile – et conservateur de sa tradition française, ingénieux et léger, dispensateur de sa richesse, raffiné, et
capable de supporter les coups durs qu'imposent une terre de colonisation
... Depuis le XVIIIe siècle et jusqu'à nos jours, bien peu nombreux furent
ceux qui ne reconnurent pas "l'esprit d'indépendance" de ce peuple des
rives du Saint-Laurent'; handwritten copy of Denis Vaugeois, 'La Nouvelle
France: creuset de la formation d'un peuple,' in *Guide de la Québécoise 1978*,
ed. Margot Gouin-Boisvert, 20, in BANQ-Q, P655-26, Fonds Vaugeois.

51 '[A] trouvé son unité, sa solidarité, son désir de durer, avant même que
la vôtre n'intervienne dans notre vie nationale,' 'l'événement charnière,'
'équilibre,' 'traumatisme,' '[e]n tant qu'historien québécois, j'interroge un
passé national qui n'est pas le vôtre. L'espace, le temps et les hommes de
mon enquête sont différents du vôtre et je suis à la recherche d'éléments
de compréhension à la mesure des inquiétudes du peuple dont je suis, inquiétudes différentes de celles qui préoccupent le peuple dont vous êtes';
Denis Vaugeois, 'L'historiographie canadienne, témoin de l'évolution et de
l'état des relations québeco-canadiennes,' notes prepared for a conference,
Sault Ste Marie, ON, 2 December 1977, BANQ-Q, P655-26, Fonds Denis
Vaugeois. Multiple other instances can be given, as in, for example, 'Con-
férence: une culture pour une société. Notes en vue d'un exposé,' Colloque
Culture et Société, Collège Jésus-Marie, Quebec, 19 April 1978, BANQ-Q
P655-26, Fonds Vaugeois.

52 'Depuis le renversement du pouvoir de 1760, alors que nous devenions une minorité nationale dominée, nos revendications en faveur des droits de la langue française n'ont eu de cesse dans notre société'; Denis Vaugeois, notes for a speech at the opening of the conference of professeurs de français du Québec, Trois-Rivières, QC, 10 November 1978, BANQ-Q P655-27, Fonds Vaugeois.

53 In an interview (7 December 2008), Denys Delâge strongly insisted on Vaugeois' ethnic construction; see, for example, Vaugeois' treatment of French-Canadian centrality in the Lewis and Clark expedition in the West in his *America: 1803–1853*.

54 'Un texte extrêmement douloureux que la tradition des Acadiens a su conserver très vivant et qui est à l'origine d'Antonine Maillet,' in 'Dossier: interventions à l'assemblée nationale. 1979,' Commission permanente des affaires culturelles, procès verbaux, 20 novembre 1979, BANQ-Q P655-5, Fonds Vaugeois.

55 '[A]nnihiler le peuple déjà formé sur ces territoires … Jamais rien ne le peut'; 'L'Amérique francophone, c'est tout le charme du rêve américain, pensé et organisé par l'esprit français. C'est l'amalgame de l'appel d'un territoire fabuleux, de la complicité durable entre l'une des plus grandes civilisations d'occident et les peuples amérindiens de cette terre'; Denis Vaugeois, Speech of welcome for Louisianans coming to celebrate the 370th anniversary of the founding of Quebec, Quebec City, 1 July 1978, BANQ-Q P655-26, Fonds Vaugeois.

56 A striking example is his use of a photo of the Rare Books Room of the modern Robarts Library at the University of Toronto on the cover of his autobiographical *L'Amour du livre*. With this choice of English-Canadian cultural richness from 'away,' he bypassed potentially delicious photos of early nineteenth-century historical collections of English Quebec such as the Literary and Historical Society of Quebec (1824) or the Rare Books Collection of McGill University.

57 See *Dictionary of Canadian Biography*, http://www.biographi.ca.

58 Denis Vaugeois, *Les Juifs et la Nouvelle France* (Trois-Rivières, QC: Les Éditions du Boréal Express, 1968), 103, 141.

59 'Juiverie internationale ou de son sous-produit la franc-maçonnerie'; 'Il n'y a aucun rapport de cause à effet entre les Juifs et la Conquête'; 'profitaient de la Guerre de la Conquête'; Denis Vaugeois, Speech by the Minister of Cultural Affairs to le Club Québec-Israël, Montreal, 1 April 1978, BANQ-Q, P655-27, Fonds Denis Vaugeois.

60 *Bulletin pédagogique* 2, no. 2 (1963); this can be compared to the Dominicans' monthly journal *Maintenant*, also established in 1962 and which had twelve thousand subscribers. See Gauvreau, *Catholic Origins*, 320.

61 Boréal Express, 'Catalogue 74,' BANQ-Q, P655-216, Fonds Vaugeois.

62 Lacoursière, Provencher, and Vaugeois, *Canada-Québec*, 4.

63 Fyson, Review, *Canadian Historical Review* 78 (1997): 347.

64 Fumaroli, *État culturel*, 19.

65 Gauvreau, *Catholic Origins*, 315.

66 'La culture est un puissant lien unificateur entre les hommes de même qu'elle est une nette démarcation entre les sociétés ... La culture est une limite, une frontière: au-delà de cette somme commune, la société considère ce qui est "autre," étranger. La culture est une mesure de différence ... Une nation peut intégrer ces groupes sans les assimiler à la condition expresse, toutefois, qu'ils partagent avec la majorité l'essentiel de la culture nationale et y contribuent'; Vaugeois, 'Conférence: une culture pour une société.'

67 'À l'heure de Chuck Mangione et de Stevie Wonder ... À l'heure ou le Ministère des Affaires culturelles subventionne une revue de bandes dessinées ... nous vivions de ce côté-ci de l'Outaouais ou de l'Autre, de ce côté-ci de l'Atlantique ou de l'autre, nous sommes tous frères dans une même civilisation ... La culture cultivée est le subconscient collectif de l'internationalisme auquel nous sommes tous conviés'; ibid.

68 '[D]e sorte que l'individu peut se situer dans une histoire, se confectionner une mémoire de son passé, s'inquiéter de son destin'; cited in Diane Saint-Pierre, *La politique culturelle du Québec de 1992: continuité ou changement? Les acteurs, les coalitions et les enjeux* (Québec: Presses de l'Université Laval, 2003), 19.

11

Remembering the Conquest: Mission Impossible?

NICOLE NEATBY

The controversy surrounding the National Battlefields Commission's plans to commemorate the two hundred and fiftieth anniversary of the Battle of the Plains of Abraham and, more specifically, the plans to re-enact the battle in the summer of 2009 ignited vociferous and passionate reactions. This controversy offers a rare opportunity to parcel out present-day collective memories of the Conquest as revealed in the French- and English-language Canadian press.[1] It also allows us to examine the ways in which the contemporary political climate served to inflame the controversy. The deliberations over the re-enactment engaged commentators of all stripes in a wider debate over a nation's 'duty to remember,' and they were informed by a specific question: are there certain battle re-enactments that are off limits when it comes to remembering in public?

Debates over how to commemorate the Conquest were a long-standing challenge in the twentieth century. Most often those in charge of organizing public events to mark what happened in 1759 have recognized the sensitivity of the issues raised by that fateful date. Unavoidably, remembering the 'facts on the ground' in public also has meant promoting a particular memory of the Conquest. The plans to commemorate the one hundred and fiftieth anniversary of the battle during the tercentenary celebrations of the founding of Quebec represented a case in point. H.V. Nelles has documented the ways in which the political circumstances of the time led to debates that brought conflicting memories of the event to the fore. A *bonne ententiste* interpretation finally prevailed, and re-enactors dressed in French and British military uniforms ended up parading on the Plains of Abraham side by side in a grandiose pageant.[2] In 1908, further reinforcing this attempt to 'neutralize' any French-Canadian nationalist sensitivities raised by the Conquest, the federal government issued a commemorative postage stamp that paired portraits of Wolfe and Montcalm, giving each equal pride of place and thus eliding any sense that there had been a winner and a loser.

In 1959, the bicentenary year of the battle, the Société Saint-Jean-Baptiste made the commemoration of Bishop Laval – the founder of the French Catholic Church in North America – as well as Generals Wolfe and Montcalm, the focus of its annual celebrations. In the 1950s context of a more assertive nationalism, this led to a renewed wave of heated debates and protests as, once again, a *bonne ententiste* interpretation of the event appeared to prevail. Gabriel Pelletier, for instance, the president of the Société Saint-Jean-Baptiste for the diocese of Quebec, argued: 'After 1959, there was no conqueror nor conquered but a new reality was emerging: a bi-ethnic and bi-cultural Canada.'[3] *Le Soleil* concurred: 'On the eve of the celebrations of the 200th anniversary of the battle of the Plains of Abraham, the racial disputes between the two enemies of yesterday are gradually fading; the two groups now collaborate to build the same nation. This is why with necessary hindsight, this celebration has nothing humiliating for us.'[4] Others, however, vehemently disagreed: 'Here at home, the Société Saint-Jean-Baptiste has found nothing better to make us proud than to celebrate our defeat. Proud of the wedding of two races? This wedding stands more as a rape.'[5] Many also criticized a commemorative stamp issued that year by Canada Post: on a red background, it featured the national emblems of Canada, Quebec, and Britain while foregrounding the word Canada, thus appearing to some to gloss over the fact that the battle had left behind winners and losers. On the other hand, there were those who felt that '[t]he Canada Post minister … simply wanted to remember a major event of Canada's history [and] the coexistence of two peoples under the same crown and in the same constitutional institutions.'[6]

The plans to mark the two hundred and fiftieth anniversary of the battle thus followed a long line of contests of memory. It is tempting to suggest that a greater awareness of these past conflicts on the part of the 2009 organizers could have inspired ways to pre-empt potential outcries. But it might be, indeed, that precedents of a different kind actually inspired them to proceed in the way they did, for other battles had been re-enacted on the Plains and had proved very popular among the public. In 1975, American re-enactors had marked the two hundredth anniversary of the attack on Quebec by revolutionaries under the command of Benedict Arnold and Richard Montgomery, who were beaten off by British and French-Canadian forces,[7] while re-enactments of American revolutionary battles were played out on Abraham's field in 1994 and again in 1998.[8] Finally, in 2004, another re-enactment of the 1775 American attack attracted tens of thousands of spectators each day.[9]

Certainly these battles did not carry with them the historical charge likely to inflame French-Quebecer and English-Canadian nationalist identities. Flush with these recent successes, the idea of re-enacting the battle that had actually taken place on the Plains could well have appealed to those in charge of commemorating its two hundred and fiftieth anniversary. Here was a great opportunity to reach out to wide audiences. Furthermore, living history, informed by the theory that one learns more effectively about the past by seeing it performed in real time, had become well entrenched in public history institutions. Another illustration of the National Battlefields Commission's commitment to this experiential approach was its plan to organize a masked ball to which the public would be invited to arrive dressed in period costume. On its website, the Commission made it clear that those who attended would be participating in a festive occasion: 'Despite the war in the colony, a few leaders find ways to entertain themselves. Dance as they did at moonlight, dressed in your most beautiful accoutrements.'[10]

Although the organizers expected an enthusiastic response from the public, the plans instead created an uproar, and nothing less than fear of violence was invoked as the main reason to cancel the re-enactment. André Juneau, the Commission's chair, announced on 17 February 2009 that the Commission had come to this decision because 'it could not guarantee the safety of families and re-enactors.' While the threats of violence were a genuine concern, the Commission's cancellation was also provoked by another type of battle: a memory war. Juneau admitted during the debate that, while he 'understood that the idea of looking back on an event that has deeply affected the province of Quebec could stir up very mixed feelings,'[11] he had been 'surprised'[12] by the extent of the outcry, and recognized that the Commission had underestimated 'people's sensitiveness.'[13] More specifically, he understood why some people unfortunately got the impression that 'we were celebrating the battle in a spirit of rejoicing.' He nonetheless found it 'odious to think that we wanted to celebrate a military defeat. We never planned to celebrate the Conquest.'[14]

Yet Juneau's other comments reveal that he did not share his critics' memory of the event: 'I am aware that we got quite the beating in

1759, in 1760 and then in 1763, but we have risen up from that after 250 years.'[15] The Commission was rightfully fulfilling a 'duty of remembrance' and could not pretend that these 'historic events' had never occurred: 'The reminder of an historical event is not dependent on victory or defeat, but on the importance of this event in our history.'[16] In Juneau's view, the Commission's mistake essentially had been in the way it presented its commemorative approach to the public, and it had not been 'ready to present the whole context.'[17] Thus, in the minds of the organizers, the re-enactment project had been a good one, and while the marketing strategy might have been misguided, the public's reaction remained an overreaction.

From the outset, the public's reactions were certainly passionate, but they were not unanimous. Francophone Quebecers were themselves divided over the issue.[18] Some were outraged and called for the re-enactment's immediate cancellation. Their reactions centred on what they perceived to be the Commission's intent, which they interpreted as to celebrate a defeat on the very ground where their courageous ancestors had spilled their blood to defend their homeland. For them, by celebrating the event the Commission was imposing a particular memory of the British victory, one that implied that the repercussions of the Conquest had, in the end, not prevented French Canadians from overcoming this defeat. Through stubborn determination, they had maintained their distinct culture and language to the present day. The image posted on the Commission's website to advertise its commemorative projects was considered a reflection of this *bonne ententiste* interpretation. It pictured the living descendants of Montcalm and Wolfe in period costumes, all smiles and shaking hands, thus suggesting that an amenable cooperation between conqueror and defeated had ensued. The ball project only served to reinforce the sense that the Commission had a jovial view of what had been a brutal military takeover.

Opponents of the re-enactment certainly did not dispute the importance of the Conquest or the need to remember it. Indeed, the editor of *Le Devoir*, Bernard Descôteaux, noted that it had been a 'turning point in Canada's history' and as such deserved to be commemorated. But this should be done through intellectual debates and analysis, 'as some institutions in Quebec are preparing to do to inform, promote understanding and provoke a reflection on the meaning of this event.'[19] Most opponents, however, felt that enough reflecting had already taken place. Their memory of the event was clear, the issue settled: had it not been for the Conquest, Quebec would have become an independent nation following the colony-to-nation trajectory. *Le Devoir* columnist Christian Rioux summed up this memory succinctly when he wrote that 1759 marked the advent of British 'colonial domination.' It was 'the starting point of the slow decline of the Francophones in Canada, a process that has never been interrupted and that thereafter seemed as irremediable 250 years later.'[20] A few, including Rioux, went so far as to stigmatize the psychological maturity of those who did not object to the Commission's plans for showing signs of self-loathing, since 'only deluded minds or masochistic' could fail to grasp 'the absurdity of this affair.'[21] For Denise Bombardier, a well-known journalist and author, commemorating the battle was to subject French Quebecers to a 'session of collective auto flagellation.'[22] The Réseau de résistance du Québécois (RRQ), an *indépendantiste* organization, declared that, for 'any normal nation,' it was unacceptable to 'have its adversaries organize ... important celebrations to commemorate the beginnings of its submission.'[23]

Indeed, many detractors argued that the Commission, operating under the jurisdiction of the English-Canadian-controlled federal government, could not but act as its handmaiden. The Commission's commemorative plans were nothing less than federalist propaganda intended to promote 'national unity' – an expression in the Canadian political lexicon referring to unity among the English and French of Canada under a federal umbrella. Pierre-Luc Bégin, the deputy director of the RRQ, explained that '[o]ur objection was not that we talked about the Conquest. It was important to talk about it. The problem was the federal government wanted to do something happy – but it was a sad event.'[24] In the weeks preceding the cancellation, journalists unearthed letters written by André Juneau that explicitly revealed his initiatives as a senior federal bureaucrat to promote national unity.[25] More damning still, the Commission's own 2007 *Report on Plans and Priorities* stated that '[t]he major events that will take place in 2008 and 2009 on the Plains of Abraham ... will provide and excellent and unique opportunity to increase the federal government's visibility in Quebec City.'[26]

A few opponents were so outraged that they believed opposition had to go beyond words, and a few individuals indicated their intention to disrupt the re-enactment with mass demonstrations. Patrick Bourgeois, founder of the separatist journal *Le Québécois* and the most outspoken member of the RRQ during the controversy, gave the Commission an ultimatum: if it had not cancelled the event by 15 February, there would be trouble. The RRQ also invited Quebecers to join its 'Comités 1759' across Quebec to organize conferences and public activities and offer transportation to Quebec City that summer.[27] Pierre Falardeau, a polemical sovereigntist filmmaker noted for his 'shock and awe' statements, warned that '[t]here won't be a party ... We have six months to organize this, it will be ugly.'[28] Some spectators, he threatened, would see their 'asses shaken,' for 'nowhere else in the world would any one accept such a thing.' While there would always be 'those who crawl, sold outs who will rejoice,' it was beyond the pale to applaud 'the Foundation Act of our misery.'[29]

Finally, the Commission capitulated and cancelled the re-enactment.[30] It also made changes to its website, eliminating the image of the two generals' descendants shaking hands. The ball was cancelled, although new events were planned to replace it.[31]

All this notwithstanding, there were francophone Quebecers who stood behind the Commission's plans, accepting that the intent was not to celebrate a defeat but rather to remember it. While some questioned the wisdom of re-enacting the battle, recognizing that it would strike a sensitive chord among French Quebecers, they still objected strongly to its being cancelled, largely because they interpreted the cries for its cancellation as politically motivated. They characterized the Commission's decision as a cowardly abdication to sovereigntist threats. In the words of journalist André Pratte from *La Presse,* who turned out to be the most vocal defender of the Commission's plans: 'The cowardice of the federalists will leave, once again, an open field to the dominant interpretation of our history, according to which the paradise of New France was transformed into Hell by the Conquest. A Hell from which we will only be free on the day of independence.'[32] As this statement makes clear, backers of the Commission's initiatives did not share this memory of the Conquest. They agreed with Pratte that it had been 'destructive yes, but foundational as well,' sealing as it did the fate of the French in North America. Their memories of the event diverged most clearly from those of the detractors over the fate of the conquered. In their view, through courage and determination, French Canadians had succeeded in overcoming defeat and preserving their language and culture. They had developed into a modern and thriving nation in the midst of an English-Canadian majority. Pratte pointed to the 'numerous moments of openness, collaboration, complicity between Francophones and Anglophones.'[33]

Like the detractors of the Commission, its backers also couched their arguments in psychological terms. To commemorate the Conquest was a sign of maturity, a capacity to come to terms with the past and get beyond old resentments. One commentator claimed that, because in Quebec 'for psychological reasons, we are unable to live with our own history,' it was 'impossible to remember it collectively.'[34] Clearly, then, the backers' reactions also carried a specific political reading of the present – namely, that since it had been possible to remain French Canadian despite the Conquest, it was equally possible to do so in the context of the Canadian federation. Although they associated the Commission with the federal government, they did not object to this association. What they did object to was Juneau's decision to cancel the re-enactment.

What about English Canadians? What first stands out is the similarity of their responses, regardless of regional affiliation. Although also attaching formative significance to events such as the French expeditions to Acadia in 1604–5 and the founding of Quebec in 1608, English-Canadian commentators tended to endorse a narrative of the Conquest as – in the editorial words of *The Walrus* – nothing less than 'an iconic moment in the country's historical narrative: literally the beginning of the story of Canada.'[35] It therefore stood to reason that the event should be commemorated in public, and the battle re-enactment seemed an ideal way to do so, if only for pedagogical reasons. In the early months of 2009, unlike their French Quebec counterparts, they did not go much beyond such generalizations to articulate more elaborate rationales for this position. Indeed, looking back several months following the controversy, Odile Tremblay of *Le Devoir* remarked that, 'since the beginning what is astounding is the low profile of the Anglophones.'[36] Of course, the fact that they argued that the Conquest marked the founding moment of Canada's history was in and of itself quite revealing. The subtext was that 1759 marked the birth of a nation-state all Canadians identified with and presumably of which they should be proud.

As many scholars have pointed out, English Canadians have distinct memories of the Conquest shaped by a variety of sources, including history textbooks.[37] A significant number of English Canadians would have been exposed to the view that the Conquest had freed French Canadians from the oppressive yoke of their French colonial masters, conferring on them fundamental liberties including elected institutions, a less arbitrary judiciary system, and the advent of the press. From this perspective, the British had acted as benevolent conquerors, allowing their new French subjects to practise the Catholic religion and speak their own language. To many English Canadians, francophone Quebec-

ers seemed to be thriving in the Canadian federation. Yet, in the midst
of the controversy, this was not an interpretation that English-Canadian
commentators invoked publicly. It was seven months after the re-enactment's cancellation before a *Globe and Mail* editorial provided a clear
articulation of this specific memory of the Conquest's repercussions. It
argued that the initial plans for the commemoration should have gone
forward, as the battle marked 'the birth of the great Canadian spirit of
cultural accommodation' and had been crucial to 'the origins of minority rights and religious freedom in Canada.' An instance of this supposed accommodation was General Wolfe's willingness 'to preserve
Quebec's unique cultural character and population.'[38] This delayed
reaction reflected a more generalized reticence on the part of English
Canadians to voice their memories of the past in public when they involved Quebec. It was likely inspired by a fear of being accused of in-
sensitivity towards a minority that has felt discriminated against for so
long or, worse still, of harbouring a lingering British colonial mentality.[39] In Odile Tremblay's words, anglophones' reactions spoke to a desire 'not to open up old wounds.' She added, presumably for dramatic
effect, that they were trying to 'avoid being lynched' and igniting 'the
bomb of history.'[40]

Once the Commission decided to cancel the re-enactment, the gloves
came off. As did francophone supporters of the event, English Canadians believed the Commission had caved in to the separatists' threats. A
National Post editorial told its readers that 'Juneau faced … a ludicrous
campaign by a noisy little group of separatists' who were determined
to see the historical re-enactment as a 'humiliation.' The *Post* criticized
Prime Minister Stephen Harper for hiding from the issue, leaving Juneau to fend for himself.[41] A commentator for the *Waterloo Region Recorder* – a small Ontario newspaper – urged the federal government to
stand its ground and let 'a peaceful, legal, educational re-enactment of
history proceed. And if there are any threats, have civil authorities in
place to arrest anyone who disturbs the public order.'[42] A few English
Canadians reacted with angry – at times vitriolic – outbursts. The reaction of Christie Blatchford in the *Globe and Mail* was a case in point. She
explained that she had experienced something close to nausea when
she heard that the Commission had yielded to a 'ridiculous, separatist-
driven furor over a planned re-enactment of the 1759 battle.' For Blatchford, cancelling the re-enactment meant forgoing an opportunity for
both English and French Canadians 'to learn more about the two generals who fought and died that day.'[43] Journalist Ian Brown also regretted

that Canadians would be deprived of an important history lesson and the opportunity to debate 'the fine points of what actually happened on the Plains of Abraham and how significant the battle was or was not.'[44] English Canadians were also much more likely than their French-Quebec counterparts to inform their readers that the 2009 re-enactment of the battle had been planned as the last of a series by the Historic Corps of Quebec to commemorate the two hundred and fiftieth anniversaries of all the battles of the Seven Years' War in North America. The first re-enactment had taken place in 2004 to mark the anniversary of the French victory over George Washington at Fort Necessity in Pennsylvania, and the most recent one had re-enacted another French victory, at Fort Ticonderoga in upstate New York.[45] The hope might have been that this would convince readers that the Battle of the Plains of Abraham re-enactment was not, as some were suggesting, meant to showcase British military might and France's humiliating defeat.

Thus, the Commission's commemorative initiatives managed to provoke the ire of commentators of all persuasions. Not surprisingly, politicians waded into the fray, and their interventions inflamed the debates. In a memory war, *when* one remembers matters as much as *what* one remembers. In a May 2007 press release, the Commission had announced plans to re-enact both the Plains of Abraham and the Ste-Foy battles. André Juneau declared: 'The public is behind us and extremely enthusiastic with the idea of experiencing, once again, the lively ambiance of the military camps and these decisive engagements of the brave men and women who helped shape our history.'[46] Adding 'éclat' to the announcement, he introduced the descendants of Wolfe and Montcalm (Baron Georges Savarina de Montcalm and Andrew Wolfe Burroughs) as co-spokespersons for the commemorative events. In 2008, Juneau conceded that he expected the event to be politicized but denied that this was of any great concern: 'There will be protestations, but there are always some during the Canada Day celebrations, therefore it is not unusual.'[47] What is particularly noteworthy is that Patrick Bourgeois was aware of the Commission's plans and appeared nonplussed. In 2008, he also exclaimed that, although the event would 'not be particularly appreciated by sovereigntists,' he was looking forward to the re-enactments, at least to the one of the Battle of Ste-Foy, during which 'the French massacred the English.'[48]

Evidently, by 2009, these protagonists saw things quite differently. What had happened? In a nutshell, plans to re-enact the battle had been taken up by politicians to score points in the never-ending national unity debate. From the sovereigntists' perspective, the timing could not have been more propitious. The Parti Québécois (PQ) had been languishing in opposition since 2003, and after the 2007 election held only third-party status. In the provincial elections of December 2008, the federalist Liberal Party was given a third mandate and, although the PQ regained the status of opposition party, the polls continued to confirm that the number of Quebecers ready to commit to the sovereigntist project had plateaued. Even among the converted, enthusiasm was at a low ebb, and there was much talk about the need to rekindle the sovereigntist flame. It looked as though history was just the ticket, especially as debates over history had made the headlines over the preceding three years. One debate in 2006 involved the Department of Education's revised high school Quebec history course.[49] Another, in 2008, pertained to the commemoration of the four hundredth anniversary of the founding of Quebec by Champlain in 1608. In this instance, Quebecers generally shared the view that the event was indisputably worthy of celebration. Consensus broke down at the Quebec border, however, when it became clear that some English Canadians, including Prime Minister Stephen Harper, remembered 1608 as the founding date of Canada. Adding insult to injury, Harper described Governor General Michaëlle Jean, a representative of the British Crown, as the last in a long line of Canadian governors, the first having been Samuel de Champlain.[50] The PQ tried to spin both these controversies into *causes célèbres*.

The debates over the commemoration of 1759 thus erupted hard on the heels of other wars waged over how one should remember Quebec's past. Yet, politicians, especially party leaders, chose at first to walk quite gingerly into the memory minefield of the re-enactment. Thus, when Premier and Liberal leader Jean Charest was asked by journalists if he thought it was a good idea to re-enact the battle, he replied rather cryptically: 'It is hard to tell what they want to do. They want to commemorate an important event of history but to go so far as to re-enact the event, I have difficulty seeing where they are going with this.' When pressed, he skirted the issue by pointing out that this was a federal government initiative in which his government would not take part. In this way, he not only distanced himself from the controversy but tried to showcase his credentials as a defender of Quebec's interests vis-à-vis the federal government. Asked if he was planning to attend the re-enactment, he curtly replied: 'I don't intend to participate in this event.'[51]

Initially, PQ leader Pauline Marois – much to the dissatisfaction of some of her supporters – did not take a public stance.[52] Soon, however, political acumen resurfaced, and the party called for the re-enactment's cancellation. PQ politicians accounted for their delayed reaction by invoking the compromising Juneau letters revealed by the press, which in their view had unmasked the re-enactment as part of a strategy to give the federal government greater visibility. From then on, Pauline Marois denounced the re-enactment as a federalist-backed initiative. 'When we saw what the federal government did with the 400th anniversary of Quebec,' she warned, 'that is enough to be worried about what they will do with this particular historical remembrance.' Marois claimed the right of the PQ 'to do our own reading of the events and analyze its consequences' – a reading that meant remembering 1759 as 'first and foremost the beginning of the end of New France' and an occasion to celebrate 'the survival, resilience and the courage of the French people of America,' who had been able to survive despite the Conquest.[53] On the face of it, this view was compatible with that of French Quebecers who supported the Commission's plans. But there was a fundamental difference. Whereas many re-enactment supporters viewed French-Canadians' survival through determination and courage as a confirmation that it was possible to continue to do so within Canada, the detractors argued that it was this very need for determination and courage that called for independence. Not surprisingly, Gilles Duceppe, of the federal sovereigntist Bloc Québécois, also called for the re-enactment's cancellation. He even presented a motion, backed by the Conservatives, summoning Juneau to appear in front of the parliamentary Heritage Committee on 25 February, ostensibly to justify his decision to cancel the re-enactment but in fact to embarrass the Liberals by bringing out Juneau's ties to the party's national unity initiatives and the notorious sponsorship scandal. Juneau's actual testimony proved unremarkable, but for the detractors it offered yet another opportunity to keep the debate in public view.[54]

For his part, Prime Minister Harper, a Conservative, tried to distance himself from the controversy, remarking that it was for the Commission to determine what kind of commemoration was appropriate. He also declared that he would not attend the re-enactment, but would send his minister of intergovernmental affairs, Josée Verner, who represented a Quebec City riding. Harper did, however, give his personal opinion that the re-enactment should go ahead, voicing a *bonne ententiste* reading of the Conquest: 'Most Canadians have moved beyond this. We're not fighting battles across the country in workplaces like this. English and French Canadians work together and we're going to continue to keep this country together forever.'[55] Liberal opposition leader Michael Ignatieff proved more forthcoming, declaring that the battle was a defeat and one should not celebrate it. Yet he believed that 'one had to rejoice over what happened after the defeat,' this being the 'surprising' reality that francophones had thrived in North America. He also tried to score political points by accusing sovereigntists of wanting 'to dominate a free debate on the meaning to ascribe to the country's history ... In a free Canada, there are at times two different visions of our history.' How one could square such double visions in commemorative events he left unsaid.[56]

The Commission ultimately did hold a few commemorative activities. When announcing the cancellation of the ball, Juneau promised vaguely that it would be replaced by 'a presentation of different actors of the period to illustrate by other means the climate that prevailed in the city before the coming of the British.'[57] As no more information was provided, one can assume that the Commission planners were still at the drawing board. In the end, not much was organized to complement the existing permanent exhibits and activities housed in the Commission's Discovery Pavilion on the Plains of Abraham. In accordance with the living-history approach, however, two special events, in which a variety of interpreters played the roles of various characters living in Quebec City before and during the British attack, marked the anniversary.[58] This time, the Commission clearly had no intention of trying to draw in large crowds. Remembering 1759 would be a low-key affair. The two special events were scheduled to take place at the tail end of the summer as the tourist season was winding down and children were getting ready for school.

On the evening of 28 August, the public was invited to attend an outdoors stage show entitled 'State of War,' featuring a series of sketches with ordinary *Canadiens*, as well as better-known protagonists such as Montcalm, Governor Vaudreuil, and Intendant Bigot. They recited texts of the period in order to 'explain the difficult conditions and the tensions that prevailed in the months preceding the arrival of the British.'[59] What stands out is the attempt by the organizers to protect themselves from any accusation of presenting a joyful picture of life in the colony. Great emphasis was placed on the difficult conditions on the eve of the British attack. A publicity sheet informed readers that '[t]he French colony's inhabitants are already suffering from the repercussions of the war. Moreover, the population is living in a climate pervaded with fear, corruption and famine.'[60] While spectators could see a few interpreters of Quebec city elites alluding to balls, every effort was made to convey to the spectators that the festivities took place 'in a false atmosphere of rejoicing' in which 'the high society ... had fun, ate and drank as if reality was totally different.'[61] To underscore the message that the Conquest had been about hardship, at the end of the show interpreters called out the names of the *Canadien* militia men who had died during the conflict. Immediately following this roll call, the mostly middle-aged crowd spontaneously applauded – a sign perhaps that this time the Commission had found the right tone for its audience? Regardless of one's memory of the Conquest, it was safe to assume that few would dispute a representation of 1759 that focused on the hardship of war.

The second event, 'State of Siege,' set in September 1759, took place on the afternoon of 30 August. The public was invited to stroll on the Plains of Abraham and go to various kiosks where interpreters in period costume would inform visitors about the 'defence system, bombings, weaponry, violence perpetrated on the countryside, desertion, Navy, Militia, Amerindians and more.'[62] Again, the focus was placed on the way people experienced the hard life during times of war. Thus, the Commission's two commemorative activities steered away from representations of the past that involved addressing the repercussions of the Conquest and, more significantly, the meaning one should ascribe to it today. While not much was made of these events in the press, in the eyes of the organizers this 'silence' might well have been welcome, confirming that they had successfully averted controversy.[63]

Off the battlefield, a very different type of commemorative initiative was organized in government-funded museums. These did not provoke controversy, either. One of them involved the Commission's working in partnership with the Musée national des beaux arts du Québec to present an art exhibit entitled 'The Taking of Quebec, 1759–1760.' It included close to forty paintings by artists of the period, depicting the Battles of the Plains of Abraham and Ste-Foy, death scenes of the generals, and drawings of Quebec City in ruins. The War Museum in Ottawa also presented an art exhibit entitled 'Landscapes of War,' which aimed to 'provide glimpses of the landscape of battles as seen by participants through a series of nineteenth century paintings.'[64] While visitors to the War Museum could obtain information about the battle in five different locations, this temporary exhibit was the only site specifically dedicated to commemorate the battle's two hundred and fiftieth anniversary. It allowed visitors to follow the military campaign step by step, location by location. Furthermore, each painting was paired with a contemporary photograph of the same location, which brought out the extent to which time had altered these landscapes. Although located in prestigious museums, and clearly identified as special events to mark the anniversary of the battle, neither exhibit attracted much public attention. This is not entirely surprising. By choosing to represent the battle through the eyes of artists – mostly of the eighteenth and nineteenth centuries – the exhibits focused attention on how a select group of individuals from a distant past visualized the event. There was no pretence here of offering a specific memory of the battle – one that might clash with those in circulation in the present day.

The Musée de la civilisation de Québec in Quebec City also held a special exhibit entitled '1756–1763, récit d'une guerre.' This exhibit focused on presenting the Seven Years' War in its wider European context. It served to make the point that the Battle of the Plains of Abraham was but one military conflict among several, thus drawing less attention to the battle as such and skirting issues pertaining to memory and meaning. One information panel entitled 'A Few Historic Reminders of the Seven Years' War in Quebec' appeared to depart from this overall interpretative approach, for its opening statement noted that the battle had 'left numerous traces on the daily life, landscape and memory of Quebecers.' Yet only one piece of evidence was provided to illustrate this larger point. Visitors learned that 'a number of Quebec families are descendants of the soldiers who fought under Montcalm or Wolfe.'

What is striking is that visitors could obtain more detailed analysis and be exposed to various interpretations of the Conquest's repercussions in the museum's permanent exhibit, entitled 'Le Temps des Québécois.' The section devoted to the Conquest featured a video, 'La Conquête de 1760,' in which three historians, Jacques Lacoursière, Jocelyn Létourneau, and Ronald Rudin, directly addressed issues pertaining to memory and meaning. And the closing statement of the video, spoken by a narrator, was in effect the articulation of a specific memory of the Conquest: 'Neither providential, neither catastrophic' it did 'reorient [Quebec's] collective destiny.' From then on it would be governed by a minority but would succeed 'in rapidly developing' and become a dynamic society.[65] As revealed by the re-enactment controversy, this position was clearly not shared by all. Yet visitors who came to the museum to remember the two hundred and fiftieth anniversary of the Conquest could avoid being confronted with potentially controversial memories of the event and leave with undisputed facts instead.

The anniversary also opened a wider discussion among commentators regarding the suitability of battle re-enactments per se – particularly over whether certain military conflicts are off limits when it comes to remembering them in public and in real time. Those who considered the re-enactment of the Battle of the Plains of Abraham legitimate typically invoked the fact that other nations regularly re-enacted battles they had lost. Why, they asked rhetorically, could French Quebecers not do the same? The examples most often brought up were the yearly re-enactments in the United States of the battles of the Civil War and in Belgium the Battle of Waterloo. Conversely, those who opposed the Battle of the Plains of Abraham re-enactment pointed both to battles that were *not* being re-enacted and to events considered by many to be morally shameful during which innocent civilian populations had been purposefully attacked. Who, they asked, would consider re-enacting the wars with aboriginals? The German victory over France? The Acadian Deportation? Or the extermination of the Jews?[66]

What stood out in these debates was that neither camp felt the need to analyse why it believed the battles or events it invoked were being or not being re-enacted. Clearly, each was convinced that the facts simply spoke for themselves. By invoking these past battles, commentators were in effect encroaching on the historian's turf. In fact, from the outset, although the controversy cried out for historians' expert contribution, they kept a remarkably low profile. Francophone historians did not produce full-length articles in the press to discuss what historical research taught us about 1759.[67] A select few, often the same ones, were briefly and sporadically quoted by journalists. Had it not been for the reporters' curiosity, historians' views would have remained almost unheard. *Le Devoir* noted with regret and disapproval that 'historians have been particularly silent' in a debate 'linked to one of the most dramatic moments of Quebec history.'[68] To fill this void, journalist Christian Rioux made a point of seeking out the views of historians specializing in Quebec, French, and British history about the existing scholarly debates over the Conquest.[69] He also asked them directly why they were not volunteering their insights on an issue that spoke so obviously to their expertise. Yves Tremblay, a military historian at the federal Department of National Defence who opposed the cancellation of the re-enactment, explained the historians' absence from the debates as yet one more confirmation of the decline of military and political history.[70] José Iguartua, who, during the 1970s had written on the Conquest, declared that, at present, 'almost no one works on 1760. Only the twentieth century is of interest today. This is what students ask for.' Interestingly, he also offered an additional, very different explanation: 'As the Quebec national question is not resolved, historians have stepped back. Our role is not to explain the future, but the past.'[71] This point, which he did not develop, should probably not be read at face value as a prescription but perhaps as a window on French Quebec historians' reluctance to wade into the treacherous waters of the nationalist debate.

A closer look at how historians contributed to the debate suggests a more qualified reading of their level of involvement. A few did participate in one capacity or another in the actual organization of the Commission's commemorative projects. New France historian Jacques Mathieu sat on its board, and the Commission hired popular public historian Jacques Lacoursière to produce a chronology of the events of the Battle of the Plains of Abraham. On the Commission's website, readers were informed that his work provided 'a wonderful opportunity to put these events into context without interpreting them. In this work, the actors and witnesses of these past events are the ones taking the floor.'[72] There were also historians who reacted to the controversy by taking a *moral* stand: all nations had a duty to remember the past, even though it could conjure up disturbing memories. Not to do so was wilfully to erase the past and thus forgo the possibility of making sense of the present. Alain Laberge, history professor at Laval University, remarked that 'commemoration is a duty of memory' which meant that 'one must commemorate events even though they are not pleasant ... To deny the existence of an event as important in our history [as the Conquest] is in no way positive ... It explains to us who we are, where we come from.'[73] Denis Vaugeois, prominent Quebec public historian and former PQ minister, concurred that one has the duty to 'know where one comes from.'[74]

Nor did all historians limit themselves to such philosophical considerations. A few took on the role of interpreters to help account for the passionate public reaction during the controversy – most often for the benefit of an uncomprehending and sometimes disapproving English-Canadian audience. They explained that, for French Quebecers, the Conquest was infused with symbolic meaning. It evoked subsequent defeats and the never-ending need to fight for survival. Unavoidably, this led these historians to attempt to establish what needed to be remembered. Early on, Jacques Lacoursière, Denis Vaugeois, and Guy Vadeboncoeur complained to the Commission about its promotional brochure, objecting to the 'jovial celebration ... being planned.'[75] Certain historians suggested publicly that, had the commemorative approach of the Commission been different, the re-enactment would have been a good idea. Vaugeois told a journalist that 'he wished that the re-enactment ... would take place.'[76] Elsewhere he noted that 'he saw it at best as being of pedagogical interest.'[77] Yet it was clear that he remained ambivalent about how best to remember the event. He did not feel comfortable using the word commemoration, as 'he believed that the term was too festive.' Commemorations, including that of 1759, should be 'historical reminders, moments of silence, moments of sadness.'[78] Historian Michel de Waele from Laval University also believed that 'the approach adopted by ... Mr Juneau and his Commission was not the best,' but he regretted the cancellation of the re-enactment because a teachable moment had been lost.[79] If one were to glean a specific memory of the Conquest from these reactions, it would be that 1759, while important enough to be commemorated, was not worthy of celebration. Its repercussions had not been positive.

Vaugeois and de Waele made even more revealing interpretive comments when they argued that the public's hostile reaction to the re-enactment had been overblown. Indeed, while deploring the Commission's jovialist approach, Vaugeois felt that 'the whole affair was aggravated by the fact that the battle ... has assumed a mythical status' it did not deserve. Vaugeois argued that 'the battle itself wasn't what caused the fall of New France'; the British takeover was settled at the negotiating table between France and Britain.[80] De Waele concurred, asserting that '[i]t is not the Battle of the Plains of Abraham that caused the loss of New France' and 'that certain Quebecers attach so much importance to this battle prevents them from understanding what happened, prevents them from understanding the little importance it had in the context of the period.'[81] Indeed, these were the positions most commonly articulated by French-Quebec historians in debates over the anniversary controversy.

What about English-Canadian historians? For all intents and purposes, they simply were not to be heard. The exception was McGill University military historian Desmond Morton, who strongly objected to the re-enactment's cancellation. Along with a few of his francophone counterparts, he believed that the public had overreacted and was misinformed. He also offered a political reading of the resulting furor, noting a 'crass maneuvering by the sovereigntists.'[82] The Conquest, for Morton, should not be seen first and foremost as the result of France's decision to let go of the colony. But neither should the Battle of the Plains of Abraham be seen as a straightforward British victory. In his view, it should be remembered as a French-Canadian victory because the evidence confirmed that the *Canadien* militia had temporarily halted the British momentum during the battle and they continued to fight after panicked French soldiers retreated. For these reasons, French Quebecers had much to be proud of and a re-enactment would give them an opportunity to celebrate the bravery of their ancestors.[83]

This limited sample of French-Quebec and English-Canadian historians' interpretations of the battle and of the Conquest reveals that they did share some memories of 1759. All agreed that the event was of great significance and should be remembered. They were all critical of the Commission's initial festive commemorative approach, regretting that it had not sufficiently recognized the sensitivity of the issue. Finally, all downplayed the role of the British in the Conquest. For some, the French Canadians of the time were not responsible for the defeat because they were defenceless pawns in a wider imperial struggle. Others viewed a commemoration of the Conquest as an opportunity to celebrate the courage of the *Canadiens* on the battlefield.

What is striking is the extent to which many of those who offered comments, including historians, drew from an old interpretative repertoire to make sense of the event – more specifically, from a set of memories that had emerged between the mid-nineteenth and early twentieth centuries. Michel Ducharme identifies several rhetorical strategies French Canadians used over this period, and argues that they served to 'legitimize the emerging French-Canadian nation.'[84] As had their ancestors, commentators in 2009 viewed the event as foundational, but, like them, they struggled with the challenge of remembering a military defeat. Some historians posited that it was France's decision to cede the colony that accounted for the British takeover. This reading absolved French Canadians of any responsibility, presented them as victims, and in the end turned 1759 into a French defeat, rather than a *Canadien* one. Another strategy recalled from the past was to focus on French Canadians as brave fighters who could be considered victors on the battlefield. Again, among the wider pool of commentators, there were also those who justified the importance of commemorating the Conquest as a way to remember that French Canadians, through their determination, had succeeded in preserving their language and culture against daunting odds. Some offered a well-used *bonne ententiste* interpretation, arguing that French Canadians had also found ways over time to cooperate with their former masters, implicitly suggesting that they could continue to do so in the future and remain part of the Canadian federation.

Yet the 2009 debates did not simply echo previously articulated memories of the Conquest drawn from the nineteenth-century repertoire. They brought to the fore a rhetorical strategy that has gained ascendancy only over the past few decades – one that presents the Conquest as a 'cataclysmic event or destructive event' that can be redeemed only by Quebec's independence.[85] The battle of 1759 is thus remembered as the event that led to the subjugation of French Canadians under an oppressive British colonial power and later under an enduring English-Canadian domination. For the time being, the Conquest might be commemorated as a testimony to French Quebecers' admirable and unwavering desire to preserve their distinct language and culture. But the only time when French Quebecers could commemorate 1759 as a true celebration would be once Quebec gained its independence. Comments made at the time by PQ politician Bernard Drainville encapsulate the links drawn between this memory of the Conquest as a cataclysm and contemporary politics. He explained that, as a sovereigntist, he 'felt ill at ease commemorating our people's defeat' and that Quebec's independence could 'put right this historical fact' and 'put a period to ... this event of history.'[86] Only independence would allow French Quebecers to forget disruptive memories of the past by rewriting history.

While the political future of Quebec cannot be predicted, the Conquest will have future anniversaries. One then wonders whether any attempt at commemoration is bound to raise passionate and divisive debates if the political landscape remains the same. And are future re-enactments of the 1759 battle ever likely to be feasible? Certainly, Americans have enthusiastically embraced the practice of playing out the Civil War battles, which have been turned into popular spectacles worthy of inclusion in many tourist itineraries,[87] even though more than half a million soldiers were killed and the Civil War still gives rise to sporadic, at times wrenching, memory wars as its causes and repercussions continue to be a source of impassioned debates.[88] The question remains, then, how can one account for their popularity? The historian David Blight argues that, shortly after the war, Americans chose to focus on the common soldiers, remembering the bravery of all who fought on the battlefield whether they donned blue or grey uniforms. They were all honourable men as they were all ready to sacrifice their lives for an ideal they believed in. Such memories allowed Americans to sweep under the carpet wrenching debates about the *nature* and *legitimacy* of their opposing ideals – most notably issues of race. This 'politics of reconciliation' in turn made military re-enactments national bonding events.[89] Thus, what has made re-enacting the Civil War possible is the ability of Americans to create a new way of remembering – one that cannot be easily challenged. This process of creation is, in fact, what Létourneau prescribes for Quebecers with respect to the Conquest when he states that 'to change such a representation takes work.'[90]

More than work was required, however, to make it possible for Americans to share a consensual memory of the Civil War – and by implication this will be true for French Quebecers as well. Politics invariably came into play. More specifically, as a prerequisite to reconciling memories of the war, a majority of Americans had to share the view that, overall, its outcome had been positive, if not necessary to ensure the future stability and prosperity of the nation. Of course, many Americans never did come to terms with the North's victory – the painful history of white and black relations since then makes this clear.[91] Today, however, few and far between are those who advocate the South's separation from the North, and it goes without saying that no one is promoting the reinstitution of slavery.

In Quebec, however, a high percentage of francophones regret the Conquest's outcome and believe they can 'undo it' through independence. The American example suggests that producing a shared memory of the Conquest that shifts the focus away from defeat would require further political developments – more specifically, changes that would leave a majority of French Quebecers with the confidence that Quebec's present and future as a francophone nation within a North American sea of anglophones can be secured. This might or might not require independence. But only when Quebec's political status fosters a collective optimistic view of the future can a new shared memory of 1759 emerge – one that would require less 'work' and allow for a proud recollection of the event by all. And only then could Quebecers view military re-enactments of the Battle of the Plains of Abraham as an appropriate, perhaps enlightening if not simply entertaining, form of commemoration.

NOTES

1 Francophone correspondents who write regularly for English-Canadian newspapers, including Lysiane Gagnon, Chantal Hébert, and Konrad Yakabuski, were excluded from the analysis.

2 H.V. Nelles, 'Historical Pageantry and the "Fusion of the Races" at the Tercentenary of Quebec, 1908,' *Histoire sociale/Social History* 29 (1996): 391–415; idem, *The Art of Nation-Building: Pageantry and Spectacle at Quebec's Tercentenary* (Toronto: University of Toronto Press, 1999); and Patrice Groulx, 'La commémoration de la bataille de Sainte-Foy: du discours de la loyauté à la fusion des races,' *Revue d'histoire de l'Amérique française* 55 (2001): 45–83.

3 See 'Un homage particulier sera rendu cette année à Monseigneur Laval et aux généraux Montcalm et Wolfe,' *Le Soleil*, 13 June 1959.

4 In 'Célébrations de la fête nationale deux cents ans après la conquête,' editorial, *Le Soleil*, 23 June 1959. See also Gérard Filion, 'Le 13 septembre 1759,' *Le Soleil*, 12 September 1959.

5 Letter to the editor, André Gingras, 'Célébrer la défaite!' *Le Soleil*, 17 June 1959.

6 Clément Brown, 'Lettre d'Ottawa: deux cents ans de coexistence,' *Le Devoir*, 12 September 1959.

7 Organized by the Arnold Expedition History Society 'with the view to rehabilitate the memory of Arnold,' it was said also to be the 'largest historical re-enactment to have ever taken place.' See *Les Plaines d'Abraham: le culte de l'idéal*, ed. Jacques Mathieu and Eugen Kedl (Sillery, QC: Septentrion, 1993), 259. For other information on the meaning and use of the Plains of Abraham, see Jacques Mathieu, 'Un haut lieu symbolique: les plaines d'Abraham,' in *Québec ville et capitale: atlas historique du Québec*, ed. Serge Courville et Robert Garon (Ste-Foy, QC: PUL, 2001); and J.I. Little, in this volume.

8 Information provided by Horst Dresler, a Quebecer now living in Vermont and president of the Quebec Historical Corps, in Ian Bussières, 'Reconstitution annulée: le Corps historique du Québec déçu,' *Le Soleil*, 14 February 2009.

9 One report claimed 'about 80,000 per day'; see Andy Riga, 'Scrapping of Quebec City historical re-enactment may have cost city millions,' *Canwest News Service*, 1 July 2009, http://www2.canada.com/topic/new/story.html. It was one of several activities organized by the Commission de la capitale nationale, the National Battlefields Commission, and the Quebec Historical Corps. The celebrations started with an *escarmouche* (skirmish) between twenty 'American' and 'British' soldiers at the Place Royale – a prelude to the battle that took place in early August on the Plains of Abraham.

10 National Battlefields Commission, '250th Anniversary of the Battles: The Commission cancels the re-enactments to avoid endangering the safety of the Plains' visitors,' Press release, Quebec City, 17 February 2009, http://www.lesplainesdabraham.ca.

11 Ibid.

12 Alec Castonguay, 'Commémoration de la Bataille des Plaines: le Bloc réclame la démission de Juneau,' *Le Devoir*, 26 February 2009.

13 Antoine Robitaille, 'La bataille des plaines d'Abraham annulée pour raisons de sécurité,' *Le Devoir*, 18 February 2009.

14 Castonguay, 'Commémoration de la bataille des Plaines.'

15 La Presse Canadienne, 'Commémoration de la bataille des plaines d'Abraham – Raconter la "moyenne claque" que les Français ont mangée,' *Le Devoir*, 24, 25 January 2009.

16 National Battlefields Commission, '250th Anniversary of the Battles.'

17 La Presse Canadienne, 'Commémoration de la bataille des plaines d'Abraham.' Elsewhere, Antoine Robitaille spoke of a *'faux pas'* that he explained by 'the rush to realize before the Christmas holidays the communication tools.' Antoine Robitaille, 'Des commandites aux plaines d'Abraham,' *Le Devoir*, 3 February 2009.

18 Although not many attempts appear to have been made to establish the general population's views about the Commission's plans, in September, following the most intense period of the controversy, one poll discovered that one Quebecer out of three believed that the re-enactment should have taken place. See Christian Rioux, 'Autopsie d'une reconstitution,' *Le Devoir*, 12, 13 September 2009.

19 Bernard Descôteaux, 'Les 250 ans des plaines – D'inutiles jeux de guerre,' *Le Devoir*, 2 February 2009.

20 Christian Rioux, 'L'odeur de la poudre,' *Le Devoir*, 23 January 2009.

21 Ibid.

22 Denise Bombardier, 'La défaite de Québec,' *Le Devoir*, 31 January, 1 February 2009.

23 'Reconstitution de la bataille des plaines d'Abraham – Le RRQ s'y oppose fermement,' *Amériquebec.net*, 14 January 2009, http://www.amériquebec .net/actualités/2009/01/14-reconstitution-de-la-bataille-des-plaines d'Abraham (accessed 31 July 2009).

24 Ian Brown, 'In Wolfe's clothing,' *Globe and Mail*, 1 August 2009.

25 See Robitaille, 'Des commandites aux plaines d'Abraham.'

26 National Battlefields Commission, *National Battlefields Commission, 2007– 2008, Report on Plans and Priorities* (Ottawa: National Battlefields Commission, 2008), 7; this priority was mentioned twice in the document on page 8. Worse still, Juneau was identified with the infamous sponsorship scandal – whereby the federal government, directly and under false pretences, allocated funds to groups specifically mandated to promote national unity and increase the visibility of the federal government in Quebec; see Robitaille, 'Des commandites aux plaines d'Abraham.'

27 The RRQ set up a website (opération1759.org) as well; see 'Le RRQ présent
    à Québec pour la "célébration" de la reconstitution de 1759 – Joignez-vous
    à l'un de nos "Comités 1759"!' *Amériquebec.net*, 25 January 2009, http://
    www.ameriquebec.net/actualites/2009/01/25-rrq-quebec-1759.qc
    (accessed 31 July 2009).
28 'Fête ou commémoration?' http://www.radio-canada.ca/nouvelles/
    Nationales/2009/01/30/005-controverse-plaines.html (accessed 31 July
    2009).
29 Quoted in 'Commémoration de la bataille des plaines d'Abraham –
    Furieux, Falardeau promet de "casser le party,"' *Le Devoir*, 30 January
    2009.
30 Juneau informed the public that he had received a hundred and fifty
    threatening emails and letters, some of which were being investigated by
    police; Castonguay, 'Commémoration de la bataille des Plaines.'
31 National Battlefields Commission, '250th Anniversary of the Battles.'
32 André Pratte, 'Capitulation sur les plaines,' *La Presse*, 13 February 2009.
33 Ibid.
34 A response by David Lépine, posted in response to an article written by
    political commentator Josée Legault, who vehemently opposed the re-
    enactment (Josée Legault, 'D'émotions et de violence,' *Voix Publique*, 18
    February 2009): 'Au Québec, pour des raisons psychologiques, nous som-
    mes incapables de vivre avec notre propre histoire donc impossible de se
    la rappeler collectivement'; see http://www.voir.ca/blogs/josée_legault/
    archive/2009/02/18/d-233 (accessed 2 July 2009).
35 John Macfarlane, 'Editor's Note,' *Walrus* (September 2009), 13.
36 Odile Tremblay, 'J'entends le Moulin, tique, tique, taque,' *Le Devoir*, 12, 13
    September 2009.
37 See the study commissioned by the Royal Commission on Bilingualism
    and Biculturalism: Marcel Trudel and Geneviève Jain, *Canadian History
    Textbooks* (Ottawa: Queen's Printer, 1970); Jocelyn Létourneau and Sabrina
    Moisan, 'Mémoire et récit de l'aventure historique du Québec chez les
    jeunes Québécois d'héritage canadien-français: coup de sonde, amorce
    d'analyse des résultats, questionnements,' *Canadian Historical Review* 84
    (2004): 325–56; idem, 'Young People's Assimilation of a Collective Histori-
    cal Memory: A Case Study of Quebecers of French-Canadian Heritage,'
    in *Theorizing Historical Consciousness*, ed. Peter Seixas (Toronto: University
    of Toronto Press, 2004); Ken Montgomery, 'Banal Race-thinking: Ties of
    Blood, Canadian History Textbooks and Ethnic Nationalism,' *Paedagogica
    Historica* 41, no. 3 (2005): 313–36; José Igartua, *The Other Quiet Revolution:
    National Identities in English Canada, 1945–1971* (Vancouver: UBC Press,
    2006); and Nicole Neatby, 'Meeting of the Minds: North American Travel

Writers and Government Tourist Promoters in Quebec, 1920–1955,' *Histoire sociale/Social History* 36 (November 2003): 465–95. More recently, Allan Greer and Catherine Desbarats have analysed how the differing French- and English-Canadian popular memories of the Conquest have been reflected in the canonical works of Canadian historians; see Allan Greer and Catherine Desbarats, 'The Seven Years' War in Canadian History and Memory,' in *Cultures in Conflict: The Seven Years' War in North America*, ed. Warren R. Hofstra (Lanham, MD: Rowman and Littlefield, 2007). See also Thomas Wien, 'Note critique: la Conquête racontée en 2009,' *Revue d'histoire de l'Amérique française* 64, no. 1 (2010): 103–25.

38 'When Canadian inclusiveness began,' *Globe and Mail*, editorial, 14 September 2009.

39 Lending support to this interpretation, although for different reasons, are comments made by military historian Jack Granatstein, who was paraphrased as stating that the whole Plains of Abraham controversy illustrates 'what is wrong with the teaching of history in Canada – namely, that we would rather not teach if there is a chance that doing so might cause offence'; Macfarlane, 'Editor's Note,' 13.

40 Tremblay, 'J'entends le Moulin, tique, tique, taque.'

41 'Harper lets down Canada on Plains of Abraham,' *National Post*, editorial, 18 February 2009.

42 'A white flag flies over the Plains of Abraham,' *Waterloo Region Recorder*, 15 February 2009.

43 Christie Blatchford, 'Battle over Plains of Abraham shows Canada's small, timorous heart,' *Globe and Mail*, 21 February 2009.

44 Brown, 'In Wolfe's Clothing.'

45 Another project initiated by Horst Dresler and the Quebec Historical Corps with the collaboration of André Gousse of the Société de Reconstitution Historique du Québec.

46 His enthusiasm was such that he added: 'The Commission is thrilled to play the role of instigator and organizer of this event'; National Battlefields Commission, 'For the 250th Anniversary of the Battle of the Plains of Abraham – In 2009, 2000 soldiers will take the park by storm,' Press release, Quebec City, 28 May 2007.

47 'La reconstitution de la bataille des Plaines d'Abraham ne fera pas que des heureux,' http://www.tqs.ca/infos/montreal/2008/06 (accessed 30 July 2009).

48 Ibid.

49 For a more detailed discussion of these debates, see Jocelyn Létourneau, in this volume.

50 See Allan Greer, '1608 as Foundation,' *Canadian Issues/Thèmes canadiens* (Fall 2008): 20–3.

51 Hélène Buzetti, 'Charest n'a pas le coeur à célébrer la défaite des plaines d'Abraham,' *Le Devoir*, 17, 18 January 2009.

52 Michel David from *Le Devoir* speculated that Marois was perhaps leery of wading into the politics of commemoration after having jumped the gun the year before when she decried the invitation of Paul McCartney to the four hundredth anniversary celebrations of the founding of French Quebec. She had been suffering from what David diagnosed as the '*syndrome McCartney*'; Michel David, 'Le syndrome McCartney,' *Le Devoir*, 27 January 2009.

53 'Le Parti Québécois dénonce la reconstitution de la bataille sur les Plaines d'Abraham – Le PQ croit qu'aucun gouvernement ne droit s'associer à cette reconstitution,' *Amériquebec.net*, 29 January 2009, http://www.ameriquebec.net/actualites/2009/01/29 (accessed 31 July).

54 Castonguay, 'Commémoration de la bataille des Plaines d'Abraham'; Robitaille, 'Reconstitution de la bataille des Plaines d'Abraham.'

55 'Harper lets down Canada on Plains of Abraham,' *National Post*, editorial, 18 February 2009.

56 Robitaille, 'La bataille des plaines d'Abraham annulée pour raisons de sécurité.' Journalists also brought to the public's attention an article published in the *National Post* on 28 August 1999 in which Ignatieff suggested that the Conquest did not turn out that badly as the British gave various freedoms to the French Canadians. See Alec Castonguay, 'La bataille des plaines d'Abraham – L'image du Québec à l'étranger a été ternie, dit Jean Charest,' *Le Devoir*, 19 February 2009.

57 National Battlefields Commission, '250th Anniversary of the Battles.'

58 A temporary exhibit was also set up to accompany the pavilion's permanent multimedia presentation, entitled 'Odyssey: A Journey through History on the Plains of Abraham,' made up of maps to illustrate, among other things, military strategy.

59 National Battlefields Commission, *Report on Plans and Priorities*, 7.

60 National Battlefields Commission, 'Take Part in the Free Commemorative Activities on the Plains of Abraham,' publicity sheet, Quebec, 2009.

61 National Battlefields Commission, *Report on Plans and Priorities*, 7.

62 National Battlefields Commission, 'Take Part.'

63 Moving into September, the Commission initiated a couple of other events, reduced in scale but just as devoid of controversy. Thus, on the 13th, it was involved in the unveiling of a monument to the French and British regiments, militia men, and aboriginals who fought on the Plains of Abraham.

Here was a commemorative initiative that ensured all sides got their fair share of recognition by way of a speechless stone. And on the 15th, the Commission organized a small, one-day colloquium involving presentations from a few experts on the period – not an activity that would attract many or risk igniting great passionate debates among the wider public.

64 From the Museum's self-guided tour brochure, entitled '1759–2009, The Battle of the Plains of Abraham.'

65 'La Conquête de 1760,' video in 'Le Temps des Québécois,' permanent exhibit at the Musée de la civilisation de Québec, Quebec City.

66 See, among others, Rioux, 'L'odeur de la poudre'; Michel Corbeil, 'Bataille des Plaines: "C'est notre histoire, que ça plaise ou non" dit Eric Caire,' *Le Soleil*, 23 January 2009; La Presse Canadienne, 'Commémoration de la Bataille des Plaines d'Abraham – Furieux, Falardeau promet de "casser le party"'; Bombardier, 'La défaite de Québec'; La Presse Canadienne, 'Bataille des Plaines – Impératif français et la Société Saint-Jean-Baptiste insatisfaits du méa-culpa de Juneau,' *Le Devoir*, 2 February 2009; and idem, 'Commémoration de la bataille des Plaines d'Abraham – Raconter la "moyenne claque" que les Français ont mangée.'

67 The exception was Martin Paquêt, 'La bataille des Plaines: une polémique de notre temps,' *Le Devoir*, 18 February 2009. However, he mostly meant to use the Plains controversy to analyse concepts of memory, social uses of the past in contemporary society, and their links to specific political contexts.

68 Christian Rioux, 'Cachez cette histoire que je ne saurais voir!' *Le Devoir*, 12, 13 September 2009. One commentator believed this silence revealed that historians were indirectly taking a position. *Le Devoir* journalist Michel David, who himself strongly opposed the Commission's initiatives, noted reproachfully that Quebec historians were 'not much inclined to denounce the event'; David, 'Le syndrôme McCartney.'

69 Rioux, '1759, "l'année des anglais,"' *Le Devoir*, 24 August 2009; idem, 'Cachez cette histoire que je ne saurais voir.'

70 He went further to make a point that he had fully fleshed out in his recently published polemical essay *Plaines d'Abraham: essai sur l'égo-mémoire des Québécois* (Outremont, QC: Athena, 2009), in which he argued that French Quebecers refused to consider narrations of the Conquest based on solid research that put into question their identity as oppressed victims. See Christian Rioux, 'Essais Québécois – Fallait-il refaire la bataille des plaines d'Abraham,' *Le Devoir*, 12, 13 September 2009.

71 Rioux, 'Cachez cette histoire que je ne samurais voir.'

72 Taken from the Commission website, http://www.ccbn-nbc.gc.ca.

73 Nadia Ross, 'Il faut se rappeler la bataille des Plaines, jugent les historiens,' *Le Soleil*, 24 January 2009.

74 François Bourque, 'A la mémoire d'Abraham,' *Le Soleil*, 20 January 2009.

75 David Johnston, 'Cancelled Plains of Abraham re-enactment no great loss:
Professor,' *National Post*, 20 February 2009.

76 Bourque, 'A la mémoire d'Abraham.'

77 Ross, 'Il faut se rappeler la bataille des Plaines, jugent les historiens.'

78 Ibid.

79 Michel de Waele interview with Tom Clark, *Power Play with Tom Clark*,
CTV, 17 February 2009.

80 Paraphrased by Johnston, 'Cancelled Plains of Abraham re-enactment no
great loss: professor.'

81 Graeme Hamilton, 'Old wounds reopened,' *National Post*, 9 February
2009.

82 Ibid. (paraphrased by Hamilton). The journalist quotes Morton directly as
saying: 'They've got to find something … the favourite notion of Quebec
nationalists is that we are being victimized by somebody.'

83 He asked rhetorically: 'Is the Battle of the Plains of Abraham such a
British victory or is it in fact a French Canadian victory?' See CBC, The
Current, 7 August 2009 podcast, http://www.cbc.c/thecurrent/2009/
200908/20090807.html (accessed 3 September 2009).

84 See Michel Ducharme, in this volume.

85 See Jocelyn Létourneau's detailed analysis, in this volume; see also Ducharme, in this volume.

86 Corbeil, 'C'est notre histoire, que ça plaise ou non.'

87 What adds to the extraordinary nature of these Civil War re-enactments is
that they date back to the early twentieth century. The first, a re-enactment
of Pickett's Charge, occurred as part of the commemorative activities to
mark the war's fiftieth anniversary in 1913. And to boot, it was re-enacted
by actual veterans of the war, turning it literally into a true re-enactment.
See 'Epilogue,' in David Blight, *Race and Reunion: The American Civil War in
American Memory* (Cambridge, MA: Harvard University Press, 2002).

88 See, among others, Blight, *Race and Reunion*; G. Kurt Piehler, *Remembering
War the American Way* (Washington: Smithsonian Books, 1995); Jim Weeks,
Gettysburg: Memory Market and an American Shrine (Princeton, NJ: Princeton
University Press, 2009); and Alice Fahs and Joan Waugh, eds., *The Memory
of the Civil War in American Culture* (Chapel Hill: University of North Caro-
lina Press, 2004).

89 Blight, *Race and Reunion*, 338–80, esp. 380. One could add that they further
'distracted' Americans by encouraging them to focus exclusively on the

war's military history. Much energy is expended among re-enactors in 'getting it right' whether in terms of military strategy or the faithful reproduction of uniforms and weaponry.

90 Létourneau, in this volume.

91 See, among others, Jacquelyn Dowd Hall, '"You Must Remember This": Autobiography as Social Critique,' *Journal of American History* 85, no. 2 (1998): 439–65.

12

What Is to Be Done with 1759?

JOCELYN LÉTOURNEAU

The title of this chapter is not meant sarcastically. It implies that the difficulty with 1759 is not historical in nature, having to do with the event in and of itself, but ideological. What matters is the use people might make – or try to make – of the event in political terms, along with the consequences flowing from their efforts to do so. Put another way, 1759 is not a problem when considered as an event embedded in time or from the point of view of determining what happened in the past, but it becomes so when these past realities are used to create a collective identity and a common cause in the present. Accordingly, one can argue that 1759 does not belong primarily to a past that we might wish to study and understand, but, rather, to a present and a future that we might wish to shape and control. This distinction allows us a clearer perspective on the virulent debates that broke out in Quebec in the spring of 2006 and the winter of 2009. The first centred around the significance attached to the Conquest in a new history curriculum, while the second focused on how to commemorate the two hundred and fiftieth anniversary of the Battle of the Plains of Abraham. Each controversy in its own way highlighted how 1759 remains, despite the lapse of time, an event enshrined in the collective imagination of Quebec. Although it is possible to reinterpret the Conquest in a way that departs from the accepted canon, revisionism inevitably runs afoul of the fear of endangering a sense of identity to which the Conquest is foundational.

Despite the widespread current interest in discovering new points of reference to underpin a renewal of the Quebec identity, 1759 stands in the way as a past experience that cannot conceivably be re-examined and rethought. In Quebec's history and its collective memory, 1759 – meaning the entire complex of events that embraces the Battle of the

Plains of Abraham, the British Conquest, and its consequences – has become sacrosanct. Nobody can handle just as they like this episode, which, through defeat, created a people. Since the mid-nineteenth century, it has been held up as the defining moment in a sorrowful historical trajectory.[1] While it might be true that the past can give rise to a variety of narratives, there are narratives of 1759 that cannot be spoken – not because they are historically inaccurate but because they call into question a sense of identity that must be protected.

Every historian is well aware that to attack the orthodox version of 1759 is to try to storm an impregnable fortress. To be sure, the event itself is important and salient. There is no way of ignoring it, or of relegating it to minor status in the unfolding of the historical process. But its transformation into mythistory has made it, for all practical purposes, inviolable. It belongs to the consecrated chronology of the *temps des Québécois*. It compels instant recognition: to cite 1759 is to say it all. There is nothing further to add, except to back away respectfully or to go on bended knee before the vision of this transcendent event. If confronted by those who might seek to advance new interpretations, the great event, through the songs of its Vestals, soon reimposes its own narrative order and the associated emotional touchstones. It lays down its own meaning, inalienable and untouchable. To interrogate 1759, no matter whether to understand it more clearly or to add clarity and perspective, is never appropriate or polite. It amounts to an affront to the majesty of an event that must always be approached with due respect and humility.

Even though historians know perfectly well that to dispute the orthodox version of 1759 is to risk excommunication, some have cheerfully risked proscription. Their names? Marcel Trudel for one, who has never hesitated to call into question the unrelievedly catastrophic nature of the Conquest and its supposedly baleful or even fatal influence over what was to become of the *Canadien* society of the time.[2] But Jean Hamelin, Fernand Ouellet, and others were also pillars – along with Trudel – of the 'Laval school,' which did not attribute to the Conquest the destructive power claimed for it by iconic figures of the 'Montreal school' such as Michel Brunet, Guy Frégault, and Maurice Séguin.[3] Although the members of the Laval school did have an audience in their own day, their voices have resounded less and less over time – current debates largely sidestep or ignore the arguments of these historians. The trio from Montreal, their memory celebrated constantly by their heirs, have enjoyed a much happier intellectual fate.[4]

Other iconoclasts include Donald Fyson, Allan Greer, Catherine Desbarats, Ramsay Cook, Louise Dechêne, John A. Dickinson, Brian Young, and Susan Mann – professional historians all. These are not minor or marginal authors – far from it – and yet their publications have made few inroads on public consciousness. The quality of their research has been overshadowed by the image of an implacable Conquest that was disastrous for a nation in search of its destiny. Although highly contested, interpreters of the Conquest from the worlds of the arts and mass communications have had a much wider influence. Take the case of Jacques Godbout, in his documentary *Le sort de l'Amérique*,[5] and Robert Lepage, in his massive architectural projection *Le moulin à images/ The Image Mill*.[6] Of Godbout it has been said that he takes delight in disconcerting his audience by putting the Conquest in a multiplicity of interpretive contexts, all the while portraying it as an event not to be treated playfully.[7] Lepage, on the other hand, makes little direct reference to the Conquest in his animated story; he presents a narrative that depends on technical effects and, consequently, that loses sight of any historical vision rooted in the lived experience of the past.[8]

There are some dissidents from the accepted interpretation of 1759 – Laurier Lapierre, André Pratte, John Ralston Saul, and a few others – whose works have been widely distributed.[9] Yet it is difficult to say just how much real influence they have had. What is certain is that their contentions have been roughly treated by a swarm of critics, more or less credible, who have no tolerance for the idea that either the Conquest or the wider historical experience of Quebec should be interpreted outside the official national canon.

The reality is that, as a historical event, 1759 has been appropriated by those who have embraced the meta-narrative of nationalism and who nurture it through the written and the spoken word. Among those who have contributed to this meta-narrative are a large number of qualified historians, some in a nuanced way and others more robustly.[10] Also central to the meta-narrative are popular historians such as Jacques Lacoursière and Denis Vaugeois, who hold a unique place as household names.[11] These two authors are especially important because they reach, through their writings and their media appearances, a large audience among those who relate to the past in a way that is descriptive and romanticized, rather than depending on critical analysis. In effect, Vaugeois and Lacoursière tell stories – such as that of the Conquest – in which the larger processes that have shaped the past are embodied in characters, in which it is easy to grasp the chain of causation, and in which the settings are spectacular and the action vivid, so that studying the past becomes much like reading a novel.[12] It would be hard to exaggerate the influence wielded by these two historians on the historical consciousness of the *Québécois*. Often quoted by politicians and cited as authorities on any aspect of national history, Vaugeois and Lacoursière have no rivals in fulfilling the role – as Pierre Berton once did for English Canada – as authors of a grand narrative.

Yet it remains true that the most influential interpreters of 1759 are not historians at all, but people belonging to the worlds of politics and the arts who play the role of professional ideologues.[13] Over the years, through a potent cocktail of abridgment, reductionism, and emotion, they have commandeered a complex event and turned it to the service of a simplistic and one-dimensional view of the past in which good and evil are easy to identify and an intractable foe – the English – is constantly landing hammer blows. The vision of 1759 currently predominating in public discourse – that of the Conquest as cataclysmic and essentially destructive – is largely the creation of these activists, who seek to use history to foster a national consciousness among the *Québécois* that is founded on a belief in destiny usurped and progress thwarted.[14]

Those who promote this interpretation, of course, have some truth on their side. The sufferings caused to the residents of Quebec City and its surrounds during the 1759 siege cannot be contested.[15] It is evident, too, that most of the *Canadiens* supported the French regime and fought for it, partly to protect their own property from the invaders. It is also clear that, despite the personal moderation of the initial British governors, residents of the colony experienced the Conquest as a profound turning point, marked by arrogance and the affronts by the Conquerors. Thus, it is entirely possible to make a historical argument for 1759 as a dramatic development, harrowing for those who experienced it. By its very nature, the Conquest certainly can be interpreted as a great discontinuity that subjected a deprived and demoralized population, especially in the areas surrounding the town of Quebec, to the mercies of an occupying power and saw the range of their options and opportunities narrowed amidst the anxiety and confusion that prevailed. But is this the only possible interpretation? Or even the most accurate – in terms of doing justice to the experience of people who lived at the time and to those who remember these events today? The answer to both questions is 'no.'

A different interpretive history of 1759 can be offered that does not minimize the impact of the Conquest but extricates it from the realm of simplistic narrative and allows it to take its place in the historic past. This alternative history is based on a view of the development of *Canadien* society and *canadianité*. It treats the period after 1759 as a turbulent era of transition, and sees the British regime from the mid-eighteenth century to the mid-nineteenth century as part of an extended process leading to the creation of a distinctive society today known as *québécois*.

In his work, Fernand Dumont has shown how, under the French regime, a society of clearly North American origins began to take root in the St Lawrence Valley during the seventeenth century and then extended to Tadoussac and the Saguenay and to the Outaouais.[16] Prudently, Dumont gave no hint as to whether this society – or 'collectivity,' as he designated it – had established a degree of autonomy from the mother country or showed signs of intending to do so. Neither did he assert that it had acquired durable institutions or a well-defined sense of identity, nor even that its members had developed a political or national consciousness. What Dumont, along with Louise Dechêne, did affirm was that New France was no pale replica of France itself. Although it was not yet an integrated or fully formed society, a collectivity was clearly emerging, aware of its French origins but its link to France tenuous. Its members had begun to develop an inchoate sense of patriotism, arising from their sense of distinctiveness on the North American continent. And this embryonic society, still pliable and open to change rather than being on a fixed trajectory, continued to evolve after the Conquest.

For the *Canadiens*, 1759 marked the most dramatic moment of a tumultuous transitional period, but it was not catastrophic. Their society was consolidated after 1759 thanks in part to the presence of an invader who became in time another founder, deeply embedded and influencing collective hopes and aspirations. During the second half of the eighteenth century, the society – already drawing on its French roots, its North American outlook, and its Amerindian influences – also became British in its institutional structures and partly in its population. Its nature, therefore, was always hybrid and complex. Neither fully integrated nor homogeneous, it was crucially defined by its tensions. Neither submerging nor reconciling its internal dissonances, it rested on the strained but inescapable interdependence of its constituent groups.

It has often been said that Canada after the Conquest was riven by a basic conflict between francophone *Canadiens*, committed to building their own nation, and the anglophone immigrants and the British rulers who imposed a cunning but highly effective form of oppression known as 'Indirect Rule.'[17] Yet, in reality, *Canadien* society was shot through with other antagonisms. Some were acute, some chronic. They pitted, for example, a declining aristocracy against a rising bourgeoisie, the great merchants against small-scale traders, the centralizers against those who favoured greater local autonomy, the Church against advocates of a secular state, *seigneurs* against farmers, the people against the elites, monarchists against republican sympathizers, Catholics against Protestants, proto-capitalists against workers. Language and religion were factors in prompting divisions or alliances, but they were not the only ones nor did they dictate the issues to be debated. There were many intertwining sources of social conflict and political strife that cannot be ascribed simply to ethnic or national rivalries, even though tensions between French and English and between Catholic and Protestant clearly intersected with many of the frictions. Although the participants themselves often used 'racial' animosities as a pretext to justify their rhetoric and their manoeuvres, the 'national question' was essentially one variable among many that affected the social dynamics. It cannot be portrayed as the alpha and the omega of the colony's evolution.

In its broadest outline, the period from the Conquest to the late 1840s corresponded with the decline of a society characterized by the vestiges of aristocracy to one in which an increasingly dominant bourgeoisie sought to attain, through negotiation and compromise – much more than through radicalism and armed struggle – a secure place of relative autonomy within the world's most impressive empire of the day, all the more urgently in the face of the expanding power of the United States. Even the rebellions of 1837–8 represented only an incident in a longer process of development. They stemmed from the deterioration of a tense situation through mismanagement rather than from any desire for independence or any sudden radicalization of political culture. Although the period from 1830 to 1848 had its moments of violence (the rebellions) and reprisals (the Act of Union), the Canadian society of Quebec – which cannot be reduced only to its francophone constituents – evolved politically and economically under British protection. Colonial governance was broadened to include an alliance of classes, groups, and individuals drawn from both of Quebec's main ethnic communities. This alliance, which over time sought to reform the colonial framework and to construct peacefully a moderate sense of *canadianité*, towered above a population that was heterogeneous from the point of view of economic conditions, political inclinations, and ethnic origins even if it was largely composed of francophone *Canadiens*. Far from having a common vision, this population was neither structured nor polarized along ethnolinguistic lines. Put another way, there was no simple division between the 'bloated anglophone usurpers' and the 'oppressed and exhausted francophones.' The reality was more tangled, and always full of surprises.

Until the achievement of responsible government in 1848, privileged anglophone-dominated networks and interest groups controlled the political system. It is also true that the large-scale commercial and industrial concerns were solidly owned by Anglo-Americans, by contrast with the small and medium-sized enterprises that depended primarily on capital of francophone origin, even though they might trade under anglicized corporate titles. The proportion of anglophones in business or the professions was far greater than their representation in the working population as a whole, which was not true of artisans or those in labouring positions. The least prosperous regions and those geographically furthest removed from the urban centres were populated by francophones, but the working class of the areas in and around Quebec City and Montreal, which experienced substantial economic growth from the 1830s onwards, was also predominantly francophone. While we should not neglect the presence of poor anglophones, especially the Irish, living 'below the hill' either in Montreal or in Quebec City, anglophones on the whole enjoyed a higher level of formal education and the advantage that the external economy – whether transatlantic or within the Americas – functioned primarily in English. They thus tended to occupy positions of higher status and to enjoy a higher material standard of living than their French-speaking fellow citizens. Anglophones and francophones, while coexisting in civil society and living side by side, also inhabited disconnected worlds between which resentment and mutual suspicion could be expressed either in discrimination and exclusivity or in overt hostility.

Yet, real as was the social separation of francophone and anglophone, it was constantly counteracted by mingling in the workplace and in the borrowings and exchanges that characterized popular culture. The gap between linguistic groups at the level of the highest political elite, while still perceptible, was powerfully counteracted by common class interests. Thus, the shared wariness of anything that smacked of radical nationalism, of any suggestion of breaking up British North America (notably any total separation of Upper and Lower Canada), or of the cutting loose of the colonies from the empire. At the level of the francophone *petite-bourgeoise*, the ethnolinguistic division was stronger and more pervasive in the absence of a level of social mobility that would have allowed these people to aspire realistically to greater power and position. This is the factor that best explains their active role in the construction of national identity and their support for the colonial autonomy that would characterize nationalist movements. For all that there was a disconnect between anglophone and francophone worlds, however, there was also a degree of cooperation in institutional matters, best exemplified by the elaboration of Lower Canada's civil code in the 1860s by a team of jurists drawn from both language groups.[18]

Overall, the society that was being built in Lower Canada under the British regime was a single society with a dualistic set of traditions and outlooks, one in which ambiguities and unresolved tensions abounded but brought neither dislocation nor paralysis. It was a society that was gradually emerging from the colonial framework, though without any likelihood of breaking radically from the British Empire. It was advancing towards rapid industrial capitalist development, promoted by a Montreal-based business elite, of both anglophone and francophone origins, that aspired to make an expanded Canada, notably by acquiring the northwest – its country and its hinterland. In matters of governance and regulation, the society strove to keep a balance between tradition (conservatism) and modernity (liberalism). Similarly, it sought to create a sense of identity that would embrace greater autonomy, together with the construction of nationality and the integration into a larger whole that the empire offered. It was a society characterized by political disputes that were sharply waged at the level of discourse but largely non-violent, pitting one against the other groups and classes that sought to assert their hegemony at the centre of power – some of them striving to use nationalism as a vehicle for mobilizing support.

One of the most important institutions in *Canadien* society was the Roman Catholic Church, which sought to safeguard its essential interests and entrench itself at the heart of power. For all that, it would never predominate, either before the rebellions or during the second half of the nineteenth century, when it came to terms with the liberal-conservatives in a relationship characterized by ill-concealed tensions. The Church did succeed in expelling from the centre of power all those who espoused radicalism or whom it judged unduly modernist, and its pervasive influence allowed it to keep a grip on the education system and nourish values at variance with the values of capitalism, putting limits on the upward mobility of the francophone population. Nonetheless, the forces of modernity – the values they propagated, the behaviours they prompted, and the forms of economic development to which they led – worked quietly but effectively in areas of development, especially in and around Montreal, whose experience mirrored that of similar areas elsewhere in North America.

This portrait of *Canadien* society takes us a long way from the notion that the Conquest brought about a protracted and general decline. It depicts, instead, a society that, from the admittedly complex and paradoxical legacy of the Conquest, went on to a phase of economic and political development that was advantageous for some (not all of them anglophones) and disadvantageous for others (not all of them francophones). We are confronted by a society that, far from falling into decay or even having to struggle for bare survival, continued to grow and to develop its distinctive texture. Despite the Conquest, or indeed because of the resourcefulness forced upon it by that event, this society recast itself according to a classic pattern – the transition to industrial capitalism, the emergence of an expanded bourgeoisie, the establishment of greater autonomy vis-à-vis the empire, and the construction of a national identity – which those who occupied places of power in Canada East gambled in the 1860s could be accomplished through building Canada *a mari usque ad mare*, within a framework of association with English-speaking Canadians. There were elements that were more distinctive in a North American context: a process of largely nonviolent transition from the *ancien régime*, gradual rather than radical separation from the imperial country, a national sensibility advancing impressively though unobtrusively, the building of a bourgeois society without giving up traditions. In short, this was a society that followed lines of development that – paradoxically perhaps – were common for the time, but also had their own peculiarities.

This version of the evolution of *Canadien* society in 'Quebec' between 1760 and 1850 at times has been dismissed out of hand, even by some distinguished professional historians.[19] It is true that to cast the British as founders rather than invaders, with all its implications, means no small adaptation of the customary narrative. To say that the British were integral to 'Us,' as opposed to being always the 'Other,' is to admit that Quebec's history can never be explained according to the paradigm of thwarted destiny. It is also to recognize that, if the British came as conquerors, they, too, were 'conquered.' In a remarkable reversal, a society in which they became a creative element eventually subsumed them.

One might assume that this iconoclastic version of the past, if publicly expressed, would gather quick and widespread popular condemnation. The assumption would be wrong. When communicated clearly by credible advocates, such a viewpoint gains an impressive and measurable acceptance among *Québécois* at large, who seem less preoccupied than the elite with cherishing an exclusive definition of identity. Or so a recent opinion survey indicates, after posing the following question: 'Are you in agreement with the following statement: the anglophones are a founding people in Quebec society?' Of francophone *Québécois*, 80 per cent answered 'yes.'[20] It is hardly surprising that a well-known analyst of Quebec's political standing, disturbed by the disharmony of this response with the assumptions that underpin his own arguments, exclaimed: '[With such a question], our historical understanding of Quebec-Canadian relations has just been turned upside down.'[21] But has the time not come to move on from a single accepted reading of the past, to develop other interpretations that might do greater justice to the complexity of the evidence, rather than simply serving the need for a sense of identity? That, of course, is where the shoe begins to pinch. For, to abandon the shaping of Quebec's history according to the matrix of a conquered people consigned by the violation of their destiny to a period of hibernation that ended only about 1960 is to do harm to the ideological giant of the catastrophic Conquest – which, in turn, forms the basis of a version of Quebec's identity that powerful interests have no desire to see revised or even reopened for discussion.

Examination of two major debates dealing with the Conquest – one directly, one indirectly – provides an opportunity to evaluate how far 1759 has come under renewed scrutiny. One of them is the controversy that broke out over Quebec's new history curriculum. In April 2006 *Le Devoir* published a scornful and alarmist article reporting that Quebec's Ministry of Education planned to introduce a new and 'sanitized' high school curriculum in which the Conquest appeared neither as a chapter heading nor even as a central point of reference in the interpretation of Quebec's history. Henceforth, wrote Antoine Robitaille, the periodization of the past would depend on two themes that were 'less political, non-national, and more pluralistic.'[22] The curriculum divisions to which he referred were 'The Emergence of *Canadien* Society,' from 1608 to 1760, and 'The Attainment of Democracy within the British Colony,' from 1760 to 1848.[23] The article unleashed an avalanche of reactions that led the minister of the day, apparently taken aback by the outcry, to demand substantial modifications to the proposed framework. By the time the revised version appeared, the coverage of the period from the early seventeenth century to the mid-eighteenth had reverted to the more conventional categories: 'The Emergence of a Society in New France (1608–1760),' 'The Change of Empire (1760–1791),' and 'Protests and Struggles within the British Colony (1791–1848).'[24]

Even these concessions did not satisfy the assailants of the ministry's initiative, who continued to denounce the 'multiculturalist and post-nationalist' foundations of the new curriculum.[25] In their view it was intolerable that the Conquest should not be studied as a determining force that imposed its own deplorable configuration on the nation that had been emerging and that drew an unmistakable line in the sand between 'before' and 'after.' It was equally unacceptable that 1759 should fail to be presented as the departure point for a dour struggle between anglophones and francophones, a conflict continuing in today's Quebec and bearing witness to the continuing oppression of the nation. Finally, it was inadmissible that the Conquest should not be interpreted from the perspective of a society already formed by the mid-eighteenth century, its entire process of development and its national aspirations torn apart by invaders who were not only alien to the earlier historical trajectory but who also fed their own vested interests by sucking the life out of Quebec economically, culturally, and – through the intermediacy of the federal government – politically.

According to those who disparaged the new curriculum, it was essential to return to a history of Quebec that put the nation at the centre and restored the proper benchmarks of the national experience:[26] French colonization in the seventeenth century; the Conquest; the Quebec Act; the struggles of the *Patriotes* and especially the rebellions of 1837–8; the Act of Union; the role of the Church after 1840; Confederation and the federal experience; the two conscription crises; the economic subordination of French-speaking Canadians; the Quiet Revolution; the report of the Royal Commission on Bilingualism and Biculturalism; the Estates General of French Canada; the rise of sovereigntism; the underhanded patriation of the Constitution; the rejection of the Meech Lake (1990) and Charlottetown (1992) accords; and the two Quebec referenda (1980 and 1995).[27] It could not have been clearer that the goal was to return to the old rallying points and to a conventional chronology of Quebec history. But is this the best way of understanding today's Quebec society in all its complexity? The answer, as already indicated, is 'no.' The difficulty with this particular 'no,' however, is that it is frequently and prejudicially taken to have proceeded not from research and rigorous enquiry but to be following a political imperative – and a cynical, subversive one at that.[28] For this reason, many of those who take an alternative view of the history of Quebec either keep a low profile or are simply ignored in public forums, unless they are explicitly impugned and in a symbolic sense convicted of treason for their lack of patriotic sensibility.

The other major controversy concerning 1759 ignited during the winter of 2009, after a decision of a federal agency to allow a re-enactment of the Battle of the Plains of Abraham to commemorate its two hundred and fiftieth anniversary. Among the critics, a consensus soon emerged that the plan was not just inappropriate but simply ridiculous. 'Do you know of anywhere else in the world,' wrote the columnist Michel David, 'where a people would cheerfully celebrate the worst defeat in their history?'[29] His colleague Christian Rioux added: 'Only the distracted or a masochist could fail to grasp how ridiculous is this whole affair. They might claim that the privileges squeezed out of the empire were sufficient to justify the colonial yoke. Yet 1759 marks the origin of the slow decline of francophones in Canada. It has been an uninterrupted process, and after 250 years it often seems to be beyond remediation.'[30] A number of commentators – a very small number – raised their heads far enough above the parapet to reflect that the argument regarding the 'paralysing destruction of future prospects' was contestable on factual grounds,[31] but their commentaries were vain attempts to resist a powerful wave that engulfed all reasoned critiques.

More fundamentally, it was not the idea in itself of recalling and commemorating the battle that had aroused the critics. Rather, they were concerned that this event and its imputed role in prompting the decay of an entire people would be misrepresented and trivialized, and its meaning misappropriated, desecrated, and demythologized by those on the 'wrong' side of the issue for their own ideological ends. That, in short, the defeat of 1759 would be repackaged as a victory, opening the door to the idea of a conquest that was beneficial and even profitable for the *Canadiens* of the day, then to the notion that the *Québécois* of today are a hybrid people, drawing strength from both French and British heritages, and finally to the contention that cooperation and healthy institutional compromises have generally characterized the relationship between the founding peoples of both Quebec and Canada despite some superficial bickering from time to time. All of these difficulties, the critics argued, could be avoided if the commemoration could just be orchestrated by those on the 'right' side. The event then could be confirmed in its *appellation contrôlée*, its sacrosanct character, and its ordained political purpose. This argument was well summarized by

Françoise David, spokesperson of *Québec solidaire*, a political organization operating within the nationalist and sovereigntist movement:

> The commemoration of the 250th anniversary of the battle of 1759 should
> be the occasion of:
>
> - reflecting on the cultural, social, political, and economic consequences
>   of the Conquest;
> - recalling the right of peoples to self-determination – that of the *nation
>   québécoise* along with those of indigenous nations here and elsewhere;
> - opening up the question of the role of armed force in statecraft, in other
>   eras and today;
> - recalling and celebrating the many forms of resistance undertaken by
>   the people in this place, against war, assimilation, discrimination and
>   the plundering of natural resources.
>
> Our proposal seeks to affirm the consensus that opposes the [re-enact-
> ment] project of the federal [National] Battlefields Commission, but at the
> same time to avoid lapsing into an anti-English chauvinism. This is why
> the kind of event we would like to see developed is one with a vision
> based on pacifism and alter-globalization, one which emphasizes the right
> of peoples to self-determination as exemplified by the inalienable right of
> the *Québécois*.
>
> What is most worthy of celebration in our history is the strength of
> popular resistance to oppression, whether military, political, or economic.
>
> In our view, the people of Quebec stand to gain by reclaiming their his-
> tory, as also by asserting control of the present.[32]

Eloquently expressed, David's statement is crystal clear in its principles and goals. Her proposal gives vigorous support to the idea of
commemorating 1759, and even celebrating it, but as an example of
the combativeness of a people. David's statement justifies celebrating
1759 as an appeal to the right of self-determination, as the key to the
realization of the national aspiration to advance beyond the phase of
mere *survivance*. This is the view of 1759 that predominated at Quebec
City on 12–13 September 2009, following an initiative by a politically
engaged hip-hop group. Biz, one of the members of Loco Locass, had
harshly denounced the plan to re-enact the battle on the Plains,[33] and
what emerged was an event that sought to highlight the traditional
symbolism and the approved rhetoric of 1759. During the continuous

twenty-four hours of the *Moulin à paroles*, 134 well-known figures read texts recalling 'from where we have come.'[34] According to the organizers of this literary marathon, the selected passages, which concluded with an unpublished piece by André Ricard entitled *La vingt-cinquième heure*,[35] were intended to 'call to mind our history and to underscore the people's resistance, from the Conquest right up to our own era.'[36] The director of this theatrical event, Brigitte Haentjens, commented that 'what we hoped for was to have these twenty-four hours contribute to identifying ourselves, to give us a memory, to show how our words have for so long defied the harsh environment, the prejudices, the battles lost.'[37] Sébastien Ricard, also a member of Loco Locass and son of André Ricard, added that 'in our view we had a duty as citizens to bring back to this country something of its own. Thus, we hope for the *Moulin à paroles* that it will represent a citizens' movement, representing the claims and the intentions of the people.'[38] Put another way, in the story of the Quebec nation, the Conquest is the unifying principle and the essential point of departure for everything else, an unforgettable injury that calls forth an eternal loyalty and an inescapable duty to remember.

Two hundred and fifty years have passed since the Battle of the Plains of Abraham. With the exception of those who adhere to the mythistory of the Conquest as cataclysm, it is difficult to know how to interpret or commemorate this episode, how even to talk about it. In today's Quebec, a society in the throes of transformation and one seeking to forge a new sense of identity that is more inclusive and pluralistic, 1759 can seem like a ball and chain. This is why neither the governments of Quebec and Canada nor the anglophone organizations in the province were willing to take an official position regarding the ceremonies that eventually did occur. Better to remain silent than to risk giving offence through word or deed. Implied, though unstated, was the cherished hope that time would efface the remnants of the battle's legacy.

Yet it is rare for time by itself to blot out established portrayals, especially when – as in the case of the Conquest – they are constantly recalled. To change such a representation takes work. The historian approaches the task through a rigorous methodology involving nuance, comparison of viewpoints, judicious generalization, and reasoned discussion. All well and good. But can the historical method really offer a path towards the future by thinking through and moving beyond 1759, when the event is held prisoner by a carefully constructed historical memory drawing on a narrow methodology that forestalls the exploration of its full complexity? To answer in the affirmative would take a lot of optimism, for when method and memory go head to head it is rare for reason to prevail over passion.

To move beyond 1759, what kind of narrative or interpretive framework would be needed? There are several possibilities. One could try to make the Conquest less charged by downplaying the need to create identity, by immersing the event in a multiplicity of contexts, or by contending that it had not really changed anything for the *Canadiens* or even significantly affected them. Clearly, though, this approach would lead to serious underestimation of the significance of an episode that cannot – unless for purely ideological reasons – be drowned in the ocean of history. Similarly, one could argue that the Conquest inaugurated a continuing process by which harmony and conciliation prevailed between francophones and anglophones. But even if this historical legacy of cooperation could provide a sound basis for reaching consensus in today's Quebec, such a contention would run into the reality of often-turbulent relations between francophones and anglophones – even today, reconciliation has not yet reached a point where the idea of a fully integrated *nation québécoise* is realistic. Moreover, one cannot ignore the fact that, at times, anglophone assertions of power were the cause of tensions and sometimes outright conflict.

Another way of escaping from a historical memory of 1759 that has proved to be more constraining than liberating would be to deny the entire notion that the Conquest and ensuing developments had crystallized in the minds of *Canadiens* an inchoate national sentiment, one that was transformed during the 1830s into an explicit national aspiration and that influences the political complexion of Quebec to this day. Any such suggestion, however, would be unduly confining, for to refuse to admit the role of national ambitions would be to ignore one of the most persistent fermentations in the historical experience of Quebec.

So, what to do? To speak about 1759 in such a way as to allow the discussion to move beyond the event does not require, in essence, any attempt to deny, contrive, or stretch the truth. All that is needed is to confront the past in all its complexity, free of any teleological or theological scheme. We need to convey accurately the sense of a past that was ambiguous and confusing, where reality was no longer clear but configured in shades of grey, where individuals did not behave according to definable roles and where entire societies were not polyphonic. The historian needs to identify roadblocks and diversions in a society's course of development, rather than relying on any theoretical model or preconceived framework, and to take an open and dynamic approach to portraying societies as malleable creations that exist in a constant state of adaptation and change.

To define 1759 in this methodological context leads inevitably to the recognition of an ambiguous conquest. It was an imperfect campaign that had equivocal results, leading not to a harsh domination but to a new beginning. Despite their intentions and their initial actions, the British simply lacked the power to constrain a subjected population and to bend them to some imperial scheme. Never able fully to assume the role of conquerors, the British themselves soon began to forge linkages with the local population, incorporating usages and customs. Willingly or not, the regime had to reach the negotiated understandings that made the colony workable. Conversely, the *Canadiens*, even though theoretically on the losing side, never lapsed into the role of the conquered. Taking advantage of certain rights that were sought and recognized, they were able – within the framework of an often-tense and convoluted relationship with the British – to build an original sense of nationality that can be defined as *canadianité*. It became increasingly firm and established over time, though proceeding along lines that were moderate rather than radical, cooperative rather than secessionist, adaptive rather than inflexible, and polysemic rather than dominated by a single discourse.[39]

It was this fluidity that ensured that nothing could unfold predictably. Rather than any basic harmony or (re)conciliation, the situation was dominated by forced coexistence and necessary compromise. The political and social environments continued to be characterized by a level of tension that led on all sides – regardless of culture or background – to apprehensions of treachery. Promotion of one's own interests to gain access to the power structure was central to the construction of *Canadien* society in Quebec during the century following the Conquest. To be sure, there were frustrations, winners and losers, resulting from a societal trajectory that did not follow any accepted model of social or national development. It did not make out of the *Canadiens*, so often seen as united in their defeat, one large and homogeneous family worshipping at the same patriotic altar. Such a pattern lacks, of course, the ability to distinguish in a satisfying way the oppressed Self from the oppressive Other, the good from the bad and the ugly. However, the historian's responsibility is clear. The business of history is not to refute or sublimate the caprices and the incongruities of the past, but to make do with them. The past, after all, promises nothing. It did not happen for the benefit of future storytellers or to fulfil their political expectations. It arose from the decisions by men and women as to what to do with their lives, intertwining their aspirations with the push and pull of contingency and circumstance. They threaded their way through the complex textures of their world and gambled to win in the unforgiving lottery of life. If the outcomes were often tangled, ambivalent, and material, then so indeed was the aftermath of the Conquest. History must bear witness to these complexities, and there is no guarantee that the result will be dramatic, inspiring, or uplifting.

So where does all of this leave the commemoration of 1759? The historian's task of investigating the complex realities of the past is entirely distinct from commemoration, which recalls the past for a present-day purpose. At present, the only accepted cause that can be served by commemorating 1759 is that of Quebec nationalism, defined according to the traditional canon, resting on the idea of the Conquest as a radical turning point. That some commentators opposed any commemoration at all was only because they feared that it might be turned to the service of another persuasion. It might be federalism, or Canadianism – or, indeed, a more pluralistic nationalism, interpreted by the conventional nationalists as a depoliticization of the past and a dehistoricization of the present. If the alternative was to have a commemoration that served any of these ends, for certain commentators it was better to have none at all. Better not to expose the Conquest to open debate than to risk damaging its pre-eminence as a tragedy and a disaster.

Yet change might be in the air. There are indications that the English could be in the process of moving from being seen as the baleful Other to gaining recognition as representing a co-founder of Quebec society. At the *Fête nationale* in 2009, for example, members of anglophone groups in Montreal sang in their own language, with keen public support. Their goal was not to colonize celebration but to show that they belonged in Quebec society. Also indicative was the ability of Paul McCartney's concert, staged on the Plains of Abraham in 2008, on the occasion of the four hundredth anniversary of Quebec's founding, which drew more than one hundred and fifty thousand people. A few critics, including a number of artists and three members of the Parti Québécois, objected to McCartney's visit, but these discordant voices were lost in the general exhilaration. In the summer of 2009, the singer Sting drew a crowd of one hundred and twenty thousand to a concert on the ancient battlefield. The reality is that young *Québécois*, whether confronted by English as a language or by the English as a social community, have an increasingly open and uncomplicated outlook that differs generically from that of earlier generations.[40]

It seems, therefore, that, quietly and unobtrusively, *à la manière québécoise*, a different kind of commemoration of the Conquest might at some point become possible. It would not associate the event with prompting the decline of a people; it would recall the way in which 1759 became a (re)founding moment for Quebec society. This process certainly entailed suffering and injury. Key moments when societies are recast are not necessarily either glorious or shameful, victorious or ruinous, triumphal or dispiriting. They correspond, rather, to moments when societies remake themselves, gaining strength through renewal – when they reorient themselves according to a new point of reference, responding to new demands, adjusting or updating their sense of identity. Taking account of the past reality of 1759 and given that its portrayals have not exhausted its complexities or the subtleties of its meaning, the event assuredly can give rise to historical work that reopens it to analysis and brings a breath of fresh air to its memory. Quebec society seems ready to embrace this phase of reinterpretation, in the interests of advancing its desire for renewal.

The year 2034, which will mark the two hundred and seventy-fifth anniversary of the Battle of the Plains of Abraham, might well signal the entire emancipation of the *Québécois* vis-à-vis 1759. Through their commemorations, they might look forward rather than back. They would do so not out of a desire to disavow the memory of their forebears but in the understanding that tradition is a legacy that offers perspective and choices, not a sense of conformity and burdensome obligation. Thus, 1759 could be revived, moving beyond the orthodoxies that have sought to set it in concrete as an inviolable heritage and opening it up to debate and commentary. In this way, the *Québécois* would accomplish a healthy transition away from a paralysing nostalgia and the dead hand of the past, towards a living memory in which each person would be at the heart of an ongoing dialogue between past and present. Recovering their ability to speak out about, and in opposition to if they wish, those who arrogated the right to be the guardians of history, they would no longer stand in a passive relationship with the past. Instead, the *Québécois* would nourish an active recollection inseparable from determining present-day courses of action. Then they would be able to move forward into the future.

NOTES

1 On the initial mythologization of 1759, see Serge Gagnon, *Le Québec et ses historiens de 1840 à 1920: la Nouvelle-France de Garneau à Groulx* (Québec: Presses de l'Université Laval, 1978). Note that, in this historiographical context, sorrow is associated not with affliction but as an ordeal decreed by Providence that eventually will lead to a joyful conclusion.

2 Marcel Trudel, 'La Conquête de 1760 a eu aussi ses avantages,' in Trudel, *Mythes et réalités dans l'histoire du Québec* (1997; Montréal: HMH, 2001).

3 See Jean Lamarre, *Le devenir de la nation québécoise selon Maurice Séguin, Guy Frégault et Michel Brunet (1944-1969)* (Sillery, QC: Septentrion, 1993).

4 It is well known that Maurice Séguin, whose works have become practically fetish objects in some quarters, has been treated with great deference by former students of his who are active in publishing and in the promotion of nationalist ideas. See Denis Vaugeois, 'Présentation,' in Maurice Séguin, *Une histoire du Québec: vision d'un prophète* (Montréal: Guérin, 1995); and Robert Comeau, ed., *Maurice Séguin, historien du pays québécois vu par ses contemporains*, suivi de *Les Normes de Maurice Séguin* (Montréal: vlb éditeur, 1987).

5 Jacques Godbout, *Le sort de l'Amérique* [script and scenario] (Montréal: Boréal, 1997).

6 Robert Lepage, *Le moulin à images/The Image Mill* (Québec: Ex Machina, 2008).

7 Louis Cornellier, 'Jacques Godbout est-il vraiment une belle guidoune,' *Cahiers d'histoire du Québec au 20e siècle* (Spring 1997): 206–9; and Serge Cantin, 'La fatigue culturelle de Jacques Godbout,' *Liberté* 206 (April 1993): 3–37.

8 Joseph Yvon Thériault, 'Mais qu'a bien pu vouloir nous dire Robert Lepage?' *Nuit blanche* 114 (April 2009): 10–13; Denis Vaugeois, 'Une fête célébrée à la sauce Canada,' *Le Devoir*, 27–8 September 2008, special edition, 'Le 400e de Québec et l'histoire.' See also the response of Philippe Dubé, 'Une histoire sans nom, sans date, ni événement,' *Le Devoir*, 1 October 2008.

9 Laurier Lapierre, *1759: la bataille du Canada* (Montréal: Le Jour, 1992); John Ralston Saul, *Réflexions d'un frère siamois: le Canada à la fin du 20e siècle* (Montreal: Boréal, 1998); and André Pratte, *Au pays des merveilles: essai sur les mythes politiques québécois* (Montréal: vlb éditeur, 2006). See also Sylvie Despatie, 'Conséquences économiques de la Conquête,' in André Champagne, *Le Québec des 18e et 19e siècles: entretiens sur l'histoire* (Sillery, QC: Septentrion/Radio-Canada, 1996).

10 The *Bulletin d'histoire politique*, a journal directed since its founding by

intellectuals who do not hide their sovereigntist orientation, represents –
along the same lines as another journal with overt nationalist sympathies,
L'Action nationale – one of the places where non-nationalist interpretations
of Quebec's past are most actively resisted.

11 See Brian Young, in this volume.

12 Jacques Lacoursière, Jean Provencher, and Denis Vaugeois, *Canada-Québec:
    synthèse historique 1534–2000* (Sillery, QC: Septentrion, 2001), chap. 16;
    Denis Vaugeois, 'Les batailles de Québec,' in André Champagne, *L'histoire
    du Régime français: entretiens sur l'histoire* (Sillery, QC: Septentrion/Radio-
    Canada, 1996); Jacques Lacoursière, *Une histoire du Québec… racontée par
    Jacques Lacoursière* (Québec: Septentrion, 2002); idem, 'Le champ des ba-
    tailles,' in *Les Plaines d'Abraham: le culte de l'idéal*, ed. Jacques Mathieu and
    Eugen Kedl (Sillery, QC: Septentrion, 1993), chap. 3; Jacques Lacoursière
    and Hélène Quimper, *Québec, ville assiégée, 1759–1760* (Québec: Septentri-
    on, 2009); and Jacques Lacoursière, *Histoire populaire du Québec*, vol. 1, *Des
    origines à 1791* (Sillery, QC: Septentrion, 1995). It is noteworthy that this last
    publication, which runs to five volumes, relies on documentation brought
    together for the launching of a popular and widely distributed historical
    review in tabloid format, *Nos racines*.

13 Among those whose interventions and publications have gathered the
    largest audience are Normand Lester, *Le livre noir du Canada anglais*, 3 vols.
    (Montréal: Les Intouchables, 2001–3); and Marcel Tessier, *Marcel Tessier
    raconte: chroniques d'histoire* (Montréal: Les Éditions de l'Homme, 2004).
    The late Pierre Falardeau, Patrick Bourgeois, and Bruno Deshaies (the
    mainstay of the website *vigile.net*, through which he disseminates his pre-
    cepts) have also figured among those receiving the most media coverage.
    Texts representing various nationalist persuasions that suffer to a greater
    or lesser degree from 'conquêtisme,' to borrow Frédéric Boily's phrase,
    have been recycled in *Les grands textes indépendantistes: écrits, discours et
    manifestes québécois, 1992–2003*, ed. Andrée Ferretti (Montréal: Typo, 2004).
    Finally, Léandre Bergeron's *Petit manuel d'histoire du Québec*, which first ap-
    peared in 1970 and sold 125,000 copies, has been republished with a view
    to capturing the sympathies of the children of the 'baby boomers,' who can
    also find all they need in *La Conquête, une anthologie*, ed. Charles-Philippe
    Courtois (Montréal: Typo, 2009), to enable them to come to a proper un-
    derstanding of the event that, according to Courtois, began 'notre grande
    débâcle nationale.'

14 For a demonstration of the resonance of this historical vision in the
    contemporary Quebec imagination, see Jacinthe Ruel, 'Clio dans l'arène
    publique: usages du passé et références à l'histoire dans les mémoires

déposés devant la Commission sur l'avenir politique et constitutionnel du Québec' (MA thesis, Université Laval, 1993); Jocelyn Létourneau and Sabrina Moisan, 'Mémoire et récit de l'aventure historique du Québec chez les jeunes Québécois d'héritage canadien-français: coup de sonde, amorce d'analyse des résultats, questionnements,' *Canadian Historical Review* 85 (2004): 325–56; and Jocelyn Létourneau and Christophe Caritey, 'L'histoire du Québec racontée par les élèves du secondaire: l'impact apparent du cours d'histoire nationale dans la structuration d'une mémoire historique collective chez les jeunes Québécois,' *Revue d'histoire de l'Amérique française* 62 (2008): 69–93.

15 Bernard Andrès, 'Québec: chroniques d'une ville assiégée, 2e partie: 1759,' *Cahiers des Dix* 62 (2008): 61–87. It should be remembered that the villagers of the area around Quebec City suffered from abuses by the soldiers of the French army and allied aboriginals, as well as from the British.

16 Fernand Dumont, *Genèse de la société québécoise* (Montréal: Boréal, 1993).

17 Claude Bariteau is one of the principal propagators of this thesis; see, especially, Bariteau, *Québec, 18 septembre 2001: le monde pour horizon* (Montréal: Québec-Amérique, 1998). See also André Campeau, 'La transformation des régimes coloniaux au Québec' (PhD thesis, Université Laval, 2001). Note that Campeau worked under Bariteau's supervision.

18 Brian Young, *The Politics of Codification: The Lower Canadian Civil Code of 1866* (Montreal; Kingston, ON: McGill-Queen's University Press, 1994).

19 There was a definable point at which a sharp reaction became evident against the intention of Quebec's Ministry of Education to concentrate, for the period beginning in the mid-eighteenth century, on the building of *Canadien* society rather than on the Conquest or the British regime. Among the most serious and recognized of the historians who led the swing in this direction were Éric Bédard, Jean-Marie Fecteau, Jacques Rouillard, Guy Laperrière, Denise Angers, Yvan Lamonde, Lucia Ferretti, Robert Comeau, and Yves Gingras.

20 Survey conducted 11–14 May 2009 of 1,003 Quebec residents by Léger Marketing on behalf of the Association for Canadian Studies and the Quebec Community Groups Network; reported in Marco Bélair-Cirino, 'Le français à Montréal: 90% des francophones sont inquiets,' *Le Devoir*, 22 June 2009.

21 Comment by Alain G. Gagnon, Canada Research Chair in Quebec and Canadian Studies at the Université du Québec à Montréal; quoted in ibid.

22 '[É]puré'; 'moins politique, non national et plus pluriel'; Antoine Robitaille, 'Cours d'histoire épurés au secondaire,' *Le Devoir*, 27 April 2006.

23 'L'émergence de la société canadienne'; '[l]'accession à la démocratie dans
    la colonie britannique'; Quebec, Ministère de l'Enseignement, du Loisir et
    du Sport, 'Histoire et éducation à la citoyenneté,' draft working document
    (Quebec: MELS, 26 May 2005), 522.
24 'L'émergence de la société canadienne en Nouvelle-France (1608–1760)';
    '[l]e changement d'empire (1760–1791)'; '[l]es revendications et les
    luttes dans la colonie britannique (1791–1848)'; Quebec, Ministère de
    l'Enseignement, du Loisir et du Sport, *Histoire et éducation à la citoyenneté*
    (Québec: MELS, 2006), 45.
25 '[M]ulticulturalistes et postnationalistes.' The last systematic critique to
    date, which brought its author considerable media coverage, was in May
    2009; see Charles-Philippe Courtois, *Le nouveau cours d'histoire du Québec
    au secondaire: l'école québécoise au service du multiculturalisme canadien?*
    (Montréal: Institut de recherche sur le Québec, 1 May 2009). The Institut
    de recherche sur le Québec, despite its official-sounding title, is an overtly
    nationalist and conservative think tank that brings together a number of
    regular contributors to *L'Action nationale*. Members of its scientific commit-
    tee have been active at various levels in the Parti Québécois. Alternatively,
    a number of critical analyses of the new history curriculum have been
    collected in two recent publications: *L'enseignement de l'histoire au début du
    XXIe siècle au Québec*, ed. Félix Bouvier and Michel Sarra-Bournet (Québec:
    Septentrion, 2008); and *Contre la réforme pédagogique*, ed. Robert Comeau
    and Josiane Lavallée (Montréal: vlb éditeur, 2008). See also the assessment
    of Christian Laville, 'L'enseignement de l'histoire à travers les lunettes
    noires de la question identitaire,' *Mens: revue d'histoire intellectuelle de
    l'Amérique française* 9, no. 2 (2009): 243–63.
26 See the documents produced by the *Coalition pour la promotion de
    l'enseignement de l'histoire au Québec*, available on the website of the Société
    Saint-Jean-Baptiste de Montréal, http://coalitionpourlhistoireduquebec.
    org (accessed 4 October 2009).
27 Michel Seymour, 'L'impossible neutralité face à l'histoire: remarques
    sur les documents du MEQ *Histoire et éducation à la citoyenneté*,' *Bulletin
    d'histoire politique* 15, no. 2 (2007): 24.
28 Mathieu Bock-Côté, *La dénationalisation tranquille: mémoire, identité et multi-
    culturalisme dans le Québec postréférendaire* (Montréal: Boréal, 2007).
29 'Connaissez-vous bien des endroits dans le monde où un peuple célèbre
    dans l'allégresse la pire défaite de son histoire?'; Michel David, 'Joyeux
    anniversaire?' *Le Devoir*, 8 January 2009.
30 'Il n'y a que des esprits égarés ou masochistes pour ne pas saisir le ridicule
    de cette affaire. Ceux-là pourront toujours prétendre que les quelques
    privilèges arrachés à l'Empire valaient bien le joug colonial. 1759 marque

pourtant le point de départ du lent déclin des francophones au Canada. Un processus qui ne s'est interrompu et qui semble toujours aussi ir-rémédiable 250 ans plus tard'; Christian Rioux, 'L'odeur de la poudre,' *Le Devoir*, 23 January 2009. One can add to the list of critics a host of names from all sectors of society.

31   '[La] défaite paralysante d'avenir.' Among the iconoclastic Quebec fran-cophones, see André Pratte, 'La bataille des Plaines,' *La Presse*, 25 January 2009; idem, 'Retour sur les Plaines,' *La Presse*, 3 February 2009; idem, 'Ca-pitulations sur les Plaines,' *La Presse*, 13 February 2009; Marc Simard, 'Dé-tournement de l'histoire,' http://www.cyberpresse.ca, 18 February 2009; and Philippe Navarro, 'Une victoire de Montcalm n'aurait rien changé,' *La Presse*, 30 January 2009.

32   Françoise David and Serge Roy, 'Pour une commémoration pacifiste et progressiste,' *Le Soleil*, 17 February 2009. In the original:

La commémoration du 250e anniversaire de la bataille de 1759 devrait être l'occasion de:

- réfléchir aux conséquences de la Conquête – sur les plans culturel, social, politique et économique;
- rappeler le droit des peuples à l'autodétermination – celui de la nation québécoise comme celui des nations autochtones d'ici et d'ailleurs;
- remettre en question le rôle de l'armée dans les stratégies politiques des États, autrefois et aujourd'hui;
- rappeler et célébrer les multiples formes de résistance des gens d'ici, depuis 250 ans, contre la guerre, l'assimilation, la discrimination et le pillage des ressources naturelles.

Notre proposition cherche à la fois à affirmer le consensus pour s'op-poser au projet de la Commission fédérale des champs de bataille [*sic*], mais aussi à éviter de sombrer dans un chauvinisme antianglais. C'est pourquoi le type d'événement que nous aimerions voir se développer en est un avec une vision pacifiste et altermondialiste, qui met l'accent sur le droit des peuples à l'autodétermination, dont celui inaliénable du peuple québécois.

Ce qu'il y a de plus précieux à célébrer dans notre histoire, c'est la force des résistances populaires face aux oppressions, qu'elles soient militaires, politiques ou économiques.

Selon nous, le peuple québécois gagne à se réapproprier l'histoire, comme le présent.

33 Biz, 'La célébration de l'aliénation québécoise,' *Le Devoir,* 22 December
    2007.
34 '[D]'où nous venons'; see the event's website at http://www
    .moulinaparoles.com (accessed 4 October 2009).
35 'Textes,' http://www.moulinaparoles.com (accessed 4 October 2009).
36 '[R]appeler notre histoire et souligner la résistance des gens d'ici depuis la
    Conquête jusqu'à nos jours'; Pierre Pelchat, 'Moulin à paroles: Labeaume,
    Picard, Snyder y seront,' *Le Soleil,* 5 August 2009.
37 '[N]ous voulions que ces 24 heures contribuent à nous identifier, à nous
    donner une mémoire, à nous rappeler le long combat de nos mots contre
    l'âpreté du paysage, les préjugés, les batailles perdues'; Isabelle Porter, 'Les
    artistes se mobilisent pour commémorer 1759,' *Le Devoir,* 31 July 2009.
38 '[N]ous pensons ... qu'il [était] de notre devoir de citoyens de donner à ce
    pays quelque chose qui vient de lui. Nous avons donc souhaité Le Moulin
    à Paroles comme une mobilisation citoyenne, une représentation du peu-
    ple placée sous la signe de l'exigence et de la signifiance'; ibid.
39 For a history of the construction of nationality and identity in this sense,
    see Jocelyn Létourneau, *Que veulent vraiment les Québécois? Regard sur
    l'intention nationale au Québec (français) d'hier à aujourd'hui* (Montréal:
    Boréal, 2006).
40 This conclusion can be drawn from Nathalie St-Laurent, *Le français et les
    jeunes* (Québec: Conseil supérieur de la langue française, 2008).

Contributors

Michel Bock is a member of the Department of History at the University of Ottawa and holds a Research Chair in Canadian Francophonie.

Phillip Buckner is Professor Emeritus of History at the University of New Brunswick and Senior Research Fellow at the Institute of Commonwealth Studies at the University of London.

Joan Coutu is a member of the Department of Fine Arts at the University of Waterloo.

Michel Ducharme is a member of the Department of History at the University of British Columbia.

Alan Gordon is a member of the Department of History at the University of Guelph.

Alexis Lachaine teaches history at York University.

Jocelyn Létourneau is a member of the Department of History at Université Laval and holds a Canada Research Chair in Contemporary Political History and Economy in Quebec.

J.I. Little is a Professor in the Department of History at Simon Fraser University.

Jean-François Lozier is Curator of Early Canadian History at the Canadian Museum of Civilization.

John McAleer is Curator of Eighteenth-Century Imperial and Maritime History at the National Maritime Museum.

David Meren is a member of the Département d'histoire at l'Université de Montréal.

Nicole Neatby is a member of the Department of History at Saint Mary's University.

John G. Reid is a member of the Department of History at Saint Mary's University and Senior Research Fellow at the Gorsebrook Research Institute.

Brian Young is James McGill Professor Emeritus in the Department of History at McGill University.

Index